MAKING
SCENES

OTHER BOOKS BY ROBERT BRUSTEIN

The Theatre of Revolt
Seasons of Discontent
The Third Theatre
Revolution as Theatre
The Culture Watch
Critical Moments

EDITOR

Selected Plays and Prose of August Strindberg

ROBERT BRUSTEIN

MAKING SCENES

A Personal History of the Turbulent Years at Yale 1966-1979

RANDOM HOUSE New York

A segment of Chapter IV, *The Panther and the Bulldog,* previously appeared in another form as part of an article published in *The New York Times Magazine* under the title "When the Panther Came to Yale," and was later republished in the author's book *Revolution as Theatre.*

Library of Congress Cataloging in Publication Data

Brustein, Robert Sanford, 1927–

Making scenes.

Includes index.

1. Brustein, Robert Sanford, 1927–   . 2. Theater critics—United States—Biography. 3. Theatrical producers and directors—United States—Biography.

I. Title.

PN2287.B728A35   792'.092'4 [B]   80–6030

ISBN 0-394-51094-1

Manufactured in the United States of America

98765432

First Edition

FOR NORMA
with whom I lived it . . . and relived it

Acknowledgments

It is impossible, in a book of this kind, to make sufficient acknowledgment of all those who contributed to its composition. My friends, my colleagues, my former students (many of whom have become my friends and colleagues) now number in the thousands, and each has played his or her important part in the events of the following narrative. Since most are already acknowledged in the body of the book, I will simply take this opportunity to say thank you, en masse, to all of them here.

But there are others who provided warm support and invaluable technical help to me during the actual writing of *Making Scenes,* whose contributions I would like to acknowledge with deep feelings of gratitude: Jan and Jeremy Geidt, Rob Orchard, Penny Pigott, Rocco and Heidi Landesman, Travis Preston, Phillip Cates, and Herb and Maggie Scarf for reading portions of the manuscript in its early stages; Robert Loomis of Random House for his uncanny editorial perception and unflagging encouragement; Sono Rosenberg for her shrewd and careful copy editing; Bernard Gotfryd and Joan Engels at *Newsweek* and the Press Department and University Library at Yale for their help in locating photographic material; and the entire American Repertory Theatre company for its understanding whenever I stole time for the book that really belonged to them. To all these—and to all those unmentioned—my thanks from an overflowing heart.

Prologue

This is the story of thirteen years in the life of an institution, but I hope it is more than that. It is also the story of thirteen years in my own life, but I hope it is more than that too. What presumptuous ambition am I claiming for this memoir? Simply that it is possible to consider the history of the Repertory Theatre and School of Drama at Yale during these years as part of a larger social and cultural pattern. Someone once remarked that if the theatre is truly doing its job, it is like a sponge, soaking up all the juices of the time. I had always believed this to be true, but I had no idea I would ever see it demonstrated so vividly until I came to Yale. Thinking we were engaged in production or training, I was to discover continually that we were also caught in the white water of history, forced forward over rapids, sucked backward into eddies.

The years at Yale during our time were unusually eventful, even tumultuous. I arrived in the middle of the sixties and left at the end of the seventies, those sparky American decades. The university was undergoing momentous changes; so was the theatre; so was the society. As a critic, I had long complained that the American theatre was cut off from American life. At Yale I could no longer make this charge. It was impossible to get through a single season without arousing some strong political, social, or personal reaction from one group or another. We intended to extend and challenge our audiences; we often succeeded in irritating and provoking them.

Much of this was doubtless my own doing, the result of my own peculiar aesthetic. To my mind, there was only one fatal sin in the theatre—to be boring. And what bored me personally was theatrical safety, domesticated passions and domestic settings, received ideas and conventional wisdom. My personal distaste for these things frequently led me into provocations. I enjoyed making scenes—and not only in the theatre. It was the only way I knew to get the blood going when somebody or something was threatening to freeze it. Brought up on Blake and Nietzsche and D. H. Lawrence, I believed with them that the tigers of wrath were wiser than the horses of instruction. I admired wisdom, but only when it was carried along by energy. Perhaps this was what attracted me to the theatre in the first place. The stage can be engaged, vital, central to our passions and thoughts; it can also be ferociously dull. To watch people failing their own imaginations is almost unendurable; it is what makes the most wretched movie more bearable than a mediocre play. On those rare occasions, however, when the theatre touches a genuine chord, when it breaks through with an original metaphor or an imaginative act, there is absolutely nothing in any other art form to match its impact.

At Yale we searched for those occasions like pigs sniffing out truffles. Occasionally, rarely, we found our treasures. Though hardly the appropriate person to record our successes, I have not been reticent about naming them in this book. There are those who will disagree with my judgments; it will be enough if they are able to acknowledge our aims. The purpose of our theatre was to awaken the imaginations of our auditors, to stimulate their appetites for the unknown. Nothing exhilarated me more than helping to achieve a moment of theatrical originality; nothing depressed me more than watching us fail. To see a member of the audience nodding would send me into despair—I much preferred an angry spectator to a sleepy one. In the same way, I hoped with our productions to bring some electricity to the university and the town. I shouldn't have been surprised when the currents started coming back.

This is necessarily a very personal book, since my own life has been so intimately intertwined with the life of the institution. There are advantages to such an approach; I also recognize the dangers. I have tried my best to keep subjective pigments from coloring my narrative, but I know I have not always been successful. I only hope I have avoided self-justification and self-exoneration. My book is an attempt to tell the truth about a time. Everybody involved in this time will no doubt have his own version of the truth. Together, we may be able to hold a little piece of history in our hands.

Contents

MAKING
SCENES

I

Entrances
1966-1967

The beginnings and endings of all human undertakings are untidy.

—John Galsworthy

At Norma's memorial service, two months before my departure for Cambridge after thirteen years at Yale, my stepson, Phillip, described how his mother had taught him to overcome his terror and ride a bicycle. She had held him on the seat by the scruff of the neck and, while the six-year-old child was loudly protesting that he couldn't possibly keep his balance, had released him, without his knowledge, to ride the rest of the way by himself. Phillip observed that Norma had behaved in much the same way toward me after I had been invited to become dean of the Yale School of Drama—metaphorically holding me by the collar and pointing me toward the unknown.

His description was accurate, except for the chronology. At first Norma was as hesitant about this particular bicycle ride as I was. An administrative post at Yale University was not one of the dreams that we had shared, and so my first bemused reaction, when Kingman Brewster offered me the job in the winter of 1966, was to say no.

Norma's acting career had ended with our marriage in 1962 (I first met her when she was performing off-Broadway in a 1959 production of Odets' *The Big Knife* under the direction of Peter Bogdanovich); my own had ended even earlier, in 1957. I had spent the past eleven years in academic institutions— the last nine at Columbia, teaching dramatic literature—and for seven of these years I had been a theatre critic for *The New Republic.* My wife and I were both passionately engaged with the theatre, and argued about it incessantly. By that time, however, our theatrical interests had become essentially critical and analytical, and my students at Columbia were either undergraduates in liberal arts or graduate students heading toward a teaching career. The notion of training theatre students, or developing a theatre company, was as far from our minds as the prospect of spending a substantial period of our lives in the city of New Haven.

For we were both confirmed New Yorkers, my wife by adoption, I by birth. We had long considered leaving the city for more pastoral surroundings, but we had never looked at houses more than commuting distance away. When I mentioned this to President Brewster during one of his recruiting visits to our apartment, he replied that this was not a problem: New Haven was really a suburb of New York, and Yale merely another New York City university. The impish way in which he delivered himself of this outlandish notion was one of the reasons we began to consider his offer seriously. Neither of us was prepared for a Yale president at once so modest and so confident, so urbane and stylish, with such an engaging, mischievous manner. Norma liked him immediately, and so did I, though in the years that followed we were never able to penetrate his guard enough to establish real intimacy.

Norma was reluctant to abandon our friends for a city so far from her beloved Bloomingdale's, but the challenge of the situation intrigued her. Kingman was willing to consider the possibility of letting me leave Yale before the end of the usual five-year appointment (I proposed a term of three years) and, in another of his charming inventions, assured me that the job would occupy my time no more than three days a week. I *think*—though I can't remember for sure—that he also applied a little moral pressure to his sales pitch, saying that here was an opportunity for some positive application of my negative criticism. For years I had been belaboring the American theatre for its failures of mind, spirit, and imagination; for years I had bemoaned the absence of great plays on our stages; for years I had deplored the low level of theatre training in America. At the age of thirty-nine, I was now being offered the chance not just to complain but to do something about my complaints, along with the chance to test my convictions concerning the value of a decentralized repertory theatre in the United States connected to a conservatory.

I was not a complete stranger to the Yale School of Drama. In 1948–49, I had been a student there, following my graduation from Amherst College— studying directing and acting, before withdrawing to work on a doctorate in dramatic literature at Columbia. My brief stay at the School suggests that I had not been happy there. I had been interested in acting since childhood, but I was just beginning to develop intellectual interests in the theatre that the School did little to encourage or satisfy. Aside from Alois Nagler's rigorous course in theatre history, there was virtually nothing in the catalogue regarding the literature of the stage. In our directing class we read Burns Mantle's synopses of the best Broadway plays of the season and transferred these to index cards, recording the number of male and female characters and the number of sets. We learned that strong entrances should be made from stage right, since people normally read from left to right, and that the focal character in a scene is best placed at the apex of a triangle. And we watched our directing teacher stage a series of student-written plays—of low aspiration and paralyzing mediocrity—in lavish sets under a huge proscenium arch.

In acting, we were taught phonetics, primarily to help us lose our regional accents and idiosyncrasies. In place of these, we had to learn a "mid-Atlantic" dialect—a quasi-British group of sounds composed of broad *a*'s and trilled *r*'s—which constituted the artificial stage speech of the time. We were asked to engage in a number of odd physical exercises in which we pretended to be typewriters and chandeliers. And we listened to recordings of other actors, especially John Gielgud and Maurice Evans, reading passages from Shakespeare. At the end of the year all these classes were suspended for a few weeks while we worked on a mammoth faculty-directed, faculty-designed production of *Faust,* functioning as spear carriers and crew labor for what we all agreed was an enterprise totally wasteful of talent, time, and materials.

I could see little value in synopsizing bad plays, and argued that directing was an art of interpretation rather than a collection of staging tricks. I protested also that acting was not a matter of imitating other performers but, rather, a compound of characterization, interpretation, and penetration, based on the knowledge of the self and the observation of life. I observed that "mid-Atlantic" was a body of water where nobody lived, therefore unacceptable as a dialect for the stage. I was considered a troublemaker; no doubt I was. But I was quickly convinced that I would have to seek my aesthetic satisfactions away from the School. I began to find great consolation in music. Because long-playing records had just entered the market, 78's were selling at a huge discount; I soon had a large collection of these obsolete discs. I also began to read that year in a systematic way, plowing through English novels, losing myself in Joyce, spending months with Proust. Also that year I fell in love for the first time, with another fiercely opinionated young directing student, now an accomplished actress. And I talked and argued and ate and complained with many of the students of the School.

It was from these people that I learned the most about theatre that year, and developed the confidence to pursue my own ideas. Although a directing student, I was relatively in demand as an actor, and so I had the opportunity to play good roles in student-directed productions of Lorca, Noel Coward, and the Restoration dramatists. The most imaginative work done at Yale while I was there were parodies of Main stage shows done in the experimental theatre. These were performed and directed entirely by students, with men playing the women's parts, in a cabaret format that worked as a release for anger and frustration. There were also bootleg productions in rehearsal at the time— unauthorized shows involving secret cells or enclaves that functioned as a theatre of the catacombs. One of these, of which I was a member, was called the Odets Group. Neither Chekhov nor Stanislavsky, nor Odets for that matter, was recognized in the formal class training, so a few of the Jewish and Italian students who had come to New Haven influenced by the social realism of the Group Theatre, with its Stanislavsky-based techniques, had to find a creative outlet. We rehearsed *Awake and Sing* for three months, under the direction of a Russian-born student named Boris Sagal. We never got to perform this, but we also collaborated on a piece for directing class called *Freight,* about a group of blacks being terrorized on a freight train by a sadistic white tramp (the School had only one black actor, so whites played the other parts). The directing teacher told the class that this strong play had "raped" his emotions, and failed the exercise.

Long before the end of the year, I knew I had had enough of the Yale Drama School, and submitted my withdrawal at the first opportunity. This was not unusual at the time; few theatre-oriented people then bothered to get their degrees from the School, not even its more famous alumni, Paul Newman, Elia Kazan, and Julie Harris. Along with six other members of the Odets Group, I helped to form an off-Broadway company called Studio 7, which played at the Provincetown Playhouse in Greenwich Village in the summer of 1949. We staged Lorca's *The Shoemaker's Prodigious Wife,* Strindberg's *The Father,* and Wedekind's *Earth Spirit,* plays that were virtually unknown at that time to most New York audiences. It was the same summer that Kim Stanley was performing at the Cherry Lane in even more recherché works, and our two Greenwich Village companies may very well have helped to spark the postwar off-Broadway movement.

My life after Yale alternated between academic study and practical theatre work. Chekhov used to say that medicine was his wife and literature his mistress. For me, the marriage was with scholarship, the illicit affair with acting. I worked on degrees at Columbia—an MA in 1950, a PhD in 1957—under such inspiring mentors as Lionel Trilling, S. F. Johnson, Moses Hadas, Joseph Wood Krutch, and Marjorie Nicolson; I spent two years on a Fulbright at the University of Nottingham; and I taught at such places as Cornell, Vassar (where Jane Fonda was one of my students), the Columbia Drama School, and, finally, Columbia's graduate and undergraduate English departments.

Meanwhile I continued to act and direct with various theatre groups as often as possible. In the summer of 1950 I joined Group 20, a theatre devoted to classical and American plays that was based first in Unionville, Connecticut, then in Wellesley, Massachusetts (where it was called Theatre on the Green). Among those I performed with in those days—many of whom were later to join us at Yale—were Nancy Wickwire, Fritz Weaver, Barry Morse, Jerome Kilty, Thomas Gomez, Max Adrian, Tom Clancy, Sylvia Short, Laurinda Barrett, Michael Higgins, Sorrell Booke, Fred Warriner, and Robert Evans. Many of these people had been trained in English acting schools (primarily at the Old Vic School), and, together with the Brattle Theatre in nearby Cambridge, we were among the earliest postwar classical acting companies.

In 1959, mildly bored by teaching English composition and dramatic literature surveys, I took a year off in order to start a professional acting career, meanwhile hedging my bets with a part-time position at the Columbia School of Drama, where I lectured and directed. I acted off-Broadway and in Equity Library productions; I did three or four television shows in New York and Hollywood, where I sat around the Hotel Montecito grousing about the weather with other New York actors; I made the rounds. But it wasn't long before I grew disenchanted with the life of a professional actor. I felt humiliated by acting agents, casting agents, and producers; I was scornful of the quality of the scripts in which so many of us were competing for parts; I had concluded that the life of an American actor circa 1959 was neither personally satisfying nor creatively fulfilling—at least for me. From that point on, I returned to teaching, finding self-expression in the writing of criticism, believing I had left the practical theatre behind me.

My dissatisfaction with the gentility and falseness of the Yale training—so reflective of the theatre I had rejected—was the reason I was first inclined to turn down Kingman's offer out of hand. What began to attract me to it, aside from the opportunity to reform the training, was the chance it offered me to combine the two major interests of my life. I had abandoned my mistress for a period of years, but I had never forgotten her. In my heart, I was still faithful to the painted jade. And I began to imagine that she might appear again, fresh and young and innocent, before my ardent eyes.

As always, Norma knew about my desires before I had formulated them, and so she began to urge me toward a positive decision. Perhaps she eventually saw a role for herself in this new career, but more important was the fact that she had recently become convinced that New York was not a proper place to bring up a teen-age boy like Phillip, much less our infant son, Danny. Both of us were losing interest in watching bad plays, and my arm had grown tired from flailing away at the meretricious Broadway product. As for teaching, it still held considerable attractions, and I was very excited by a new seminar in modern drama I was holding for seven brilliant Columbia undergraduates (four of whom were later to accompany me to Yale). But I would be able to teach at the Drama School, too, besides channeling my energies into practical theatre work. So, with Norma holding me firmly by the collar, we began our long thirteen-year bicycle ride.

Certain questions still remained to be answered. The Yale School of Drama had undergone a number of administrative changes since my departure seventeen years before—for one thing, it had evolved from department status, under the jurisdiction of the School of Fine Arts, into a full-fledged graduate-professional school with a dean of its own—but the faculty was essentially the same, and the training hadn't changed much either. I believed in radical surgery. Would I be allowed to perform this operation on the School? Kingman assured me that I was free to introduce whatever changes were necessary, within the limits of contractual obligations and rational procedure. He seemed unusually open to suggestion. What I didn't know was that a few months earlier he had received a petition signed by virtually all the drama students, protesting the uncreative atmosphere of the School, and demanding that a new dean be appointed immediately to restore the place to its former eminence.

Kingman, independently, had become convinced that he would either have to dissolve the School or transform it. It was because these options were so drastic, I think, that he came to me instead of to the candidates recommended by the faculty—Walter Kerr and Howard Taubman. Kingman knew the title of one of my books, *The Theatre of Revolt,* though I wouldn't swear that he had ever read it. The title may have sounded sufficiently inflammatory to persuade him that I was a firebrand with the appropriate revolutionary credentials. My book was actually a study of metaphysical rebellion in the drama, rather than of social or political revolt; it embodied my conviction, in fact, that trying to change society was impossible without a change in the basic nature of humankind.

Still, *The Theatre of Revolt* did embody many of my aesthetic and philosophical beliefs, particularly a commitment to modernism, and an Ibsenite conviction that gradualism was a form of compromise. For me, the theatrical ideas of seven great modern dramatists—Ibsen, Strindberg, Chekhov, Shaw, Pirandello, O'Neill, and (together with Artaud) Genet—had almost become the basis for a personal religion; they were later to inform our aesthetic at Yale. The distinction I tried to make between revolt and revolution was a difficult one—revolt having to do with ideas and the imagination, revolution with political action—and I was not always successful, in later years, in explaining this distinction to my critics on the right and the left. But in 1966, with the Vietnam war just starting, American society was still stable enough to tolerate change without being threatened or inflamed by it; and Brewster was determined to distinguish his presidency by revitalizing the torpid areas of the university.

By then it had become perfectly obvious that the School of Drama was one of those stagnant ponds, and so, when I told Brewster that I couldn't consider the job without the power to make sweeping changes, he applied immediately for a grant from the Rockefeller Foundation that would help support additional faculty. When he asked me to join him at the foundation to outline my plans to the officers, I at first demurred. I was not a fund-raiser, I told him loftily; it was Yale's responsibility to supply the funds. Kingman assured me that he would not have hired me if he wanted a fund-raiser. He only needed my brief appearance in order to secure the grant, and added that he did not expect me to be much involved in the fiscal needs of the school. Satisfied by his explanation, I accompanied him to the foundation, blissfully unaware that this was to be the first of at least a hundred such visits; Kingman's assurances about my freedom from fund-raising were to prove as dependable as his other assertions about how simple my future task would be.

Kingman Brewster at this time had been in office for only a year, but he was already known as "the King." He had assumed the presidency shortly after the death of Whitney Griswold, who brought him to Yale from Harvard (where Kingman was a professor of law) to serve as his provost. Brewster was a fascinating mixture of qualities that divided people's opinions about him. I for one found him extremely charming, and never quite understood why so many Yale alumni took such a personal dislike to him. There was always a lot of grumbling about Kingman as a "traitor to his class," especially after he opened Yale to women and minority groups, and, of course, his statements about black revolutionaries during the Panther trials were not designed to endear him to the hearts of the Old Blues. But although Kingman was later to develop blind spots in certain areas, he rarely imposed his will on others. He was a wonderful listener rather than a generator of new ideas, capable of recognizing originality when he saw it and clearing its path. Thus, although he formulated no striking educational theories while in office, he possessed something almost as important in a university president—the capacity to absorb a number of points of view and synthesize them into a program.

Kingman's own convictions were hard to identify. As a student at Yale, he had been editor of the *Yale Daily News,* where he endorsed the America First movement and its opposition to United States participation in World War II. This marked him as a conservative, but then he astonished everybody by refusing a tap from Yale's most exclusive secret society, Skull and Bones, because of its undemocratic structure. This was typical of Kingman's internal contradictions and his unpredictable political postures. When I first met him, he was a firm supporter of the Vietnam war and a registered Republican. Within a few years, he was to join the antiwar movement and lead his students to Washington, and, of course, to become the leading spokesman for the legal rights of black revolutionaries.

Kingman was a natural patrician, destined—it was said—to be the first appointed president of the United States. Of stocky build, which sometimes (after too many alumni dinners) verged on portliness, he had the suggestion of jowls and the set jaws of a Yale bulldog, but he was nevertheless a strikingly handsome man, always impeccably tailored in an English style. Kingman had a way of sniffing after he had composed a phrase he liked, as if inhaling the fragrance of his own witticism—a mannerism that, along with his clothes, was frequently copied by his young administrative associates, most of whom resembled him physically as well. Not an electrifying public speaker, Kingman conversed, in private, in soothing, mellow tones that made it a sensuous experience to be in his presence. Conversing with a visitor in his office, he would sit back casually in a high-backed desk chair, and, while the grandfather clock ticked a languorous accompaniment, hypnotize the auditor with his rolling dialogue—twisting his wedding ring, interjecting a sudden sniff, rubbing his eyebrow—until, rising from his chair, he indicated the interview was over. I was always reluctant to leave his presence after our business was completed: that ticking clock and that sonorous voice created an atmosphere in the room that worked on one's spine like a massage.

His greatest gift, during the eleven years of our association, was his confidence in me. I provoked a lot of controversy, particularly in the early years, and Kingman's office was often bombarded with angry letters. But whatever his own opinions about the given situation, he always remained supportive, as he did with his controversial chaplain, William Sloane Coffin, despite personal disagreements with him. Kingman rarely visited our theatre; I can't say he either appreciated or understood our work. His main interest was in the visual arts—painting, sculpture, and, especially, architecture. Normally a model of democratic tact, he was an autocrat when it came to university buildings; no decisions regarding the exterior look of Yale could ever be made without his approval. I suspect he looked on the new Yale architecture as his monument; he certainly took great pride in the construction undertaken during his administration. The Kline Biology Tower, the Old Campus renovations, and, preeminently, the British art gallery—these were the achievements that stimulated his ardor, not music or literature or theatre or a new program in the humanities.

Kingman believed that a major obstacle in the way of attracting distinguished faculty to Yale was the city of New Haven, which, whatever it was like in the past, had now become something of a cultural and aesthetic wasteland. In Kingman's mind, Yale had the obligation to provide some of the artistic life that the city lacked, and it was partly for this reason that he encouraged public performance in the schools of music and drama, where theory had always prevailed. He believed that Yale also had a responsibility to the nation to provide it with not just "leaders of men"—in its traditional role of developing bankers, corporation executives, lawyers, engineers, doctors, and architects—but also scholars, musicians, painters, sculptors, and theatre artists.

Partly for these reasons he endorsed my plan to create a new professional theatre on the grounds of the university. To me, it seemed an inevitable—indeed, an essential—step. When the School of Drama was founded in 1927, following George Pierce Baker's move from Harvard, the central locus of theatrical activity, whether for art or entertainment, was Broadway, but the same theatrical conditions did not continue during the years of Baker's successors. The American theatre began to develop alternatives—not only off-Broadway, which existed during the early years of the century, but off-off-Broadway and the decentralized resident theatre movement. Despite these developments, however, the School of Drama continued to prepare its students as if nothing but Broadway existed, even after Broadway had ceased to be a hospitable place for the serious American drama. Moreover, the School's training procedures had become antiquated, and, as a result, students considered them useless for providing either practical opportunities or viable alternatives. It is a melancholy fact that by the fifties and sixties only a very small proportion of Drama School graduates (most of them designers) were entering the American theatre profession.

Some were going into college or high school theatre departments, some into business, some into advertising. The School had largely lost its reputation as a training institution or a breeding ground for talent. Acting students, for example, were accepted not through auditions but on the basis of academic records and recommendations. My plan was to transform the place from a graduate school, devoted to fulfilling requirements and granting MFA degrees, into a professional conservatory, concerned with developing artists for the American stage. The Master of Fine Arts degree would still be offered after the satisfactory completion of three years of work, but passing courses would no longer be the goal of the work; instead, the student would be encouraged to develop his or her talent. The shift was subtle, but it was important. It suggested a commitment to growth rather than to academics. It was perfectly conceivable, for example, that a gifted acting student might complete three years at the School, playing leading roles and even entering the company afterward, without ever having completed the degree requirements. The degree would be important to the student, not to the School, and it was up to the student to obtain it. Our emphasis would be on training—and training for a well-defined purpose.

This shift to a conservatory structure raised certain problems for the university, though it never seemed to bother Kingman. Yale was a system of schools and colleges administered by deans and, as such, was bound to feel uncomfortable with a professional school that subordinated its academic function. A conservatory of this nature could survive in the university only by sufferance, and would always be particularly vulnerable at Yale, which considered undergraduates the central constituency. It also meant that undergraduates would have much less access to the School than they had in the past, when anyone who registered was allowed to join the acting classes with the drama students. The undergraduates had their own program in theatre administered by the Drama School, which we were to improve as the years went on; and they had many outlets for acting and directing, including the Yale Dramat and the numerous dramatic societies in the residential colleges. But they always objected to being segregated from the graduate-professional activities of our acting and directing students. The objections were understandable but, to my mind, unanswerable. Because of its professional thrust, its selective admission process, and its collaborative nature, the School of Drama would never be able to satisfy undergraduate demands as easily, say, as the School of Art, with its system of lecture courses. As long as it guarded its own integrity and autonomy, the School would always seem a little peripheral to the rest of the university. Indeed, nothing could guarantee its survival except the support of the central administration.

This support remained firm and constant as long as Kingman remained president. Whenever I mentioned the odd nature of the School in an academic setting, he simply shrugged. He approved of my changes, and he didn't seem to care whether they fit a neat pattern within the university. He did, however, refuse one of my requests for change; I didn't want to be called a dean. The title made me uncomfortable; it smacked of academic robes and punitive behavior. How do you communicate with creative people in something called the Office of the Dean? But Yale was an institution administered by deans, and Kingman couldn't release me from the office without violating the charter of the university. I was stuck with the title and, worse, I was stuck with the psychological impact of the title on the minds of faculty and students alike. It created subtle barriers, difficult to overcome, and it affected perceptions of me in a way I couldn't change.

Nevertheless, the dean of the School had another title more appropriate to the situation—director of the Theatre. This was helpful, considering my plans for the formation of a professional company at Yale. In my mind, the company had become the key to the training. If the American theatre had lost its way, then schools of drama were obliged, I thought, to break a new path. It was essential to create a professional model in order to inform the training, determine the aesthetic, develop a laboratory, and provide a potential avenue of future employment. The analogy I proposed to Kingman was the School of Medicine in its relationship to the Yale–New Haven Hospital. Yale faculty participated in both these institutions, while students took classes in one and practiced internship in the other. Like the hospital, the professional theatre could help to bridge a gap between the academic and the urban community; and like the practicing doctors, the practicing artists could provide an up-to-date source of instruction for young people in the field.

Professional instruction was crucial to the realization of the conservatory idea. Kingman had already made it possible through his earlier decision to abolish future tenure appointments at the School. This was a brilliant if controversial move; without it, I doubt if I could have proceeded at all. The School's tenure policies were unquestionably responsible for many of its problems, particularly its stodginess. Tenure was originally invented in order to protect academic freedom, not to sink creative people into an atmosphere of staleness and paralysis. To offer lifetime protected positions to instructors in a professional School was to encourage separation between theory and practice; it was to substitute security for growth. Tenure discouraged practice by rewarding academic achievement instead of artistic endeavor, and since art is a process of continual change, people who did not practice their profession were not really prepared to teach it. A professional company at Yale would provide instructors in all the areas of theatre—acting, directing, design, playwriting, stage management, dramaturgy, technical production, and theatre administration—and while it wouldn't guarantee that all would be inspired teachers, they would certainly be lively and informed, and what they couldn't give in continuity of instruction would be provided by a permanent resident staff.

My hope, at the time, was to involve everybody at the School with the Theatre and everybody at the Theatre with the School, so that the two related structures would ultimately become interdependent, indistinguishable, one. This took years to accomplish, and ran into unexpected difficulties of a kind to be later described. But bringing in professional people had one immediate advantage; it exposed the tenured faculty to new developments in the theatre. This was important because a few of them had become curiously isolated in New Haven. An elder, respected faculty member, for example, surprised me by saying he had not seen any New York productions for years, including Peter Brook's *Marat-Sade* (then considered one of the most seminal shows of the decade). He wasn't alone; most of the others hadn't seen it either. Too busy. Too many committees. Too many classes. Too far to go. A few years later I would find myself making some of the same excuses for my failure to get out of New Haven. How easy it was to lose track of the advances in your field.

The last and most important reason for forming a permanent company at

Yale was to state as strongly as possible that the Yale School of Drama was now devoted to training students not for teaching careers, not for college theatre, not for Broadway, not for television, not for the movies, but rather for the resident theatres that were just then beginning to burgeon in the larger cities of the country. I thought that resident theatres had much in common with universities—both were nonprofit institutions representing a real alternative to the profit-making corporate world. If one informed the mind, the other informed the imagination; both were at their best when challenging, provocative, adventurous, taking risks. Why wasn't it possible for the university to provide not only a library for learning but a living library for art—offering not only the best that had been thought and written but the best that was being invented and created? I began to envision not only professional theatres and art museums in places like Yale but also resident dance and opera companies, symphony orchestras, string quartets—an alliance of art and learning that would make the university a cultural capital. I had no idea, at the time, how easily nonprofit institutions could be drawn into the vortex of the prevailing system or how shaky were their values.

From the beginning, however, I had in mind a professional theatre to be staffed primarily by people who had completed the training at the School, who shared *its* values. The idea was hardly a new one. In Europe, theatre conservatories were common enough in relation to professional companies—the Old Vic School, for example, which trained young actors for the Old Vic Theatre. In the United States, too, George Balanchine and Lincoln Kirstein had developed the New York City Ballet Company out of the School of American Ballet, while such musical training grounds as the Juilliard School and the New England Conservatory continue to provide musicians for such orchestras as the New York Philharmonic and the Boston Symphony. As an idea for theatre, however, the conservatory notion was a relatively new concept in America, and not as readily accepted. People tended to think that actors were discovered in a Hollywood drugstore rather than trained in performance studios. And since Broadway drew its talent from casting calls rather than from schools or workshops, the organic relationship between a conservatory and a professional theatre had to be continually justified, articulated, and explained.

When I outlined the idea to Curtis Canfield, former dean of the School, he assured me that the acting students would never stand for it. This surprised me, since I thought that anybody would welcome the opportunity to supplement the work done in all-student projects with contact with experienced professionals, both in the classroom and onstage. Didn't young actors partly learn from watching distinguished performances? Didn't young directors partly learn by assisting distinguished artists? What I hadn't anticipated was the American resistance to the European master-apprentice system. We had always been plagued by the belief that acting was a matter of instinct, which gifted people pulled out of the air, instead of a technique to be learned, as one learned the violin or the harp. And we were just heading into the late sixties, when all notions of "authority" would come under question, and any kind of apprenticeship would be considered an unacceptable form of self-subordination.

There would have been no problem had I been able to entrust these students from the start—as I learned to do soon after—with responsible roles in the professional productions, but I had inherited two years of students whose talents were then unknown to me, who had developed under an entirely different system. The incoming actors would have the opportunity to start their training from scratch; those already at the School would have to keep some continuity with the old program lest the changes prove unsettling. For this reason I consented, against my better instinct, to approve certain projects (a student production of *Hamlet,* for example), that were clearly beyond the reach of the participants as well as to feature a traditional faculty-directed project (Dean Canfield's production of O'Neill's sea plays with an all-student cast) on the Main stage. Before long, I would learn just who among the students could be entrusted with good roles with a professional company, and who among them was capable of designing, directing, managing, and writing plays for a professional theatre. But until I had more familiarity with the talents of the second- and third-year students, I planned to offer them a compound not only of method and practice but of apprenticeship and observation as central components of the intensified approach to training I hoped to introduce.

For these reasons I ignored Dean Canfield's warning and brought my proposal to the Drama School acting students in the spring of 1966 (some months before I officially took up my duties at Yale). As Canfield had predicted, this group received my plan without much enthusiasm, even with some traces of hostility. Some of my ideas—such as increasing the number of acting faculty from two to eleven, and the number of contact hours from eight to twenty-five per week—were appealing to the student actors. But my proposal to invite visiting companies and eventually to form our own caused considerable consternation. One young actor (ironically, he would join our company when he graduated) coldly rejected the idea that professionals could teach him anything, either on stage or off. "We can play the roles as well as anyone you bring in," he said, with the others nodding their approval. "That is, unless you bring in someone like Morris Carnovsky." It was more than youthful arrogance. These students actually believed they were equal or superior to anyone acting on the stage. A few months later an instructor showed his class the Olivier film of *Henry V,* and, receiving no response, asked who thought he could do it better. Almost all in the class raised their hands.

At this particular meeting the best I could do was assure the acting students they would benefit from the changes. But at the same time that they were objecting to playing supporting roles in professional productions, Stella Adler was objecting to their playing any roles at all, even in the student projects. Stella had been one of my first new faculty appointments. A good friend of Norma's and mine for a number of years, she had been running a studio in New York where she gained a reputation as a brilliant, inspiring teacher; she had taught Brando, De Niro, and Pacino, and she had taught my wife, who later assisted her at her studio. A leading actress with the Group Theatre, Stella was one of the few who had actually worked with Stanislavsky in the Soviet Union. Her disagreements with Lee Strasberg over what she took to be his misapplication of Stanislavsky theory were a continuing source of lively debate in New York theatrical circles.

Stella had done little acting in recent years, and had stopped altogether after an ill-fated production, in England, of Arthur Kopit's *Oh Dad, Poor Dad.* She didn't have a lot of respect for most directors, and she didn't think much of most critics either. Stella's ambiguous attitude toward acting inevitably communicated itself to her students. It was to her the most ennobling—but also the most difficult—of the arts. As a result, some of her charges tended to consider performing an ordeal; it was said that if you could get through Stella's training, nothing would ever frighten you again. Whatever she thought about the terrors of acting, however, she certainly demonstrated, through her own example, that a great actor had to be a great human being. Ageless, magnificently beautiful, heavy-lidded and white-maned, she dressed like a French courtesan and lived in an apartment furnished like a Venetian brothel, but she had the regal dignity of an English queen. Stella Adler struck admiration, love, and fear into the hearts of all who knew her—at once the most intelligent and seductive of women, witty and scholarly, generous and loving, one of the great myths of the American stage, whose boards she shunned as a result of wounds of which she never spoke.

When I finally agreed to Kingman's offer in March of 1966, Stella was the obvious choice to head the acting department. She stood at the very heart of the American theatre—which, in one sense, meant that her techniques were designed for realism. But she also knew and appreciated Shakespeare, and she had a deep understanding of Ibsen, Strindberg, and, especially, Chekhov, all of whom she taught in a famous script breakdown course. I believed that Stella would help us navigate the extremes of artificial, English-style "rep" acting, on the one hand, and narrow Actors Studio naturalism, on the other. I wanted to develop an actor capable of playing any role ever written, from the Greeks to the most experimental postmodernists. Of all the New York acting teachers who had come from the Group Theatre, Stella was clearly the most versatile, the most demanding, the most passionate—and, I thought, the most open to a continually changing theatre.

I arrived at her apartment in March, accompanied by Jeremy Geidt, whom I had just persuaded to teach acting also; later he was to become one of the key figures in our acting company. Jeremy had performed extensively with British companies, had taught at the Old Vic School, and had come to the United States as a member of the English satirical group called The Establishment. He seemed eminently qualified to train in a variety of areas, including Shakespeare, mask work, satirical improvisation, and games theatre—an unlikely mishmash of styles, which pleased me. Upon our arrival in Stella's luxurious Fifth Avenue living room, she eyed Jeremy suspiciously. She distrusted English actors because she found them mannered, lacking in truth. Over tea, however, Jeremy quickly disarmed our hostess. Endowed with the barrel chest of a Toby jug and the delicious vocabulary of a foulmouthed sailor, Jeremy assailed Stella's ears with his salty theatre anecdotes and his obscene jokes. For a few moments she looked at him quizzically; soon after, they were fast friends.

Stella had not yet decided to commit herself to Yale. She worried about the travel, the salary, the classroom space. After an hour of discussion, I asked her point-blank if she would accept the job. "I'll do it," she said, fluttering her eyelids and pursing her lips, "I'll do it . . . *for you.*" Only two things stood in the way. She insisted on teaching all her classes over a period of a day and a half a week, and she wanted to be assured that the acting students would not perform in public for the first two years of training.

Stella had a way of getting whatever she wanted, and she had already reduced the two of us to jelly; still, this last seemed to me an excessively stringent demand, and I resisted it. Jeremy and I believed that acting students learned as much from getting up in front of an audience as they did from scene work and exercises; we couldn't imagine a program in which actors were prevented from acting. I feared that the students wouldn't be able to imagine it either, and that Stella was asking for trouble. Nevertheless, she remained firm. Stella was convinced that performance was earned only after strenuous training; otherwise, the actor only calcified bad habits. In this she was following Stanislavsky, who had prohibited his students from performing for an even longer period. But I didn't think she was being sufficiently sensitive to the impatience of American students or their need to display their talents. Stella remained steadfast on the issue; so did I. Finally, we compromised. Students would be asked to refrain from public performance only during their first year of training—and they would be given the chance to act before an audience at the end of that year, in a faculty-directed project.

Stella, Jeremy, and I held auditions for the incoming class at the Establishment Theatre in New York, with Norma popping in from time to time to look the candidates over. We saw about two hundred and fifty applicants that year (in future, the number of applicants would more than double) out of which we chose a class of thirty (in future, the first-year class would number fourteen). I was amazed at Stella's concentration during those arduous auditions. I was also amazed at her energy; long after Jeremy and I had flagged, Stella was still fresh. She was, moreover, patient and generous even with those whose lack of talent was embarrassing. Whenever some tongue-tied dolt would start annihilating the letter scene from *Two Gentlemen of Verona* or Mercutio's speech in *Romeo and Juliet,* Jeremy would reach unobtrusively under the table with his two hands and pretend to be pushing the detonator on a couple of sticks of dynamite. But Stella lavished as much of her charm on those without any gift as on the most talented candidates; and everyone who did an audition for her seemed dazzled by the experience. Among the ones we chose that spring were Talia Shire (then called Talia Coppola), Stephen Mills, Jan Egleson, and

Ken Howard—the last, a splendid blond giant from Amherst who made Stella's eyes light up.

Aside from Stella and Jeremy, I made other appointments to the faculty during those spring and summer months, including Gordon Rogoff as associate dean, Arnold Weinstein in playwriting, Herman Krawitz and Harvey Sabinson in the new department of theatre administration we were forming, Rhoda Levine in movement, Jan Kott in dramatic literature, Arthur Pepine in stage management, and Joseph Papp in directing. Papp was coming down from a disappointing year with the New York Shakespeare Festival, and for a brief moment I thought I saw the chance to bring him to Yale on a full-time basis, as a teacher and director. But that same year, he started his work at the Public Theatre and in a few short months had completely reversed his fortunes through a policy change that found him producing new American and European plays instead of Shakespeare. Naturally, this began to occupy him so completely that he was forced to share his teaching with Gerry Freedman, a former colleague at the Shakespeare Festival.

Rogoff went on salary in the spring, and prepared the way for me, during a trip he took to London in June, to meet with a number of English theatre artists whom I also hoped to invite to the school as teachers. These included the directors Peter Brook, Michael Elliott, William Gaskill, and John Blatchley, the designer Jocelyn Herbert, and the voice teacher Cecily Berry—but all refused my invitations. Either they had prior commitments or they disapproved of America's growing involvement in the Vietnam war. I did, however, succeed in persuading the fine English designer Michael Annals to join the design department, headed by Donald Oenslager, and I also enticed Jonathan Miller to the school for a few months as a lecturer and director.

I was embracing the new job in earnest, finding the most enjoyment in recruiting faculty. I had no administrative experience whatever, and the unfamiliar tasks of being a dean were already changing my life, even before I officially took office on the first of July. For the first time, I began to wake up in the middle of the night, remembering something I had forgotten, and make notes on a pad beside the bed. My nocturnal restlessness brought sharp looks, and occasionally sharp jabs, from Norma, who valued her uninterrupted slumber. "Don't sleep like a great man," she said one night, quoting Stella's immortal remark to Harold Clurman, "just sleep." But sleep was never to be the same again for me. The waking hours were much too full of anxieties.

Norma herself was displaying certain anxieties about the future. Our visits to New Haven in the spring had been personally supervised by Kingman, who took great trouble to organize dinner parties with people he thought we might like to meet. Among these were John Hersey, then master of Pierson College, and his charming wife, Barbara, who quickly became two of our closest friends in New Haven. But Norma remained very worried about the formality of life in this community, where, she had heard, the center of social life was the Lawn Club, and invitations to tea or dinner were personally delivered to your door by New Haven matrons wearing white gloves and Peck & Peck suits. In New

York our friends were mostly cantankerous intellectuals and artists, who often concluded an evening with a screaming quarrel. By contrast, New Haven struck us both as rather decorous. Would Yale be able to accept our outspoken, freewheeling style? And was this sedate community prepared to accommodate the kind of provocative theatre we were hoping to establish?

The unspoken worry was over being Jewish in an essentially Gentile community. Brewster, patrician though he was, had no apparent difficulty with people of other racial or religious groups, but Yale itself had traditionally been a protected Wasp enclave, and vestiges of anti-Semitism still remained. Stella certainly noticed a difference during her first visit to the Drama School: John Gassner was the only Jew on the entire faculty. Furthermore, the two or three homosexuals were in the closet, leading hidden lives as exemplary family men. "How can you have a theatre," she asked, "without Jews and homosexuals?" And without them, how could you have a university or a cultural community? At one of those early dinner parties Norma and I felt obliged to attend in New Haven, one of the guests—a curator of old maps—fixed us with a frozen smile over dessert and said, "I hope you're not coming here expecting to find the Promised Land?" We found this a curious allusion. Neither Norma nor I had ever been oversensitive to anti-Semitic innuendo, but then neither of us had ever before lived in such a rarefied community.

Norma was also worried about *where* we were going to live. Her strong nesting instinct, coupled with a childhood dread of moving, made housing an important issue. Kingman, sensing this, took a personal interest in finding us a proper home. He had one particular place in mind, an imposing, three-story quasi-Tudor dwelling on a private street, which the architect Eero Saarinen had renovated for himself and his wife just before his death. Aline Saarinen had sold the house to Yale at a conveniently low price when she moved from New Haven, and now Yale was willing to sell it to us.

The university, however, had been extremely careless about maintaining the house during the two years it was uninhabited. The heat had been shut off; the walls and ceiling were cracked; dirt and plaster dust were everywhere. The living room, moreover, had been redesigned to focus attention on Saarinen's furniture, so that the windows (along with a view of two glorious giant birch trees) had been blocked off with plastic sheets. Kingman showed us through the house late one cold afternoon, illuminating our passage with his cigarette lighter. We were shivering and depressed, but Kingman, elated as always by architecture he liked, was in a very high mood. "I love this place," he announced, extending his lighter into the cold, dark corners of each plaster-laden room. "I *hate* this place," responded Norma, and refused even to investigate the third floor.

The next day, when the sun was out and the air had warmed a little, I persuaded her to give the house a second chance. This time she began to see some possibilities, though she continued to be daunted by its size. We made the purchase soon after with the help of a generous Yale mortgage, and moved in May. Within a few months Norma had transformed it, with her genius for homemaking, into a warm, attractive, spacious environment. We lived there for the next thirteen years, never really managing to fill the space or to find any intimacy in its huge public rooms.

On the same day we moved, we were invited by former Dean and Mrs. Curtis Canfield to a reception for us and for alumni of the school. Curt and Kitty had been extremely gracious to us since my appointment (he had been my drama teacher at Amherst when I was a student), and this reception was intended as a kindly gesture, designed to make us feel at home among the graduates of the institution I now led. Norma and I were surrounded by packing boxes, and covered with the grime of moving. We were also a little shy about meeting lots of people we didn't know. Both of us would have much preferred to spend the afternoon in the tub, but it was impossible to refuse. On the way to the punch bowl, Kitty—with Norma behind her—stopped to speak to a middle-aged alumna ahead of her in the line. "Have you met Mrs. Brustein yet?" asked Kitty, preparing to make the introduction. "No," replied the woman, obviously unaware of Norma's presence, "Thank God, I've been spared *that.*"

Norma was amused by the incident, but I took it as an ill omen. And as it turned out, our relations with the "old" alumni, as distinguished from the students who finished under us, were never very cordial. For this, I must accept my share of blame. Before coming to Yale, I was hardly known for diplomatic behavior, but I sure made a mess after I arrived. When my appointment was announced, I took the opportunity to sound off freely about the shortcomings of the old School and how I proposed to cure them. In my eagerness to announce a new program, I made many remarks that no doubt wounded those who loved the old traditions, and I wasn't at all reticent about characterizing what I took to be the failures of the past. Since most of those at Yale when I was a student seemed to share my lack of regard for the old program, I believed, foolishly, that they would welcome my efforts to improve the School. I had underestimated the power of time in changing perceptions, and the power of nostalgia in altering memory.

Still, I don't really believe that things would have been much different even if I had proved more circumspect in my remarks. A profound change was about to take place, which the press was beginning to notice, and any change implies a criticism of the previous pattern. How could the introduction of a new program, a new curriculum, and a new faculty be interpreted as anything other than the repudiation of an old program, an old curriculum, and an old faculty? Some of these criticisms I intended, others were imagined by the alumni. As a result, an adversary relationship developed almost immediately, which was to continue until our departure thirteen years later.

This hostile attitude was intensified by a few buckets of paint. Like all incoming deans, I had been given a small budget to make some minor alterations in the facility. Since my predecessor had already used his fund to gold-leaf the theatre, I decided to use the money to give the entire place a bright new coat of paint. There was nothing symbolic about this decision, nor was there anything significant about the shade we chose. The walls and ceiling of the School were peeling, and the beige and green colors of the public rooms made the whole facility look dingy and institutional. In an interview I gave at the end of my first year—typical of the imprudent things I was saying—I recorded my impressions of the School upon my arrival: "It was like entering King Tutankhamen's tomb; closets stuffed with eighteenth-century costumes that were never touched or used; prop rooms that were constantly kept locked; musty, gloomy interiors; beige offices with horrible lighting fixtures; a peeling theatre built along the dimensions of a Shubert house." In an effort to cheer things up, Norma added some colorful posters contributed by a friend of hers from Posters Unlimited, and chose to paint the greenroom and University Theatre a shade of bright red, a common enough color in New York theatres.

Howls of pain and outrage! The new red color confirmed the suspicions of the old alumni—and some of the university community as well—that the School had been captured by a wild, irresponsible radical with links to the KGB. Nor was this reaction limited to older people. The Yale Dramat (the undergraduate theatre club) was incensed that we had chosen our paint without consulting its board members, and wrote an angry letter protesting my arbitrary procedures. I was quickly learning about Yale protocol—and also about the traditional tension between the Yale Drama School and the Yale Dramat. This dated back to that fateful day when George Pierce Baker—the new boy in town from Harvard—had first invaded the turf of Monty Woolley—the professor of English who advised and directed the undergraduates—and started a row between them whose reverberations were still being felt.

Although I tried from time to time to placate the "old" alumni, I sensed that the damage had been done, and my efforts would all prove fruitless. I spoke to alumni groups; I arranged testimonials with them for departing faculty; I let them speak to our students on "career" day. Each time I was assured, "Well, it's a start." After a few years, I grew tired of annual "beginnings" and made an ending. There was no profit in the effort, and my heart wasn't in it. Most of these people weren't in theatre anyway, and they had never supported the School in any conspicuous way. Their annual giving varied between $7,000, when they were pleased with the administration, and $6,000, when they weren't—hardly worth exposing oneself to insult for. Why, Paul Newman had just pledged $50,000 by himself, on the urging of Joe Papp, to help start our resident company. I decided to turn alumni affairs over to a well-loved former faculty member of the School, and give my attention to serious fund-raising, which I now recognized as my personal obligation if I wanted to see my programs through. And with the addition of two new departments—theatre administration and dramatic criticism—to the existing five divisions of the School—acting, directing, design, technical production, and playwriting—I had my work cut out for me, especially with my plan to start a new professional theatre.

For this reason, the Rockefeller grant secured by Kingman was of great significance in that first year. This was a declining grant of $340,000 dispensed over five years, designed to provide seven new faculty positions (at $20,000 each) until the teachers being supplemented reached retirement age. I managed to stretch the number of new faculty from seven to twenty-two by combining part-time professionals, on partial salary, with full-time people generous enough to work for less. From the previous administration I had inherited a $75,000 grant from the American Broadcasting Company for a television writing program. I wanted the money but was uninterested in TV, so I persuaded James Hagerty of ABC to let us call the program "Writing for the Camera." This allowed us to include film-making—and, more important, to invite gifted young playwrights to the School on fellowships, for the ostensible purpose of studying film but for the actual purpose of writing plays. During this year a commercial television network was contributing to the support at the School of such experimental theatre writers as Sam Shepard, Megan Terry, Barbara Garson, Lanford Wilson, and John Guare, which seemed to me absolutely proper and oddly appropriate.

My final task in the spring, before decamping for a Martha's Vineyard vacation, was to introduce myself to the older faculty at the School. It was a trying experience for all. Some of these people—notably John Gassner, professor of playwriting and dramatic literature—were genuinely friendly and helpful. Others did their best to put a good face on what they obviously considered a bad situation. It was weird enough to find myself in a position of authority, but some of these faculty members had been my instructors when I was a student at Yale, and it was no longer any secret how I felt about *that* experience. I tried to assure the more worried members of the faculty that the changes being contemplated would not disrupt their own routines too seriously —especially since most of them were on an academic schedule (four to six class hours weekly), which could be easily accommodated within our expanded training program. Only one faculty member—a young playwriting instructor —resigned in protest against my appointment. But many of those remaining were plainly unhappy about the prospect of sharing their students with these new mavericks from New York.

Most of these teachers had been at the School since the early days of George Pierce Baker, and were therefore on the verge of retirement. My problem was to find assignments for them that were, at the same time, meaningful for the teacher and harmless to the student. One of them, Constance Welch, had started at Yale with Baker in 1927; now she had one more year before she reached the mandatory retirement age of sixty-eight. Miss Welch had been the sole acting instructor at the School for almost forty years, teaching both voice and performance to every acting student in the program. It seemed sensible to me that she should devote her final year to the graduating class, which she had already followed through two years of training, while Stella and Jeremy would take over the incoming group and the second year. This may have been sensible, but it caused resentment among the alumni. Much admired by her former students, Miss Welch was seen as a martyr to the revolution, and when she retired, in June of 1967, I was accused of having forced her out. The fact that her appointment was mandated by university regulations did not convince the alumni who believed that I, somehow, was in a position to postpone her departure. That was a feat that even Kingman Brewster would have been unable to perform—at least, at the time (mandatory retirements were not to be dropped until future years). But the alumni attitude suggested not only a certain bad will but also a belief that I had been invested with extraordinary powers. It was not hard to see why, since Kingman had given me considerable freedom to develop my programs. Hiring, for example, was entirely in my hands during the early years until each department was consolidated enough to make its own recommendations. So were the curriculum and the catalogue, which I wrote virtually single-handedly. And it was I who decided on promotions and raises.

My academic autonomy (some would call it tyranny) as dean was a departure from traditional university practice, where decisions are usually made by committees, and my artistic autonomy (some would call it despotism) as director was a departure from resident theatre practice, where power is shared with a board of directors. I recognized the danger of absolute power, which Lord Acton has told us corrupts absolutely, and I know that I sometimes misused this power—not absolutely, I hope. But I also recognized that a new artistic program needs decisive leadership, which democratic procedures tend to hobble. I had seen too many adventurous artistic directors fired by their boards, and too many strong programs watered down by committees, to have much faith in consensus politics in regard to aesthetic or intellectual matters. Later I began to share these powers with the faculty and the students, and had to learn the lesson all over again when, in one of the most painful episodes of my life, I was forced to reassert a claim to leadership in order to save the institution from falling apart. I hope I was always open to advice and counsel, and I know I was always willing to credit a good idea. But in those years I jealously reserved the final decision on any issue that might change the nature of the School or Theatre.

Soon after arriving on Martha's Vineyard for the summer, I received a bulky collection of computer print-outs, full of weird numbers and odd symbols. This was the School of Drama budget, and it was like nothing I had ever dealt with before. While I was engaged one morning in trying to make some sense of the figures, I was visited by Philip Roth, who, seeing me bent over this strange document, immediately began improvising a sketch about bureaucratic procedures and the bizarre humanoids who performed them. To Roth, we were in the land of Kafka, taking up positions before the locked door of the Castle. Dealing with budgets *was* a new experience for me, and it was bound to turn me into a different breed of human creature. But there was another way in which I found myself changing—I was looking at Roth, for example, with more than a friendly regard. I knew he was halfway through a new comedy called *The Lone Ranger* (never completed). Would he let me look at the manuscript for our first season at Yale? The Vineyard was loaded with talented people who might have plays, and I was learning to overcome my shyness about approaching them.

I next discovered that Jules Feiffer (also a Vineyard neighbor) had just completed his first long play. It was called *Little Murders,* and it dealt, pro- phetically, with the brutalization of the urban landscape. It didn't take long to persuade him to let us have this play as the opening work of the new season; Jules and I spent much of the summer choosing a director and interviewing actors for the forthcoming production. Robert Lowell was also engaged in theatrical activities, writing a new adaptation of *Prometheus Bound,* which he graciously offered to us at Yale. It contained references to the Vietnam war and the Johnson administration, both very much on Lowell's mind since he had publicly rejected an invitation to a White House party for the arts (an invitation that I had also declined, and for a similar reason). On the island, too, were John Hersey, William Styron, Lillian Hellman, Art Buchwald, and many others whom I was to importune at one time or another for theatrical material for our theatre.

Kingman was also on the island. We saw each other, during the summer, on the beach and at dinner—somehow the conversation almost invariably turned into an argument about the war. Kingman and his wife, Mary Louise, were both supporters of our intervention then, arguing that if we didn't defend freedom in Vietnam, then all of Southeast Asia would fall to the Communists. My stepson, Phillip, all of fourteen that summer and very querulous, pro- nounced the domino theory an insufferable excuse for the presence of troops where they didn't belong, and he startled Kingman and Mary Louise by the vehemence with which he disputed their position. Arguments were beginning to heat up all over America on the subject of the war. Youth was finding a voice and a cause; tempers were inflamed; social events were turning nasty.

Most of my vacation time, however, was occupied with interviewing and hiring new faculty, revising the course catalogue, and designing the theatre season. In 1966 we had not yet formed a resident company. We would be doing plays, but what was later to be called the Yale Repertory Theatre was still a distant dream. What we started with was a production apparatus, not an ongoing organism, a fact reflected in the way it was described. During the first year the season was produced by "The Yale School of Drama." In the second year we called ourselves "The Yale School of Drama Repertory Theatre." But only in the third year, when some of our own people had been developed and the idea was taking root, did I have the temerity to use the name the company was to have thereafter—"The Yale Repertory Theatre."

Whatever we called it, the new theatre had to have a season. *Little Murders* would not be ready for production until October, so we decided to open the year with a production by a visiting company, the first of many to be invited over the years. Gordon Rogoff had told me of a lively Philadelphia-based group called the Theatre of Living Arts, which had just done an experimental production of Beckett's *Endgame,* under the direction of its founder and leader, Andre Gregory. On Rogoff's recommendation, we invited this group to perform at Yale in early September. Immediately a problem arose. Greg- ory's brilliant designer, Eugene Lee, had left the Drama School, not under the most agreeable circumstances, the year before I came, and the technical department, insulted to find Lee back at Yale, was refusing to work with him on the set. The problem was resolved when Lee agreed to do his own design work in the early hours of the morning, when the irate faculty members would have been spared the ignominy of his presence.

Endgame proved to be a profoundly original, profoundly controversial production, which encouraged us all about the daring of the resident theatre movement. Lee's splendid set was a four-sided cage made of transparent mesh and a steel floor that rattled painfully when it was walked on; and the production was performed in vaudeville style, preceded by an overture consisting largely of Nelson Eddy and Jeanette MacDonald duets. In Gregory's interpretation, the relationship between Hamm and Clov (powerfully played by David Hurst and Ron Leibman) evoked memories of all the great American comic duos from Laurel and Hardy to Abbott and Costello, and underlined their symbiotic dependency on each other. As a result, the play has never been funnier or, in my opinion, more powerful. Ron Leibman's work, especially, was a revelation; I was full of admiration for his manic daring. And in David Hurst, he had the ideal partner for his tragic tantrums and comic pratfalls.

Endgame pretty much divided the New Haven audience during the one week it was performed. Most of our students were electrified by the acting and excited by the direction. But a few spectators were shocked by a moment in the play when Hamm and Clov made masturbatory motions. At a symposium we held after one of the performances, some Yale professors attacked the production not only from an aesthetic but from a moral point of view, complaining about "bad taste" and "obscene" gestures. Arnold Weinstein rose to his feet, incensed. "What kind of people are you anyway," he shouted at the astonished audience. "You ought to be ashamed. You've just seen an inspired production and at least two great performances, and all you do is complain about some dirty gestures!"

Some of the faculty at the school were shocked as well, and not only by *Endgame.* Curtis Canfield—having read the script of *Little Murders,* which includes a long speech by the protagonist describing an obsession he once had with photographing shit—took me aside to warn me about the consequences of doing such a play in New Haven. "The clergy, Bob, *the clergy,*" he exclaimed, waving his arms the way he did when he was agitated. "For your own good, you have to be more careful about what you put on stage here." He suggested cutting the speech, and when I protested that aside from the censorship issue this would do serious damage to the play, Curt replied, "Well, can't you persuade the playwright to change the word to *crap?*"

By any other name the shit would not smell sweet—but as it turned out, our potential confrontation with the clergy didn't materialize. *Little Murders* was never produced at the Yale Theatre. Before we started production, I learned that Jules Feiffer had been assuming we would move the whole thing to Broadway if it was successful, with a commercial producer, and this forced me to make my first painful decision. I had conceived of our professional work as an alternative to Broadway, not a supplement to it, and with our very first production we were on the verge of becoming a tryout house. I was eager to see American playwrights reach a larger audience, but there was a subtle difference between doing a play because it had no apparent commercial possibilities and doing it because it needed testing for a Broadway run. Whatever contracts would be signed between a playwright and a producer subsequent to production at Yale, we couldn't be a party to prior agreements and still be true to our purpose. I knew this position would not be easily understood—by neither writers nor actors, nor even by most critics. And it was not very practical, either, for an indigent, nonprofit theatre that had the opportunity of sharing in the author's royalties in the event of a success. But I knew that if I didn't make our position clear from the start, we would always be subject to compromise thereafter.

This put me in a quandary. Jules was a close personal friend, and had given us his play as a gesture of friendship. We had, moreover, already put a considerable amount of time into preparing the production. I feared that I was being excessively rigid over a principle that few seemed to understand. I tried to resolve my own conflict by asking Jules to postpone his Broadway production until the following season, by which time the New York version would have developed an independent life of its own. When he, quite understandably, refused, I felt I had no choice but to release the play.

It was my first experience with the powerful, almost irresistible lures of the commercial system; it was hardly to be my last. I battled these pulls and pressures throughout my whole stay at Yale, always unhappy with the way my principles were affecting my personal relationships. At times, I felt like Ibsen's Brand, sacrificing my family, friends, and personal happiness for an unrealizable ideal. Still, I was in the grip of an idea, and if I compromised its premises, what was the sense of coming to New Haven? At least, this unpleasant incident helped us to develop a policy regarding production of new plays; before we accepted them, the playwright had to agree to postpone a potential Broadway production for at least one season—a demand we did not extend to production off-Broadway or at other nonprofit resident theatres. The real solution to this nagging problem would not arrive until we had developed a permanent company, for when actors were in rehearsal with another play, it would be impossible to transfer their current production to a Broadway house.

Having lost *Little Murders,* we had a gaping hole in the beginning of our season; rather frantically, I began shopping around for a substitute. At an Open Theatre workshop in New York, I found one—a work-in-progress called *Viet Rock.* Written and directed by Megan Terry in collaboration with the members of the Open Theatre, *Viet Rock* was the first play, to my knowledge, to deal with the issues of the Vietnam war, and to approach them through the youthful medium of rock music and scorching satire. The work of another visiting acting company, *Viet Rock* was not the homegrown, Yale-developed creation I had hoped would open our first season, but it had undeniable attractions, aside from its subject matter. Still in a formative stage, it could be rehearsed in New Haven at the beginning of the term, and thereby give our students the opportunity both to observe an interesting experimental work in the process of evolution and to engage in workshops with the cast.

The four-week rehearsal period eventually gave birth to a stimulating, if somewhat crude, piece of theatre which, in retrospect, had more significance as a media event than as a stage achievement. Controversy surrounded it from the first. Following an uneventful opening, the second-night performance was disrupted by two former students of the school who came to the theatre with the apparent intention of making a scene. One of them, a black, interrupted the play to complain that there were no colored people in the cast. Muriel Miguel, a full-blooded American Indian, shouted back from the stage, "What about me? I'm not exactly white!" The heckler was removed from the theatre by a campus policeman; later he told the *Yale Daily News* that he had been ejected because of his color. I heard mumbling that I had arranged the disruption in order to get publicity for the theatre. This was ironic, considering how hard I had been working to keep the New York critics away from *Viet Rock*, but it was typical of the suspiciousness with which we were now being regarded.

The local press was divided on *Viet Rock*, though it went on to a moderate run off-Broadway. Some critics found it exciting and "relevant" (a word just coming into fashion then); others thought it obscene or tasteless or both. Kingman received some letters from Yale alumni and the New Haven Chamber of Commerce protesting this play, especially after *Endgame*—there was a general impression we were bringing on an avant-garde holocaust. Walking together on College Street, Kingman told me of his growing correspondence; he was worried that we were getting too political. "Would you do a play by William Buckley if he gave one to you?" he asked, half jokingly. I replied that I would consider any play for production, providing it had quality. Kingman was a little disturbed, but he made no further effort to influence our policy. He was having enough trouble with the uproar being caused by William Sloane Coffin.

I myself was not completely happy with *Viet Rock*. For one thing, the completed work was politically simplistic; for another, it was not very well performed. I didn't know when I invited the Open Theatre to Yale that it was in the midst of one of its factional disputes (the group tends to splinter every few years), and that half the actors I saw in New York had been replaced. Some of the actors possessed a raw, sinewy power; others had more nerve than craft. I had written about the workshop version of *Viet Rock* with approval in an article called "The Third Theatre"; in a later article, to the chagrin of some of the company, I had to qualify my enthusiasm. I was divided between my admiration for these young performers and my concern over their lack of training, especially since they were currently serving as models for acting students at Yale.

Those most directly influenced by the methods of *Viet Rock*, as a matter of fact, were not the actors but the directors at the school, many of whom were just beginning to get very interested in performance group techniques. As a result, a few of these student directors began to compete with the acting teachers for influence on and control of the student actors. These young people believed that Stella's methods were old-fashioned, and that they were more qualified—by politics, culture, age, and temperament—to guide their own contemporaries than these relics from another epoch. For her part, Stella had little use for her critics in the directing area. She didn't have much use for directors anyway, but to her, these young people were "pishers"—still wet in the diapers—whose influence on the actors was like the blind leading the blind.

It was the beginning of generational conflict. For a while I tried to accommodate both demands on the acting students because the theatre I wanted required both the confident hand of experience and the passionate anarchy of youth. A resident company invulnerable to new ideas was in danger of becoming a museum, while a theatre that pulled itself out of history was likely to become insular, narcissistic, self-absorbed. I desired a theatre that was technically expert without being artistically stiff, and I wanted an acting training that would prepare the students for all kinds of theatre, from classical plays to free-form improvisations. What I didn't realize was that, lacking a single acting teacher sympathetic to all these styles, the acting students would be subject to confusing influences, pulling them in several directions. To Stella's dismay, we began to discuss the possibility of "ensemble groups," to be led by a student director in collaboration with a student playwright and designed to evolve a theatre piece as a collective effort with actors. These ensembles would be instituted the following year, but Stella continued to insist that the actors be excluded.

During this first year at Yale I was exploring many avenues for the School, hesitant to preclude anything that might have creative issue. Only later was I forced, by circumstance, to choose a consistent, well-defined direction for the training. I had come to my position out of a background that was liberal in politics, philosophy, and educational theory. I was, therefore, still eager to make room for dissenting opinions and alternative ideas, though not at the expense of my decision-making powers. It was for this reason that I set up a weekly "bull session" with students and faculty in the university theatre, designed to air gripes and grievances, as well as to circulate information. These sessions, good-natured enough at first, were to grow increasingly acrimonious in the coming years, but it was clear from the start that the main aesthetic issue dividing the School was the conflict between the technique and ideology of performing groups, with their open-ended preparations for a single "relevant" work, and the goals of resident repertory theatres, with their five-week rehearsals of a sequence of already written plays.

My own preferences were clear enough. But I still believed that the experimental energy of performance groups was a necessary component in vitalizing a theatre devoted to text. I liked what the Open Theatre had created with Jean-Claude van Itallie on *America Hurrah!* and I was impressed by Peter Brook's reinterpretation of Shakespeare with the Royal Shakespeare Company. My belief in a synthesis between the past and the future—between tradition and experiment, between text and performance technique—was reinforced by the next production we did at Yale: *Dynamite Tonite!,* an "actors' opera" with words by Arnold Weinstein and music by William Bolcom. *Dynamite Tonite!* was not a new work, but it was the first to be produced entirely under the auspices of our new theatre. Originally produced by the Actors Studio Company at an off-Broadway house in 1964, the play had run into a cruel press and closed in one night, when the producer (Lee Strasberg and his associates) panicked. Although a critic on the second-night list, I had been invited to the opening by Arnold Weinstein; otherwise I would never have seen it. I felt a personal loss when the production was withdrawn so quickly.

In early 1966 I created a series on public television called *The Opposition Theatre,* devoted to the kind of new plays then being developed by American writers. This gave me the opportunity to gather together some of the original cast of *Dynamite Tonite!* and present the play in a half-hour version. It was my first experience with producing and (in the light of later problems) casting was deceptively easy. We got William Redfield back as Smiley and George Gaynes as the Enemy Prisoner. Barbara Harris was unavailable to play Tlimpattia again, so Rae Allen did her part. In place of David Hurst, the original Captain, we cast Eugene Troobnick, and instead of Anthony Holland as the Sergeant, Alvin Epstein. The original production in the Studio had been done by Paul Sills, who was replaced by Mike Nichols at some point in rehearsals. Our version was directed by the author, Arnold Weinstein. I mention this, because almost every one of these people, many of them previously associated with Paul Sills's Second City troupe, were ultimately to join our work at Yale.

The success of this abridged TV version—which used a single piano instead of a cabaret orchestra—encouraged me to produce the full-length opera on the stage. By luck, the entire television cast was available again, with the exception of Rae Allen, who was replaced by Linda Lavin. Most fortunate of all was the availability of Paul Sills, who managed to restage the play in little over two weeks. Paul knew the actors; the actors knew the work; and so the rehearsal period was spent not in exploring the text so much as in exploring physical relationships among the company. For our students this proved an invaluable demonstration of "games theatre," a technique invented by Paul's mother, Viola Spolin. During one session the actors simply threw a basketball around from hand to hand; during another they went through the entire play just touching each other; during another they spoke their parts while handling all the props. It was a brilliant lesson for our students—both for those who came to observe and for those who participated—in how well actors work together when they share the same values and backgrounds. As for me, I began to dream about a repertory theatre in which all the great plays would be performed by Second City actors, developing a strictly American style.

With *Endgame* and *Viet Rock,* I had merely been an observer of the production process. With *Dynamite Tonite!* encouraged by Paul's open collaborative nature, I began to make some active contributions. The cast was imported, but the School provided the production with three of its cast members (the shell-shocked soldiers) and with a wacky Rube Goldberg design, featuring a crazy locomotive that entered through a tunnel every time a bell rang to load and discharge explosives. I devised a filmed prologue, selected and edited with the help of our instructor in film, Mike Roemer, consisting of clips from the Marx Brothers, Charlie Chaplin, the Three Stooges, et al, and also a group of filmed sequences—projected every time a character opened the door of the bunker— from the battle in *Alexander Nevsky* to clips of World War II. This prologue ended with a list of credits, and with the announcement that the whole evening had been produced by "The Yale School of . . ."—the last word being obliterated by a mushroom cloud and a loud explosion.

I was very proud of this production, but once again it divided the press and the audience, even some of the students. A sweetly innocent satire on the cold war, distinguished by Weinstein's goofy syntax and Bolcom's remarkable eclectic score, *Dynamite Tonite!* was about an imaginary war being fought between two countries very much like Freedonia and Sylvania in the Marx Brothers' *Duck Soup.* Part serious, part comic, part opera, part musical comedy, the work was entirely sui generis, and the fact that it was performed by actors who could sing, rather than (the usual case with opera) singers who can't act, made it seem odd and idiosyncratic to people who couldn't identify the style. "What is this?" asked one irate Drama School alumna who buttonholed me in the lobby during the intermission. "It's not a comedy. It's not a musical. What is it anyway?" "Well," I answered, "it's an opera." "Some opera," she remarked. "Why don't you do something to please the audience for a change. Look, the house is only one-third full." And she flounced out of the theatre without another word.

As a matter of fact, *Dynamite Tonite!* did please a few people and developed a passionate coterie, but it was never a popular success—not when it was first performed off-Broadway, not in its Yale version, not when it later moved off-Broadway again for a brief run, not even when we revived it at Yale in 1975 to celebrate our tenth anniversary. But I loved it, and I love it still. As for pleasing audiences, I certainly had no aversion to full houses, but I had few illusions that we would ever be a popular theatre. As I told the president when I first outlined my plans to him, it was not our purpose to entertain the city of New Haven. We were functioning in a university and therefore wanted the same privileges as a laboratory scientist or a literary researcher. It was our responsibility, I thought, to explore, to experiment, to develop new techniques, to rediscover neglected works—in short, to perform the theatrical equivalent of basic research. The practical applications of this research might not be immediately apparent, but it was the university's responsibility to provide the facilities, tools, and tolerant atmosphere to permit such work to proceed.

Besides, New Haven already had its own community theatre—the Long Wharf, which had been founded in 1965 by two School of Drama graduates, Jon Jory and Harlan Kleiman. In its second season when I arrived at Yale, the Long Wharf had not yet developed the popularity it was to have in future years under Arvin Brown, partly because Jory and Kleiman were proving too unconventional in their programming for local tastes (resident theatres at this time still retained their original spirit of adventure). The Long Wharf's current season was devoted entirely to new plays—always a dangerous policy with regional audiences. As a result, the theatre was losing about $5,000 a week, along with most of its community support.

At Yale we found ourselves that first year in the unfamiliar position of attracting most of the press attention and a significant proportion of the audience, despite our controversial season. Possibly for that reason, some members of the Long Wharf board initiated discussions with Kingman Brewster concerning a merger with Yale—without the knowledge of Jory or Kleiman. When Kingman apprised me of these negotiations, I had mixed feelings. The advantage of such a merger was the acquisition of a much needed facility. But there were disadvantages, too: the remoteness of the Long Wharf Theatre from the Yale campus, the difficulties of transportation, the implied obligation to provide a more popular season. I was also disturbed about being a party to the loss, through merger, of a struggling nonprofit theatre, and the elimination, through intervention by the board, of the very people who had founded that theatre.

I told Kingman that I was willing to consider the proposition, provided I could be assured of maintaining my independence from the board. But before the discussions proceeded any further, and my own moral position was put to the test, the whole business was leaked to the New Haven *Register,* probably by somebody closely connected with the theatre. A great furor ensued about a "Yale takeover" of a valuable community operation. There were editorials and letters to the editor, followed by a highly successful campaign to raise money to "Save the Long Wharf." Publicly embarrassed, the board withdrew its offer to Yale, and halted the negotiations.

I was relieved. I also felt compelled to correct the impression created by the *Register,* and not denied by the board, that I had initiated these discussions and deliberately tried to swallow up a defenseless theatre in my monstrous maw. My published denial caused embarrassment for Kingman, who wanted good relations with the town. He couldn't understand why I just didn't keep my mouth shut. I replied that I had been asked by a reporter to comment on a story false in some of its details. "Couldn't you just say, 'No comment'?" he asked, showing a little exasperation. Of course I could have. It just never occurred to me. "You had to protect your hurt little pride," charged Norma later, giving me her most scornful look.

My capacity to offend the community was apparently undeterred, and when we opened our next production—a contemporary version of Ben Jonson's *Volpone*—I managed to do it again. By this time, David Hurst and Ron Leibman had joined us, since Gregory's company in Philadelphia was disintegrating, likewise because of interference from his board. We had student designs again, and advanced students in supporting parts. And to direct the new production, we imported Clifford Williams from the Royal Shakespeare Company. Williams set the play in a Fellini-like Venice, populated with denizens of *la dolce vita*—a concept that was at times effective and stimulating, at others facile and irrelevant. I had been trying to articulate a position regarding reinterpretation of the classics which encouraged contemporary directors to treat the sacred texts with the utmost freedom, as long as they preserved the original spirit. A few years before, I was vigorously opposed to tampering with the classics. Now I had become persuaded that the traditional interpretations were putting everybody to sleep, and that a new metaphor was required for every new production.

Although I continued to insist that this metaphor be linked to a fresh but faithful investigation of the text, this was a thin, precarious line to tread, and my position, as expressed in an article called "No More Masterpieces," was much criticized. Williams's *Volpone* was hardly proof of my theory, but I regretted the way the whole idea was being dismissed as a result of this one production. The purists in the English department thought I had helped to open the doors to cultural barbarianism, while John Simon became convinced that I had taken leave of my senses. I should have realized that humanists have a vested interest in "masterpieces"—they are the precious metals of a huge research industry. I shared this interest myself when I was an English professor. But years of reviewing stale classical productions had convinced me it was better to run the risk of violating a well-beloved play than to produce it in a conventional, stodgy fashion. I wanted the contemporary theatre to offer the same startling freshness to an audience as the play had when it was originally produced, and if it failed, well, the play was always available for another production.

Yale was able to provide a much more satisfactory example of classical reinterpretation with the final production of that year—Robert Lowell's adaptation of Aeschylus' *Prometheus Bound*. This production was significant in many ways—for one thing, it was the occasion of our first grant from the National Endowment for the Arts. Although *Prometheus Bound* was not completed when we responded to the invitation to apply, the award was made on the basis of Lowell's reputation—$10,000 to the playwright and $15,000 to the theatre. This money made it possible for us to invite Lowell to the school for the year to hold classes with student playwrights while he was participating in rehearsals of his play. Later I learned that the grant had almost been canceled. President Johnson, enraged to discover that a government agency had awarded money to someone he believed had insulted him, demanded that the award be withdrawn. To the credit of the endowment—then under the chairmanship of Roger Stevens—Johnson's efforts were resisted. But this represented the first attempt by government to politicize the decisions of the agency. (Not, however, the last.)

Cal Lowell and I were in agreement that the ideal director for this play was Jonathan Miller, who had recently directed Lowell's *The Old Glory* at the American Place Theatre in New York. The two men complemented each other strangely—Lowell taciturn and soft-spoken, mournful and reserved; Miller dynamic, convivial, hyperactive, marvelously funny, a cascade of anecdotes and insights always pouring from his lips. It was Jonathan's idea—after a number of American actors had refused the part—to offer Prometheus to the British actor Kenneth Haigh, the original Jimmy Porter in *Look Back in Anger,* in the hope that some of that brittle rage might be appropriate for this demigod in chains. The cameo role of Io he offered to Irene Worth (she accepted immediately, her only question being "Who does my wig?"). As Ocean and Hermes, we cast our two new resident actors, David Hurst and Ron Leibman (who had just finished playing Volpone and Mosca); and with two more professional actors and three students from the School our cast was complete.

Our resident designer, Michael Annals, was responsible for the design—an awesome creation so huge we had to remove the entire stage floor. Miller had set the play in an undesignated country during the seventeenth century— probably Spain during the Inquisition, though he wanted this to remain vague. Annals provided statue-bearing niches and platforms of tortured, aging brick that went upward and downward as far as the eye could reach. "It's supposed to suggest a structure far larger than you can see," explained Miller in an interview, "sort of a brick kiln, a Pharos or huge lighthouse on the Mediterranean going up thousands of feet into the sea; no specific time, but some sort of decaying seventeenth-century culture that has gone bad. The characters are prisoners, they put on the play in this eternal imprisonment as a punishment."

I was a little embarrassed by the monumentality of the setting—especially since I had been advocating simple designs. Still, it was important to the director's concept, and there was no denying that it was awe-inspiring. Our design students worked closely with Annals on both his sets and costumes, extending the work they had been doing with him all year in the classroom. I observed with pleasure how effectively their own imaginations were stimulated through association with this bold, poetic young designer. In one of the photographs I have from that year, you can see a bearded young man intent on sculpting a piece of statuary for the set. It is a first-year designer named Santo Loquasto, who was later to design our production of *Bacchae* as a third-year student, then to become our resident designer, and then to go on to a distinguished career as one of the leading scenic artists in the American theatre.

Rehearsals for *Prometheus* were highly concentrated, yet loose and relaxed. Ken Haigh, usually high-strung, felt immediately at home with Miller's humor and intellect, and Irene Worth set about her tasks with that joyous wonder she always displays when a director is asking her to make new departures. As for the students in the cast, they were electrified by Miller's animated manner, by the flood of ideas that flowed from his lips in perfect grammatical sentences, interrupted only by an occasional soft stammer. Like all the other Yale productions of that year, *Prometheus* was rehearsed in a variety of fugitive spaces around the university so as not to disrupt student classes and projects. In the last week it moved from the Annex on Park Street into the University Theatre, where the final process could be observed by all the interested students.

Everything was proceeding smoothly, so there had to be a snag. It arrived on schedule in the form of a complaint from Actors Equity. We were told to remove Kenneth Haigh forthwith from the cast. American actors had recently become sensitive to the way their talents and their luster were being overshadowed by visiting British performers. Because of this, and because Americans were prevented by British Equity from acting in England, the American actors' union had insisted on a clause in its contract with LORT (League of Resident Theatres) barring aliens from performing with nonprofit companies unless they had resident alien visas. (No such prohibition existed on Broadway, where producers were allowed to hire a large proportion of aliens, provided they constituted no more than 30 percent of the cast.)

For the first time in my life I was being treated as a manager—which is to say, an adversary in a labor dispute—and I didn't like it. I had somehow assumed that organizations like Equity would be among the first to recognize our service to actors, through training and career opportunities, and offer cooperation in a common cause. Equity had already made a few concessions to us regarding the use of students in professional productions (later it was to grow more knowledgeable and relaxed about the special needs of resident theatre companies); but at this time, its leadership was under considerable pressure from the membership, and on this issue, it refused to budge. We were given an ultimatum: Fire Kenneth Haigh, or the American actors in the cast would be told to go out on strike.

I didn't believe it was possible to replace Haigh at this late date and still preserve the quality of the production; and it wasn't possible, for a variety of scheduling reasons, to postpone the date of the opening. We were at an impasse. Then, we discovered—when our managing director finally examined our Equity contract—that we weren't subject to the LORT alien rules, since we were not yet a LORT company. In setting up the house, Equity had obliged us to sign a Broadway contract. This meant that by Equity's own regulations, we were entitled to employ not just one but as many as three or four aliens for the play.

When I informed the Equity official of our discovery, he said he would call me back. Within the hour, he phoned to say that if Yale insisted on sticking to the letter of its contract, then Equity would withdraw its concession to allow students to perform in professional productions. In short, if we didn't fire Haigh, we would have to fire the students. As an Equity member myself, I was stunned, and a little ashamed. To me, the union seemed to be acting against itself. What I didn't understand was how inflammatory the issue of aliens had become to a large portion of the Equity membership.

Two of the three choral Seabirds in the cast were students—one from the second year and one from the third—and a first-year student was doing a walk-on. Rather than replace them with Equity actors, I had to propose that all three join the union themselves. This made me queasy. I didn't feel so bad about the third-year student, since she was about to graduate, but the other two were still in training, and something in me rebelled against asking matriculating students to join Equity in order to perform on the university stage. Quite a few of our students already had Equity cards when they first came to the school, or acquired them during the summers, but their membership was suspended during the training year, and, anyway, union status for them was a voluntary choice rather than an expediency forced on them by events. I felt compromised, and I felt I was compromising the students, breaking some unformulated covenant in order to save a production. None of the students involved seemed disturbed by the problem, and responded graciously to our proposed solution. We supplied the initiation fees, and paid the students by applying their salaries to scholarships. Thus we managed to satisfy Equity, at some moral cost to everyone involved.

Labor troubles aside, the rehearsals for *Prometheus* were a delight. The director had a firm grasp on Lowell's ideas and a strong concept of how to make them work in the theatre. Miller was inspired by the memory theory of Frances Yates, which holds that each culture remembers the past by imagining a theatre and associating parts of speech with parts of the stage. Using the seventeenth century as what he called a "booster message center," men could thereby argue their way back to antiquity. The *Prometheus* production scrupulously refrained from making the gods recognizable—Ocean became a self-serving, tired, wheedling old man; Hermes was a storm trooper out of anti-Nazi movies from the forties; Hephaestus emerged as a crippled Negro, who buzzed and hummed while he hammered wedges into Prometheus' side—but the ancient Greek gods were nevertheless always present in the form of cracked statuary well above the heads of the other characters.

Miller was anxious to let the action resonate in the minds of the spectators without urging them toward any single interpretation. A lot of good rehearsal ideas, in fact, were thrown out because they were too precisely analogical. Originally, for example, Miller wanted to open the play with Prometheus adjusting his own gag in his mouth, screaming in pain while Hephaestus tortured him, then removing the gag as if nothing had happened. The torture itself was to be done not through any physical contact but through analogy: Hephaestus was to break some twigs at the feet of Prometheus as a metaphor for breaking his limbs, while his beating of a leather pallet would signify the painful driving in of a wedge. This device was too distinctly Oriental to satisfy Miller, and it was therefore discarded, much to my regret. The torture scene was finally performed in relative darkness.

Other devices were preserved. In Lowell's text, the daughters of Ocean are changed to three Seabirds; Miller enlarged their roles further by turning them into recording angels who inscribe Prometheus' utterings and prompt the other actors while functioning also as questioners and observers. The wandering Io—whom Zeus had raped and then beset with flies—became, in Miller's hands, the victim of a kind of celestial malaria, vibrating with heat and delirium. As for Prometheus, he emerged less a savage titan, raging against his fate, than a bitter, self-hating young man, scornful of himself and of the gods, often reluctant even to give the heavens the benefit of his indignation. The result of all this was a thoroughly modernized version of the ancient play, with contemporary resonances echoing all forms of tyranny (including America's treatment of the Vietnamese), but a version that nevertheless maintained a certain historical distance.

I found the production a welcome example of the kind of resourceful, though respectful, intelligence I hoped to see applied to the classics—insightful without being chic, historical without being traditional. I felt privileged to bring together such distinguished artists as Robert Lowell, Jonathan Miller, Irene Worth, Kenneth Haigh, Michael Annals, and the others on a single project. I thought it augured well for the future of a poetic theatre.

The production opened to considerable fanfare, since I had been persuaded (with a small rebuke from my puritan conscience) to turn the occasion into a formal event. The honored guests received printed invitations and arrived wearing evening gowns and dress suits. A number of theatre celebrities attended, including David Merrick, who in the lobby during intermission offered his opinion that "The name of the game is still entertainment." Following the performance, beef and shish kebab were served to company and friends at Pierson College, John and Barbara Hersey playing host. The press reaction was mainly enthusiastic, and respectful when it was not. And the students, some of whom had been complaining about the usurpation of the University Theatre by professional production, were proud of having such a distinguished work on the Yale stage.

As for me, I felt a mild anxiety vitiating my pride in the event, a certain ambivalence about its success, which the formal opening only compounded. I had few apologies to offer about the productions we had done that year, but I felt a little apologetic about the way these productions were being perceived. With customary brashness I had stated that New Haven offered us the important opportunity to evolve our work in peace and quiet. Yet, with my consent, we had become the subject of a press blitz, the center of loud and bright attention.

I had made some effort—not enough—to turn this attention away. Since I had come to Yale making arrogant proclamations about changing the face of the theatre, I should not have been surprised to find the journalistic juggernaut wheeling around in my direction. Stupidly I thought I could turn this to my own advantage without suffering any consequences. It was foolish of me to implore the cultural editor of *The New York Times* not to send a reviewer to *Viet Rock* and thereby honor "our efforts to develop the craft of the theatre away from those conditions that have hitherto been impeding the development of that craft." But couldn't I foresee that he would refuse when I was admitting local reviewers to our productions and granting interviews to reporters from his own newspaper?

I was obviously growing very ambivalent about the role of the press—consciously on behalf of the institution, unconsciously on my own behalf. As a theatre, we needed to attract fiscal support; as a school, we needed to attract good students; both required a certain amount of publicity for the place that the press was more than willing to provide. I naïvely believed that I could monitor the coverage we received by cooperating with those newspapers and magazines dedicated to collecting information, and by refusing to speak with those devoted to collecting personalities. Already I was trying to discriminate among reporters as later I would try to discriminate among reviewers. I remember bringing down the wrath of a writer for a women's fashion magazine when I made an effort to explain why I wouldn't give him an interview. "You're in the press bag now," he exploded, "and you won't find it easy to cut your way out."

I'm still trying to understand my personal attitude toward the press. In truth, I disapproved of all the attention I was getting; in truth, I enjoyed it too. I was becoming a celebrity, and it felt good—so good it had me worried. I knew I would have to watch myself very carefully in future. I was worried about my soul, but I was also worried about my ass. Celebrity status would obviously make me the focus of a lot of hostility. When the hostility inevitably came, I complained about it bitterly and with considerable self-pity—significantly enough, in another press medium, an article written about the School in *The New York Times:* "I've never been the object of so much hatred before," I moaned. "When you're a critic, someone sends in a hate letter and you can reply scathingly, wittily or not at all. But when you're inundated with hate, you feel as if you're drowning a little. . . . With *Dynamite Tonite!* and *Viet Rock,* I felt as if certain New York critics were reviewing *me*—which was unfair to the actors, directors, and authors."

Unfair to me too, I was doubtless thinking. For the first time in my life I was feeling vulnerable. I had made a number of enemies during my career as a critic, but before, I had always been able to defend myself. Now my typewriter was sitting on my desk attracting cobwebs, like a powerful weapon that couldn't be discharged. Too combative by nature to accept this condition for long, I soon broke the locks on the arsenal and began to sound off on the state of the theatre, the state of the nation, and the state of criticism, as if I were still holding my old job on *The New Republic* (actually, I did hold it for another year until my position became untenable). I never learned to accept my welts like others in similar circumstances; I still preserved the right of reply if I thought the Theatre or I was being badly used.

As a result, throughout my thirteen years at Yale, I proceeded to have both public and private exchanges with unfriendly reviewers, which often only exacerbated their hostility to our work. This had started with Walter Kerr during my years as a critic, and continued even after he had praised *Prometheus Bound.* I was objecting not that he had commended the production ("a perfect project for a serious university theatre") in those faintly patronizing tones that he usually reserved for us, but that he had chosen to come up from New York at all. "We're grateful for the review," I announced. "We hope he never comes again. Whether he liked it or not, I felt it was a mistake for him to cover the play, thereby imposing upon us the hit-or-miss pressure of Broadway." This was high-sounding and, I believe, sincere, but it was also brash and ungracious. Worse, it was unrealistic. Ten years later, I would be begging him to come to our productions—which suggests something of my compromised attitude toward the press.

The year ended with an unpleasant event—the so-called flag case. Four drama students, influenced by *Viet Rock,* had staged another play by Megan Terry called *Keep Tightly Closed in a Cool Dry Place.* Since the School production was effective, they took it on the road in the spring—first to the Exit Coffeehouse in New Haven, and then to the New Dramatists Workshop in New York. In New York all four were arrested. At one point in the performance they had used the American flag as a blanket, and one outraged witness protested to the police. The American Civil Liberties Union agreed to take the case, and I offered to testify in their defense.

The New Haven *Register* carried the story on its front page, accompanied by a photograph of the four students and me descending the steps of the courthouse juxtaposed against another of Chuck Connors reenacting the famous Iwo Jima flag-raising scene on television. The caption beneath the Connors picture read, "He honors the flag." The caption beneath our picture read, "They defaced the flag." We shouldn't have expected better of such a conservative newspaper, but I wrote in protesting to the editors that they were prejudging a trial that had not yet taken place. An apology was printed, but the mischief had been done. The next day Norma received a call from an anonymous local patriot who called her a "Commie pinko whore" and made threats against my life. A number of similar calls were made before the week was out.

At the university the reaction was more polite but no less indignant. Most of the flak exploded at a resident college of which I had recently been made a fellow. Since I had been too busy during the year to take tea in the Master's House or to eat in the dining hall with the students, I tried to compensate for my delinquencies after we had opened our final production. At my first meal my partner at dinner, a professor of physics, fixed me with a sour stare and asked, "Why do you encourage your students to dishonor the flag of their country?" I mumbled something about the right of students to treat the stage as a forum for free expression, as he would no doubt like the classroom treated, but I obviously left him unsatisfied.

At future dinners I parried enough questions of a similar nature to make me wonder whether I should remain in this particular college. Finally I severed my connections with it after another similar incident. The master of the college had asked me to talk to the fellows and students about our plans for the school, and I had agreed, provided that any questions be directed to the content of my lecture. After I had concluded, the first question from the floor was "Why do you encourage your students to desecrate the flag?"

As a matter of fact, I was then encouraging my students to get the case dismissed on a technicality. I believed that the flag ruling was very probably unconstitutional, and would ultimately be overturned. But I feared that the young people involved—none of them very political—would end up as martyrs to a test case. With the help of their lawyers, and the cooperation of a sympathetic prosecutor, the case was dropped before it came to a trial.

In my first annual report to the president and fellows of Yale University I wrote of "an exhausting but very often exhilarating year." Even today, that seems like an accurate way to describe it. I spoke of two areas of potential problems—limited finances and limited facilities. The first was responsible for inadequate scholarships programs; the second was causing difficulties for rehearsal and performance. I would devote the coming years to solving the funding problem. The facility problem would not be solved until 1969, and then only after it came close to disrupting the entire school.

But aside from these potential danger areas, the situation was fairly satisfactory, so I am surprised to find myself brooding (in an interview conducted at the end of that year) over a prospect of ultimate failure. I suspect I was having forebodings over the consequences of the aloof, embattled niche we had carved out for ourselves: "This identity, this concern for our development, may result in our cutting ourselves off from the community," I reflected, "but I feel the crisis in the theatre has forced us more and more into an increasingly radical position. I started out to reorganize a school. I discovered that I couldn't have a school without a company into which to feed the best students—a company to serve as a model. Next, I discovered that you can't build such a company until you have an audience that responds to the work and is interested in the kind of development the company is committed to. Of course, you can't have the audience until you have the community, because an audience is a community in miniature. You can't have a community until you have a country, and you can't have a country until you have a civilization. The disease is at the roots."

"To be blunt," I added, "though I'm sure we shall succeed in part, I very much doubt whether we can realize the initial vision at present, given the fact that the culture is so much against it. Our culture thinks it's for art, but it's against art. I think that more and more we are discovering that all the current talk about the cultural explosion is empty rhetoric. In every city where advanced theatre has been tried, it has failed for one reason or another. Philadelphia's Theatre of the Living Arts has just lost its driving force. Andre Gregory was fired. The Actors Workshop closed. There were two different managements in two years at the Pittsburgh Playhouse. William Ball was fired and now John Hancock has been fired. The Front Street Theatre in Memphis was recently on the verge of collapse. Lincoln Center has just lost its second artistic director, Herbert Blau. And there will be more. . . ."

These remarks are pretty dark, even if you disregard my customary pessimism; they are also somewhat prophetic. But even with the fatigue and foreboding of that first year, I was feeling pretty good. The students were entering a solid, if evolving, training program. The Theatre was taking root, and subscriptions had almost tripled. The foundations were becoming interested in our work. The productions, if not all of high quality, were all ambitious. And although I had managed to alienate a substantial portion of the Yale–New Haven community, we still had the blessings of the administration.

Norma and I had decided to spend three years setting up the program and establishing the Theatre before returning to our lives in New York. The next year would be devoted to the second step: forming a permanent company and improving the training program further. We had sown the seeds of our advances. Unaware that we had sown the seeds of our disasters as well, we broke for the summer and entered the next year in a state of high expectation.

II

Forming a Company 1967-1968

My curse on plays
That have to be set up in fifty ways,
On the day's war with every knave and dolt,
Theatre business, management of men.
I swear before the dawn comes round again
I'll find the stable and pull the bolt.

—W. B. Yeats

That summer, we were back on the island of Martha's Vineyard, and I was learning how to conduct my administrative business in the mornings while continuing to scratch for clams, search for fish, and scramble up tennis games in the afternoons. It was a summer devoted to selecting a season and forming a permanent company for the Theatre as well as making certain adjustments in the faculty and curriculum of the School. I was trying to institutionalize our gains without losing our forward momentum.

Gordon Rogoff had proved as inexperienced administratively as I was, and much too independent intellectually to bury himself in bureaucratic tasks, so I asked him to shift to the directing department. The position of associate dean was now open. It was a thankless and time-consuming job, similar to an executive officer on a ship; it required someone sufficiently devoted to an idea not to feel degraded or humiliated by a subordinate role. I thought I had found the right person after interviewing Howard Stein, then an assistant professor of playwriting at the University of Iowa. I had known Stein when we were both students at Columbia, and we had many friends in common. Although his background was essentially academic, he was known for his dedication to the theatre and loyalty to his students; he also seemed to have a genuine passion for what we were trying to do at Yale. Best of all, he had no measurable limit to his energies and no apparent vanity, which made it possible for him to concentrate on the often menial duties of the office without exhaustion or resentment. Once appointed, he established a routine of ten- and twelve-hour days, sitting inside a glass office that kept him continually visible, and continually available, to students, faculty, and visitors alike. In order to avoid confusion about the nature of his duties, we changed his title from associate to administrative dean, a position he was to hold for the next eleven years.

Also joining the faculty that year in the playwriting and criticism areas was Richard Gilman, the drama and literary critic. Gilman had no academic degrees, but he was a born teacher. I first met him when he was reviewing plays for *Commonweal* magazine, whence he had gone on to become the theatre critic of *Newsweek*. Having abandoned that job, he was now looking for an opportunity to teach, reflect, and write more extended essays and books. I had taught a course in modern drama at the School during the first year; this year I would teach the classical drama. I asked Gilman to teach the modern, and to be the critical voice in Arnold Weinstein's Playwrights Workshop. What I hoped was to alternate the two dramatic literature courses with Gilman—as I had done at Columbia with Eric Bentley—but I could never get him interested in teaching classical drama. His course in modern drama proved immensely popular—at one time it was being taken by over eight hundred Yale undergraduates—and I had to accept the fact that the contemporary field was where his passions and interests lay.

Other faculty appointments made around the same time included Stanley Kauffmann—movie critic again for *The New Republic* after a short stint as theatre critic for *The New York Times*—to teach the ABC course in film; Jean-Claude van Itallie to conduct some seminars in playwriting; Jacques Levy to teach directing; and Bobby Lewis to back up Stella Adler in the acting area. Later that year I appointed Larry Arrick as a directing instructor and, more crucially, as resident artistic director of the new permanent company—a title he was to hold for only a few months in the spring until we both recognized it was a misnomer.

For it took me the better part of that year to realize I would have to be much more actively engaged with the work of the Theatre if it was ever to become the institution I had in mind. In the previous year I had been a producer— choosing plays, selecting artistic staff, and casting roles with separate *en suite* productions in mind. Now that we were working with a permanent company, my role was destined to change. I knew that a company couldn't function properly without unity, cohesiveness, and a well-articulated aesthetic, but only gradually did I begin to realize that the qualities I desired for the Theatre could not be defined by anyone but me.

By choosing the season and casting the company that summer, I had already usurped some of the functions of an artistic director; but for some reason I was hesitant to assume the title. The resident theatre was still in its infancy, and its hierarchical structure wasn't yet clearly delineated. Each organization was finding its own form; none could be a model for another. At Yale we had begun with a producing apparatus. Now we were developing a permanent company. I had not yet made the transition fully in my own mind. I still believed that if you had interesting plays, imaginative directors, and gifted actors, you had all you needed for effective productions. Like most critics, I was too accustomed to sitting out front and judging results to be bothered with the delicate process that created the finished product. Part of me still wanted to remain out front, but I found I couldn't really form the company until I had personally entered the process.

Choosing the season was always the first step in this process, and on paper, at least, our season that year was impressive. We had decided to open with *'Tis Pity She's a Whore,* a relatively obscure, philosophically precocious, phantasmagorical Jacobean tragedy by John Ford. Seldom revived, it had a singular depth and power—also, it seemed to me, a singular appropriateness for our times. Our second production was to be a new play by Joseph Heller—not yet titled—which extended the antiwar lunacy of *Catch-22* into a Pirandellian theatrical conceit. And for our third presentation of the season we were planning to bring Stella Adler back to the stage as Arkadina in Chekhov's *The Sea Gull.*

The Sea Gull was an example of the familiar repertory staple we were pledged to avoid unless we could find a new channel into the play. But during a visit to the Soviet Union, Stella had met a director who was proving successful in reinterpreting Chekhov—Georges Tovstonogov of the Leningrad Gorki Theatre. Stella was so taken with Tovstonogov that she was willing to undertake one of the most difficult roles in drama, providing he agreed to direct it. Fortunately, he was in New England that same summer, participating in theatre seminars at the American Shakespeare Festival. It was at Stratford that we—communicating haltingly through a translator—agreed on dates and arrangements for a Yale production of *The Sea Gull.* Tovstonogov, excited by the prospect of working with Stella, was perfectly agreeable to any other cast members I selected (I had Kenneth Haigh in mind as Trigorin and Alvin Epstein as Konstantin Treplev), but he couldn't come to this country again without getting clearance from the Soviet Minister of Culture.

Having planned English, American, and Russian plays, we decided on an Italian one for our fourth production—Pirandello's *Henry IV,* directed by Jacques Levy of the Open Theatre, in celebration of the playwright's centennial anniversary. And for our fifth and final offering, we chose a German-English collaboration, Brecht's version of Shakespeare's *Coriolanus,* directed by Carl Weber, a former member of the Berliner Ensemble. I looked over this international schedule with pride: Shakespeare and Ford representing the Renaissance; Brecht, Pirandello, and Chekhov representing the modern period; and a new American play by a brilliant novelist. This would be a strong indication of the intentions of our theatre, and the directors we were recruiting gave promise that the plays would be treated well.

At the very moment my pride was inflating, the air was going out of my plans. But still unaware that very little this year was destined to turn out as expected, I went about the business of choosing a company capable of performing in the plays we had scheduled. I recruited as our leading lady Kathleen Widdoes, an actress I had long admired for her beauty and range, offering her Annabella in *'Tis Pity* and Nina in *The Sea Gull,* in addition to smaller roles in the rest of the season. Kathleen had a daughter the same age as my son,

Danny; she also had a husband, Richard Jordan. In order to make it possible for her to be with her family at Yale, I cast her husband opposite her in *'Tis Pity,* in a role I had intended for Sam Waterston. I had never seen Jordan act, but one of the things I was hoping to do at Yale was to provide the opportunity for actors to lead stable family lives.

Of the people we had worked with our first season besides Kenneth Haigh, only Ron Leibman had agreed to return, and then only for a short stint in the Heller play. The new members that year were Michael Lombard, Paul Mann, Anthony Holland, Barry Morse, Jeanne Hepple, Estelle Parsons, John Karlen, Harris Yulin, and Stacy Keach.

Keach was an important addition to the company, since he was signed to play Starkey in the Heller piece, Baron Belcredi in *Henry IV,* and the title role in *Coriolanus.* I had been enormously impressed by Keach's performance in *MacBird,* which I had recently reviewed with great enthusiasm. What struck me about his talent was its versatility. Playing MacBird, he found not only the extended, heightened, satirical side of the character but also the root on which the parody of Lyndon Johnson was based, namely, Macbeth. Here was an American actor, I thought, capable of playing all the great repertory roles— and playing them with a combination of emotional involvement and impersonality that gave them a contemporary stamp. These were perfect qualities for Brecht's *Coriolanus;* they were appropriate also for countless plays from Sophocles to Beckett. Tragedy with a twist of cabaret, that was what I wanted to show the acting students, and Keach was the perfect example. When I introduced myself to him backstage at *MacBird* and told him about our company, I was interested to learn that Keach had also been a Drama School dropout. He was intrigued by the prospect of returning to Yale as a professional actor (partly because his brother, James, was now a student there), and I was certainly intrigued by the strength he would give our company.

My pleasure in *MacBird* was not limited to Keach's performance. I had, in fact, been praising Barbara Garson's play ever since I first came on it in pamphlet form circulating through the underground. At a Columbia teach-in, following an early escalation of the Vietnam war, I gave the work its first public reading; even some of those opposing Johnson's policies were shocked by its scandalous nature. Many found the play to be infantile and libelous, and my endorsement of it brought rebukes from friends and enemies alike. I knew that *MacBird* was irresponsible, particularly in its blithe assumption that Johnson had arranged for President Kennedy's assassination, but I believed the play to be valuable less as a historical tract than as an emotional cathartic for our unrelieved feelings of frustration over the current political situation. Johnson was single-handedly conducting an illegal war in Southeast Asia, and he was justifying his usurpation of Congress's war-making powers through the fraudulent machinery of the Tonkin Gulf Resolution.

That very summer this resolution was being defended before a congressional committee by Johnson's under secretary of state, Nicholas deB. Katzenbach, in testimony that caused not only an unpleasant incident on Martha's Vineyard but one of my rare confrontations with Kingman Brewster. Since Katzen-bach was a summer resident of the island, a number of Vineyard literati, including William Styron, Lillian Hellman, Philip Roth, John Hersey, Henry Beetle Hough, Jules Feiffer, John Marquand, Daniel Lang, and myself, had taken out an advertisement in *The Vineyard Gazette* protesting his testimony before the committee and imploring him "as a civilized and humane man" to speak out against "President Johnson's indefensible diplomacy of violence." We had framed our statement with great care, after numerous meetings at a number of homes, trying to moderate the indignation we were feeling with a properly courteous tone.

I soon learned that our action had deeply angered Brewster, who was a close friend of the Katzenbach family. I had been invited for drinks at Kingman's house, and was asked to come a little earlier after the ad appeared. Arriving, I found him in the company of his good friend and Yale classmate McGeorge Bundy, then a close adviser of President Johnson, though soon to become the head of the Ford Foundation. After making introductions, Kingman handed me a drink and took me aside to tell me how we had all committed a serious breach of etiquette; we had embarrassed the Katzenbachs during their summer vacation. "In the summer," he added, "we should leave our politics in Woods Hole." I asked him what he thought Woods Hole had done to deserve that, and if this made the Vineyard into Berchtesgaden. He reddened at this remark, and he looked angry when I added that remaining silent in the current atmo-sphere was tantamount to being a "good German." I was sorry to be curt with Kingman. Neither of us wanted to quarrel. But I thought he was wrong, given his position, to criticize my actions. Actually, it was quite unusual for King-man to question the political behavior of his associates; I sensed he was fulfilling an obligation to a friend. Later I learned that he had also tried to rebuke John Hersey for adding his name to the statement, but that John had been even more direct in his rejoinder, saying he was not accustomed to being told what he could or could not sign.

In that summer of 1967 the war had been escalating for a year, and as a result, people were escalating their resistance to it. I had joined the peace movement immediately after Johnson had increased the number of "advisers" in Vietnam. I was among the original signatories of the Resist statement. I joined the various marches in and around the White House, sitting with Norma at the foot of the Washington Monument and singing "Give Peace a Chance." I participated in teach-ins and moratoriums, spoke at rallies, de-fended those being indicted for civil disobedience. It was an unfamiliar role for me. I was not by nature a politically engaged person, but I knew from the start that this was an evil war and could only create evil for the entire country.

One expression of this evil was the contentiousness that was beginning to enter personal relationships. We were divided into camps and factions, aflame with righteous indignation every time we met someone with opposing views. Opposition to the Vietnam war provided the intellectuals, and then the aca-demics, with a unity rare among such groups, and the strength we drew from being in agreement for once tended to make us intolerant. We had the moral advantage of being a minority in the country, combined with the psychic advantage of being a majority in the community. This put us in danger of becoming bullies. My own distaste for the war was partly caused by my distaste for what I perceived to be America's violent nature. It would take some time to discover that violence might also be present in those protesting so warmly for peace.

I didn't realize this at first. Quite the contrary, I took considerable satisfaction in finding myself part of a noble political cause whose righteousness was beyond dispute, and my opposition to the war was beginning to inform both my writing and my theatre work. To watch the peace effort grow from a small group of protesters—marching past signs reading "Burn Commie Professors" —into a large inter-university movement was to have one's faith restored in the possibility of community: the theatre was one place this community could be gathered. I didn't have much faith in art as an instrument of lasting change, but I did believe that the public art of theatre was an instrument of social collectivity, where audiences and artists could share an emotion of multitude. I considered myself, in short, a cultural radical, not a political one. I had no special attraction to plays of protest or propaganda, particularly those that tried to manipulate the truth for the sake of persuasion. But I believed it the central obligation of the theatre to soak up the pressing concerns of the time, confronting audiences with their own fears, hopes, and anxieties: engaged, not activist, volatile, not inflammatory, contemporary, not fashionable. Obviously, the war was on everybody's mind, so the war would inevitably become a major subject of the American theatre—even if the American theatre was impotent to end it.

Given the rather complicated nature of my politics, I should not have been surprised, I suppose, to find myself identified by the more rabid elements of the movement as a submissive liberal whose theatre not only was failing to affect social injustice but, in some way, was helping to perpetuate it. The more inflamed the antiwar movement grew, the less it was willing to countenance complexity. Life became a melodrama, a battleground of moral extremes, and people were divided into those who agreed entirely with your position and those who had to be converted or silenced. Still, it was something of a shock to discover, on my return to New Haven, that one who was considered a radical on the Vineyard was now considered the conservative of Yale. The first sign of my new characterization came during a visit to the Theatre, in early September, by the San Francisco Mime Troupe.

I had invited this company to perform at Yale while we were rehearsing our first production, as part of a continuing policy of bringing in visiting troupes. I had never seen the Mime Troupe perform, but I knew of its reputation, and I had had some conversations with its founder, Ronnie Davis, during a visit to San Francisco in 1965. Davis had been an original member of the Actors Workshop, but had broken with Herbert Blau and Jules Irving when he found them insufficiently interested in new performing techniques or contemporary

American plays. Davis was an activist, whose politics eventually issued in an improvisatory form of commedia dell'arte street theatre, designed for working-class audiences, who, I later learned, were sometimes exhorted to turn on their oppressors and revolt.

At Yale the San Francisco Mime Troupe performed a loose version of a Goldoni play, after which Ronnie Davis informed the spectators applauding the curtain call that if they wanted to end the war, they would have to take to the streets with guns. This was my first encounter with the more violent side of the Vietnam protest, and I was shaken. How could we criticize the violence of our government if we advocated violence ourselves? Just a few weeks before, in the course of giving some lectures at colleges in the finger-lakes district, I had participated in a silent vigil for the victims of the Vietnam War. A crude wooden gun was passed from hand to hand. When it reached me, I impulsively splintered it across my knee and my eyes grew moist. Were guns to be our future at home as well as overseas, brandished by friends as well as enemies?

I was disturbed also to see Davis and his group so sullen and remote when we visited them backstage after the show. They had been invited as comrades and had come as belligerents. During a reception in the greenroom, the troupe refused to mix with our students or our company. Perhaps because we were members of an "Establishment" university, we were the enemy, and all our efforts at friendship were coldly rejected.

During this time 'Tis Pity She's a Whore was in rehearsal, under the direction of Kenneth Haigh, who was now a resident alien, therefore acceptable to Equity. Haigh was not an inevitable choice for this project. He had been given the assignment as a result of one of those bargains that are sometimes struck in the theatre—he would agree to play Trigorin in The Sea Gull only in return for a directing opportunity with the company. I knew nothing about Haigh's capacities as a director, but I respected his artistry and intelligence. In our first year, he had conducted a rigorous seminar in verse speaking that proved considerably successful with the acting students, despite some grumbling about his short temper and impatience. None of the other directors I had approached were willing or available to direct the Ford play. Giving it to Haigh was risky, but then he knew the play and loved it; he understood how to make verse sound both natural and rhythmic, and he might turn out to be a gifted director. Perhaps he was just the one to induct our new company into the mysteries of Jacobean drama.

I had a special reason for doing 'Tis Pity She's a Whore, which I carefully outlined to Haigh before I hired him. The play had always appealed to me partly for its intellectual and philosophical precocity. Ford was a precursor of Nietzsche and Dostoyevsky—not to mention Camus and the Existentialists—in his understanding that if God is presumed to be dead, then anything is possible, not excluding incest and murder. What had previously bothered commentators, and made productions of the play a rarity, was its bloody Tussaud sensationalism—the hero, Giovanni, appears at the end with the heart of his mistress-sister, Annabella, skewered on his dagger. It occurred to me that circumstances had now arranged themselves in a way that might make this gory theatricality meaningful to an American audience. *'Tis Pity* could be treated as a hallucinatory experience—a violent trip by two spaced-out adolescents flipping on peyote or LSD. Drug use was causing extravagant enough things in the Yale community to make this comprehensible. One undergraduate, believing he could fly under the influence of LSD, had leaped from the window of his college and punctured his spleen. Another student, thinking his car had wings, had plunged off an embankment and been killed. Many others were entering mental institutions, having suffered psychotic breakdowns from bad trips. As for sensationalism, the Manson murders were soon to make the violence of *'Tis Pity She's a Whore* look feeble by comparison.

My proposed concept was to drench the production in a vapor of acid—to look at its reality through the eyes of the feverish protagonists. This would require a subjective design, in the manner of a hallucination, and a style of acting that was extreme and extended. Haigh listened to my ideas with tolerance, interest, even some excitement—and then proceeded to ignore them completely.

To this day, I can't define the interpretation that Haigh substituted, but it certainly had no contemporary associations; quite the opposite—I suspect it was an attempt to pull the play out of history altogether. The visual setting was very abstract—an arrangement of jagged, semiperpendicular cliffs, difficult for the actors to navigate—and the costumes were designed as unisexual gowns, most of them white, which gave the characters an extraterrestrial appearance. Haigh was not very preoccupied with the design; what really interested him was the acting.

But he was hamstrung by the fact that this was the first production of our newly formed company. They were not only unfamiliar with the play and with the verse, they were also unfamiliar with each other. As husband and wife, Richard Jordan and Kathleen Widdoes had no difficulty acting together as brother and sister—they proved a handsome Giovanni and a moving Annabella. But the other parts were approached in a variety of styles, not all of them appropriate to the play. One strong exception was Anthony Holland playing the goofy, vain, insensitive clown, Bergetto, who executed his death scene—the first comic death in dramatic literature—with pathos and humor.

The most rewarding role in the play was, oddly enough, the most difficult for me to cast—that of the tool villain, Vasques. I had the perfect actor in mind to play the part, but he was hard to locate. Eventually I managed to track him down in Hollywood, where he was waiting for a movie or a television show. He expressed great excitement over the prospect of joining our new company, and was interested in the role I offered him—until he read the play and discovered that Vasques was not the "lead." He told me that he would be happy to come to Yale, but couldn't we change the play to *Cyrano de Bergerac?* If so, he would be happy to play the title role.

I replied that *Cyrano* was not on our schedule that season, but that Vasques was a very juicy opportunity for a good actor—a character with the implacable nature of Iago, cold and detached, a demon of cruelty. He said he would think about it, and, after a few days, called back to tell me he had decided to accept my offer, despite the strong objections of his agent. "This is just the sort of thing I should be doing," he said. "Send me a contract quick before I change my mind." Three weeks later the contract had still not been returned, and my calls were not being answered. Finally his agent got in touch with me to say that the actor would not be coming to Yale; he had just been offered an important role in a film being made for television. When I protested to the agent that this was mighty short notice, considering the fact that we were about to go into rehearsal, he said the movie was too wonderful an opportunity to refuse, and offered to send me a copy of the script to prove it. I told him *'Tis Pity She's a Whore* was at least as good an opportunity for the actor, and offered to send him a copy of the play to prove it. With that our conversation ended. The actor sat around his swimming pool, waiting for the shooting date of his film. It never arrived; the film was not made.

We managed to fill the part of Vasques, despite the short notice, with an accomplished repertory-trained actor who played it perfectly well, but lacked the edge the other would have provided. Losing the one I wanted was a disappointment in other ways. I had naïvely assumed, after the experience of casting my television series and our first productions at Yale, that it would be easy to attract talented actors from the commercial theatre with the promise of challenging classical and modern roles. This was one of my earliest disappointments among many more to come, and I never learned to accept them with equanimity. Naturally, I had selfish reasons for feeling dejected: I had to form a company, I had to cast plays. But I was also worried about what this signified for the American resident theatre movement. I had always assumed that the only thing preventing good actors from joining repertory companies was the absence of the proper conditions. Now I was learning that the stage was not the magnet I had always believed—that, in fact, it had a powerful competitor in television and the movies. Was it possible that American actors actually preferred *Rawhide* to *Hamlet?* It was one of the first indications I had of the irresistible attractions of the commercial system.

On the other hand, *'Tis Pity She's a Whore* did not turn out to be the kind of distinguished opportunity that actors gnash their teeth to lose. The only thing memorable about it—apart from a few isolated performances—was the fact that the New Haven *Register* refused to print the title. We had composed an ad for the paper preceding the opening and submitted the copy on Tuesday. When it appeared the next Sunday, we were flabbergasted to see the phrase "a Whore" in the title crudely marked out and replaced with the word "Bad" —whether by the editors or by a puritanical typesetter. *Newsweek* had a lot of fun that week with the city of New Haven and a bizarre Jacobean play at Yale called *'Tis Pity She's Bad.*

The production demonstrated that our new company was not yet an ensemble. No doubt it was foolhardy of me to expose a group of actors still unfamiliar with each other to an unfamiliar text. With our next production, however, we began to look more like a company, doing work that came more easily to American actors—a play by an American author.

The author was Joseph Heller, and the play was (finally) called *We Bombed in New Haven.* I had secured this play for our theatre, as I had scouted *Little Murders,* through my friendship with the playwright, which dated from an enthusiastic review I had written of *Catch-22* for *The New Republic.* When Heller first told me of his plans to write a play, I was very excited; I thought he was the most original comic talent of our time. Soon after, he sent me a draft of the first act with a scenario of the rest. He was obviously cooking, though the writing was a little crude in this early stage. The play reminded me of Pirandello (an author Heller denied he had ever read) in its formulation that the characters were acting—sometimes consciously—according to the dictates of a prearranged script. Heller's first draft had vitality, sweep, and theatricality; I found it very promising. I advised him to tighten up the first act and complete the play as soon as possible. We scheduled it for November and started looking for the right director.

I soon found my man in Larry Arrick. Arrick, a former associate of Paul Sills at Second City, had recently been working around Broadway and off-Broadway, never too satisfied with his conditions. He was about my age at the time, mild-mannered and good-humored, balding and a trifle hunched. A chain-smoker, he always kept a cigarette dangling from his lips, like a Bill Mauldin character, and there was often keen speculation as to whether the lengthening ash would fall on the floor or on his shirt front. Larry was devoted to new American plays, actors, and improvisation—in that order. He had a shrewd editorial intelligence, which, combined with his enthusiasm for good writing, made him a natural collaborator with new playwrights. He worked very closely with Heller, but it soon became clear that the loosely written style of the first draft was pretty much what Joe intended for the entire play. Nevertheless, Arrick agreed to direct the production, provided that Heller approve his very free approach.

What Arrick proposed was to use the text as a springboard for improvisation rather than as a finished text, with the actors inventing additional dialogue at will. Heller, obviously taken with Arrick, agreed to the idea, and I approved it as well. The play seemed to us unfinished, and Joe seemed disinclined to work on it further. Larry's suggestion not only suited his own working process but seemed appropriate to Heller's Pirandellian structure.

We had the good fortune to have some actors in residence who had been trained in improvisation, among them Ron Leibman, Anthony Holland, Michael Lombard, Estelle Parsons, and Stacy Keach. Some had been citizens of Second City, which was an improvisatory group; others instinctually used improvisation as a basis for preparing a role; all shared the ironic, satirical, freewheeling style required for Arrick's approach. Stanislavsky had proposed improvisational paraphrase as a method of building character and establishing behavior. American actors had expanded this method into a creative process of their own. It was well known, for example, that the famous car scene in

On the Waterfront—between Marlon Brando and Rod Steiger—had been totally improvised by the actors under the direction of Elia Kazan. The comedy of Nichols and May, and of Woody Allen, proceeded entirely from improvisation. And actors like Dustin Hoffman and Alan Arkin, for example, invariably supplemented their roles with dialogue of their own invention.

Heller stayed away from this rehearsal process pretty much until the final week, although he was teaching classes at the school. At forty-four, he was a little heavier than in later years (his jogging was to slim him down considerably), and his hair, though already graying, had not yet developed such a prominent curl. Heller always kept an orange Stim-u-dent in his mouth for periodontal purposes; that, and his hooded eyes, gave him the look of a hard-boiled movie gangster. This was all part of the cynical pose he liked to adopt when speaking to young people. Whenever his class asked him why he had written this play, Heller would answer, "What else? I wanted to make a million dollars." To an interviewer, he gave an only slightly less mischievous reply: "Right now I want to make every woman cry and every man feel guilty when he has to go home and face his sons." When pressed, he offered, somewhat sheepishly, what was probably his true motive: "I meant to write a very good play."

Heller gave a number of interviews during the rehearsal period, his joking manner concealing a genuine anxiety; he was a lot more nervous about the experience than he cared to admit. When he dropped in on rehearsals (infrequently), he chewed his Stim-u-dent into splinters, and left without a word. The next day we could expect a whole sheaf of revisions through the mail— changing "Oh" to "Ah" or "Alas" to "My God." These were more like textual emendations for publication than script revisions for the stage; Heller was not prepared to make the radical rewrites that the theatre sometimes demands. Arrick and the actors therefore began to depart more and more from the written text, and the first run-through was a wild, freestyle variation on a theme by Heller that left us wet with laughter. Joe it left wet with panic.

Heller had not entirely understood what Arrick had meant by "improvisation." *"They're changing my words,"* he shrieked in genuine authorial distress. After a while he managed to accommodate himself to some of the changes introduced by the actors, though he insisted on reinstating most of the script. "I'm learning," he told an interviewer who asked him what differences he had discovered between the novel and the theatre. "I'm learning that I wrote a script and not a production. In novels the writer defines and limits his characters, but not in plays. If an actor has any talent and is working with a good director, he will fill out bare words in the script."

This was indeed a discovery, but still he remained very, very nervous. After the run-through, he decided to avoid rehearsals altogether—"Otherwise I think there will have to be some unpleasantness." A week later he was back demanding that Michael Lombard, playing the Major, shed his Southern accent ("I don't want the audience to think he's Johnson"). For Heller, his experience with the theatre was proving a new and not altogether pleasant adventure. "Listen, who's nervous," he told the same interviewer. "I'm a veteran of the theatre now. After two weeks' experience I've learned a lot. I've learned how to suffer excrutiating torture without making a sound while they blow my play."

That interview appeared in an alternative Yale newspaper called *The New Journal.* On the page facing it was a full-page advertisement endorsed by the Yale Draft Refusal Committee and signed by hundreds of students, declaring their determination to refuse induction in the Vietnam war. The Resistance Committee had purchased a block of seats for the opening of *We Bombed in New Haven.* It certainly seemed an appropriate benefit for the movement. For the play concerned a group of air force personnel fighting in an unnamed war for an unnamed cause, gradually being blasted away by an unnamed enemy. The final scene—which I found very moving—showed the weak-willed hero, Captain Starkey, trying to find a replacement for one of the dead soldiers. The first candidate turns out to be his own son. Since the replacement is destined for certain death, Starkey helps his son to escape through a window and calls for the next candidate. This, too, turns out to be his son. Each time the boy escapes, he reappears at the door until, pale and shaken and solitary, Starkey is forced to send him off to his death.

This scene, which I found so powerful, others found extremely offensive. It almost caused a disruption on the opening night. The more radical students at the School—most of them in the criticism department—had decided that Heller's play capitulated to the war instead of resisting it. They interpreted the passivity of Starkey's son before his fate as a rank distortion of the way their generation was behaving. These students were urging everyone to refuse induction, and Heller's ending signified to them an acceptance of induction.

The students were planning to gather in the orchestra during the final scene, and shout "Hell no, we won't go," after which they intended to chase the actors off the stage into the greenroom. I got wind of the plan from one of them, and tried to reason with the group during the intermission. Four students were involved—two were from my old Columbia seminar. The leader was a Chilean in the directing department who had brought in an outside agitator from the Students for a Democratic Society. The students seemed embarrassed when I spoke to them, but they were also genuinely troubled. They were obviously convinced that Heller's play was counterrevolutionary, and I suppose the presence of celebrities in the opening-night audience (Paul Newman among them) had aroused their suspicions that I had joined the Establishment. I was there with Jules Feiffer, whose antiwar credentials were impeccable, and between us, we managed to persuade the students that disrupting the play would hurt their cause more than help it. But they were not reconciled to the situation, and they eyed us both in a way that I found strange and new. We were over thirty and not to be trusted.

Everybody agreed that the performance was brilliant; many had doubts about the play. Heller was in agony on opening night, and didn't conceal his pain even when taking a bow with the actors. That look I was to see again on the faces of other established nondramatic authors persuaded to try their hand at plays. Exposing your work to the public, with critics and spectators sitting just a few feet away, is an experience considerably different from the solitary act of writing and publishing fiction, and it can be scary. Heller left the next day without a word; I was not to hear from him again for some years. But while he had given up on Yale, he had not given up on the theatre. *We Bombed in New Haven* was done on Broadway the following year in a revised version with a couple of stars (Jason Robards and Diana Sands) and two members of our company (Ron Leibman and Anthony Holland) in the cast. It had a new director, who no doubt adhered more faithfully to the script. It was generally thought to be inferior to our production, and it was not a success.

The Yale production, on the other hand, was a moderate success, despite the mixed reception of the play. It sold a lot of tickets and pleased a lot of people—for us, it had the more important value of unifying the company and providing it with a style. Arrick's rehearsal procedure and amiable personality proved very appealing to the actors; he enjoyed himself, too, speaking of a new sense of fulfillment after years of frustration in the commercial theatre. Arrick and I shared many of the same literary interests, the same vocabulary, even the same friends. I was looking for an artistic director to shepherd the company while I ran the School and tried to raise money. I believed I had found the right person in Larry Arrick, and within a couple of months I was to offer him the position.

Meanwhile the remainder of the season was running into unexpected troubles. Both Jacques Levy, scheduled to direct Pirandello's *Henry IV,* and Carl Weber, scheduled to stage Brecht's *Coriolanus,* were unable to commit themselves during the periods assigned. Weber had just been offered what he considered a very juicy directing opportunity—*Cyrano de Bergerac* at the Vivian Beaumont—and wanted to withdraw from his commitment to us. I was puzzled by his enthusiasm (obviously shared by many American theatre people) for this romantic and charming but overdone warhorse, especially in the light of his experience with Brecht and the Berliner Ensemble. But since Levy was unavailable to direct *Henry IV* in the December slot to which we had been forced to move it, I offered Weber the Pirandello play, and released him from *Coriolanus.*

The cause of these scheduling snags was *The Sea Gull.* The deterioration of East-West relations was threatening to destroy our plans for this production, and, with them, our hopes of bringing Stella back to the stage. Although Tovstonogov had agreed to come to Yale, we were unable to persuade the Soviet authorities to let him out of the Soviet Union. Howard Stein had recently made a special trip to Canada to see Madame Furtseva, the Soviet Minister of Culture, during her visit to Expo '67; but she had brushed by him curtly, refusing either to hear or acknowledge his request regarding Tovstonogov. Subsequently we sent long and eloquent communiqués to her, which she never answered. Then we began to pull every string available. Sol Hurok carried one of our letters to the Soviet Union. Bobby Kennedy wrote a letter on our behalf. So did Lillian Hellman. No reply whatever.

In an effort to gain more time for negotiation, I moved *The Sea Gull* from the third slot to the fourth, thus creating scheduling problems for Jacques Levy. I was building a house of cards; every move affected something else. In late December we received a letter from Tovstonogov, replying to a letter I had sent him in early October; at the rate our correspondence was proceeding, our *Sea Gull* would not be ready to begin production until 1985. With Tovstonogov's exit visa still in doubt and designs not yet begun, we finally had to admit that this production wasn't destined to take place, at least in the foreseeable future. We canceled it with considerable sadness, mourning another casualty of the times and the power of politics to strong-arm the pitiful weakness of art.

In the theatre, however, there is little time for regrets; we had another production to stage. We were in the midst of rehearsing the Pirandello *Henry IV,* with Ken Haigh playing the title role—and playing it with a febrile, mercurial, lacerating savagery that was electrifying. His concentration was so intense, and acoustical privacy so minimal in the university theatre, that he not only insisted on total silence from the drama students in the auditorium but demanded that they wear sneakers when they walked through the adjacent greenroom. (Not surprisingly, his demand was not very graciously received.) The rest of the parts were played very well by the company and the students in the cast, but *Henry IV* was essentially a one-man show, with Haigh giving a demonstration of virtuoso acting to be matched on our stage only two or three times in future.

There was some danger for a while that Haigh's performance would be obscured by the production. Weber had wrapped a social-political skin around the play in the form of filmed interludes between the scenes—shots of Henry on his throne intercut with clips of crowds cheering Mussolini's speeches. Aside from its inaccuracies (*Henry IV* was written before Mussolini came to power), Weber's approach confused the play, which is not a political study of Fascism, but rather a metaphysical examination of how humankind takes refuge from painful reality. We looked at the film a lot during technical rehearsals, with Haigh glowering impatiently at us from the stage—we shortened it, repositioned it, finally abandoned it.

The production was very well received, but it left the company grumbling. Most of the actors had been obliged to spend four rehearsal weeks and two weeks of performance playing small, unfulfilling parts. I knew that actors were usually willing to accept supporting roles if they also had the opportunity to play some leads, but this was only true in a system of rotating repertory where the various parts were alternated in the same week. Because of all the demands on the university theatre—the locus of acting projects, classes, parties, lectures, and the activities of the undergraduate drama society—our company was able to play only twelve weeks of the year in two-week runs, interrupted by four weeks of nonperformance. It was far from an ideal situation, and it caused the first signs of dissension in the company's ranks.

Detecting this, I agreed to Arrick's suggestion to substitute *Three Sisters* for the canceled *Sea Gull.* Chekhov's beautiful play could hardly be considered neglected or experimental, and I was not convinced that Arrick had anything particularly original to add to it. But it had the immediate advantage of providing splendid roles for virtually every member of the company. Normally, I would not have considered producing a play like *Three Sisters* unless we had a compelling reason to do it, but keeping actors satisfied was now becoming as important as making a strong theatrical statement. I also owed it to Arrick, in his new position of artistic director, to let him participate in the choice of plays, and I was confident he would use this occasion to restore the company's morale.

The production of *Three Sisters* had some fine performances, the most satisfying being that of Richard Jordan as Kuligin, who revealed himself as an accomplished character actor after an undistinguished season playing juveniles. But the evening left me with the sinking feeling that we had fallen into the very errors we had pledged to reform. There was something stale about this production; I didn't think Arrick had proved the necessity of doing the play in this traditional manner at this particular moment in history. A few of the students not only found the production conventional but considered the play reactionary, because they said it showed Chekhov accepting the misery of existence without making any effort to change it (I thought Heller, charged with a similar stoicism, would be pleased to find himself in such distinguished company). To these radical students, Chekhov was a quietist. When they did their own cabaret version of *Three Sisters* in the Experimental Theatre, they ended the play with the protagonists shaking their fists at the audience, shouting *"We must work!"*

Our *Three Sisters* was given a critique by Michael Feingold, then a second-year student in criticism (and also one of those who had come with me from Columbia in 1966). The critique—an exercise devised to let the Doctor of Fine Arts candidates in criticism express their opinions before the entire student body, faculty, and company—was used by Feingold as an occasion to deliver a savage attack on the entire undertaking while informing the professional actors of their serious limitations in vocal control, movement, and characterization. At the conclusion of his presentation, which he gave in a shy, halting manner, twisting the buttons on his jacket in reticence and discomfort, he had left a lot of blood on the floor. Some of the actors slammed out of the room in a rage; Arrick's face was ashen. My judgment in permitting this kind of public abuse was seriously questioned. After Feingold's performance, we decided to abandon the "bloodbath," as it was coming to be called, and have the criticism students leave their written impressions of production on reserve in the library, where the professional actors could have the luxury of ignoring them.

Feingold's critique reflected, I think, a widely shared dissatisfaction in the School not only with *Three Sisters* but with the entire season. By contrast with the excitements of the previous year, this one must have seemed rather stodgy and flat. For one thing, all the plays of the first season—with the exception of *Volpone*— were either new works or adaptations, while all the plays of the second—with the exception of *We Bombed in New Haven*—were classics. Then, scheduling problems and other difficulties were preventing me from matching exciting directors with the plays we had chosen for them, with the result that most of the work was looking rather orthodox. Obliged to satisfy tastes other than my own, I was beginning to realize that building a company required making choices I didn't always find agreeable. I also began to suspect that these choices weren't even practical. *Three Sisters,* for example, had been chosen especially for the actors—and for Larry Arrick as artistic director—but it was ironic that most of these actors decamped for other jobs soon after the production.

The students expressed their opposition to our procedures in another way —through the work they did in the ensembles. Under Gordon Rogoff's supervision, these ensembles were made up of first- and second-year students in directing, playwriting, technical production, design, and administration—and students in acting, too, over the repeated protests of Stella. The object was to experiment in various modes of collective creation, under the influence of the techniques of the Open Theatre, evolving a project over a much longer gestation period than the customary four-week rehearsal. The structure and purpose of the ensembles were not the same as the structure and purpose of repertory theatres, but they had the potential to achieve the same goals. I imagined that the more successful ensembles would leave the School as nuclear units of full-fledged theatres, ready to start producing in any city in the country.

A few of these units developed significant work, particularly those associated with an imaginative playwright, but none of them survived. Most were afflicted with conflicts of leadership, ideological squabbles, and lots of wasted time. This was hardly unexpected. A cohesive group does not materialize upon demand, within a preordained period. Still, we were learning that, in conformity with the dictates of Parkinson's Law, extended development periods are not always preferable to shorter periods of intense rehearsal. As a result, the ensembles were beginning to absorb a great deal of time and a great deal of energy that should have gone into the classroom. Members of the acting department seriously questioned their value, a debate that divided these teachers not only from the directing faculty, but from most of the student body as well.

One of these ensembles, moreover, was led by our Chilean. It was remarkable to see the hypnotic control the Chilean was able to exercise over his middle-class charges, especially considering how simpleminded his pronouncements could be. A typical product of this ensemble was a twenty-minute scene in which a solitary actor, stripped to the waist, performed yoga exercises while sitting cross-legged on a mat, during which he intoned a single line over and over like a litany: "There is one fact and one fact only and that fact is the oppressed."

Each time the line was spoken, the actor cast a searching glance over the faces of the people in the room. A few students stood up in place to express their silent agreement. Others walked out, saying to the actor, "It's not true." The rest departed for their next class without a word. It was a provocative moment—it was also a fundamentally false one. The theatre involves conflict —which is to say, it asks us to entertain at least two possibilities in opposition. If there is only one fact, then there is no theatre; all that is left is propaganda. It was significant that only one actor held the stage to make this ideological point.

I was amused to find myself regarded by these students as an Establishment figure with an expanding waistline at the same time that some others in the university were calling me the "Red Dean." It was true that I was beginning to turn away from the "third theatre," as I had called the avant-garde movement in an earlier essay. I feared it was becoming an uneasy compound of revolutionary politics and media fashion. But at the same time that I was growing critical of such groups as Tom O'Horgan's La Mama company and Richard Schechner's Performance Group, I still remained committed to what I considered genuine experimental theatre, and especially to such exploratory playwrights as Sam Shepard. I began to perceive two central failings in the avant-garde that I couldn't reconcile with my former advocacy of it: the way it substituted raw energy for skill, and the manner in which its actors were beginning to eclipse the playwright. I also couldn't accept its way of justifying these developments politically, as a form of participatory democracy in which any discipline or craft was regarded as a tyrannical restriction on the free imagination.

Attracted by the vitality and adventurousness of the youth movement, disturbed by what I called its "anarchic side . . . which can make a hash of culture if it starts to run wild," I had cast myself in an unplayable role, especially when everybody was beginning to choose up sides. Nonverbal theatre versus language; modernism versus classicism; performance groups versus resident companies; improvisations versus texts; actors' theatre versus directors' theatre; youth versus age—the oppositions were everywhere, and I was still making an effort to accommodate anything that promised a little quality. I admired the energy and brashness of youth; I also respected the discipline and skill of experience. I wanted a theatre that explored the future without rejecting the past. In my effort to unify, I encouraged factions. Trying to mediate, I divided.

As a result, a leadership vacuum was beginning to form, which various people would soon rush in to fill. I believed in pluralism, and I believed that a university was obliged to encourage diversity and dissent. For that reason I held off imposing my will (though I had no hesitation expressing my opinions) on students and faculty. I had to agree with the directing department that the acting training devised by Stanislavsky, valuable though it might be, was not fully appropriate to the new theatre, and I had to agree with the acting department that the ensembles were virtually preempting the formal training at the school. The two departments were going off in opposite directions, and I was trying to support both their positions without taking a stand of my own.

Diversity and dissent were all very well, but I was running a conservatory, not a progressive school, and my policies were leading to chaos. What appeared to be freedom for some was for others a form of restriction. The ten weekly hours assigned for rehearsing ensemble work had mushroomed into twenty, sometimes thirty, additional stolen hours, and the directing faculty was not making an effort to police the situation. The student actors, pulled in two directions, were beginning to complain about losing their voice and movement classes, while the student directors were beginning to scorn the actors' allegiance to "old-fashioned" and "conservative" teachers. It was common then to reject any form of self-subordination, even that of student to teacher; a favorite motto of the School was "Don't park your individuality at the door." Inevitably, discipline grew lax, and when the students were asked to display professional attitudes in regard to promptness and attendance at rehearsals and classes, they complained that they were much too tired.

A typical instance of the tensions growing among us was the time a student director objected to letting the acting faculty witness a run-through of his final project. Most third-year students at the school had the opportunity to present a "thesis" in the form of a fully designed production, an extended role, a major production assignment, etc. Third-year directors presented a complete production in the Experimental Theatre. Faculty members had always appeared during the last week of the rehearsals to help the acting students involved with any problems; this year, Bobby Lewis had been assigned to watch the dress rehearsals of the third-year shows. Incited by the director, the cast simply refused to cooperate. At one scheduled run-through the actors spoke the play so softly it couldn't be heard; at another they didn't even appear onstage. Bobby appealed to me for help; I appealed to Gordon Rogoff who was heading the directing department. Rogoff replied there was nothing he could do; it was up to the students; you don't park your individuality at the door.

Partly as a result of incidents like this, Stella Adler told me of her determination to leave the School at the end of the year. She had been taking the train to New Haven each week for almost two years now, carrying her heavy carpetbag and wearing her floppy hat, and the trip was beginning to take its toll on her boundless energy. The real reason she wanted to quit, however, was that she wasn't getting much satisfaction any more out of her classroom work. The new class that year had some talented people in it, including Jill Eikenberry and Henry Winkler, but some of the incoming actors were criticizing her methods, and sometimes the class was half empty. Stella had no patience to argue with her students over training, or to compete with the "pishers" who were trying to influence them. In her own Studio, she was accustomed to strict punctuality and considerable deference; she never permitted smoking or slouching in her classes; and she was bewildered by the restive, undisciplined, sloppy behavior of her students at Yale. It was not that Stella was opposed to political engagement. In her Group Theatre days, she had marched in demonstrations herself (reportedly wearing a mink coat and carrying a poodle). But she resented the way student radicalism was affecting the development of actors. Anyway, this was a new kind of politics. It was aimed at the immediate family as much as at the society outside, and it was making people say unpleasant things. The one thing Stella could never tolerate was discourtesy, and she refused to tolerate it here. "Too chaotic," she said, shaking her head. She submitted her resignation, to take effect at the end of the year.

The company actors were also starting to abandon ship around the same time. They had first come to Yale full of excitement, prepared to participate in an ambitious new venture that included for some of them (like Paul Mann and Jeanne Hepple) training young actors in the classroom, and had been met, almost immediately, by competitiveness, envy, even insult. This was a year of growing student unrest all over the country. Such was the political climate that small issues, normally resolved with a little reasonable discussion, were exploding into massive resentments and confrontations. Many of the students befriended the professional actors, but a small group (always that same small group) glowered at them continually as if they were trespassers. Also, the actors did not have enough opportunities on stage to compensate for this unfriendly treatment. A few fat roles would at least have given them professional satisfaction, but in our final production of the year *(Coriolanus)* most of them had no more than two or three scenes. There was no adhesive in the situation, so when other offers came toward the end of the season, they saw no pressing reason to reject them.

Stacy Keach remained to play Coriolanus, and Barry Morse to play Menenius. Ron Leibman would have made an ideal Aufidius, but he had already gone off to New York; we cast Harris Yulin in the part. As Volumnia, we brought in Nancy Wickwire, a strong classically trained actress who—like Barry Morse—had been in the Group 20 company. The other roles were filled by students.

The play was being staged by Larry Arrick, now fully installed in his new position as artistic director of the theatre; we both agreed on a promising young third-year student named Jeff Bleckner as co-director. This was a more responsible assignment than the assistant directing duties usually entrusted to the students, but Arrick knew this was going to be a gigantic undertaking, and he needed all the help he could get. The set was a massive construction, dominated by planes and peaks and scaffoldings, so difficult to act on that we decided to rehearse on a mock-up. The only space large enough to hold this was Ingalls Rink, a huge arena for the hockey team on Prospect Street, which had been designed by Eero Saarinen as a bizarre piece of architecture known locally as the Yale Whale. The acoustics in this building were appalling, so all we could rehearse there were the physical aspects of the production—blocking, swordplay, encounters between warring armies. From the beginning it was obvious that the first production of Shakespeare at Yale was going to be a spectacle.

It was also obvious from the beginning that Arrick was having troubles. He didn't seem to have the juice required to direct the play. The reception of *Three Sisters* had disappointed him, and like most depressing experiences, it had drained his energy. As a result, he wasn't showing much enthusiasm for *Coriolanus.* My original plan was to do an American version of the Brecht production at the Berliner Ensemble—an economic interpretation that treated the conflict between patricians and plebeians as motivated by the high price of corn. But with Carl Weber in New York doing *Cyrano,* we had lost our German connection, and Arrick wasn't particularly interested in Brecht's adaptation. Consequently we decided to do the original play. In a number of meetings held in my office, I tried, without much success, to get Arrick to articulate a concept for his production; Larry wasn't particularly interested in directorial concepts. This left us with the prospect of a rudderless Shakespeare, with no more purpose or direction than the productions I had been criticizing at the American Shakespeare Festival.

After two weeks of desultory rehearsal, Arrick told me that for the sake of his health, he would like to turn the show over to his co-director, Jeff Bleckner. He would help in any way he could, but he was not capable at that moment of taking full responsibility for a large and complicated production. Bleckner, though young and inexperienced, was obviously gifted, and he was trusted by the actors. He had not done much preparation on the play, but considering the way Arrick was feeling, we really had no choice in the matter, so rehearsals proceeded under Bleckner's direction.

The play opened in the middle of a Yale maintenance workers' strike. The primary issue was wages. After Yale had agreed on increases higher than those enjoyed by any other employees in the area, the strike was about to be settled when the radical students joined in "support" of the workers, urging them to reject Yale's offer. At the Drama School, the only workers on strike were Dominic and Sophie, the janitor and the cleaning woman, both of them eager to return to their jobs. But some drama students, inflamed by the heady experience of supporting two people they knew against what they called the "exploitation" of the "underprivileged" by the "university bosses," asked me to close down the Theatre in sympathy with the strike. I replied that we were about to open a production of a play. Far from from closing down the theatre, I was trying to recruit student volunteers to clean up the auditorium in preparation for opening night.

The next day some signs appeared in the greenroom: "Don't be a scab!" "Support Dominic and Sophie in their struggle for a better life!" "Refuse to clean the Theatre!" These admonitions were ignored by the students helping to tidy up. That night we found garbage strewn all over the lobby. All of us joined in removing it the next morning. By afternoon more garbage had appeared, this time dumped over the seats of the auditorium.

Entering the Theatre on opening night, I saw two of our students handing out to the audience leaflets denouncing Yale. One of them was supposed to be performing—in fact, he was due to appear onstage in less than five minutes. "David," I said, in some consternation, "what are you doing here? You'll be late for your entrance." He replied, with a touch of disdain, that some things were more important these days than mere plays. "That may be," I replied, hearing my voice turn a little squeaky, "but you agreed to act in *Coriolanus,* and you have an obligation to honor that commitment. Have you decided to go on strike too?"

"No," he answered guiltily, "but I support the workers. I feel badly that I crossed the picket line."

I reminded him of the half-hour regulation, a sacrosanct law of the theatre that requires actors to be in their dressing rooms thirty minutes before places are called.

"I'm wearing makeup," he answered. (He was indeed, which made him an odd-looking strike supporter.) "All I have to do is put on my costume."

I began to sputter: "But you should be backstage. You're getting all confused between politics and art. There's no conflict there."

"There's a conflict all right," he answered, eyeing me coldly. "You're on one side and we're on the other."

"David, don't get paranoid," I told him. "I'm not your enemy."

He looked at me skeptically for a moment, then went inside the theatre to perform the play.

Coriolanus opened without further incident. It neither provoked the audience nor scandalized the critics. It was, in fact, one of those shows that win audience and critical approval precisely because they contain nothing very original or challenging. It satisfied few of the people in the cast, and it certainly didn't satisfy me. It was a production that bore no particular stamp; it was a production that could have been offered by any theatre in the country.

I knew I was failing my purpose. I was also failing to maintain the momentum we had built up in our first season. Having recruited a potentially strong company, I had lost them to various causes but primarily through my failure to excite the actors with a sense of the importance of our mission. Most of them had already departed, and after *Coriolanus,* Keach and Morse would leave us too. Some of the prize acting faculty were also leaving, unprepared to tolerate the growing tensions at the school. The students were jittery. A few of them would soon drop out as well. I was losing my constituency. I feared I was losing my way.

I was also about to lose my artistic director. During *Coriolanus,* Arrick sent me a letter: "I have not been happy here," it read, "I have not functioned well here. I had hoped that the atmosphere of Yale would increase my creative powers and channel my (heretofore) prodigious energy into an approach to my work that I had only dreamed of in my professional life. This has not been so. The reasons are many. I would prefer not listing them right now. . . . My impulse is that I should not return next year."

Arrick then went on to list four possible alternatives for a theatre at Yale: (1) a permanent company of ten professionals and three journeymen, doing mainly new plays chosen according to Arrick's taste and sensibility; (2) a company of third-year students and recent Yale graduates, supplemented by occasional guest artists, doing plays that drew on the youth of the ensemble; (3) a workshop company, developing a single project over the course of a year in the mode of performance groups; and (4) a professional company producing new and classical plays in the same manner as before, "only better." Of the four solutions he proposed, the last one seemed to him the least attractive. "I might like to direct a play or two. I don't want to be the resident director of such a theatre."

Arrick's letter helped to crystallize my own anxieties. The plays he suggested were pretty interesting ones, and the actors he proposed were largely people I admired. But it was now clear that despite many areas of agreement, we had certain differences about the purpose of the Theatre that would eventually create a clash between him, as artistic director, and me, as producer. The fault was entirely mine. I had believed that I could appoint him to a position of artistic authority without relinquishing my control over the selection of the plays, the makeup of the company, the approach to the productions. His letter reinforced our mutual suspicion that we were occupying the same space. What I had offered him was a job without teeth, where he would be continually subject to my sensibility, my aesthetic, my taste.

I was learning that I could not surrender the leadership of the theatre, partly because it was so closely related to the School. I had invested Arrick with a fancy title when he was actually functioning as a resident director under my artistic control; no wonder he began to wilt under this arrangement, and chafe under this constraint. The powers I wanted to preserve for myself were the powers of the artistic director. Now I would have to claim this title, along with its responsibilities, and reassert my right to the Theatre.

I told Arrick of my decision to continue as we had been—"only better." For his first three solutions made it his Theatre, the fourth made it mine. The next year I would assume the title of artistic director, along with that of dean. Arrick agreed to return to the School as a teacher—and possibly to direct a production or two if the occasion arose. And thus we resolved, in a guardedly friendly fashion, the issue dividing us.

In my annual report for that year I spoke of "mixed pleasures and pains." The pleasures were mostly financial. Our box office had increased by 30 percent, and some of our economic problems were being relieved, temporarily, through grants from individuals and foundations. The Rockefeller Foundation, which had led the way with its $340,000 award to the School, now came through with a $300,000 grant to the Theatre, thus becoming the first major contributor to our professional activity. And the expiring Yale-ABC grant had been picked up by a most unusual benefactor—the movie producer Joseph E. Levine.

The American Broadcasting Company had finally caught on to the fact that its money was not going to television courses but, rather, to supporting playwrights, despite our tactical catalogue descriptions ("Writing for the Camera"). I wasn't willing to lose this valuable program or the interesting writers it attracted to the School if it was possible to identify another donor. When

Mike Nichols came to lecture to our students, I told him of my problem. He provided the solution with a single telephone call to Joe Levine.

Levine, at the time, was riding high on the crest of his success with Nichols's film *The Graduate*, and would probably have bought Mike the Triborough Bridge if he had asked for it. At Nichols's suggestion, I asked Levine for $100,000 ($25,000 more than the ABC grant), and, to my astonishment, he agreed—probably the fastest money I ever raised. All that he required was that I visit him in New York, and tell him more about the program.

A rotund, volatile, dynamic individual whose rasping voice bore traces of a Boston accent, Levine was then the head of Embassy Pictures, an independent enterprise he was about to sell to a conglomerate, Avco, in a multimillion-dollar deal. Surrounded by trophies, mementos, signed letters, and autographed photographs of himself and his wife with all his stars, the diminutive Levine was almost lost behind a huge office desk, on which he drummed continually with his thick, ring-laden fingers. He was so delighted with his own success that it was impossible not to share his pleasure. I took an immediate fancy to him, and listened with fascination as he regaled me with movie anecdotes and outlined his grandiose plans for future "pitchers." He promised to mail the check immediately. Departing from Levine's office suite, still dazzled by my quick success, I met Mike Nichols in the lobby, preparing to go up. "Well," he asked me in his laconic way, "how does it feel to have sold out?"

If this was selling out, it felt good, but despite our success in raising money that year, I was still not very satisfied. The major reason, aside from my feelings about the productions, was our sadly limited facility, which I likened in my report to "crowding hundreds of temperamental people into a tiny room, each fighting for a space." I implored the administration to find a solution for this problem, warning the president that "a new space must be quickly found if the restiveness we experienced this year is not to grow explosive."

One additional facility did come through toward the end of that year—a converted fraternity house, called Vernon Hall, not far from the School. It didn't answer our need for another first-class theatre, but it did make an important impact on our work in future. Besides providing additional classrooms, a studio theatre, offices, and rehearsal spaces, Vernon Hall had a dining area in the basement that was to double, the year following, as a cafeteria for students during the day (we called it the Drama Deli), and as a cabaret on weekend evenings. The cafeteria couldn't make its way financially and closed after two years of operation, but the Cabaret proved to be a very appealing place for short plays, satirical sketches, and musical offerings—it was later to have a powerful influence on the style of acting and writing at Yale. The Cabaret also managed to provide for the community a place to meet and eat in the late evening hours—not an inconsiderable thing in a city where virtually nothing stayed open after 10 P.M. Naturally, when it opened the next fall, it was immediately embroiled in controversy.

One more positive thing happened before the end of the season that helped to relieve my melancholy over our various failures—the beginnings of a new magazine, edited by students in criticism under the supervision of the faculty. The first issue of *yale/theatre*—underwritten partly through a generous $2,500 grant from William Styron and partly through the Alumni Fund (which I applied with malicious pleasure to the project least designed to please the old grads)—was devoted to the subject of Greek drama, and included articles by Jan Kott, Jonathan Miller, and me, among others, along with articles and reviews by some of the DFA students in criticism. What sparked this issue was the Yale production of *Prometheus Bound,* and future issues would frequently be inspired by other productions in the Theatre. From the start, *yale/theatre* (later called *Theatre*) filled a need for an intellectual journal of the stage, but like all the other things we did, it had a training function as well, providing a laboratory for students in criticism similar to the way the professional theatre functioned in relation to students in playwriting, acting, directing, technical production, administration, and design. It represented another step forward, and perhaps for that reason, I ended the year in a mood of relative complacency.

"I would like to say," I wrote, concluding my annual report, "that, in spite of all the difficulties I am sanguine about next year. We have already taken many steps to solve as many of the problems that came up this year as possible. The professional season promises to be the most exciting and vital one we have yet produced, with seven premiers of new plays, a new adaptation of a classic, and a visit by the Living Theatre with four plays in repertory. The cabaret will be offering a variety of dramatic, musical, and literary evenings that are certain to enrich the night life of the Yale community. The students, despite their many gripes and groans, are really an imaginative and a cooperative lot. To a large degree they have been responsible for whatever has been accomplished over the last two years, and they remain an invaluable source of ideas, of talent, of healthy ferment, yes, and of comfort during these difficult periods. We are in a constant state of communication; morale is generally high; and we all sense that we are involved in something valuable and effective."

Sanguine about next year! A visit by the Living Theatre!! Healthy ferment!!! I must have had my brains soaked in formaldehyde, my head buried in sawdust.

The next year was to be our Armageddon.

III

Armageddon
1968-1969

Please do not shoot the pianist. He is doing his best.

—Oscar Wilde, *Impressions of America*

September of 1968 was unpleasantly warm. Yale students lounged on the steps of their colleges in T-shirts and jeans, whacked out by the heat, lacking even the ambition for a game of Frisbee. The air was thick and still; sounds of rock music blasted over the campus through the open windows.

At the School we were preparing for a visit by the Living Theatre. In a welcoming speech delivered soon after they arrived, I told the students of this and other plans for the year. The speech was positive about the coming programs of the School, gloomy about the political outlook of the country. The murder of Martin Luther King had seriously affected the hopes of black people for a peaceful process of integration. The hopes for a reasonable settlement of the war had also been dashed first by the assassination of Robert Kennedy, and then by McCarthy's failure to win the Democratic nomination. The horrors of the 1968 Chicago convention lay in our mouths like ashes; the candidates, Humphrey and Nixon, looked like the mangled parts of a broken-down electoral process.

"We are confronted," I told the students, "with a choice between two faceless party hacks, both sharing the policies of a discredited President. The young are caught between a loathsome war and the absence of regular channels through which to express dissent. Dissent itself is in real danger of a coming repression. Violence and racism seem to be our only inheritance; black grievances are being ignored; the sentiment of the country against the war is being squelched. . . . As a result of these tensions, it is inevitable that many of you will become more alienated or more radicalized. Frustration and anguish will mount, and any authority will seem to be corrupt or malevolent. But the sign

of your maturity is your ability to distinguish those who support your legitimate aspirations from those who do not. . . . Those of you who are in revolt
are rebelling not only against something, but on behalf of certain values—
courtesy, decency, generosity, peace. It is crucial that no matter how beset you
may become, you try to maintain those values in yourselves."

I pleaded with the students to apply themselves to meaningful work and a
common purpose; I tried to explain how what we were sharing at Yale was
one of the methods of bridging the "deplorable gulf" of the generation gap.

Obviously, I was expecting trouble. There had already been radical rumbles
at the School, and I had learned enough in the last few months, after the
explosion at Columbia, the student strikes in France, and the events of the
Chicago convention, to know that a contagion was spreading throughout the
world to which nobody was immune.

I had also begun to realize that the visit of the Living Theatre might prove
an immediate source of difficulty, though I had been unaware of this when I
first invited the company. It was in the previous winter that I had learned—
through Saul Gottlieb, who was handling the American arrangements—that
the Living Theatre was returning to the United States after four years of exile
abroad. And at that time it seemed entirely fitting that the Yale Drama School
be the first stop on its national tour.

For I had been one of the warmest supporters of the Living Theatre when
the company was situated off-Broadway. My own inaugural as a reviewer for
The New Republic had coincided with its most controversial production—Jack
Gelber's *The Connection*—so I had been in a position to help defend this, and
other embattled Living Theatre productions like *The Brig,* against hostile
reviews in the daily press. *The Connection,* in fact, had been saved primarily
by the weekly reviews—mainly by Donald Malcolm in *The New Yorker,* but
also by Harold Clurman and me—and the long run it enjoyed thereafter was
a sign of both the growing power of the off-Broadway movement and the
growing influence of the minority critics.

But Julian Beck and Judith Malina, who led the Living Theatre, had run
afoul of the Internal Revenue Service at the height of their success. Partly out
of conviction, partly out of carelessness, they had failed to pay federal taxes
on their box-office income. They had also broken some locks that the government put on their theatre, in order to stage a final, unauthorized production
of *The Brig* for the benefit of their actors. A trial followed, at which a number
of us were invited to testify, and the Becks were fortunate enough to have a
friendly judge who was prepared, given the first opportunity, to drop all
charges. Unfortunately, however, the Becks saw the trial as an opportunity to
dramatize their politics and "humanize" their case—which meant that the
proceedings became a pretext for something I was later to call "revolution as
theatre," the first such example I was to witness. Judith Malina, wearing a long
judicial gown she called her "Portia costume," conducted her own defense,
examining a number of witnesses (including her husband, whom she questioned about her menstrual cycles), indicting the American system of justice,

exhorting the spectators to take action in the courtroom, and, finally, exhausting the patience of the judge entirely. After he had been identified six or seven times as a malignant symbol of cruelty and injustice, and after he had given them repeated warnings to desist from making a travesty of the trial, he found Julian and Judith guilty—not of the government's charges, which he dismissed, but of contempt of court. They got prison terms of six and three weeks each.

Their martyrdom achieved, their theatre defunct, the Becks went abroad in 1964, leading a troupe of gypsies and nomads all over Europe. In the subsequent years the Living Theatre developed an almost legendary reputation for its exploits; it was said that the company had discovered an entirely original style. Although I had had only a nodding personal acquaintance with the Becks, I was a great admirer of their theatrical dedication, not to mention Julian's talents as a designer and Judith's as a director. Their return to these shores seemed to me an admirable opportunity to expose their work to my students, especially since they were offering to perform four different productions in sequence before the start of the regular Yale Repertory Theatre season.

After having extended the invitation, however, I was disturbed to hear that the Becks's activity in Europe had not been entirely theatrical that summer. It was not just that they and their actors had joined the French student revolt, but that they had helped to occupy the theatres of their French theatrical hosts, Jean-Louis Barrault and Jean Vilar. This seemed to me an odd repayment for the hospitality they had received. At one point I had the opportunity to withdraw my invitation. I was strongly advised to do so, and for a while I was sorely tempted. But still in the grip of certain liberal delusions, I decided to overcome my fears, cross my fingers, and provide the company with a platform.

When the Becks arrived in September, I barely recognized them. They had changed both inside and out. "Julian Beck's features," I wrote in an article about them, "now contained an ascetic calm usually associated with Hindu gurus and Confucian monks, while his wife, Judith Malina, had taken on the look of an unprotected street urchin, her eyes sometimes ablaze with fervency, sometimes limpid with compassion for all martyrs, not excluding herself." The rest of the company was equally exotic. Attired like hippies and gypsies, their clothing collected from every corner of the earth, they astonished New Haven with their blatant life styles. The men were almost indistinguishable from the women in regard to their dress, hair length, jewelry, and drug consumption, and the numerous children who accompanied them (few of them certain of their parentage) were just as beaded, bangled, long-haired, and stoned.

It was obvious immediately, as soon as the company arrived, that the Living Theatre had come to the United States not only to revolutionize the American stage but to start disruptions in American universities and civic centers. The Becks had always been anarchists in theory; now the social and political conditions of the time had turned them into activists. As a result, they were no longer primarily concerned with creating coherent theatrical productions.

What possessed them now was their missionary program. While we were preparing a season of plays, the Living Theatre was organizing a season of acts, with the express purpose of evangelizing the young for a special kind of nonviolent revolution.

In some of our drama students, and in some of the Yale undergraduates, they found pliable material, and they were soon able to manipulate these young, middle-class minds with the skill of accomplished hypnotists, using a weird blend of sensation, suggestion, and guilt. Visiting companies had previously been invited to the school in order to supplement our training with other theatrical approaches. With the Living Theatre, it was all or nothing. You could not accept its techniques without rejecting everything else you had ever learned, possibly including your toilet training. I was interested to note, however, that the rehearsal and performance process of this company was quite similar to that being practiced at La Mama and the Performing Garage; the Living Theatre was obviously the primary source for performance group techniques. The debate we had been having—between the aims of the resident theatre, with its orientation toward the playwright, and the aims of the performance group, with its orientation toward the acting ensemble—was about to erupt in open warfare.

In four short years, the Living Theatre had almost totally abandoned text; written language was now considered an obstacle to breaking down the barriers between life and art. During their New York period, the Becks had always been daring in their approach to classical and modern plays, but they had also always been attracted to these plays. Now there was virtually no trace in their work of a playwriting intelligence. I doubt that either Judith or Julian would have joined their more rabid followers in saying "Fuck Shakespeare. Fuck Euripides" (which I heard shouted at a symposium later that year in New York), but they were not far from it. The Becks believed that anything blocking your personal freedom, including written language or characterization, was psychologically repressive, if not politically authoritarian: "I dig Shakespeare sometimes," Judith Malina once said, "But I also want to speak in my own voice, in my own person. I mean there's Hedda Gabler and there's Judith Malina, and I want to be Judith Malina." And wanting this meant clearing away the obstacles; any theatre antiquated enough to produce written plays was ripe for destruction.

While in residence at Yale, the Becks proselytized among our students with lectures, seminars, demonstrations, and table talk. During one such meeting —a formal debate before the School—I tried to dispute their assumption, central to anarchism, that human instinct is essentially decent and generous, and twisted only by external social laws. I thought the events of the twentieth century had been enough to lay Rousseau Romanticism in the ground forever, but my professorial arguments proved no match for their Pied Piper appeal. The Living Theatre's style of life was proving so alluring to our students that some of them began to imitate it; one first-year actor actually left with the company when they departed from New Haven. It was hard to deny that years of practice had endowed these people with a symbiotic unity and natural grace that were singularly appealing. By contrast, we older people at the School must have looked awkward and morose, and the work of our theatre staid and unexciting.

My admiration for the appearance of the company was tempered by a vague sense, which steadily grew sharper, that they were in the grip of an unacknowledged totalitarianism. Playing upon a general sense of emptiness in a world without absolutes, where even individual salvation was proving difficult, they declared their allegiance to freedom and self-expression—but it was constraint and control that were more in evidence; nobody was ever allowed to break the pattern of manipulated consent. Love and brotherhood were continually on their lips, but no actors in my experience ever bristled with so much hostility or so effectively stimulated the aggression of others. As for love and brotherhood, all I saw was herd-love and brotherhood among the anonymous. The return of the Living Theatre described a full circle insofar as the company had taken on the very authoritarian qualities it had always denounced, the very repressiveness that had driven them from the country four years before.

These qualities were prominent in everything they did, but most conspicuous in *Paradise Now,* the production that caused the greatest furor in New Haven. In that work the Living Theatre virtually abandoned any effort to create an artistic imitation. Audiences were invited over the footlights to join the performers; other performers in the house wandered among the spectators. The actors proclaimed their inability to travel without a passport, to smoke marijuana, or to take their clothes off—all to a mass of Yale undergraduates who, seeing the actors peel down to loincloths, thereupon stripped down to their underwear, and lit up joints. Mass love zaps and petting parties materialized onstage among couples of various sexes and sexual inclinations; and after the endless, loveless, sexless public groping was finally over, everyone was exhorted to leave the theatre and convert the police to anarchism, to storm the jails and free the prisoners, to stop the war and ban the bomb, and to take over the New Haven streets in the name of the People.

As the bedazzled audience streamed out of the theatre on opening night, roaming up and down York Street on their appointed mission of liberation, I was experiencing a keen sense of dismay, which was only exacerbated by the reactions of some of my colleagues and friends. I remember encountering Michael Feingold outside the theatre that night, his eyes glistening with excitement; I think he must have taken my disapproval as an indication that I was a traitor to the avant-garde. So did Gordon Rogoff, who was championing the Living Theatre both at the School and in the pages of *The Village Voice.* Arnold Weinstein, intoxicated by the impact of *Paradise Now,* began calling me an "enemy of the new" when I argued with him over its value. As for the Becks, they treated my resistance to their work with melancholy condescension—another blind authority that would have to be overthrown.

Within twenty minutes the performers and spectators—having swarmed out of the theatre in their loincloths and Jockey shorts—encountered a few astonished New Haven policemen, who thereupon took ten of them into custody for indecent exposure. Following a minor scuffle, Judith Malina and Julian Beck, plus a few others in a similar state of undress, were led off to the county jail for the night while Norma rushed home to collect whatever blankets and towels she could find to keep the victims warm on this September evening. When they were released the next day, Norma tried to reclaim our property only to be told that the articles had been converted into wearing apparel for the Living Theatre, and anyway property was theft. (Norma, enraged, replied that theft was theft too!)

The Becks had been released on their own recognizance, along with the other new inhabitants of the county jail, after promising the New Haven police that future performances of *Paradise Now* would take place entirely inside the theatre. The New Haven Fire Department, however, also had to be placated; aware that the number of spectators was exceeding the capacity of the auditorium, the fire chief insisted that attendance at the remaining performances be limited to those with seats. By this time the whole of Yale, New Haven, and the surrounding countryside was eager to see the show; tickets were free; and there was no way of containing the crowds that wanted to enter the theatre.

The theatre's total capacity was six hundred seventy; more than three times that number appeared at the next performance. With the police prepared to enforce the Fire Department's ruling, we were about to experience the most frightening moment of the entire week. People were massed up and down the street waiting to be let in; firemen were posted at every door; police were waiting for the first sign of disturbance; and the Living Theatre, inside the building, was beginning to shout "The theatre belongs to the People."

The waiting crowd outside picked up the chant, "The theatre belongs to the People." A few of those within were trying to open the doors. The policemen holding them outside tensed; the mood was turning ugly; anything could have sparked a full-fledged riot. Suddenly the doors on the side of the theatre burst open, and three burly men in porkpie hats ran in, shouting, "The theatre belongs to the People, the theatre belongs to the People." They were campus police. Having gained entrance, they barred the doors and stood in front of them with their arms folded. The crowd quieted down; the actors went on with the show; and the riot was averted.

When the visit of the Living Theatre was finally over, some of us took our first deep breath in weeks. We had managed to avoid a calamity, but we had not escaped unscathed. The community was polarized between those who believed the company was the bright hope of the future and those who thought it had brought disgrace on Yale. The New Haven *Register* ran an editorial that called the event "disgusting fig-leaf theatre . . . on the level of Minsky's" and the president of the local television station personally took to the air to attack me for having instigated it: "Is this the best Yale University can offer?" he asked rhetorically, "Is even mediocrity appropriate?" I replied on the air that, as an official of a commercial station, he was hardly in a strong position to talk about mediocrity; but the Living Theatre scandal had given voice to all the unarticulated anger seething against the new Drama School regime. In an article called "The Rape of Yale," published in the *Yale Alumni Magazine,* a right-wing Old Blue named Julian Dedman inveighed against me for bringing to Yale "a coterie of New York professionals known as the Jewish Mafia" who had given the School a "reputation for gutter theatre"—"befouling the U.S. flag" and inviting "the so-called Living Theatre, a group that specializes in nudity, writhing bodies, and clutching genitalia." It was small comfort that Kingman was even more roundly condemned in this article than I was, partly for ever hiring people like me in the first place to perpetrate these monstrous deeds.

Naturally, I had to defend the Living Theatre against this sort of Arrow Collar harrumphing. I also felt obliged to testify in defense of those who had been arrested on the opening night of *Paradise Now.* I appeared at the trial along with Jules Feiffer, another disconcerted witness of that evening; we did what we could to keep the Living Theatre from suffering any legal consequences for its harmless sortie into the streets. The major concern of the court on this judicial occasion was to determine whether anybody's genitals had been exposed during that fateful night. When the police failed to make a positive identification (of the alleged culprits, not of the alleged genitals), the defendants were finally freed, though Judith Malina was fined $100 for interfering with an officer (she had thrown her entire ninety pounds into an effort to free her husband from the bondage of the law).

At the same time that I was discharging my civil libertarian duties in public, I was privately trying to figure out what made the company's behavior so troubling to me. I published these musings in *The New York Review.* "The Living Theatre," I wrote, was "the theatricalization of campus revolts, confrontations, and occupations . . . of those numerous quasi-revolutionary gestures by which students are persuading themselves today that they are having a significant impact on their times. That these gestures are aimed not against the Pentagon or napalm-producing factories, but rather against the university itself (for all its faults, still one of the last outposts of civilization and humaneness) only indicates that the desire for effectiveness *somewhere* far transcends the desire for effective change. But it also indicates that, with the day of protest upon us, the conditions necessary for the creation of great art may well be over, at least for a time. As one gifted acting student told me, upon withdrawing from Yale: 'I don't give a shit about art. I want to create events.' "

It was a relief to express my feelings in prose; I certainly wasn't expressing them very well at the School. There, "events" were completely obliterating reasoned discourse and theatrical development. I imagine that after the Living Theatre excitement our own season must have seemed pretty anticlimactic to students, but still I was unprepared for the series of shocks and convulsions that attended each of our productions. For a while they threatened to bring the activities of the School to a halt and the work of the Theatre to extinction. I had announced a "theme" for the season—"the theme of violence, examined in its revolutionary, racial, official, and random phases." For most of the year we lived that theme in action.

Our first production was a play by Jules Feiffer called *God Bless,* which came to us, this time, without a Broadway producer. A satire on Washington politics and radical revolution, *God Bless* was about a hundred-and-ten-year-old statesman who has survived innumerable political administrations, both Democrat and Republican; by the end of the play, he has survived a revolution as well. In the final scene he is negotiating with black and radical leaders—who have occupied Washington and taken over the White House—regarding who gets to talk on television first. The first act was lowered on the blowing up of the Washington Monument; the production was almost blown up as well.

Black and radical elements at the university were extremely angry about being satirized in this manner. We got a few bomb threats and a lot of threatening rhetoric. At one bull session, following the final performance, our resident Robespierre, the Chilean, delivered a scorching attack on Alvin Epstein, who had rejoined the company that year to play the ancient statesman; among other delicious remarks, he called Epstein's acting "an obscenity." This particular meeting made Norma very angry. She thought that "someone" should have stood up in defense of Alvin; she obviously meant me. When I argued that everyone has a right to be heard, she bristled: "Your friend, not to mention a fine actor, was being insulted in public, and all you could do was hold your head in your hands." Rancor was beginning to erupt in every corridor of the School, and I was still trying to preserve the privileges of dissent.

Since Herbert Marcuse's theory of "repressive tolerance" was one of the standards of intelligence at this time, my position only further enraged the radicals. It certainly didn't quiet things at the School. Our situation was sufficiently restive to attract the attention of the *Yale Daily News,* where it was described by a young reporter named William Henry III as ripe for tumult: the old School, wrote Henry, was run "like a Prussian military academy. The answer was always no, and students never dared voice dissent. Under Brustein, heated argument about the operation of the School has been accepted, even sought. Thus the School has faced turmoil on nearly every major question." Henry ended his piece with a warning: "Because of his open, permissive approach to dissent, he may be subject to more overt controversy than Canfield ever faced."

The next issue to arouse this controversy was the opening of the cabaret. Having acquired the space from Kingman, I had managed to wangle $10,000 out of Susan Morse Hilles for renovation funds. With this, Vernon Hall was painted, equipped with lighting instruments, a working kitchen, and a small stage, to emerge soon after as Yale Cabaret, an after-hours bistro featuring a selected menu of cakes, coffee, salads, and sandwiches. For our first offering, we announced *An Evening of Kurt Weill Songs* (later to tour the country as *The Kurt Weill Cabaret*) performed by Alvin Epstein and Martha Schlamme. Once again our Chilean marshaled his troops for action. He declared that the Cabaret belonged to the People (meaning his own ensemble), and that it was up to the People to decide how the space was used. It was intolerable enough to find pig professionals befouling the University Theatre. The People must now make certain to protect the Cabaret from similar defilements. They would turn themselves into a guerrilla force, occupy the Cabaret, expel the professionals, and raise the flag of freedom on the stage.

The Cabaret had been planned as a place for students and professionals to work together—as they were doing in the University Theatre—or apart, depending on the project. It was a space that naturally invited experimentation, and a number of student projects had already been scheduled there, including a concoction by the Chilean's ensemble called *The American Pig.* There was really no issue here, except a conflict over power. It was important for me to maintain authority over the selection of the Cabaret programs—partly to preserve the educational status of the facility, partly to ensure its quality. The threat to occupy the Cabaret was a direct challenge to my authority, and it put in serious jeopardy the whole student-professional relationship we were trying to build at the School. It could also have affected the future use of the space, which, if it became a subject of contention, would have been removed from Drama School auspices and turned into a graduate student lounge.

I met the Chilean's challenge with a little muscle, informing him and his troops at a School meeting that in the new *University Guidelines,* page 24, were to be found clearly defined regulations regarding the occupation of Yale buildings: the offending students would either be suspended or expelled. Feeling slightly embarrassed over this unusual announcement of my administrative powers, I then opened the meeting to a discussion of what had caused the Cabaret crisis in the first place. Apparently, the acting students felt they weren't getting sufficient opportunity to act. The ensembles—designed to absorb their energies for most of that year—were, for various reasons, in serious disarray, and few were issuing in performance, though they rehearsed incessantly. Also, they were failing to fill the training gap left by the departure of Stella. For one thing, the student directors were ignoring our plan to complete three different projects in three different styles (the very notion of "style" was being rejected as an externally imposed, therefore inhibiting, concept). As Stella had prophesied, "the blind were leading the blind"; the directing faculty was failing to supervise the ensembles properly; and, as a result, a number of actors were left with nothing to do—always a potentially volatile situation.

For this reason, some students were beginning to feel abandoned and ignored. I tried to show how the Yale Repertory Theatre was an extension of their training, not a rival or a threat. I reminded them that three recent graduates were in the acting company that year, and that Jeff Bleckner had graduated into the position of resident director. Our second professional offering, moreover, was scheduled to be a repertory of three plays, drawing on young talent in every area: the American premiere of Edward Bond's *Saved,* directed by Bleckner, with Yale graduates playing leading roles; and two short plays written by students in the School, directed and acted almost entirely by students. (One of these, a two-character by David Epstein called *They Told Me That You Came This Way,* had begun in workshop, and had the distinction of featuring, in its successive productions, two students who later became leading television stars—Ken Howard and Henry Winkler.)

I hoped that this would prove a tangible demonstration of how we planned to bring more and more students—both those in training and those who had graduated—into the professional company, without losing professional quality. But I did not succeed entirely in overcoming the doubts and suspicions growing at the School, and the Cabaret crisis was only one symptom of a pervasive restiveness. That crisis subsided quietly; Alvin Epstein and Martha Schlamme opened their show without further problems, to considerable applause from the community; and the Cabaret enjoyed a productive year, with many strong student contributions. But the whole affair convinced me that I would have to be more responsive to student grievances, especially those regarding performance. With this in mind, I organized a student grievance committee, known as the Committee of 21, since it represented all three years of each of the seven disciplines at the School. And with this in mind, I decided to seek another play in place of the one we had scheduled for our third production of the season, Ronald Ribman's *The Inheritors.*

The DFA students had been objecting strongly to the Ribman play on aesthetic grounds, but this was not the reason I canceled it. I personally liked the play; it simply didn't provide enough roles for students; and given the failure of the ensembles to engage their energies properly, I was now determined to provide the actors with more performing opportunities. In keeping with my efforts to be responsive to all shades of opinion, I had formed a new Play Committee to advise me on the schedule of the Theatre; it was composed of representative students and two faculty members from directing and playwriting (Gordon Rogoff and Arnold Weinstein). This was now empowered to find a suitable replacement for the canceled Ribman play.

By what seemed at the time to be an extraordinary stroke of luck, a new play reached us which everybody agreed was a remarkable piece of writing: Sam Shepard's *Operation Sidewinder.* It even had a subplot appropriate to our season theme of violence and revolution, since it revolved around an attempt by black revolutionaries to put LSD in a U.S. Army water supply. We optioned the play immediately, with the full concurrence of the Play Committee, assigned Jeff Bleckner to direct it, and began to cast the roles from among our professional company, student body, and (when two black students mysteriously refused to accept them) outside actors.

Our time was limited, and so were our means. For these reasons, we were unable to construct some of the complicated machinery that Shepard had stipulated—notably, a giant mechanical sidewinder snake supposed to move around the stage under its own steam. These considerations aside, we intended to give the production our best possible effort, out of respect for what all of us considered a real advance by a continually developing playwright who was rapidly becoming America's most original young dramatic writer.

Operation Sidewinder had been cast and designed, and was in rehearsal for about two weeks, when I received a statement signed by six of the seven black students at the School (the dissenter was a special student from Nigeria). The

document charged that the Drama School had "failed to live up to its obligation or responsibility as a learning, growing, pioneering venture in American
theatre through an ignorance and refusal to acknowledge the Black contribution that has been made, is being made, and will continue to be made to theatre
in this country and around the world." This accusation was followed by eight
tersely stated "demands," the first one being "either no reference to Blacks in
the Sam Shepard play . . . or no production of that play."

The six remaining demands on the list concerned increasing the black
population at the School: more black faculty, more black students, more black
actors in the company, and the creation of a black workshop in acting, directing, and film-making. The students also demanded a strict accounting of a
Ford Foundation grant we had recently acquired for black and certificate
students, and insisted on full tuition plus $4,000 in living expenses for each
black student, not to mention additional funds for travel "to share black
theatrical experiences." The statement concluded with a request that I respond
to all these demands within a week "so that we might inform the rest of the
Black community of your new position."

Some of this touched on important and acknowledged issues. We had long
been aware, for example, of the need to increase the number of black students
at the School, and, since we usually received so few black applications, were
trying to solve the problem through aggressive recruiting practices. Other
demands, however, like the establishment of a black workshop, would have
created a segregated unit at the School in contradiction to its whole purpose
and philosophy. Negotiations on these various issues would continue for many
years, and substantial progress would be made on many of them. But the one
demand on which I refused to budge was the proposal to cut or cancel *Operation Sidewinder.*

Unfortunately, this was the one demand that meant the most, at the time,
to the black students. Their reasons became clearer in a letter they later wrote
to President Brewster: "The production of this play by the Yale Drama School,
following as it would have the presentation of *God Bless* in which a black
revolutionary was a 'sell-out,' would have indicated . . . racism in its most
subtle form. Furthermore, Shepard's play represents an incomplete picture of
the black man in his more current, more sophisticated stereotype—the Black
Militant—the 'Let's Destroy Everything' image. It trivializes and makes a
mockery of the black man's struggle for dignity and liberation in this country."
By the time they wrote this letter to the president, the students were also
demanding a black play in the schedule of the Yale Repertory Theatre, performed by an all-black cast, to be chosen exclusively by black students.

I met with these students on the day they had appointed, accompanied by
Norma. She was there to answer questions. After teaching black ghetto kids
at Lee High School for a year, she had set up an acting workshop for them
in a room at the School; and our own black students, protesting that they had
not been consulted and that the class was being conducted by a white woman,
wanted an explanation. Furious, Norma read a two-page description of her

work with the high school kids, and then announced that she was handing over the class to our black students; let them teach it. They responded with something resembling panic. They simply wanted information, they said; they didn't want to change the makeup of the class.

After Norma had been mollified, I told the students that all of their demands were negotiable—with the exception of the one regarding *Operation Sidewinder*. (I also expressed strong reservations about the idea of segregating our own students in an all-black workshop, which seemed to me directly contrary to our shared desire for an integrated School.) Howard Stein reviewed our efforts to attract more black faculty to Yale, which thus far had failed—at least five black teachers, including Lloyd Richards, had refused our offers to come to the School. We described our efforts at recruitment and how we planned to improve them. And without revealing the exact terms of the Ford grant, I gave the students a general idea of how it was being allocated.

But the discussion kept coming back to the issue of *Operation Sidewinder*, perhaps because it was the one issue on which I gave no sign of yielding. I had shown the play to Ronnie Johnson, chairman of the New Haven Hill Parents Association, who was then at the School working up a Cabaret project; I thought he might tell me what the students found so offensive in it. He was just as puzzled as I was ("What do they want?" he asked me, "a bunch of Mod Squad niggers?"); and when he asked them at the meeting to define their objections, they responded that they would submit their answer the following day. The meeting broke up peaceably.

The answer did not arrive the next day; in fact, a whole week went by without further incident. In the meantime I made an effort to speak informally with individual students, in the belief that we could communicate better when not ranged against each other in a room. I had been particularly close to one of these students, a mild-mannered third-year actor, and to my surprise, he began to speak with considerable bitterness about the humiliation he suffered being a black student in a predominantly white institution. Nobody at the School, he said, understood what it meant to be black, and he was always being insulted by careless remarks. As a Jew, I knew something of what it was like to feel like an outlander; I also knew it was possible to be oversensitive to casual rejoinders. But this was the first time I learned of the chagrin that many of these students were continually feeling, for whatever reason, at Yale.

The following Tuesday, my secretary wrote on my appointments calendar the names of all the black students, followed by the word "Etc." "Etc." turned out to be three black faculty members from other departments of Yale, a city planning student from the School of Art and Architecture, and a popeyed, wispy-bearded, explosive militant from town who, I later learned, was under indictment for conspiring against the lives of public officials and for having attacked another city man with a machete. I found the presence of this militant to be a violation of what I still believed to be a trusted relationship with the black students, and I began to bristle.

The black faculty members were the first to speak. Each offered an account of his objections to the play. One, a member of the English department, rewarded me with his detailed judgment on the low quality of the work; he found it unworthy of presentation in an academic institution of higher learning. He added: "The play is full of stereotypes about black men. For example, the Cadillac in the play is a stereotype, and so are the black leather hats the revolutionaries wear; and the use of the word 'spade' in Act Two is offensive."

I refrained from saying that what I found offensive was having to listen patiently to his pretentious, uninformed remarks; apparently, our play choices were now to be influenced by anybody who had ever earned a degree or had ever held an opinion. Instead, I said that in the United States—and especially in a university—it was intolerable to pre-censor or suppress a work of the imagination, either for aesthetic or political reasons. By this time it was becoming clear enough that everybody in the room had a different reason for disapproving of the play. The middle-class faculty and the drama students were objecting that the blacks in *Operation Sidewinder* were depicted as militants, while the militant was objecting that the revolutionaries in the play did not succeed in overthrowing the United States.

I argued that what Shepard had in mind with these characters was not to provide a cross section of black life in America—in all its manifold forms—but rather to give us a specific portrait of a particular type, as shaped by his dream imagination. I said that the theatre was not obliged to be an extension of sociology, in which every group was accurately represented; I made a case for the autonomy of art in being free from social or political pressures. I tried to convince my colleague in the English department that if this play were to be withdrawn because he didn't like it, then one day a book of his might be withdrawn because somebody else didn't like it. People would soon be telling us what we could teach, what texts we could offer, what themes we could assign. For me, the only issue at stake was academic and artistic freedom.

At the very moment that I was descanting on free speech and the academic virtues, the militant broke in, his eyes popping wildly, and said, "They call me violent, they call me irrational. But if you proceed in doing this libel on black people, I'll show you what violence and irrationality really is." I sat up straight in my chair. My eyes began to pop as well. I cleared my throat, wiped the sweat from my brow, and made an effort to mumble something coherent about how little threats can accomplish. There was an embarrassed silence. The black students and faculty were obviously as uncomfortable as I was. Finally the meeting broke up—after I was given an ultimatum. I had until Thursday to cancel the play.

In the days preceding the next scheduled meeting with the black students, I sought counsel from a number of people, including the department heads of the School and the officials of the university. Some counseled capitulation, others urged me to resist. The provost asked me whether this was really an issue on which I wanted to go to the wall. When I said yes, he replied that he was glad because he really wanted to see the play now. Not normally a theatregoer, his curiosity was aroused by the controversy. As for Kingman, he was very amused over the fact that it was his radical dean who was receiving all this radical flak.

At the next meeting we held to discuss the issue, I invited Christopher St. John, the actor we had hired to play Blood, Shepard's black revolutionary. He was puzzled by the student reaction to the play, and wanted to learn more about it. The militant was also present again, and St. John regarded him carefully, no doubt picking up character hints for his role. We rehearsed everybody's objections again. And again I rehearsed my reasons for refusing to cancel the play. But this time I thought I might have located an acceptable compromise. Couldn't the students use the stage of the University Theatre, following each performance of *Sidewinder,* to present their point of view, either through direct address to the audience or through another play? "The best way to deal with something you don't like," I added, "is not by trying to suppress it but rather—"

My remarks were broken off by the militant, who had risen slowly and menacingly to his feet. "Mr. Brustein," he said, "what you are attempting to do here is what has taken place all over America. You sit here and insult our intelligence at this moment by trying to describe what our actions should be as black people. You see, we have the capacity to determine our own destiny. So don't sit here and predestinate us and tell us what our tactics should be out of some paranoid idea. This shows a total insensitivity on your part this morning to sit here and broadly insult us. Take everything that is said here and educate yourself to the needs of black people. And I just refuse to even dignify your existence any longer with my presence."

With this, he rose to his feet and walked out, followed somewhat hesitantly by the entire group. Only St. John stayed behind for a moment, shaking his head sadly. "I've been through a hundred meetings like this," he said. "It's so stupid. Don't worry. They'll be back."

But they didn't come back, and now the School was becoming badly split on the issue. Feelings were running high, inflamed by rumors that the theatre might be bombed. When I held a School meeting to try to restore some calm to the atmosphere and give both sides a chance to state their positions, the black students staged another walkout during my initial presentation. This incensed some of the white students, who felt that discussion was yielding to coercion. I pleaded with them not to let this problem divide the School. I had already made up my mind about how I was going to resolve the *Sidewinder* controversy. I didn't want the black students to feel they had lost not only their protest but the affection and respect of their fellow students.

In further meetings with faculty and students, however, I learned that a resolution was far from being achieved. Rogoff and Weinstein, for example, both of whom had voted in favor of *Operation Sidewinder* as members of the Play Committee, were now urging me to cancel the production. When I tried to point out inconsistencies in their position, they told me that personal opinions were less important than placating the black students. Two older white radical students, with whom I had warm relations, also urged me to withdraw the play, in view of the fact that this was a time of crisis. "A lot of students feel blacks have been oppressed for two hundred years, and should be given what they ask for as a form of reparation. The play doesn't matter. It's more important to give the black students a sense of self."

"Does that mean we should burn the books?" I asked them.

"No," one answered. "Just put them on the shelf until a better time."

The next day, Jeff Bleckner, who was directing *Sidewinder*, came to tell me that he was under a lot of pressure from his friends at the School to stop rehearsals on the play. He looked haggard. He was obviously not sleeping well. He admitted that being a recent graduate of the School, he felt suspended between the students and me, and felt somewhat embarrassed at his new status as a "member of the Establishment." He was also becoming convinced, he added, that our open-stage approach to the play, without mechanical elements, was not what Shepard intended.

Arnold Weinstein, a passionate advocate of the black demands, was now calling Shepard in New York, urging him to withdraw his play from Yale. He also gave Sam's phone number to the black students, who went down to see him at his apartment, and apparently persuaded him to yank it. Upon discovering this, I called Shepard and begged him not to withdraw his play. I tried to explain the importance of the principle I was defending, and the importance, too, of defending us both against the imputations of racism. Sam was not convinced. Apolitical himself, he was reluctant to expose his work to such a highly charged political atmosphere. More important, Shepard suspected that Jeff Bleckner had lost his commitment to the project, and would therefore be unable to direct it properly. That afternoon I received a call from Shepard's agent, telling me that his client had decided to withdraw *Operation Sidewinder* from Yale. He no longer believed this was the proper atmosphere for his work. I thought to myself: Is it the proper atmosphere for any work?

Under the terms of our contract with Shepard, we had a legal right to produce the play, even without his consent, but I wouldn't do this for a number of reasons. Chief among them was the fact that one of the principles I was trying to defend was the artist's freedom from external constraints. Staging *Operation Sidewinder* against the playwright's wishes was just as much a violation of this principle as trying to suppress it. I realized that I was defeated —and on an issue of supreme importance to me. I had lost the fight for freedom of the stage at Yale. Before meeting with the company to inform the actors of Shepard's decision, I walked around the block three times, profoundly dejected, talking to myself. I was rehearsing a speech of resignation.

In the company meeting, however, I discovered a powerful sentiment in favor of continuing with rehearsals. This was particularly strong among the three black members of the cast. One of them got up to make an impassioned speech: "I've been in jail in Georgia," he said, "I've served time on a chain gang. I've been manacled and beaten and spat on. I would never act in a play against my race. And this play is not against my race." The other actors rose to their feet and cheered. I recognized the moment from all those old show-business movies where, when the theatre is about to be closed down and everything seems lost, the company unifies, pools its resources, and gets the curtain open on time. The show would go on after all.

We turned to Jeff Bleckner. His response was crucial. If he agreed to continue work on the play, Sam Shepard would undoubtedly change his mind about withdrawing it. Bleckner hesitated for a few moments, pale-faced and trembling, then replied that he was unable to give his answer at that time. Too many pressures. Too many complications. He left the room on the verge of tears. I guess he hadn't seen the same movies.

The show did not go on. Paralyzed by the events of the past few weeks, pressured by the students, ambivalent toward me, Bleckner was simply suffering too much to continue working. When I told Shepard of what had transpired at the company meeting, he was fascinated and encouraged, but it was much too late to find another director. The production was canceled.

I scheduled a School meeting the next day in the Experimental Theatre in order to give the black students a further opportunity to explain their demands, and also to announce that one of their demands had already been met, albeit unwillingly, with the withdrawal of *Operation Sidewinder.* I was half tempted not to make any public announcement of the cancellation so that audiences might come to the theatre expecting to see a play, and watch the curtain rise on an empty stage—a symbol of the future in an atmosphere of this kind.

I was prepared to tell the student body of my decision to resign. Instead, I found myself delivering a tirade, with a passion compounded of equal parts anger and despair, which poured from my heart like water from an open faucet. "I want to add just one more thing," I said. "I want to talk to you about a problem which is afflicting us. It is not a problem motivated by race, though it has just taken a racial form. It is a problem for which I blame a lot of you, both black and white. We have reached a point where decision-making at the School is being influenced not by reason and counsel, but rather by threats, coercion, disruption. We are heading toward anarchy and chaos, when there will be nothing on our stage but empty noise. I came here to try to help make works of art; I believed that most of you wanted to help make works of art too. That is now proving impossible, and the reason is your infatuation with power politics. I don't think I am going to tolerate this anymore; the tail has begun to wag the dog. You have not, as a body, supported me on a single important issue, and for all your vaunted idealism, you have not been able to recognize a major point of principle, without which there is no sense remaining either in the theatre or the university. You are an intellectually precocious generation, but you have serious ethical blind spots. You have been overindulged and overpraised for qualities that on close examination are not altogether praiseworthy. I, for one, intend to indulge you no longer. Either there will be a radical change in your behavior, or there will be a radical change in mine. That's all I have to say at present—" (a student raised his hand to make a comment) *"and no more discussion!!!"*

As I flounced out of the room, I heard—to my vast astonishment—the sound of thunderous applause, mixed with shouts and whistles. Jeremy Geidt ran into my office to embrace me, his face wet with tears. Norma told me she had been waiting for this moment for almost three years. Students filed by my window, waving and smiling; many sent me warm letters of support. For almost the first time since I had come to Yale, I had made a popular statement —to the effect, ironically, that I no longer wished to be popular, that I was turning my back on participatory democracy.

That afternoon I called Gordon Rogoff into my office, and told him I had decided not to reappoint him the following year. Since this was the end of December, and he was taking a leave of absence beginning in January, this meant that for all intents and purposes he was through at the School. Arnold Weinstein submitted his resignation soon after, undecided about whether to make it effective as of January or June. I urged him to make it effective immediately, though I later granted his request to stay on through the spring to finish production on one of his plays.

The break with Rogoff was highly controversial and much publicized, since he had been my first appointment. Both of us made rancorous comments. He had a lot to say about my conduct of the School; I had a lot to say about his conduct of the directing department. But the root of our conflict was a disagreement about policy which at this time could not be reconciled. Rogoff's ensemble approach, with its emphasis on the slow evolution of a group creation, was a perfectly viable way to develop works for the stage, but it was finally obvious to me that it disrupted the formal acting training and that it was in direct contradiction to the process of interpreting written texts with a resident company. It also encouraged a competitive and resentful attitude toward the Yale Repertory Theatre—"Brustein's theatre," Rogoff and his students used to call it—which was preventing the two institutions from cooperating with each other. "The artistic and educational differences between us are so profound," I said in my statement, "that they have affected the proper functioning of both the Theatre and the School. Although he is well qualified to run a program along the lines he advocates somewhere else, the complex program as designed at Yale cannot accommodate purely autonomous activities."

For his part, Rogoff charged me with being intolerant of dissent, and accused me of preventing him from teaching his spring courses (he had asked to cancel his leave and I had refused). He raised the question of whether the theatre exists to serve the School or the School the Theatre—publicizing a debate that was to be resolved only (years later) when the two institutions finally entered a close working relationship. It was an issue that had to be raised, but could only be settled in practice. My position, as published in *The New York Times* story announcing our split, was that "no great theatre school has ever existed . . . without being connected to a theatre," to which Rogoff responded (in the same story), "Never to my knowledge has a theatre been built out of a school—he's bucking history." As for Arnold Weinstein, he limited his public remarks to the immortal statement that "the whole issue is too complex to brave the epistemological vicissitudes of journalism."

Eighty-three drama students signed a petition demanding the reinstatement of Rogoff, and ten took the opportunity to leave with him—among them the Chilean and four members of his ensemble. One of these, the granddaughter of a wealthy New York woman publisher, had been radicalized during her first few moments at the School. She entered my office with a large tear painted beneath her eye to announce, in a loud voice, that actors must be liberated from "dumb critics" and that people who do not enjoy total freedom "will be forced to use violent means to regain what has been taken from them violently." They were all eager to tell me of their exciting new plan to go to New York City and create guerrilla theatre in the subway system.

I thanked them for their statement, which I had listened to with studied indifference, and bade them Godspeed in their new undertaking, which, I was sure, would draw large captive audiences. They eyed me with cold contempt and left. In succeeding weeks I was accused by a variety of people in a variety of places of tyranny, conservatism, censorship, suppression of dissent, and maintaining a "high cultural bias" which imposed irrelevant external standards on student work. *The Yale Daily News*—criticizing my "authoritarian, repressive policies" where once it had criticized my "open, permissive approach to dissent"—wrote an editorial calling for my resignation: "Brustein has told drama students they can leave if they don't like the school," it read. "As vital as he has been to the reputation of the Drama School, perhaps it is Brustein, rather than the students, who ought to consider leaving."

I *had* considered leaving, I thought wryly, every day for the past two and a half years. What the *News* didn't know was that my recent actions were the direct result of a decision to stay. I had come to the brink of resignation and stepped back, surprised to discover I had staked more on this venture than I realized. If my programs were to succeed, I would finally have to accept the conditions of leadership. I had never fired anybody in my life, and it was not in my nature to tell people they had the option of supporting the School or leaving it. But I had taken the bit in my mouth and I was chewing it hard. What had begun in dissent had ended in disruption. My open invitation to students to debate every decision was making collaboration impossible. I now knew with my heart as well as my head that training theatre people and developing theatrical productions were not democratic procedures, and that the individualistic-narcissistic thrust of the time (called "doing your own thing") could be death to a collective effort. Having recognized this, I had to stop the machine in its tracks, and turn it in another direction. This required me to undertake a radical change in my own character, one that Norma had always strongly encouraged. I would finally have to take my head out of my hands.

During the reign of Lyndon Baines Johnson, when all authority was under question and student governance was the main issue confronting the university, this was a dangerous course to run. It was the cause of my conflict with Rogoff (who identified my attitude with the Johnson bumper sticker "Love it or leave it"), and it also caused conflict between me and my most intelligent students, between me and my closest friends. In short, my popularity was short-lived, as I knew it would be. On the other hand, I enjoyed the support of a large number of the faculty, of not a few students, and, most sustaining of all, of my wife, whose feisty nature was fired up by the anticipation of battle. My confidence was also reinforced by the fact that creative activity was now beginning to yeast and bubble at the School, where before it had been dormant. Perhaps the students were at last finding an appropriate outlet for their seething energies.

All of this ferment followed the cancellation of *Operation Sidewinder,* but theatrical though it was, it couldn't substitute for another production at the Rep. That substitute soon came from a totally unexpected quarter when Larry Arrick entered my office, very excited, with Paul Sills close behind, to say that Sills had a dynamite idea to suggest as a replacement for our canceled offering. Sills, at that time, was conducting a student workshop in improvisation and, as a close friend of Arnold Weinstein, had been an amused observer of our recent tumult. He took a place on the couch and, gazing out the window abstractedly, said in his most laconic manner, "We just tell stories, fairy tales." Then he fell silent.

I pressed him for a little more detail. "We go to Grimm, see?" he went on, "and we just tell the story out of Grimm's fairy tales. The actor says, 'Once upon a time,' and then he transforms himself into the character he's describing, getting bent over and squeaky-voiced as he says, '—there was a wicked old man.' I did some experiments with it in Chicago. It's a natural. The audiences love it."

"Now wait a minute," I said. "You mean to tell me you just tell a fairy story on the stage?"

"Sure," Sills answered. "These are stories that touch something deep, something fundamental in the audience. Otherwise they wouldn't have lasted so long. And the technique is very liberating for the actor. He can play dozens of parts in the course of one evening. All you have to do is announce who you are at the moment, and the audience will buy it. They eat it up. I want to try the technique with Chekhov stories sometime, maybe even a Tolstoy. I believe it will work with all the great stories."

The idea sounded a little thin to me, but I wasn't in a position to quibble. We were little more than two weeks away from the opening of a scheduled nonexistent production. Sills was confident that he could work the evening up in a very short time. He didn't require much in the way of physical setting or costume, and he had at his disposal a very accomplished group of actors, including Mildred Dunnock, Alvin Epstein, David Spielberg, Michael Lombard, and a number of advanced students. This company responded to Sills's idea with enthusiasm, treating it as a valuable opportunity to work out a brand-new process. It was satisfying to watch a seasoned realistic actress like Millie Dunnock commit herself so generously to something untried and unproven, and fascinating to see Alvin Epstein, who had been trained in mime, getting the chance to do a number of animal transformations. Sills selected six fairy tales to make up the evening, including "Godfather Death," "The Goose Girl," "The Blue Light," "The Bremen Town Musicans," "Clever Gretel," and "The Marriage of Sir Gawain." All I contributed was the title: *Story Theatre.*

I was worried that the University Theatre—a large proscenium house— would overwhelm this delicate work. Wouldn't he be happier with the smaller, more intimate Experimental Theatre? Sills scratched his head. "The University Theatre is certainly a limitation," he admitted. After pausing a moment, he added, "But I prefer the limitation."

Since Sills's imagination was of the kind that is sparked by limitations, the University Theatre proved to be no difficulty at all, and *Story Theatre* provided us with our first real popular success of the season. *God Bless* had been received with little enthusiasm. Bond's *Saved,* like all our Bond productions, left audiences and critics divided over its pitiless values. The repertory of student plays had only a mild reception. But *Story Theatre,* in the first of its many incarnations, touched a chord in audiences that was to reverberate whenever and wherever it was staged. The next fall we put some of these stories on public television, and the season after, Sills restaged the show (with a different cast) for Broadway. Every season thereafter, for the next few years, we included at least one Story Theatre presentation in our schedule, including tales by Ovid, Flaubert, Isaac Bashevis Singer, and Joseph Conrad. And Sills's direct, presentational Story Theatre style was to have a more lasting influence on our directing and acting students than the techniques of any of the performance groups, including the Living Theatre.

During *Story Theatre,* we were free from disruption for a time, though I was involved in another confrontation during a symposium in New York (sponsored by the Theatre for Ideas) called "Theatre or Therapy." I participated in this discussion, along with Nat Hentoff, Paul Goodman, and Judith Malina and Julian Beck, before it was thoroughly wrecked by some high-spirited members of the Living Theatre troupe. Beginning with shouted obscenities at the speakers ("Fuck all liberal intellectuals and their fucking discussions"), they then went on to take over the lectern, the platform, the whole hall, emptying women's pocketbooks on the floor and accusing the audience of racism and warmongering. The ensuing pandemonium gave me considerable amusement—and not a little satisfaction, since it recapitulated the events we had experienced at Yale for those who still remained skeptical of the reports —and I later chronicled the happening as if it were a Marx Brothers movie. It was a relief to be an outside observer for once of revolutionary fermentation. Before too long, however, we were able once again to create our own home brew.

The occasion was a production of Euripides' *Bacchae.* We had planned a contemporary production, directed by Andre Gregory and designed—a resplendent egg-shaped cage—by Santo Loquasto. I had always been powerfully affected by this ancient play, but my desire to do it this season was induced by a famous recent incident—the confrontation between antiwar hippies and bayonet-wielding troops on the steps of the Pentagon. Since that event we had experienced something even more relevant to the theme of *Bacchae*—the visit by the Living Theatre. The conflict between the drunken, ecstatic followers of Dionysus and the ordered, uptight subjects of Pentheus struck me as almost identical with the relationship between the rampaging Living Theatre and the various civic and academic centers it was disrupting, including our own. It occurred to me that a production of this play might be a good way of theatricalizing and objectifying these recent experiences.

Since Gregory had been asked not only to direct *Bacchae* but also to replace Gordon Rogoff in his teaching assignments, he was not exactly overwhelmed with love and friendship upon his arrival. Some students wanted to meet him at the train station and send him back to New York. Many of the same students had been cast in the Chorus of *Bacchae*. Rather than afflict Gregory with a hostile student cast, I suggested that we rehearse the Chorus and the principals in different places at different times, using different directors, and combine the separate units in the final weeks, when tempers might have cooled. Gregory readily consented, and while he was rehearsing the professional company, Stanley Rosenberg, a movement teacher who had studied with Grotowski, began taking the Chorus through strenuous physical exercises.

As I should have realized from the start, the student cast soon began to feel competitive toward the professional company. The Bacchic Chorus was supposed to be anarchic, irrational, and violent, and—unable to separate art from life—the students almost came to blows with David Spielberg, who was playing Pentheus. Rarely have two such separate worlds been asked to share the same stage—the principals working with language, text, characterization, and interpretation, the Chorus writhing about in various degrees of performance group contortions. The physical production was spectacular, and Alvin Epstein—playing Dionysus with a huge live boa constrictor coiled around his torso—was hypnotic and sensual. But the generational conflicts between the School and the Theatre—not to mention the artistic conflicts between ensemble techniques and the styles of repertory acting—boiled over into a few unpleasant greenroom episodes, and onto the stage itself.

For all this, the time of serious disruption was over for us, partly because I had decided to buckle no more before the fractious moods of the radical left, partly because the entire School was now engaged in energy-consuming activity. Productions were springing up everywhere, and although a number of these (particularly the third-year directing projects) were dedicated to the spirit of Gordon Rogoff, they were also a significant demonstration of what could be accomplished when art, not politics, prevailed. My stepson, Phillip, visiting one weekend from Putney School, was able to spend an entire Saturday, from noon to three in the morning, just going to Yale productions. He saw a matinee of the Weinstein-Bolcom opera, *Greatshot,* on the stage of the University Theatre, followed by a first-year acting project, a third-year directing project, a playwright's workshop, a Cabaret performance, and finally, a one-man show by one of our students at a local coffeehouse. I was never more proud of my students than when they were working well, and I was rarely to be more proud of them than in those last creative months of that year: "In spite of our dissension," I told them, "or perhaps because of it, we have entered an exceedingly fertile and imaginative period in our history as a school."

As a result of the new calm, I managed to do a lot of things that had been put aside and forgotten. I was able to listen to Mozart again, with a thrill I had not felt for a long time. I was able to read a book without falling asleep over the pages. And I was able to take a week off during spring vacation to do some writing at Yaddo. In that glorious artists' retreat in Saratoga, where the grounds were still frozen and the trees still bare from a murderous winter, I engaged in some quiet reflecting on the last few months. I was slowly getting over a serious case of shell shock. Before I left New Haven, I had driven the car around front, in my usual fashion, to pick up my five-year-old for school, and had driven right past him, absentmindedly, leaving him weeping furiously at being abandoned on the porch. At Yaddo I found the time to pull myself together, to write, and to laugh again—particularly at the sight of Phil Roth teaching four-letter words, phonetically, to a decorous woman writer from New Zealand. It was time for healing; it was time for reconstitution. I was trying to come to terms with a new personality.

I was also trying to define my feelings about the radical young. In a couple of articles I wrote that week I made an effort to defend the values of art and learning in a time of growing politicization. Like many people of that time, I had believed we were blessed with a very special generation endowed with unusual moral passion and superior intelligence. Now I was not so sure. Events at the School, and at other universities, had begun to persuade me that something in the movement was going very wrong. My criticism of New Left radicalism seemed to some like a defection and a betrayal, and it brought reactions from friends and foes alike, including my old colleague Eric Bentley, who wondered in print if I was not "going over to the enemy" as a result of having become a dean. My reply reflected some of my more recent agonies:

"I do not share," I wrote to him, "the current reflexive assumption that radical movements are necessarily more humane or more compassionate than other movements. I hear the SDS affirm this, but I see no evidence in fact. When I hear of a Columbia professor having his arms pinioned by students about to occupy a building and being hit in the face with a club, or the gentle lady president of Radcliffe being terrorized by students protesting a minor disciplinary action, I do not automatically think of the courteous Marxism espoused by Brecht, but rather of the bully tactics used by the Nazis against the educational institutions of another corrupt liberal regime, the Weimar Republic. . . .

"I loathe the Vietnam war, and I continue to support the Resist movement in its efforts to end that war. My question is whether the assault on the universities is helping to end the war—or to deflect the nation's attention from it. With university news getting such prominence these days in the media, the atrocities in Vietnam get elbowed off the front page, and so does the attention of legislators who begin to pour their energies into making laws against disruption. . . . While the great ROTC controversy of 1969 occupies the campus activist at Yale (and elsewhere), the Olin Mathiessen plant (and others) just down the street continues to pour out armaments that will be sent to Vietnam. . . . The assault on the universities sometimes looks less to me like honest idealism than a grownup version of the bully game called 'get the guy with the glasses.' "

The assault on the universities to which I was referring had been going on for a year; it was just then beginning to touch Yale, occupying much of Kingman Brewster's attention. Brewster's amusement over my problems soon vanished when he began to experience his own, for there were ample signs that the difficulties the Drama School had recently experienced were minor compared with what was in the wind for the rest of the university. First, there was the governance issue, where students demanded a pivotal role in deciding on faculty, courses, and discipline. At one of many mass rallies held in Ingalls Rink that spring, Yale students voted—in the presence of Brewster, helplessly looking on—to participate in Yale College faculty meetings. A few distinguished professors—most notably, the historian C. Vann Woodward—spoke up against this motion, but to no avail; it was carried overwhelmingly, with the support of many young instructors. Brewster looked wanly in my direction, making small gestures with his hand as if signaling me to speak. He obviously needed all the help he could get.

I felt I was unpopular enough already on these issues, and kept my seat. (In an article called "The Case for Professionalism," I had argued heatedly against student participation in faculty decisions, except in an advisory role.) But I knew I had failed Brewster at a time when I could have helped him, and it made me feel bad. I wrote to him the next day, apologizing for my cowardice, and promising not to repeat it in the future. "You must have felt somewhat abandoned last night," I said, "and I'm sorry that I helped contribute to that feeling."

At another mass rally in Ingalls Rink the Yale community voted on the burning issue of whether to maintain ROTC on the campus. This was a source of considerable anger in most academic institutions at that time; and the Yale ROTC building had already had a few small fires. I agreed with those who wanted to banish ROTC from the campus, since a university was no place, I thought, for military activity. But I wasn't happy with the way the subject was being debated. Members of the Yale Corporation were subjected to abuse and insult, and so were all those who disagreed with the radical position. When the vote was taken, it turned out to be a tie—remarkable, considering the thousands of people voting—but the administration decided to disband ROTC anyway.

Brewster's most serious crisis that year came from the School of Art and Architecture. Its Department of City Planning, which had close links with the black community of New Haven, had by this time become totally radicalized. The department had voted (governance being equally shared between students and faculty) to admit twenty students in the incoming class, ten of whom were black or Spanish-speaking. The trouble was that the dean of art and architecture had put a strict limitation on the number of new students in the department. When unauthorized letters of acceptance were sent out, the dean appealed to the president, who thereupon proceeded to relieve the chairman and the assistant dean of their administrative duties, as well as to fire two faculty members. Soon after, the Department of City Planning was disbanded, Kingman's house was picketed, and the building housing the School of Art and Architecture (a modern structure designed at great expense by Paul Rudolph) was virtually gutted by fire.

Brewster was working very hard at this time to keep the governance of the university in the control of the departments and the administration. "We are and intend to remain," he wrote to the black students of the Drama School, "a largely faculty-run institution." To preserve these powers, he had to fight certain strong misconceptions that were currently confusing educational with electoral institutions. Students demanding a representative voice in the "decisions that affect our lives" were comparing the academy with the democratic state, as if the primary function of the university were to govern and to rule. But while the relationship between the administration and the faculty did have certain political overtones, they could no more be considered the elected representatives of the student body than the students—who were admitted after voluntary application on a selective and competitive basis—could be considered freeborn citizens of a democracy: the relationship between teacher and student was primarily tutorial. That the bad reasoning behind this analogy was not more frequently questioned indicated the extent to which some teachers were refusing to exercise their roles as professionals. Faculty members were becoming more and more reluctant to accept the responsibility of their wisdom and experience and, therefore, were often willing to abandon their authoritative position in order to placate the young.

With student governance shaping up as such an inflammatory issue on campus—not to mention the ROTC presence and the question of black recruitment—Brewster was expecting trouble ahead. Universities all over America were being occupied; Yale would undoubtedly be next. In preparation for this, Brewster proceeded to draw up a document that would announce in advance the strict consequences following any disruptions or occupations by students. This "scenario," as it was called, was designed to alert the radicals, and particularly the SDS, to what they might expect from the university in the event of any violent actions, so as to avoid the mistakes made at Harvard and Columbia when, lacking any other disciplinary measures, the police were called in to oust the students from occupied buildings. Brewster's scenario was enthusiastically endorsed by the faculty of Yale. But the next year was to be a test both of the scenario and the faculty's resolve when the bombing of Cambodia, the escalation of the war, the trial of the Black Panthers, and the Kent State massacre would threaten the very survival of the university.

In this same year, Brewster was confronted with a problem of quite a different sort when Joseph E. Levine pulled up to Woodbridge Hall in a long, black, chauffeured limousine. Levine had made an appointment for a lunch that would include Kingman, me, and the vice president of Avco industries, the new owners of Embassy Pictures. It took place at Mory's—barely a block away from Brewster's office, though Levine insisted on driving him the entire distance in his Cadillac. After we had dined on Blue Point oysters and New England chowder, Levine came to the point of his visit. His new bosses at Avco had been extremely impressed by the Yale-Levine program called "Writing for the Camera," and wanted to make a substantial contribution to the university: four and a half million dollars to build a new theatre!

We had been looking for another facility since 1966; the offer from Avco-Embassy was unquestionably a temptation. But we were accustomed to looking for a quid pro quo. What would Kingman be required to do in return? Nothing, answered Levine. Only serve on the board of Avco-Embassy. Kingman said something about the demands on his time. Levine replied that the meetings of the board took place only once a year—they could easily be held at Mory's. Brewster then said that, as a matter of policy, he served only on the boards of educational institutions. Levine replied that American movies were very educational. Why, Leonard Bernstein and Mike Nichols had already agreed to join. He would be in very distinguished company. Brewster promised to give the matter his most careful consideration, and send his answer soon in a letter.

Walking back to his office with Brewster, after the limousine had departed, I told him that it was apparent enough to me that he had no intention of joining the board of Avco-Embassy, but just in case he was considering it, he should know that among the many things manufactured by Avco Industries were missiles for Vietnam. Apart from the moral implications of accepting such a gift, there was no sense constructing a spanking new theatre complex if it were to be blown up on the day of dedication. Brewster confided to me that he didn't intend to accept this offer. He would write a courteous letter to Joe Levine, thanking him for his kindness and pleading a busy schedule.

Some months later, when I called Joe Levine to get his grant to the playwriting program renewed, he turned me down curtly. "Your president," he sputtered, "your president . . ." Kingman had never sent his reply to the Avco-Embassy offer, and this omission had humiliated Levine in front of his new boss. I felt very bad about this—and not only for Levine. The grant was crucial to our young playwrights. I called Brewster, who was vacationing in Eleuthera, and he immediately sent off a letter of apology. But it was too late. The grant was not renewed, and we wouldn't have a similar program again until CBS picked it up in 1973.

The rest of that spring was spent trying to fulfill our promises to the black students at the School. I had turned down their demand for a black workshop. What I suggested in its place was a "black-and-white workshop"—open to all our students—designed to examine relations between the races while preserving our integrated standing. This proved acceptable and was instituted the next year. Renewed efforts at recruitment increased the number of black applicants from thirteen in 1968 to sixty-six in 1969, while the number of black acceptances rose from seven to twenty-one (three of these being young ghetto kids trained in Norma's workshop). We also managed to augment the black faculty and staff. Lonnie Elder and Joseph Walker were appointed playwrights in residence, Woody King became a liaison officer, and Ken Mills—a Marxist professor of philosophy—offered a course in the School on society and the arts. Most important, the celebrated dancer Carmen de Lavallade was invited to join the company and supervise the movement classes, and another black woman would give a supplementary course in Afro-Caribbean dance. Finally, the Negro Ensemble Company agreed to visit the School in the fall of 1969, performing its fine production of *Song of the Lusitanian Bogey*.

All this proved a partial solution to the problems of our black students; we also found a partial, if temporary, solution to our facility problems. Paul Mellon had just given a large sum of money to Yale for a new museum to house his vast collection of British art. One of the buildings purchased for the site was the Calvary Baptist Church on the corner of Chapel and York streets. Brewster, convinced at last that our recent difficulties were largely due to overcrowding, offered to lend us this building as a theatre, with the warning that Yale would take it back in a year when the Mellon gallery began construction.

Even as a temporary facility, this was a gift and a godsend. The church had certain acoustical problems, and it had no storage or fly space, but we were all convinced it would more than serve our needs once we had made certain minor alterations. Anyhow, we were in no position to quibble; in our emergency situation, we would have gratefully accepted the men's room at the Hotel Taft. The church was half a block from the School; it had a basement area that could serve as a greenroom, as a lounge, and as dressing rooms; and it had space in the auditorium for more than four hundred seats. I took a certain sardonic pleasure in remembering that, just two years earlier, we had been refused the use of the church basement because the Baptists were frightened we might be performing obscene and irreligious rites. Now we had the opportunity to confirm their fears. After a ritual of deconsecration—and a summer of alterations—we were ready to perform in a primitive but functional professional theatre.

I announced the acquisition of this space to the school toward the end of the academic year, expressing again my conviction that a training program could have little value or meaning without the presence of a closely linked professional company. I had to admit, however, that the events of the year had not confirmed my beliefs; a synthesis of School and Theatre, each with its own separate purpose, was something we had not yet achieved. There was much confusion between process and results, between the ends of training and the ends of production, and we had yet to work out a way to amalgamate conflicting needs and demands.

"The solution, as I see it," I proposed, "is to separate the company out of the School—to provide it with its own facility—and to invite the participation of those students who will profit from such participation without feeling the usual competitiveness, as well as those who truly want the experience of work, and don't feel insulted at being assistant directors or supporting players. This would reserve the present facility entirely for School work. With the company as a near neighbor of the School, and not another tenant threatening the present occupants with eviction, or moving them out on a sublease, a lot of the advantages of the company will still obtain, and a lot of the disadvantages will disappear. So there we are—at the crossroads. Next year you may either take advantage of this company on your doorstep—or ignore it, as the case may be. But you should know that your formal training and development will continue to be organized toward it, and that that is the true and ultimate development of the School."

The year had been a difficult one for me—possibly the worst yet of my life. But it had also proved beneficial in forcing me to define the goals of the School, and my own relationship to those goals. I had tried to be a mellow, reasonable administrator and had presided over uprisings, disruptions, and cancellations. I no longer felt very avuncular. The School had settled down when I took a strong position. Could it be that this was really what the students wanted, for all their talk of freedom and individuality? Whatever the truth of the matter, I had determined on my course. We had survived the worst. If I could just hold the rudder firmly enough, we would survive the future too. It had taken three years just to make a start. By my original timetable, the job should already have been finished and the family back in New York. Still, we were about to add ten more graduating actors to the company for a total of thirteen former students, along with two directors, a resident designer, and a literary manager from the student body. At last, we were in a position to show, in a meaningful way, how the training extended into the professional company.

The final theatrical event of that year was a postseason production of *The Sea Gull* on the lawn of Bill and Rose Styron's home in Roxbury, Connecticut. Norma and I joined some students in the cast of the play—Norma playing Polina, I playing Shamrayev. Each act took place in a different part of the grounds, with the spectators moving their portable chairs to watch us perform under a blossoming apple tree (view of a lake), on a verandah, against the exterior wall of the house. (We called this process "location theatre.") It was a sparkling day. The spring foliage and fruit trees were all flowering, and everyone seemed happy. I felt a great harmony working with my students in those lovely surroundings. It was something I was to experience many times in future when I directed or performed with them at the Rep. We were doing something we were born for—acting in a great play, in the lap of nature, our heads clear at last of those noisome swamp vapors that had swirled about us all year long.

IV

The Panther
and the Bulldog
1969-1970

The wolf also shall dwell with the lamb. and the leopard shall lie down with the kid.

—Isaiah 11:6

Bill Styron was having troubles of his own. His novel *Confessions of Nat Turner,* a considerable critical and popular success when first published, was now being assailed by black and Communist critics as a falsification of a great historical figure. Some were offended by the homosexual incident in the book; others objected that a black hero had become the fictional property of a white man. To the world, Styron maintained an attitude of imperturbability, but inwardly he was seething. He was also deeply hurt. He truly believed he had made an honest effort to create a positive, if complicated, portrait of a significant American, and now he was being abused for failing to produce racial propaganda. Wherever he appeared, on lecture platforms, in seminars, in symposia, he was subject to reckless charges of racism. At Yale he was mocked publicly by black undergraduates.

All that year, New Haven was preoccupied with problems concerning blacks —chief among them, the approaching trial of the New Haven Black Panthers. A leading Panther official named Fred Hampton had recently been shot to death by Chicago police under suspicious circumstances, and when, in another incident, Bobby Seale, chairman of the party, was extradited to New Haven to stand trial on charges of murder (along with eight local party members), blacks and whites together began to perceive that the U.S. government was harassing and persecuting this revolutionary party.

The Seale trouble had begun the previous spring after he had been invited to speak at Yale by a young administration student at the Drama School, the wealthy daughter of a prominent member of the Yale Corporation. Under the influence of Arnold Weinstein, she had become a rabid supporter of all black causes, and on that occasion, she insisted that I give Seale the University Theatre for his speech. When I refused—on the grounds that our facilities were for theatrical rather than political purposes—she took this as confirmation of my racial "insensitivity," and appealed to the Reverend William Sloane Coffin, who allowed her to schedule the speech in Battell Chapel. It was during the time of Seale's visit that spring that he allegedly gave the order to "off the pig" when asked by local Panthers how to deal with a suspected FBI informant named Alex Rackley. Soon after Seale's departure, Rackley's body was found —tortured and mutilated—in Middlefield swamp, and Seale was implicated in the murder through the testimony of another Panther, George Sams. Implicated with him were a number of other New Haven Panthers, including the popeyed militant from the *Operation Sidewinder* controversy who had made such a stir in my office the previous year.

Race and war were the compelling issues of this time, and while the Panther defenders were marshaling their forces in preparation for the trial, the peace movement was also making a major effort in the area. In October of 1969 a Moratorium Against the War was held on the New Haven Green, which was attended by fifty thousand students, faculty, and city residents, as well as by Richard Lee, mayor of New Haven, and Kingman Brewster, president of Yale.

Brewster had come a long way since his domino days. In his speech on the green, he announced that he was now firmly opposed to the war, though he had obviously reached his present position with difficulty: "Let us admit," he told the crowd, though emphasizing that he spoke for himself, not Yale as an institution, "that it is not easy to abandon the anonymous masses of South Vietnamese who have relied on us. Let us simply say that their interest as well as ours can no longer be served by the perpetuation of terror and death." Along with the other speakers, he called for the withdrawal of American forces from Vietnam. But before the speeches began, a black student—moderator of the Black Student Alliance at Yale—made a dramatic effort to demonstrate there were other, more important issues confronting the American people than foreign wars. Grabbing the microphone from the hands of a scheduled speaker, he began to inveigh against the harassment of blacks by New Haven policemen. "With all due respect for the moratorium," he said, "I say we have also had enough."

In those weeks not only politics but culture was being served at Yale. *Butch Cassidy and the Sundance Kid* had its world premiere at the Roger Sherman Theatre in New Haven, as a benefit for the film program at the School of Art and Architecture. At a large dinner party in the President's Room of Woolsey Hall, President Brewster and his wife played host to Paul Newman and Robert Redford, the stars of the movie; George Roy Hill, its director; and Barbra Streisand, one of its producers. Norma and I were invited too, partly in recognition of Newman's recent grant (in the name of the Nosutch Foundation) to the Yale Repertory Theatre. After dinner we all drove to the Roger Sherman in limousines, and were mobbed upon our arrival by hundreds of New Haven movie fans who, in their enthusiasm, began to rock the cars. We were in a limousine with Streisand, who was panicked by the crowds eagerly pressing against the windows for a look at her face. "Harry," she whispered fiercely to her agent, "you didn't tell me it was going to be anything like this! You said '*Yale*,' Harry! '*Students*,' Harry, not mobs. You should have told me, Harry! I wouldn't have come!"

Other, less entertaining incidents from that time:

A gentle, reticent young man, hired to serve as press director for the Theatre, committed suicide in his garage by turning on the exhaust in his car. An acting student was found on Chapel Street, naked, directing traffic with a Bible in his hand. Another acting student, stoned out, was discovered sleeping in the middle of Yale Bowl. A playwriting student was picked up on Route 95, walking on the highway, dazed, drunk, and barefoot. Two students from Norma's undergraduate acting class were busted when police found marijuana in their room, following a small fire. Professor Nagler's class in theatre history was disrupted by three Yale Weatherpeople protesting the treatment of the Chicago Panthers by halting his lecture on scenic devices in ancient Greek theatre.

But the event that most engaged the attention of the Yale community that fall was the occupation of Wright Hall on November 6 by members of the Students for a Democratic Society.

Brewster's faculty-approved "scenario" regarding disruption of university facilities by physical force, coercion, or intimidation had been mailed the previous year to the entire Yale community. Since the directive was very precise about the consequences of disruptive actions, the radical students, naturally, felt compelled to test it. They occupied a university building and held a university official prisoner overnight. The provost spent most of that evening standing on top of a Yale police car with a bullhorn, warning the students that if they didn't abandon the building forthwith and release the official, they would be subject to suspension or expulsion. When they failed to emerge until the following morning, the provost suspended them all on the spot.

The Executive Committee of Yale College—composed of faculty members and college deans—was convened immediately to examine the case; it was chaired by Georges May, dean of the college and professor of French. After two weeks of deliberations, the committee announced that it was prepared to make its recommendations known to the entire Yale College faculty for the purpose of a vote. What the committee thereupon proposed was to remove the suspension, administer a strong rebuke to the offending students, and warn them that if the action was ever repeated they would be dealt with severely.

As this recommendation was being read to the faculty assembled in Sprague Hall, I carefully scanned Kingman's face. He seemed impassive and controlled, but I believe I saw a barely perceptible wave of shock pass over his features at the committee's findings. He had worked hard to develop a strategy to preserve Yale from the kind of earthquakes shaking most other universities in the land. He had consulted with the faculty, which fully endorsed his plan.

Now, with its first test, the "scenario" had been scuttled. Rather than take punitive action against the SDS students, the Executive Committee had elected to strand the president.

As Brewster rose to make his response to the recommendation, the thought passed through my mind that he was going to resign. In the text of the scenario, Brewster had already mentioned the risk "that a faculty reversal of a President's judgment would seriously impair the President's usefulness and fitness to continue." That is precisely what had just happened. Would Brewster feel unfit to continue? If so, he gave no sign at that meeting. Instead, he courteously acknowledged the efforts of the committee, and said he looked forward to the ensuing debate.

That debate continued for a period of two weeks, attracting more than local attention. On the weekend separating the committee resolution from the faculty vote, Norma and I went to Washington on a march, to join a few hundred thousand people gathered near the Washington Monument in protest against the war. After the demonstration dispersed, a young radical handed us a copy of the SDS periodical, *New Left Notes,* where we read a front-page story about the Wright Hall occupation carrying the headline: *Racist Yale Gives In!* Among those who signed it was Mark Zanger, the excitable Yale radical who was the model for Mark Slackmeyer in Garry Trudeau's *Yale Daily News* comic strip, *Doonesbury.* The article exposed Bill Coffin as a "witting tool of the imperialist Yale bosses" in their grab for "super-profits," and proudly announced that the university had been forced to surrender before the student occupants of Wright Hall.

We convened in Sprague Hall a few days later to vote on the recommendation of the Executive Committee. Seated next to me was a young man I had never met before, though it was obvious he knew me. I found him remarkably witty and intelligent, and not just because he had read my articles. The acid comments he made, behind his hand, on what he regarded as the cowardice of his colleagues were amusingly caustic. He urged me to say something in support of the president. I told him I was preparing some remarks for the next meeting, when amendments to the resolution were scheduled for adoption. The vote was then taken on the committee resolution to rebuke, rather than suspend, the students. It was approved by a wide margin. I voted against it. The man beside me voted with the majority. It was my first encounter with A. Bartlett Giamatti.

The motion on which I was preparing to speak at the next meeting had been proposed by the "liberal moderates" on the faculty. It was an effort to restore some credibility to the president's scenario against coercion after the faculty had effectively undermined it. Under the pretext of expressing appreciation for the hard work of the committee, this motion was designed to reaffirm the rules against occupations and intimidations, primarily so that Brewster would not feel completely powerless in the face of the next episode. In support of that motion I read a lengthy prepared speech.

Part of it went as follows: "What is not sufficiently understood about the president's scenario is that it was meant to provide a *buffer* between students and police, to avoid a confrontation between two forces or powers. If academic sanctions cannot be made to apply, the university may be forced to turn to civil sanctions to protect itself against its own destruction; and, as everyone agrees, the use of outside police against university students is an intolerable and unacceptable condition. Academic sanctions, however, can obviously not be applied unless they are accompanied by credibility, and if this credibility is in danger, then the possibilities of real violence are unquestionably increased. I do not believe that a suspension of a suspension will convince the SDS that the university means to apply its sanctions in future. . . .

"The history of academic faculties, during this century, in the face of internal and external threats to their existence, has not been a very noble one. In Germany and Austria, many university professors looked on silently while students beat up the Jews in their midst; in Falangist Spain, they watched without comment while the rector of Salamanca, Miguel de Unamuno, was removed from his post and placed under house arrest after he made a courageous speech to a Franco general in defense of the free intellect; during McCarthy's time in America, they trembled and kept silent while their numbers were being picked off for the outrageous crime of having opinions and convictions. Will history record that America, in the sixties and seventies, had its universities destroyed because their faculties were unable to defend themselves against the incursions of their more violent students? . . . . Support of the present motion, and its overwhelming endorsement, will, I believe, preserve both the humanity of this faculty and its sense of justice; and will besides help to reestablish the university teacher as a figure with the courage of his own authority, and therefore worthy not only of a student's love, but of his respect."

It was the first speech I had ever made before a large assembly of Yale College faculty, and I was nervous. As a professor in the English department, I had a legitimate right to speak at this meeting, but I was identified with another School. And while it was one thing to talk this way to my own students, or to write articles on the subject, it was quite another to administer rebukes to distinguished scholars. I knew that my speech was not likely to fall gently on the ears of a large faculty body, exhausted by an extended series of meetings and bewildered by its new role as a disciplinary agency. Still, I had made a written pledge to Kingman not to fail him when the occasion rose again, and I was worried over how these meetings might have affected his resolve. I continue to believe—though this is only a hunch—that the Wright Hall incident and its aftermath undermined Brewster's determination to establish strong administrative procedures at Yale. If his actions after this event tended to be more stratagems and expediencies than principled and consistent decisions, then this may have been because he had lost confidence in the faculty's capacity to support him.

My speech was received with more favor than I had expected, though it enraged one faction, which instantly put me down as a faculty conservative. Along with a number of compelling remarks made by other "liberal-moderate" faculty members, it helped to carry the motion reestablishing support for the President's scenario, which became an amendment to the Executive Committee's more lenient recommendation in the hope (inevitably to be disappointed later) that some of the damage might be repaired.

My recent experiences had reinforced a conviction that we were not helping the young by continually yielding to their demands. It was a natural impulse for youth to test limits. It was less natural, I now believed, for their elders to dissolve these limits by declaring an "amnesty" following every trespass. The collapse of my generation before the pressures of the young was leading to the collapse of professionalism itself. In their praiseworthy resistance to authoritarianism, some students were also beginning to resist all forms of professional authority, questioning whether anybody had the right to "impose" a body of knowledge, law, experience, or judgment on the mind of another. This would soon make the very act of teaching impossible. For a time, I had been awed by this lively, rebellious generation. Now I suspected that the assault on authority was standing in the way of education, and I was beginning to doubt whether these students were quite as well informed as they boasted.

My new role as a "heavy father" did not come easily to me—especially since I still considered myself, secretly, another one of the kids. But much as I valued the affection of my students and contemporaries, I was finally admitting there were things I valued more. I certainly didn't enjoy being rejected by certain liberal magazines and periodicals that used to welcome my articles, any more than I enjoyed being the subject of scurrilous graffiti in Drama School johns. It was no fun to be pegged by the reactionary Al Capp as a former radical reclaimed for the conservative cause, nor was it pleasant to hear my friend Lillian Hellman describe an address I made about the need of the young for limits as "the most conservative speech I ever heard." Still, I was in the grip of a powerful current that, in my new sense of conviction, I had no impulse to resist. Formerly an aloof, fastidious observer, I had now become an actor in a significant drama, and like any other performer, I was obliged to expose my character whenever onstage. If some of the audience were unhappy with me in this new role, I was a lot less unhappy with myself. And I had the important backing of Norma, who never liked me better than when I accepted the consequences of my authority, though she continued to accuse me of spoiling our child.

While the university was in the throes of debate the Repertory Theatre had been in the throes of construction, and around the same time the faculty completed its deliberations, we finally completed satisfactory renovations on our new church facility. A raked platform stage had been built over the baptismal font, the acoustics had been improved with soft absorbent hanging panels, a crude lighting system had been installed in the balcony, uncomfortable but inexpensive folding chairs had replaced the wooden pews, and new front doors were decorating the façade. (In a fit of mischief, I had these painted red.) We were ready to begin our fourth season. For the opening production, we selected Richard Brinsley Sheridan's *The Rivals,* directed by Alvin Epstein.

The Rivals is a fine comedy, but not one that I would have normally chosen for the season. There was no compelling reason, in the fall of 1969, to do a play about romantic anguish and mistaken identity. The play was scheduled because this was Alvin Epstein's first directing assignment with the company, and I thought he had earned the right to choose his own project. Alvin, in turn, was attracted to *The Rivals* because he thought it was tailored to the talents of our young company as well as to our older resident actors, Jeremy Geidt and Betsy Parrish. Neither of us, in short, had decided on the play for its own sake, which was probably a mistake. I was continuing to learn that satisfying a company is not a strong enough reason for mounting a production.

The Rivals was acted and directed very well, drew enthusiastic notices, and pleased its audiences. I found it pretty tepid theatre. Epstein handled the play with considerable style and grace, but he surprised me a little—considering his own unconventional approach to acting—with a production reminiscent of the Old Vic in the 1950's. Using an English vocal coach, he had the company speaking in cultured British accents and arranging themselves in choreographed patterns, particularly in the opening scene, where the actors walked through the audience singing eighteenth-century music. Even the English were beginning to abandon this kind of theatre now; and soon Jonathan Miller would do a *School for Scandal* at the Old Vic which revealed the seamy underside of eighteenth-century life by featuring pregnant servants, brutal men, and unwashed women. Alvin's hunch was correct about the appropriateness of our actors to the play, and the entire cast acquitted itself with considerable expertise. But where was the American style we had been trying to develop over the past three years? By what imperative did this evening exist? We had devised a charming period entertainment, with pleasant music, handsome Wedgewood settings, lovely costumes, and much good-natured laughter. But in these extreme times an offering of this sort struck me as an escape, a sign that we were somehow failing a vital function.

I didn't utter these puritanical thoughts aloud, and my secret apprehensions didn't prevent me from joining the cast for the last three performances, in the part of Sir Anthony Absolute. Jerome Kilty, who originated the role for us, had to leave for another assignment; I had already played Sir Anthony twelve years previously at Group 20. As Kilty's understudy, I now had the chance to act again, as well as to demonstrate how seriously I took my understudy assignments. During two brushup rehearsals, the cast was very helpful in taking me over the rough spots, and I had the opportunity to experience personally how well Alvin worked with actors. I did a matinee and two evening performances. At the matinee my five-year-old son came to see me with his mother. During the prologue he waved at me as we marched through the audience, crying "Hi, Daddy!"—and in the scene where Sir Anthony disinherits Jack by saying "He's anybody's son for me," Danny shouted in considerable proprietary dismay, "*I'm* your son!"

During these months, Danny's father was also trying to formulate some coherent descriptions of the aims of the Theatre and the purpose of the School.

For the first time, the students were being informed about the kinds of theatre for which we were *not* training—street theatre, guerrilla theatre, black theatre, "poor" theatre. This was a clear repudiation of our past eclectic patterns. Other programs—the drama program at New York University, for example —were providing satisfactory training in performance group techniques. Our program would be designed exclusively for repertory theatres doing classical and modern texts. I was trying to preserve a balance between the works of the present and the works of the past. We believed in a relevant theatre art, but tried to distinguish this from a narrowly topical approach. We did not think that "relevance" consisted in straddling the newspaper headlines with each production, or in repudiating two thousand years of cultural achievement. As it turned out, the current season was heavily weighted toward the classics; future seasons would sometimes be weighted toward new plays. But the idea was to have the past refresh the present and the present the past. We chose Janus as the symbol of our theatre, the god of beginnings and endings, whose two heads look backward and forward simultaneously. Henceforth, the spirit of Janus, if not his physical image (we never found a satisfactory design) would preside over our work at Yale.

We also began to emphasize the need for standards, which meant that the faculty was now obliged to make judgments on the development of talent. This was difficult in a small school where student-teacher relationships are close and cordial—but it was important. It was also important to reestablish the authority of the teacher without suppressing student ideas, a precarious balance of power that required continual attention. I knew that little could be accomplished when suggestions became insistences and insistences hardened into demands, so I made it clear that coercion would not be tolerated, and disruption would be met with swift action: "If you can't find a way to change the situation here," I told the students, "short of locking me in my office or heckling the faculty members in the classroom, then we will put all the resources of our excellent placement bureau at your command to find you a place somewhere else." I was trying to preserve the privileges of dissent while protecting the security of the School. But more important, I was trying to say that our central purpose was the development of talent for the creation of dramatic art. Only a drama, I reminded the students, is called both a "work" and a "play." We were there both to work and to play—to channel our abundant energies into the labors and pleasures of theatre.

My exhortations were unnecessary. The students were already working that year, and working very well indeed. The activity begun the previous spring had intensified in the fall. Playwrights, directors, actors, and designers were all discovering how to join in collective effort. The playwright, Robert Montgomery, found his director in David Chambers as Ron Whyte did in Tom Moore and David Epstein in Michael Posnick—relationships that were to last beyond the years at Yale. *Subject to Fits,* Montgomery's fascinating fantasia on Dostoyevsky's *The Idiot,* was given its first performances that year in a Yale workshop, before it went on to production at the Public Theatre and at various resident theatres. And that year a young Jesuit brother, A. J. Antoon, emerged as one of our most promising directors, staging a blazing production of Strindberg's *Dance of Death* in a nearby church, and a Story Theatre version of Chekhov and Tolstoy stories in a workshop version influenced deeply by Paul Sills.

Meanwhile, Sills was continuing to sharpen his Story Theatre techniques—his new efforts formed the basis for our second Repertory Theatre production of the season, *Ovid's Metamorphoses.* I had tried to encourage Sills to proceed with his ambition to direct some Chekhov stories, especially after seeing Antoon's version in workshop, but after agreeing at first, he then grew more interested in restaging the Ovid stories, which he had been developing over the summer with some actors in Chicago. When Sills arrived in New Haven that fall, however, he told me he now had lost his appetite even for doing another production of *Metamorphoses.* He was willing to rehearse the company in the play during the first week, then allow Larry Arrick (who had worked with him on the first *Story Theatre*) to take over production for the next few weeks, and then return to clean the whole thing up in the final week. I was not overjoyed at this prospect, since Sills had already agreed to do the show himself, and the actors were looking forward to working with him again. But I had learned enough about his artistic process to respect his wishes. Sills did not perform well when he was bored or tired.

Instead of rehearsing the cast for a full week, Sills stayed only three days, and he didn't return to the production until the day it closed. By that time, *Metamorphoses* was Arrick's show and it carried his imprint. This deeply disturbed Sills—a perverse reaction, I thought, since he had chosen to abandon the production to Larry—but it was not difficult to understand Sills's objections. As translated and adapted by Arnold Weinstein, *Metamorphoses* threw off a lot of flash and dash and color, but it had lost the childlike simplicity of the original *Story Theatre,* and now looked a little like American musical comedy—I was reminded of *One Touch of Venus.* What it did display, abundantly, were the high spirits and musical gifts of the young company—and, especially, the beautiful grace of Carmen de Lavallade, playing such nymphs as Europa and Galatea.

Carmen had come to us that year on the crest of a distinguished career as a dancer with Alvin Ailey, Martha Graham, and Robert Joffrey, among others. By common consent, she was—and still is—one of the most exquisite women in the world, with long jet-black hair, large limpid eyes, and a lithe graceful body. In one of those fateful decisions that dedicated artists sometimes make in mid-career, Carmen had made up her mind to change her profession. She was growing older and, she feared, less supple; she was afflicted with occasional aches in her back and limbs after a grueling session of movement. Anxious that her life as a dancer might not last much longer, she had determined to become an actress. Carmen began her new career with certain limitations, which included a lack of acting experience and a light, somewhat inflexible voice. Nevertheless, she set about the business of training herself—using the voice and acting teachers of the School—with a single-minded dedication that testified to an extraordinary self-discipline. This discipline Carmen brought with her from the dance world. She not only embodied it herself, she demanded it of her acting students whom she was now giving classes in movement. Carmen, like Stella before her, was astonished at the sloppy habits of the young people in training. Her refusal to tolerate this behavior went a long way toward helping to establish new attitudes of discipline at the School. The model she herself provided of hard work, taste, patience, artistry, and continual good humor was certainly among her most valuable contribution to our world over the next ten years.

Carmen performed admirably in *The Red Shoes,* a children's show we did that year, so Bobby Lewis decided to cast her in his production of Strindberg's *Crimes and Crimes* at the Yale Repertory Theatre. This decision proved somewhat premature—Carmen was not yet prepared to undertake a taxing emotional part, and her performance as Henriette, the hero's mistress (which she played with a West Indian accent) never quite took wing. Still, the experience was important to her development as an actress, and her development was important to our theatre. Carmen took some knocks from the critical fraternity (though she received a good notice from David Rabe, then reviewing occasionally for the New Haven *Register*). So did the rest of the production—deservedly, since the concept was not well formulated and the evening was rather stiff. But in spite of its failure, the production did not depress me, because it was accomplishing certain things that only a resident theatre can achieve when the company is working together on a continuous basis toward a particular goal.

Alvin Epstein played the leading role in *Crimes and Crimes,* as he did in our next production, Gogol's *The Government Inspector.* Then in his second full year with the company, Epstein was emerging as a central actor and director with the Rep, gradually becoming a confirmed partisan of the resident theatre movement. I prided myself on having had a part in his conversion; it was I who first persuaded him to abandon the commercial theatre. My powers of persuasion were not successful immediately; I had been working on him since he first played with us in *Dynamite Tonite!* (1966), after which I had failed in my efforts to recruit him for our company. I remember a walk we took together through Central Park in the summer of 1967, when I tried to convince him he was that rare American bird, a genuine artist of the theatre, and therefore owed an obligation to his talent, not his career. At the time, Alvin believed his future lay on Broadway; I believed that Broadway had ceased to offer interesting opportunities for creative actors. "Whose career," I asked him, "would you want for your own?" He pondered this a long time. The only name he could offer was that of Jason Robards, an actor who had already forsaken the theatre for the movies.

Epstein had trained with Etienne Decroux in Paris, had performed with the Habimah Theatre in Israel, and had returned to the United States to hold placards for Marcel Marceau. Like many American actors, he was not very familiar with the literature of the stage, but he had one of the most extraordinary intellects of anybody in theatre. He also possessed a marvelous ear for music and was, besides, an accomplished mime. Although he did not believe that mime was useful for actors, and refused to teach it to our students, it was clear enough how mime always reinforced and extended his own performances. Whether he was playing Lucky in *Waiting for Godot* on Broadway, or the Fool to Orson Welles's King Lear at the City Center, Alvin always managed to demonstrate that he was an artist to the tips of his fingers. It was my job, once he had decided to join us at Yale, to arouse that sleeping intellect and expose it to the great drama he had never read. These plays literally took him days to ingest, as if he were absorbing the material into his bloodstream. But once he had read the play, he was ready to reconstruct it on the stage, often in a startlingly original manner. His laborious reading of plays always reminded me of the concentrated way he ate a lobster, a process that never took him less than three hours to complete. He would extract every ounce of meat from the creature, meticulously removing tail, carcass, claws, and feelers in careful order. Then, just as meticulously, he would reconstruct the lobster on his plate, whole and complete, except for the nourishing parts he had added to his digestive system.

Epstein's gentle temperament—which grew explosive only when his artistic process was being blocked—made him an ideal colleague and a warm friend; and I watched his development as a repertory actor and classical director with something approaching paternal pride. His Khlestakov, in *The Government Inspector,* however, was not one of his great performances. Just as he was moving toward the unexplored surrealist reaches of the part he was hit by a bad virus, and the period away from rehearsal short-circuited his process. Even then, his interpretation was strong in its manic foppishness, and his scenes with Gene Troobnick, playing the Mayor, were hilarious. During the course of this production, Henry Winkler also got a chance to display his comic versatility. Winkler had been cast as Dobchinsky, one of Gogol's twin buffoons; playing Bobchinksy was another young student, then suffering from unrequited love. When his girlfriend left New Haven without him, the lovesick student packed up and followed, with no notice whatever. Henry offered to play both characters, an idea jokingly suggested earlier by Bobby Lewis who (totally bald and round as an apple) proposed to draw his face on the back of his head and speak both parts. Winkler managed the feat by twirling around the stage at lightning speed, rattling off speeches with a verbal virtuosity that delighted the audience and amazed the company.

These audiences, by the way, were getting younger with each passing year. Students had the opportunity, through a YRT pass and rush system, to see plays at the Rep for less than two dollars. This was cheaper than a movie, and a lot more convenient for those without a car. As a result, large numbers of college students began subscribing regularly to the Rep—by 1979 they would constitute over 60 percent of our total audience—and they imparted an invaluable electrical charge to the atmosphere of the performance. The company enjoyed playing for spectators that were there by choice, and not out of some mistaken cultural piety, and the students enjoyed the relaxed nature of these theatrical occasions. It was significant—considering the conventional wisdom about the moviegoing habits of undergraduates—that in New Haven at that time the movie houses were empty and the theatres were full.

Subsidizing these student subscriptions was necessary, but it helped to exacerbate our financial problems. All that year, I was worrying about money; the well was threatening to run dry. In one more year the Rockefeller grant to the School would be all used up, and the Rockefeller grant to the Theatre was already coming to an end. I was accustomed by now to priming the pump with annual fund-raising, but never quite on the scale that now seemed necessary. In an effort to clear some time for these fiscal duties I improvised a new kind of leave of absence called an "administrative leave." I would continue to run the Rep, teach my courses, and look for grants, but the decanal duties at the School would be assumed by Howard Stein as "acting Dean." The leave was, frankly, a subterfuge; I still made all the important decisions behind the scenes. But dropping the title of Dean for one semester relieved me of certain time-consuming duties like student counseling and faculty hand-holding, which Stein was perfectly well equipped to assume.

Before too long, the cash-flow problem was temporarily solved. Among other windfalls, Harvey Sabinson (then a faculty member in theatre administration) persuaded David Merrick, an old adversary of mine, to give us a 17 percent interest in the profits of *I Do, I Do* (this varied between $2,000 and $20,000 annually, depending on the popularity of the musical with dinner theatres). And during my winter vacation, in Barbados, I had the good fortune to encounter once again the munificent Joseph E. Levine.

Levine's anger against Yale had cooled with the passage of time, and his attitude toward me was cordial. We spent a few days of that vacation exchanging toasts at dinners in the home of some mutual friends. I managed to get him up to Yale, a few months later, to speak to the drama students about his checkered career as a movie producer. The turnout was large; even the radicals wanted to hear about Sophia Loren. Levine, walking with the aid of a cane, gave a colorful talk, in that rasping voice of his, about his early days as a theatre owner, as a distributor, and finally as the mastermind of "Joseph E. Levine Presents . . ." The students obviously loved it, and Levine loved the attention. During a dinner party at our house that night, Levine grew expansive under the influence of some very good wine, and began to talk about endowing a School of Film at Yale. Kingman Brewster was present—having felt guilty enough over his previous lapse to accept our invitation—and he and Levine raised their glasses to the future. Also present were our good friends Fredric March and Florence Eldridge, whom Levine had wanted especially to meet. Levine had come with his wife, Rosalie, and his adopted son, Richard, a young man in his twenties who collected expensive antique cars. At one point, Richard Levine asked Florence Eldridge how old she was. Sweetly ignoring the discourtesy of the question, Florence replied that she was now in her seventies. Richard thereupon paralyzed the entire table by saying, "How does it feel to be living on borrowed time?" Norma dropped her plate.

This dinner party, and subsequent social encounters, softened Levine's heart to the point where he made a pledge of $100,000 to the Yale Repertory Theatre for the following year. Norma and I received the pledge one late spring day while attending a birthday party for Levine at his still-unfinished house in Greenwich, Connecticut. We ate lunch on tablecloths decorated with the architect's blueprints; our food was served on trowels and plasterboards by waiters dressed like carpenters. Later we swam in a sumptuous Olympic pool, equipped with a Jacuzzi, where we were served snacks off replicas of New York hotdog stands. The beach house was made entirely of white marble, with a model of it nearby, molded out of chicken liver. Overhead a biplane floated through the sky, trailing a banner that said *Happy Birthday Joe.* Afterward, the two hundred guests were invited into a huge screening room to see Levine's latest movie. He was obviously sitting on a helluva lot of money, and he seemed to have no qualms about spending it.

It was my job to keep Levine interested in our theatre—not an easy task, considering that he had no use either for classical or experimental plays. Of all our offerings that year, I thought that *Transformations,* a trio of short new works by Yale playwrights, might be the least painful, so I invited him and his wife to the opening as my guests. Included in the evening were plays by Lonnie Carter, David Epstein, and Jeff Wanshel; the director was Richard Gilman. All of these playwrights had been Gilman's students at one time or another, and after doing some apprentice work with Joseph Chaikin's Open Theatre in New York, he had expressed a desire to direct at Yale. This was obviously an appropriate project. The production was simple and clear enough, but neither Carter's farcical punning nor Epstein's epiphanies nor Wanshel's whimsy apparently appealed to Levine. He left the theatre without a word, but I didn't give up. The next thing I invited him to was my own production of Molière's *Don Juan.*

This was my first assignment as a director at the Rep, and like most of the things I did there, it was an understudy role. Andre Gregory, originally committed to direct *Don Juan* in an adaptation by the classics scholar, Kenneth Cavander, was forced to drop out because of a conflict in his schedule. I embraced the project with pleasure; Don Juan was a figure who had intrigued me ever since my days in graduate school when I wrote an essay on Mozart's *Don Giovanni* for a doctoral seminar taught by Lionel Trilling and Jacques Barzun. The Molière play seemed to me uncertain in tone and confusing in form—I much preferred the Mozart–Da Ponte opera—but the legend of this seducer-hero, which persisted through dozens of versions after its first appearance in a play by Tirso de Molina, was much more important than any single variant on it. It had inspired a seminal essay by Kierkegaard called "The Immediate Stages of the Erotic," which exercised a lasting influence on my own thinking. Kierkegaard had convinced me that Don Juan was not just a literary invention but a character that fulfilled some deep need in Judaic-

Christian culture. He had assumed the importance of a myth, embodying the force of seduction in a sexually repressed society—much as, in Greek theology, Poseidon represented the force of the sea and Aphrodite the force of sexual love.

It was my intention to stage this myth; indeed, to show the myth in the very process of being formulated. For this purpose, it was necessary to turn our theatre back into a church, and perform the play against the background of a Black Mass. A young student named Jeffrey Higgenbottom provided a spectacular design that called for the distressing of the entire auditorium. Over the existing stained-glass windows were placed black-and-white windows, depicting obscene orgies instead of religious scenes. And in front of each of these windows—not to mention over the entire length of the stage—were suspended plaster statuary in various attitudes of torment, molded from every character in the play, with the significant exception of Don Juan. On the stage itself were placed a reredos, an altar, a sarcophagus, and a pulpit, from which long speeches were spoken as if they were sermons. The idea was to treat the Molière text as a play-within-a-play, stage-managed by a group of hooded celebrants engaged in a ritual that reenacted the life and death of Don Juan in a Black Mass, as the life and death of Jesus is reenacted in the Christian Mass.

The audience was to file into the theatre to find a ceremony already in progress—a blasphemous ritual sacrifice, with a text provided by Aleister Crowley and an eerie sound collage by Richard Peaslee. Following the killing of a young lamb, the celebrants would draw the characters of the play out of the darkness—first, Sganarelle to speak his comic sermon on tobacco from the pulpit, then Don Juan, led onto the stage in a trance by a hooded lady in a black silk cape. This mysterious Specter—symbolizing the unattainable female that he seeks in every woman he seduces—would appear at significant moments in the production; at the climax of the evening, she would turn out to be Death itself. I was admittedly taking considerable liberties with the play. In our version, for example, Don Juan met his retribution not by being hauled down to Hell by a stone statue but through the intervention of the Specter. After Don Juan was forced into her embrace by the statue, the Specter opened her cape to reveal her internal organs in a state of deliquescence, then lifted him onto the altar, and—to the accompaniment of earsplitting sounds on the church organ—fell on top of him and literally loved him to death. At this point, Don Juan was turned to stone himself—another piece of statuary in an attitude of torment. And as the Specter rose from his body, her face a white mask, the hooded celebrants gathered around this frozen figure to repeat their ritual over a human sacrifice, with Sganarelle screaming to heaven in fury and terror for his wages.

When I described this concept to Kenneth Cavander, his own face went white. He absolutely refused to have anything to do with it—not because he was a Molière purist, but rather because he was a modern occultist. He warned me against tempting dark destructive forces. What was an interesting theatrical idea to me was to him a frightening supernatural reality. He reminded me of what had occurred when I invited the Living Theatre to Yale, which he interpreted as a stimulus to violent reverberations. He warned that I was about to bring on an occult catastrophe. With this, Cavander withdrew from the production, though he granted me permission to make any changes I wished in his script, and vainly continued to try to dissuade me from my course.

My other collaborators on *Don Juan,* however, were more cooperative, and the sessions with the designers were particularly exciting. I relished the opportunity to restore our building to its original purpose with this production (to show how even a seducer can play out his passion in a church), and I leaped at the opportunity to put our unused church organ back into operation. Higgenbottom's costumes were entirely black and white—the only spot of color was a red rosette near Don Juan's heart which became a bloody stain on his white statue. And with such talented actors as Alvin Epstein playing Don Juan, Gene Troobnick playing Sganarelle, Carmen de Lavallade playing the Specter, Jill Eikenberry playing Dona Elvira, John Cromwell playing Don Luis, Henry Winkler and Joan Pape playing Pedro and Carlotta, and David Ackroyd and James Naughton as the two avenging brothers, we had a powerful and integrated cast.

The Theatre was running smoothly, the School was running smoothly. What was now in ferment was the university.

For the day of the Panthers was approaching—a trial that would soon confront Brewster with the greatest crisis of his administration. The only major university that had not yet experienced a serious disruption, Yale was now expected to be at the center of the worst such storm in history. A crowd being estimated at anywhere between twenty-five thousand and a million people was preparing to descend on New Haven during the weekend of May Day to demonstrate against the trial; the potential for trouble was enormous. Brewster held meeting after meeting with college masters, faculty members, students, and city officials, desperate to find some strategy that might save Yale from the impending destruction.

Similar meetings were held, informally, in many Yale classrooms during those days; within a few weeks, the faculty would vote to formalize these discussions in scheduled classes as a way of avoiding panic. Education and politics were developing an uneasy relationship; the academic air was being mixed with an atmosphere of extremism. In the middle of April, four hundred Yale students called a four-day moratorium on classes in support of the Panthers, demanding that Yale contribute $500,000 of its endowment to the Panther defense (other ideas proposed at that meeting included shutting off the city's water supply, blowing up Beinecke Library, holding Kingman Brewster for ransom, and asking one student a month to commit suicide in protest). The next day my doctoral seminar in dramatic literature was interrupted by a visit from a member of the Branford Liberation Front, a radical cadre of students from the residential college in whose oak-paneled Fellows Room our class was being held. He climbed through the leaded window and looked accusingly at the students listening to a report on John Webster's Jacobean tragedy *The White Devil.*

"What can we do for you?" we asked.

"You shouldn't be holding classes today," he answered. "You should be talking and thinking about how to free Bobby Seale."

"*Should?*" I queried.

"There's a reality happening out there," the student answered, "and you should be dealing with it."

"There's a reality happening in here, too," I replied. "It's called learning. Each day is composed of twenty-four hours, so there's plenty of time for political activity without interrupting our class."

One of my students courteously asked the young man to sit down and join the class. He listened to the report for about ten minutes, possibly under the illusion that a "white devil" had something to do with racism, then left by the door.

The School of Art and Architecture, in trouble since the problem with the City Planning Department the previous year, was also threatened by angry visitors. The fire had made all the floors above the gallery unusable, so temporary offices and classrooms, constructed out of sheetrock, had been moved to the ground floor. This outraged the aesthetic sensibilities of some of the students, who responded by drawing obscene graffiti on the white walls of the sheetrock. The dean of the School, newly appointed that year, was the celebrated architect Charles Moore, and one day, when I was seeking his advice over lunch about how to treat the exterior of the church, I noticed that he looked uneasy. "Look," he said, when I asked him what was the matter, "I probably shouldn't be here right now. In a few minutes, they tell me, my students are going to tear down the temporary offices. They find them ugly." He looked at me, a veteran of similar wars, with a mournful expression. "Do you think I should be there when they start to demolish the place?" I told him I didn't think it mattered in the least whether I witnessed the tumult or not, so he might as well enjoy his lunch. He resigned his office at the end of the year, and returned to private practice.

A few days later, pressures increased on the entire university. On April 21, the Moratorium Committee called a mass meeting in Ingalls Rink for the purpose of shutting down academic activity at Yale out of sympathy for the Panthers who were on trial. All presumption of guilt or innocence in the murder of Alex Rackley was now being swallowed up in a general indignation caused by the harassment of the Panthers throughout the nation, the extradition of Bobby Seale, and, most recently, the six-month contempt-of-court citations handed out by the presiding judge to David Hilliard and Emory Douglass, two Panther officials, for minor infractions of courtroom rules, even though both sentences were suspended when the men apologized to the court. Just a week before, some Panther speakers had urged Yale students to demonstrate their revolutionary commitments by getting guns and occupying Beinecke Library, where the university stored rare books.

The turnout at Ingalls was huge—the estimate was forty-five hundred—with every bleacher in the hockey rink, and most of the playing space, crammed with excited students and faculty, as well as wandering reporters carrying movie cameras and tape recorders. The meeting was addressed by a number of speakers, including the Reverend William Sloane Coffin, the Panther lawyer Charles Garry, Kenneth Mills (the Trinidad-born Marxist philosopher), and a representative of a women's liberation group. The most startling appearance of the evening, however, was that of the principal speaker, the Panther chief of staff, Dave Hilliard.

Hilliard entered the rink, accompanied by a number of muscular, glowering black men in leather jackets who took up positions on the floor and along the aisles of the bleachers. Four burly men in black berets stood behind Hilliard as he took the platform to tumultuous applause and a standing ovation. "There is a very basic decision facing racist America," he began, "as to whether we will allow this country to become openly fascist, or whether we will wage revolutionary struggle to bring order to the disorder of this country. When black men are snatched out of courtrooms and taken to prisons, then brought before judges and reprimanded as if we were criminals to apologize for wrong-doings that were meted out against us, then I see that somewhat as a compromise. But there are distinctions between revolutionary compromises and reactionary compromises. That statement was necessary to allow us another day of freedom."

Hilliard paused. "But just because we were crafty enough to outwit the stupid demonic persecutors of black people in this country, we're going to take the opportunity to say *Fuck the judicial system!* Next time we're going to rot in jail rather than compromise. And that's my confession to Yale."

"We have a revolutionary brother in Berkeley," Hilliard continued. "The brother is charged with four counts of attempted murder of pigs. And I don't think that's wrong. Because everybody knows that pigs are depraved traducers that violate the lives of human beings and that there ain't nothing wrong with taking the life of a motherfucking pig."

The cries of *"Right on"* were now getting mixed with some boos from the crowd. The boos began to mount in volume as more of the audience absorbed what Hilliard had just said. "That's the best thing that happened here tonight," Hilliard continued. "Those boos. Because you give me room to tell you people my real feelings. . . . I knew you motherfuckers were racist. I didn't have any doubts."

The boos hardly diminished in volume after this outburst, and this made Hilliard's anger blossom. "Boo me right on out of this motherfucker. Boo me right back to Litchfield jail. Go boo me again, racists! . . . . Go on back to your humanities classes, go back to your psychology classes, or your English 3 or whatever it is." The booing stopped at this, perhaps because some of the students were embarrassed by Hilliard's remarks about their racial attitudes and academic obligations.

"Because we know this is a real situation—because we're suffering," Hilliard said, after the crowd grew quiet. "We're dying in the streets, we're facing the threat of torture in the electric chair, and I say Yale has a long way to go if they don't think we're hostile and that we're not angered by the inactivity of a bunch of young stupid motherfuckers that boo me when I speak about killing pigs. I say Fuck you!"

The boos had begun again, louder than ever. Hilliard regarded the crowd stonily. "Boo. Boo. Boo," he joined in. "Boo Ho Chi Minh. Boo the Koreans. Boo the Latin Americans. Boo the Africans. Boo all the suffering blacks in this country. You're a goddamn fool if you think I'm going to stand up here and let a bunch of so-called pacifists, you violent motherfuckers, boo me without me getting violent with you."

His tone suddenly grew restrained. "Because"—he paused to let the audience absorb the full impact of his words—"because I understand that although you don't agree with what I have to say, you should be intelligent enough to tolerate that rather than boo me."

At this, the black students and faculty ranged in the stands behind the platform rose to their feet and applauded Hilliard; and this brought a number of white students to their feet as well. In this more friendly atmosphere, Hilliard went on to remind the crowd of the potential for race war, and to tell of those who believed it was inevitable in this country. "I think that such a war might just be headed off," he said, "but that statement is supported when you all boo me."

Having reminded himself of his bad reception, Hilliard began to warn the crowd: "If there's any assassinators in the audience, if there's anyone crazy enough to come up here and supplement that booing by sticking a dagger in my back or shooting me in the head with a Magnum, then let's do that, because I know that will be the one spark that will set off the reaction that will civilize racists in this country and hopefully in the motherfucking world."

Hilliard paused to consult with his strategists on the platform, none of whom looked happy at this turn of events. When he spoke again, his tone was milder, more humorous.

"Now you got me talking to you like a crazy nigger—you got me talking like your mothers and fathers talk to you. I've called you everything but long-haired hippies. . . . And now I want to compound my sin by calling you long-haired hippie Yale motherfuckers. Fuck you."

The booing had stopped, but now the crowd was puzzled. Was Hilliard serious or putting them on? Hilliard resolved the question by holding out his arms and saying, "Now I'm going to take it all back—I take it all back, everything I said to you. On the grounds that you repudiate your boos." The assembly responded to this new "revolutionary compromise" with deafening applause. Good-natured liberalism was about to prevail, after all. Hilliard began to shout in the mike: "Power to the people! POWER TO THE PEO-PLE!" The crowd took up the chant, rising to its feet and holding up clenched fists.

Now there was considerable activity erupting behind and to the left of the speaker's platform. A young white man in shirt sleeves was seen struggling with Hilliard's bodyguards, and the black men stationed around the rink moved swiftly from their positions. Suddenly the man was being struck by the bodyguards. Soon he was on the ground, and the bodyguards were kicking and stomping him. Although the struggle was visible to those of us in the bleachers, the crowd on the floor received word of it slowly, and responded like a ripple of water turning into a wave. The crowd began to shout its dismay, and Hilliard announced that a "reactionary" had been prevented from taking over the platform. The "reactionary" was now completely encircled by blacks, who continued to stomp on him until Ken Mills and some students helped him to his feet.

Hilliard told the shouting crowd: "I think that was a humane response to all those who try to block the legitimate struggle of black people in this country. I think that anybody who takes the opportunity to come up here and run me or any other individual off the platform deserves that kind of treatment —and if they don't want that, then keep their motherfucking asses down."

Hilliard's remarks, predictably, were greeted with boos, and Hilliard, also predictably, returned to his refrain about the importance of tolerating different opinions. But the mood of the crowd had changed; it was not to be mollified so easily. After a few attempts at jocularity ("It's lucky I wasn't smoking pot or dropping LSD because I would have kicked his motherfucking ass too"), Hilliard wisely decided to finish his speech and leave. Collecting his bodyguards around him, he concluded by cursing Yale students because "you only want to be entertained" and shouting "All power to all except those who want to act like motherfucking racists."

The beaten man was on the platform, carefully taking notes off the speaker's lectern and throwing them on the floor. Responding to appeals from the floor, the committee allowed him to have his say. He stood silently, with his head bowed. His shirt was torn and his face was dirty, but there were no signs of blood on his body. He allowed three minutes to pass in silence. Then he began to pace up and down shaking his head. The audience was growing restive. A few students began to shout witticisms.

Finally, after about five minutes, he came up to the mike and blew into it. The crowd applauded. Silence. He hit the mike a few times with his fingers, popping the loudspeakers. More jokes from the crowd. Now he began to scrape the lectern with his fingernails. It occurred to me that he was executing an extraordinarily eloquent act of theatre. He would turn himself into a mute testimony, and then leave.

But then he spoke. He had a pronounced foreign accent. (I later learned that he was a student from the School of Architecture, a citizen of Lebanon, of Greek extraction; he ended up in Bellevue, brought there when he tried to force his way into an art museum after it had closed, reportedly to look at a painting that reminded him of home.) "A small step for mankind," he said, "a big step for me—whatever that implies or invokes. . . ."

More silence. "Louder," someone shouted. Many laughed. The young man spoke again, more incoherently. Then he said, "This is a privileged position I have at the moment. Of course I'm hopeful that I'm worthy."

A professor of psychiatry joined him on the platform. "I'm Ken Keniston. I'm a psychologist. I think this fellow is in trouble."

"I'm not in trouble," the man replied. He stammered a little. "I think it is you who are in trouble. I think it is all of you."

Keniston put his arm around the student. "I'm going to ask all of you for the greatest understanding and sympathy at this point—and silence and respect—while we try to help this guy." There was sympathetic applause from the crowd as Keniston, with the aid of some students, helped the young man off the platform and out of the hall.

Ken Mills regained control of the meeting. "I hope at this point we can be calm," he said, "and get back to the business we are trying to deal with . . . and that business, of course, for us here at Yale is a consideration of what we are going to do about the defense of justice for the Panthers and to retain whatever humanity we still have left. . . . Yale is now the target and the question now is how to prevent that kind of holocaust and destruction that in many ways nobody here wants and yet that arises out of the nature of conflict and injustice in our society. I call for an acclamation that shows you are serious, and that the shutdown is *now.*"

At this point a number of students took up the call of *"Strike!"* and were joined by many, though not all, of the crowd. The students then left to attend late-night meetings at their individual colleges where nine out of the twelve colleges voted to shut down academically and to open their facilities to out-of-town demonstrators on the weekend of May 1. From that point on, the large majority of Yale students stayed away from class, some to attend teach-ins, some to discuss the issues with the residents of New Haven, some to train as marshals and hold down violence on the weekend. In this way they hoped to express their dismay over the American legal system, to save Yale, and to demonstrate a sympathetic concern over the plight of the Panthers on trial.

On the next day we held a general meeting at the School of Drama to determine our own position vis-à-vis the strike. Acting Dean Howard Stein presided. The meeting was passionate and highly charged. Rumors had begun to circulate about the kind of activity to be expected on the weekend, and many of the students were fearful over the potential for violence as well as angered by the society they believed was responsible. Like the majority at Yale, the students of the School were eager to prevent a conflagration from starting in New Haven at the same time that they were looking for ways to express their feelings about the condition of black people. For this reason, our students were torn between shutting down operations altogether (the position of the radicals) and "redirecting" the School's activities (the position of the moderates) so that classes and productions could continue, with some of them focusing more directly on America's political dilemmas.

The black students at the School sat quietly, though with obvious impatience, as the white radicals began to append their own concerns to the matter at hand. Before the end of the meeting, most of the black students had left. There was considerable debate about whether Yale should be trying to "free" the Panthers or simply working for a fair trial. I took this opportunity to say that I was not convinced, as some apparently were, that the aspirations and desires of the black community were necessarily identical with the goals of the Black Panthers. As for those who wished to express solidarity with the Panthers rather than help ensure that the trial was a fair one, they should try to remember that the Panthers were openly dedicated to the extermination of "pigs" and to a Maoist revolution through violent means, and that their attitude toward Jews was far from tolerant. I also felt compelled to remind the students that somebody had committed a particularly brutal murder of a black man, that two of the defendants had already confessed to complicity in the crime, and that (no matter how discredited such testimony might later prove) these were certainly sufficient grounds for a trial.

One young actress, not terribly talented, was annoyed by my remarks. She had been in my office just a few days earlier to complain about her obligation to attend voice classes. I remarked that she should have welcomed those classes, since she had a pronounced lisp. She denied it. I pointed out that she was lisping her denial. "It only happenth when I'm ekthited," she lisped. At the School meeting, when the issue came to a vote, she waved her fist at us —excitedly—and screamed, "I thay thtrike!!!"

The students voted not to shut down but rather to "redirect" the activities of the School for an indefinite period. Although this vote was not binding on the administration, Dean Stein agreed to a modification of the existing training, providing it was voluntary on the part of instructors and students, and providing the existing class schedule was preserved. In this way, students who wished to continue training could still pursue their work in class, while others had the option of staying away and functioning through direct political action or through their area of expertise, the theatre. Some students wanted to engage in guerrilla theatre tactics on May 1; others wished to reenact daily the proceedings of the court, using the transcript as a text; still others went into training as marshals.

Carmen de Lavallade expressed her concern over the black high school kids who were beginning to roam the city streets, many of them getting arrested for breaking windows and snatching pocketbooks; she suggested that drama students bring rehearsed productions to Lee and Hillhouse High to keep the kids in school and off the streets. Inevitably put into question was the "relevance" of upcoming School productions, including the acting projects and the Rep production of *Don Juan*. But although a few students were eager to convert all of our activity into political action, the great majority insisted on preserving the freedom of individuals to choose their own ways, and all classes and projects continued in a normal fashion.

I went from the School meeting to the Theatre. Our rehearsal had been delayed, as many of our scheduled activities would be delayed over the next week for crises and meetings. I was eager to hear the opinions of the company concerning the strike, since what had just transpired at the School was bound to affect our work. We worried over the possible risks of proceeding with the last few performances of *Transformations,* fearing that a public display of business-as-usual would enrage Yale's more radical students. Despite personal anxieties, however, the company voted unanimously to continue with the performances as well as with rehearsals of *Don Juan.*

Following the vote, one of the box-office staff broke in. "Aren't you going to do *anything* to support the strike?" she asked.

"What do you suggest we do?" I answered.

"Close down the theatre," she said, "and give the place over to black groups. Or contribute box-office receipts to the Panther defense."

"Well, if we cancel performances at the church here, we'll have no way to pay our salaries (I won't mention the breach with our audiences). You know, your own salary comes partly through box-office receipts. If you're willing to give up your paycheck this week, I'll ask the others how they feel about it, so at least we can be generous personally instead of asking the Theatre to do it."

"That's not the question," she said. "I can't stand it that the theatre is doing nothing at all for the Panthers."

"Well, you have your options," I said.

She exercised one, and quit.

A few days later a meeting was held in Sprague Hall, where, after lively debate, the Yale College faculty voted to "modify" indefinitely the "normal expectations of the University" in a motion that concluded, "We feel that the suspension of the normal academic functions of the University would allow all those concerned and interested a chance to discuss the issues and the ramifications of the issues and to plan what direction we should take in this crisis."

It was at this meeting—conducted while nine hundred shouting students demonstrated outside the building—that Kingman Brewster uttered the sentence that was to dog him forever and to cloud the remaining years of his administration: "In spite of my insistence on the limits of my official capacity, I personally want to say that I am appalled and ashamed that things have come to such a pass that I am skeptical of the ability of black revolutionaries to achieve a fair trial anywhere in the United States."

Brewster's statement instantly called down the wrath of judges, lawyers, officials, Yale alumni, and Vice President Spiro Agnew, creating an explosive impact on everyone who heard it. It didn't disturb me particularly, despite my disagreement with its content, partly because it was so clearly offered as a personal rather than an institutional position, partly because it was so obviously an effort to defuse the rage against Yale. It achieved its immediate purpose. The university was now perceived by the moderates, and even by some of the radicals, as an ally rather than an enemy in the May Day demonstration. But the longer-lasting effect of Brewster's statement was to shake the confidence of the alumni in his leadership, and this was to jeopardize and hamper his future fund-raising efforts. As so often happens, the media seized on this remark to the exclusion of anything else he had ever said or done. I've never known a single utterance to be repeated so often after it was made, or to burn so deeply into people's minds. I fear it will eventually be chiseled on his gravestone.

I was sympathetic to the effort of the university to preserve itself by whatever means, but I knew it would someday have to pay the price. For this reason, I continued—along with a few older members of the faculty—to insist on issues of principle, quixotic as this may have seemed at the time. We voted against the faculty resolution to modify academic expectations indefinitely, and we challenged Brewster's decision to open up Yale on May Day as a haven for out-of-town demonstrators. Some of us feared that in urging us to use our class time to discuss the Panther trials, the faculty had voted away a share of our academic freedom; we worried about the potential danger to students in keeping the university open in the face of potential riots; and we didn't agree that Yale had any obligation to offer hospitality to radical demonstrators protesting a legitimate trial. These were arguably rigid positions to take at a time when flexibility was required. But we didn't insist that they be followed, only that they be *heard*. People were beginning to talk like military strategists rather than disinterested scholars. I couldn't imagine the future of any university where truth was sacrificed to expediency, which refused to tolerate the expression of a contrary opinion.

Still, my position tended to isolate me considerably during the days that followed—which shouldn't have surprised me. What did surprise me was the way academics, who normally never agree on anything, were now insisting on a single point of view. During a teach-in on "Revolution and Language," conducted two days before the fateful weekend, my contribution to the panel discussion was to observe the similarity between such phrases as "off the pigs" and "the final solution"—both were the kind of euphemisms described by Hannah Arendt as phrases designed to dehumanize people in preparation for destructive acts against them. Robert Jay Lifton, professor of psychiatry and noted psychohistorian, accused me from the floor of trying to "polarize" the community with observations of this kind. I replied that what he called polarization I called simple disagreement, and our community was in a sorry state when we all had to adhere to a uniform point of view.

The next day I was walking down York Street behind a student I recognized; he was a dropout from the graduate philosophy department who, the previous spring, had tried, unsuccessfully, to revolutionize the Drama School. Casting a mean look in my direction, he raised his fist and said, "Power to the people!" I nodded neutrally and continued on my way. Once again he turned: "Power to the people!" I failed to respond. Then he stopped and faced me: "We're going to give you something special this week to write about for *The New York Times.*" I thanked him, and then inquired whether the "people" included anyone who might disagree with his position. He turned silently and walked away, his clenched fist held aloft.

A few days later a band of roving students banged on the doors of the Theatre demanding to be admitted, and shouting, "Shut it down!" The same afternoon I was called away from rehearsals by Dean Stein. My wife was in his office, and she was under obvious strain. She had just received a phone call at home. Somebody had asked "Is Brustein there?" and when she offered to take a message, then said, "Tell the pig he's going to die!" Similar calls, I was told by the Yale police, were being made to other members of the Yale faculty, but this was not much consolation. When birdshot shattered my neighbor's window that night, narrowly missing one of his children, I took my wife and son to sleep in a Howard Johnson's Motor Inn.

I have been accused by a number of sensible people of having been unduly alarmist about that weekend, especially in view of the fact that nobody was actually hurt. That may be, but it is hard to deny that the potential for violence was enormous. Two hundred and eighty riot shotguns had just been hijacked from an unguarded truck outside of New Haven; $2,500 worth of mercury had recently been stolen from the chemistry lab, and mercury was used in making blasting caps for homemade bombs; explosives had been discovered in the apartment of a Yale Weatherman dropout living in the city; and there were rumors abroad that a hundred radical shock troops from the University of California, as well as a gang of Hell's Angels, were coming to town expressly to "burn Yale." Thirty percent of the entire Yale community, including 50 percent of the freshmen, were alarmed enough to leave town for the weekend. And the mayor, the police chief, and the governor of Connecticut were sufficiently alarmed to post National Guard troops in the downtown area, along with four thousand federal troops on the outskirts of New Haven—deterrents which, in the opinion of the police chief, "substantially reduced the possibility of violence."

I reduced the possibility of violence for myself and my family by taking refuge for the weekend at the Styrons' house in Roxbury. It was eerie enjoying a social evening in such tranquil pastoral surroundings when, thirty miles away, New Haven was being boarded up in preparation for disaster. Among the guests at dinner that night was my amiable antagonist, Robert Jay Lifton, who undertook to explain to me why the Beinecke Library had become the focus of radical wrath. It was impossible to justify spending money on rare books when there was so much poverty in the land. Controlling myself with difficulty, I asked Lifton to take a walk with me around the grounds and, with considerable heat, asked him why he thought that the university, designed as a center of truth and learning, should be held accountable for the failures of the social system. He replied—in that patient, rational, unruffled manner of his that sometimes drives people to smash windows or crack up cars—that the university was now so corrupt it was appropriate that it should be destroyed.

I was not a witness to the events that followed, but from all accounts, the weekend came and went without any serious consequence. A bomb placed under the bleachers at Ingalls Rink, probably by a right-wing group, exploded shortly after most of the demonstrators had left a concert there, resulting in only minor injuries. The Branford Buttery was burned and hacked with an ax by some of the visitors enjoying the hospitality of this radicalized Yale college. A fire was started in the Law School, and ten small fires were extinguished elsewhere on the campus. On the New Haven Green, a lot of angry rhetoric flowed. Jerry Rubin advised a crowd to go home and kill their mothers and fathers, while inveighing against some local figure he called "Kingman

Brewer." In the most serious incident of the weekend, the National Guard sprayed tear gas on fifteen hundred or two thousand enraged demonstrators who marched on the courthouse after they had been misinformed, by an unidentified black man, that some Panthers had been arrested by the police.

But on the whole, the proceedings were relatively peaceful, and the estimated crowd of thirteen thousand to fifteen thousand demonstrators fell far below the numbers that had been predicted. The Panthers had decided to cool the weekend, and worked bravely and tirelessly for that purpose. The Yale marshals, at risk of life and limb, helped to pacify the crowd whenever it threatened to turn into a mob. Some of the Yale faculty, including many doctors from the Medical School, lent aid and comfort to the injured. The New Haven police, under Chief James Ahern, acted in an admirably restrained manner, arresting only thirty-seven people in the two days of demonstrations. The black community kept the kids off the streets. With a huge sigh of relief, New Haven shopkeepers began to take the boards off their windows, and Yale initiated a week-long process of housecleaning. In his Battell Chapel sermon, Chaplain Coffin announced, "We did a helluva job . . . a Christian job. We licked them with love."

Brewster's strategy had worked beyond his wildest expectations; miraculously, nobody had suffered serious injury. Even the buildings remained intact, except for the damage to Ingalls Rink and some broken windows in the ROTC office. True, the graffiti had certainly multiplied (on our theatre, somebody posted a sign saying, "The Drama School closed its doors on the revolution"). But Yale came away from May Day relatively unscathed, except for a surfeit of self-congratulation. The students and faculty were mighty pleased with what they had accomplished; some called the experience of the preceding weeks a much better education than anyone could ever have received in a classroom. Then the awful events of the Kent State massacre and the invasion of Cambodia exploded, mobilizing the campus to strike once again. But in spite of efforts by the radicals to keep the university shut down academically and opened up for political education during the summer, the president issued a directive reconvening classes, and a few students and faculty returned to their regular duties. A campus hero now, Brewster announced that he would lead a Yale delegation to Washington in order to discuss ways of ending the war with members of Congress who had Yale affiliations.

We even managed to open our production of *Don Juan* on time. It was a grand success, both with critics and with audiences, few of whom questioned its "relevance" in a time of crisis. The final scene was even more terrifying than we had anticipated, because—at the precise moment when Don Juan was being turned to stone, with the organ crashing and the lights flashing—a bat flew out of the belfry, zooming back and forth over the heads of the spectators. Many believed it had been planned.

V

Out of It
1970-1971

You say that every voice in the faculty of philosophy is against you. Dear Brandes, how else would you want it: Are you not fighting against the philosophy of the faculty?

—Ibsen's *Letters*

Once again Norma and I decamped for Martha's Vineyard, but this time the company remained together. The Yale Repertory Theatre had received an invitation to perform at the John Drew Theatre in East Hampton, and a summer season was planned under the artistic direction of Larry Arrick. Arrick had become a true convert to Story Theatre, and together with a group of senior and junior actors from the Rep, he created a rapid-fire sequence of Story Theatre productions over an eight-week period: an evening of Philip Roth stories; a double bill of Bram Stoker's *Dracula* and Dashiell Hammett's *Flypaper;* another double bill of Isaac Bashevis Singer's *Gimpel the Fool* and Gustave Flaubert's *St. Julian the Hospitaler;* and a new edition of Ovid called *Olympian Games.*

The summer group represented the nucleus of the company that was to perform in New Haven during the coming year. It was staffed entirely with people who had been trained at the School, or with people who were currently teaching at the School. We had long dreamed of an organic theatre, composed of those who shared similar theatrical values, a common vocabulary, and the same training experience; this now seemed to be coming closer to realization. The Story Theatre technique, whatever its other virtues, had a unifying power, and the success of the summer season helped to cement bonds among the members of the company in a way that was never quite possible in the frozen isolation of a New Haven winter. The actors lived together, worked together, ate together, swam and played tennis together; they even exchanged a few wives, husbands, and lovers. By the end of that summer, they had grown in artistic confidence and physical grace, the faces of the young people developing structure and definition, their bodies gaining strength and muscularity.

Norma and I were outsiders that summer, for reasons not hard to understand. We had chosen to spend July and August on the Vineyard, and let Arrick take responsibility for the East Hampton season. Neither of us was prepared to face another year at Yale without a few months' rest and recreation, even though the temptation to share in the summer activities of the company, and enjoy their camaraderie, was strong. When we arrived to watch the dress rehearsal of each show, we were greeted warmly, but there was always, nevertheless, a slight reserve in the air, as though we were encroaching on a mystery. Arrick had created company unity by generating a certain exclusiveness. Those not part of the process were considered part of the audience.

Considering how possessive I had recently grown about the Rep, I didn't enjoy these visits much, but I still took pride in the achievements of the company, and looked forward to building on these when we returned to New Haven. I decided to open the season with a *Story Theatre Repertory,* consisting of *Olympian Games* in alternation with the Singer and Flaubert stories, both redirected by Arrick; and I spent the rest of the vacation planning and casting the remaining plays in the schedule. My other labors that summer, apart from organizing the School curriculum and writing the catalogue, consisted of entertaining and being entertained by Joseph E. Levine.

I was trying to extract from him the money he had pledged to the Rep. That $100,000 was absolutely crucial to our budget, but not a dollar had yet been sent to the Yale Development Office. I thought it more politic not to mention the money during our meetings; instead, I tried to make myself conspicuous in the hope that seeing me often would remind him of his pledge. I was at a loss to understand what was wrong. Could it be that he didn't have the cash? Nonsense. That July he had sailed into Edgartown harbor in a seagoing yacht that was over a hundred feet in length. In those waters it looked like the *Queen Mary.* The very night he arrived he invited a number of Vineyard friends to attend a lavish shipboard party in celebration of the newly decorated interior.

When we came on board, we found Levine in a fury. The posh and snooty Edgartown Yacht Club had refused to let his boat tie up alongside, and he was now threatening to buy up the entire beach front nearby and turn it into a pig farm. After he calmed down, he led us through the several cabins of the sumptuous craft, proudly pointing out where Rosalie had installed the crystal chandeliers and where she had replaced the ripped-out teakwood with flocked wallpaper. The carpets were of thick, deep piling, and the beds so soft you could barely extricate yourself from the downy comforters. After the tour we were served dinner on deck by uniformed stewards and, as usual, the drinks were generous and the meal was delicious. Vineyard salts, cruising by the yacht in their unvarnished skiffs and peeling lobster boats, gawked incredulously as we lolled on the poop deck of this mammoth floating hotel, consuming canapés and martinis, and listening to Frank Sinatra on stereo cassettes.

Norma made an effort to repay Levine for his hospitality a few days later by throwing a large party for him at our home in Lambert's Cove. All of our Vineyard friends were invited and all of them came, including Renata Adler, a former movie critic for the *Times* who was visiting Lillian Hellman. Levine took an immediate shine to her, and rather irritated this shy, gentle woman by continually inquiring why such a nice Jewish girl was not yet married. Near the end of the evening, sitting woozily on a chair in the middle of our living room, he tapped for attention with his cane on the floor and announced, in a very loud voice, "Joseph E. Levine . . . is drunk!"

He was kidding his celebrated credit "Joseph E. Levine presents"—but by the end of the summer, Joseph E. Levine had still not yet presented. This was very worrying. We had a problem with cash flow, and there wasn't enough money in the till to finish the first part of the season. When we were invited to Greenwich to perform in September as a preseason benefit for the new high school, I accepted, largely because I remembered that Levine's new house had been built in Greenwich. Five hundred people attended the event. I was conscious only of one. Having determined that Levine had accepted his invitation, I made certain the theatre playbill included a line (featured beneath the title and written in bold letters) that the New Haven season of the Yale Repertory Theatre was being made possible "through a generous grant from Joseph E. Levine."

The performance we did for the benefit was called *Two Saints,* and it consisted of two Story Theatre presentations from the summer, *Gimpel the Fool* and *St. Julian the Hospitaler*. Gimpel is a charming folktale of a holy Yiddish simpleton, whose credulity is such that everyone takes advantage of it, but whose innocence finally triumphs over those who would betray him. We played this first. During the intermission Levine came over to me and whispered in my ear: "Don't you think," he said hesitantly, "that this show is a little too *Jewish* for Greenwich?" I gave a start. For a few dark moments I thought I had blown the entire pledge. But the essentially Gentile audience obviously adored both the plays, and gave us a standing ovation at the end of the evening. During the reception afterward Levine's round face was wreathed in smiles. "You need money?" he asked me. I allowed that we could use a little cash. "How much you need?" I told him, "As much of the pledge as you can give now. In a few weeks, we won't have enough to pay our actors' salaries." "I gotta sell some stocks," he replied. "I'll send you a check in a few weeks."

In a few weeks the check arrived, as promised—for $25,000.

It was less than I hoped but enough to get us started, and I was grateful for it, though a little anxious over being so dependent on Levine's capricious largesse. We opened our fourth Yale Repertory Theatre season soon after with *Story Theatre Repertory,* which New Haven audiences found as charming as did audiences in East Hampton and Greenwich. As for me, I thought our adaptation of the stories lacked weight as dramatic pieces, but the production showed the advances of the summer in displaying the various histrionic, musical, and dancing gifts of the company. Alvin Epstein played Gimpel with an aura of simple idealism, and David Ackroyd made a strong and sinewy St.

Julian. *Olympian Games,* also in this repertory, though fluffy, was integrated by the ensemble work of the actors, the two most memorable episodes in the evening being Tereus and Procne (with Carmen de Lavallade ravishing as a ravished Philomela) and Baucis and Philemon (featuring Alvin Epstein and Betsy Parrish as a gentle old couple transformed into trees by the gods). Although the evening had an undeniable sensual appeal, the lightness of the treatment continued to disturb me. I still believed that the Story Theatre approach could support something deeper and perhaps darker than legend, mythology, fairy stories, and folktales.

On the other hand, *Story Theatre Repertory* inadvertently reflected a new atmosphere at Yale that fall, which President Brewster described as an "eerie tranquillity." People had grown tired of the endless tumult of the radical years, and wanted some respite in quiet and relaxation. Although we didn't realize it at the time, 1970 marked both the highwater mark of student radicalism and the beginning of its decline. Nixon was about to defuse the antiwar movement by putting an end to the draft, an act of low cunning inspired by his understanding that to most students involuntary induction into the armed services was as much an issue as peace in Vietnam. And the Kent State killings had made it clear that officials were now ready to use firearms against demonstrators. Besides this, a moderate backlash was building up against the more extreme elements of the movement, especially after the explosion on Eleventh Street, in New York City, which killed some Weatherpeople using a brownstone as a bomb factory, and the bombing of a building at the University of Wisconsin, which resulted in the death of an innocent graduate student.

As a sign of this backlash, a faculty group at Yale, previously sympathetic to the radical demonstrations, were now urging students to work for change through the electoral process. An antiwar candidate, Joseph Duffey, was running for a Senate seat in Connecticut, and they were worried that a peace demonstration planned for Halloween might jeopardize his chances. Their letter urged the Yale community to stay home, reminding us that "the American public, [though] a majority . . . wants all our troops out of Indochina by 1971, overwhelmingly opposes demonstrations." Kenneth Keniston added: "Our best sense of the best tactic is to support an effort to try to change things politically."

This was a significant change from the time when many in this group were admiring the blisters on the palms of the Venceremos Brigade. But there were others sufficiently distrustful of this "eerie tranquillity" to offer their own warnings. One group, which I helped to organize, drew up a statement opposing all forms of violence, whether perpetrated by society against the Vietnamese and blacks or by the radical young against society. We protested, in this statement, against "America's lapses into brutalism, racism, and destruction," and identified ourselves as "vigorous opponents of the Vietnam war and of racial discrimination," adding: "At the same time, the very principles that originally brought us to this position compel us to oppose not only an immoral war and racial oppression but also the appeal to violence in the name of radical morality and revolutionary idealism. We believe that the bombings and burnings that have recently broken out in this country are mirror images of the very destructiveness we are pledged to resist."

Although this statement looks tame enough today, it caused considerable division among the Yale faculty members who were invited to sign, and underwent a good deal of revision before it was thought fit to circulate. Some people, like Robert Jay Lifton, flatly refused to endorse the statement, afraid that it would play into the hands of "the radical right and lead to considerable misunderstanding about the extent of violence among antiwar students." Others, like the late Alexander Bickel of the Law School, found it unsuitable from the opposite position; he sent a blistering letter charging us with "wildly exaggerated condemnations of this imperfect but, really, not quite debased society." Despite these objections, the statement eventually appeared in the *Yale Daily News* endorsed by three hundred sixty-four Yale faculty members, most of them happy at the chance to go on record against the actions of extremism everywhere.

There were other signs that year of changing attitudes. When a film called *Bright College Years,* by Peter Rosen (a former student in art and architecture), appeared at the York Square Cinema, nobody went to see it, even though it depicted the events of May Day, including hordes of undergraduates (some of whom might have recognized themselves on the screen) shouting "Free Bobby" and raising clenched fists. As a student reviewing the movie for the *Yale Daily News* put it, "Maybe we have all been too embarrassed to say anything. Maybe we have all been too ashamed by how little we actually achieved last spring. Maybe we have all been made mute by the fact that some of the already tried Panthers confessed that they killed Alex Rackley, and thus for them at least, the case wasn't a political trial after all. Maybe issues weren't as clear-cut last spring as we had thought they were then." This was a remarkably percipient statement, suggesting that perhaps some "education" might have come out of this affair after all. But at this time nobody was protesting the unfairness of the Panther trials any longer, or demonstrating against the inadequacy of the judicial system. A few of the defendants had been convicted following their confessions, but Bobby Seale was free as a result of a hung jury.

While this review was proof that minds could sometimes be changed in a university, the new mood of "eerie tranquillity" did not lead to any significant political discussion or self-examination—only to that "mute" embarrassment mentioned by the student reviewer. As for the vaunted educational opportunities of May Day, the only conspicuous sign of learning was the silence. Still, even the silence said something—that Yale might once again be ready to tolerate a little intellectual complexity. The politicization of the community had liberated a lot of energy, but it had not been particularly protective of the privileges of dissent.

I had suffered my own form of politicization, and I continued to be obsessed with the prevalence of violence in American life. For better or worse, this obsession informed our next production at the Rep, a seventeenth-century bloodbath by Cyril Tourneur called *The Revenger's Tragedy.* I decided on this work for two principal reasons—because of its feverish imagery and because of its peculiarly modern treatment of role-playing. Ben Jonson, Tourneur's brilliant contemporary, had described the process in a passage I cited in the program: "I have considered our whole life is like a play; wherein each man, forgetful of himself, is in travail with expression of another. Nay, we insist so in imitating others, as we cannot (when it is necessary) return to ourselves." This insight, which Pirandello was to develop three hundred years later, struck me as peculiarly cogent in regard to Tourneur's use of disguise. The hero, Vindice, begins as a critic of the corrupt pageant he witnesses; then, gradually, he enters it, first as an actor, then as a playwright and a stage manager. Finally, he is swallowed up in the action and "forgetful of himself," is consumed entirely in his role and cannot return to himself—his mask, or disguise, usurps his face.

Obviously, I had other things in mind than the theatrical implications of this idea: "Like so many of today's radical avengers," I wrote in a program note, "Vindice begins with an authentic grievance against his violent society and an honest determination to purify it. To do this, however, he must 'put on the knave for once,' and use the tactics of the world he abhors. . . . Having lost his initial purpose somewhere along the way, he inadvertently becomes identified with the objects of his vengeance. . . . The revenger's tragedy is that he cannot escape the cursed circle he has sworn to break. We have chosen, in this production, to examine the moral and physical transformation of an idealist into a knave."

I was still in the grip of a social idea. But in my eagerness to make a contemporary point, I imposed a concept on the actors that didn't help them much in finding connections to characters who were already rather abstract and allegorical. The dramatis personae of the play includes such type-figures as Lussurioso (Lust), Ambitioso (Ambition), Supervacuo (Idleness) and Spurio (Bastardy)—not to mention Vindice (Vengeance). How do you play a single character trait, even if it's active? It was important to provide the cast with intentions, objectives, and character elements that would help to anchor them in reality. Instead, I encouraged them to approach the text as if it were a morality play, extending a single quality obsessively. Lussurioso, for example, would be nothing but Lust—a walking erection who can't keep his hands off himself or others. Generously, the actors tried their best to give me the results I wanted; but trained in a realistic Stanislavsky technique, most of them were stranded by my concept.

More disappointing was my failure to realize the central thematic idea—that Vindice's face is usurped by his mask—primarily because Kenneth Haigh, who was cast in the role, was reluctant to use any mask at all. My plan was to have Vindice wear a full latex mold over his face every time he went into disguise. At the end of the play, having been responsible for so many deaths, he would be unable to remove the mask from his face, like the character invented by Marcel Marceau whose hideous clown grin becomes involuntarily affixed to his features. I don't think it was a bad idea, but I should have abandoned it the moment I sensed resistance from Haigh. The actor was understandably worried that a mask would inhibit his facial expression. We experimented with various versions of the mask throughout rehearsal, gradually exposing more and more of Haigh's lower face, until we finally had little more than a helmet for the upper features which Haigh put on and off like a mask in a Restoration play.

This permitted him the freedom to articulate Tourneur's febrile verse, but it made a hash of the concept and helped to confuse the production. Santo Loquasto's set was a black geometrical box made of plexiglass, and the costumes had an exaggerated grandeur in the manner of Hieronymus Bosch—both contributed to the gory pageantry, which concluded with a scene in which a skeleton led the characters through a spasmodic dance of death. But in spite of its visual splendor, the production divided reviewers. Although all praised Haigh's authority, some didn't like the play, some didn't like the acting, some didn't like the direction. I agreed secretly with the last.

A few of the critics took this occasion to rebuke me for imposing an alien concept on Tourneur's play; since the concept had not been realized in the production, it was obvious they had read the program notes. The risks of providing program notes are well known to people in the theatre. Reviewers invariably want to crib from them or argue with them. Literary material, for some reason, attracts more attention from reviewers than stage action; there is always the danger they will review not what they see but what they read. Nevertheless, we had an obligation, built into the nature of our theatre, to extend the audience's perception of a play beyond the production itself. Just as a theatre event is a transaction between a writer and his collaborators, so a play is a transaction between the writer and his culture. It was the job of our doctoral students in criticism to research these transactions, and to share their discoveries not only with the actors and directors but with members of the audience as well, by providing dramaturgical material in the form of essays, literary selections, and graphics. Our first literary manager, Michael Feingold, was particularly adept at collecting program material, but before long it was a function gracefully performed by all our DFA's. We even managed to obtain a grant for dramaturgy training from the National Endowment for the Humanities, which helped us develop many of the literary managers later employed by other resident theatres. Part of their apprentice work at Yale was to provide material for our handsome, informative souvenir program.

I must admit, however, that my own program note for *The Revenger's Tragedy* managed to obscure rather than clarify my production. It also revealed the extent to which I was still affected by the past two years. Whenever a bomb went off in a ROTC building or a policeman was killed by a revolutionary or a black was killed by a policeman or Nixon escalated the war, I had this unmanageable compulsion to make some statement about violence. The success of the peace movement, I believed, depended entirely on its being peaceful, just as the effectiveness of the Student Non-Violent Coordinating

Committee (SNCC) depended on its remaining nonviolent. I had no patience with people who didn't understand this. A Yale faculty friend of mine, for example, had written an article in *Partisan Review* recalling the "Revolution and Language" symposium of the previous spring, and charging that I had made the mistake of confusing euphemism with metaphor in complaining about the phrase "off the pig." "The Panther phrases are the metaphors of argot," he wrote, "a secret language designed to identify members of a group and intensify their communication through exclusion of anyone outside their circle." I found this an exceedingly precious distinction, which treated serious, dangerous behavior as if it were a subject of academic linguistics. I replied by sending him some newspaper clippings concerning the sharp rise in gun attacks by black revolutionaries on policemen, two of whom had recently been murdered in Harlem. "Did these men die from metaphor?" I asked him in a tart note which managed to cool our relationship for a while.

Exchanges like this one caused Norma to begin calling me "The Great Right Father." Why did I always have to have the last word? Couldn't I just shut up already? She had pushed her husband beyond the boundary of his customary nature, and like Lady Macbeth, she couldn't seem to stop him now and wasn't altogether happy with what she had created. It wasn't my position that bothered Norma. She shared many of my opinions about our contemporaries and whipped off quite a few caustic notes herself. It was my style. If I had to quarrel, she said, at least I could quarrel courteously; no need to isolate ourselves entirely from the Yale community. I wasn't as fearful of ostracism as she was. I was working too hard to worry about a social life, and, anyway, I still continued to receive a lot of supportive letters whenever I took a public position. But I should have thought more about Norma, who suffered greatly for my sake. Anyway, even if I was capable of heeding her cautionary advice, it came too late. By that time, I was emitting a bad smell, like Flower the Skunk in the Disney movie who sends everyone scurrying in various directions as he walks blithely to his destination, striped tail proudly aloft.

In an article in *The New York Times Magazine* called "The Yale Faculty Makes the Scene," Thomas Meehan discussed the prominence of such "teacher-celebrities" at the university as Erich Segal, Charles Reich, Robert Jay Lifton, Kenneth Keniston, Robert Penn Warren, and me. Segal had written a best-selling novel called *Love Story;* Reich, Lifton, and Keniston had each produced popular studies about the attractive style of the radical "kids"; Warren was a well-beloved teacher, as well as a great poet; I was the heavy. Meehan made very positive remarks about the Drama School and my own role in helping to advance it, but he also quoted "an angry member of the Students for a Democratic Society" as saying, "You know the Sara Lee slogan in the TV commercials—'Everybody doesn't like something, but nobody doesn't like Sara Lee?' Well, around here that might be paraphrased to read, 'Everybody doesn't like somebody, but nobody doesn't dislike Robert Brustein."

I took no comfort from the confusion of the double negatives. I was hurt. Still, I managed to keep my tail aloft. In the same article—also in later articles of my own called "Cultural Schizophrenia" and "The Decline of Professional-ism"—I added some baking soda to my Sara Lee reputation by attacking a few of the very "faculty swingers" that Meehan was interviewing, criticizing their "Consciousness III" compulsion to dress, speak, and behave like the kids. Norma, mortified by the Sara Lee remark, was imploring me once again to shut up already. Despite the affection that had now developed between the drama students and me, I was no campus hero to Yale undergraduates, and my alleged hostility to undergraduate drama only reinforced their dislike.

I believe my position regarding undergraduates and theatre was consistently misunderstood—but it's not hard to see why. Partly attracted to Yale by the growing reputation of the Drama School, young people had entered the college expecting to take our courses—only to discover that the classes they coveted most were reserved for graduate-professional students in training. A number of offerings in our catalogue were always available to undergraduates, includ-ing those in literature, criticism, technical production, and (to a limited degree) playwriting. I personally taught a large lecture course each year in classical or modern drama, which enjoyed a sizable undergraduate enrollment. The trouble was that our programs in acting and directing were closed to all but our own students, unless the undergraduate elected, and was qualified, to combine his final year at the college with his first year at the Drama School.

The undergraduates at Yale had their own acting and directing classes, taught (until we upgraded the undergraduate drama major with professional teachers) by our own students in theatre. And they continued to have a number of outlets for public performance at the Yale Dramat and the residential colleges. But it goes without saying that our own acting and directing pro-grams were always more in demand; and I was never able to explain (though not for want of trying) why they couldn't be opened up to nonprofessional students. The difficulty lay in communicating to these students that the theatre was a discipline like medicine or law; and like the schools of medicine and law, the School of Drama was devoted to training people for a profession. Our own students had been carefully selected, from among a large number of applicants, on the basis of talent and dedication. How could they share a class with undergraduates who were there seeking additional credits for a liberal arts program? Professional students in acting usually engaged in twenty-eight con-tact hours of training each week, along with countless hours of rehearsal and performance. How could they work in a class with undergraduates who elected two or three hours of acting along with their language, literature, and science courses? It was not just a question of talent and dedication, it was also a question of experience—rather like throwing a young piano student, just learn-ing scales, into lessons with students prepared for recitals.

The difficulty was compounded by the fact that the School of Art and the School of Music had opened their classes to undergraduates—giving large lecture courses along with private instruction. But with acting, we were teach-ing a collaborative art where the group is held at the level of its least talented member; it wasn't like teaching the violin or painting. I tried to explain all this, but none of my explanations would suffice. And since Yale College is the center of the Yale universe, the School of Drama was soon considered exclusive, uncooperative, recalcitrant, an unavailable resource for undergraduate activity. The irony was that this extraordinary surge of interest in theatre was largely stimulated by the very School they felt excluded from.

I was, besides, thought to be indifferent to undergraduate performance. This enraged a number of students, particularly since I was known as a theatre critic and my attitude was regarded as a form of judgment. The truth is that I didn't have a great deal of respect for the Yale Dramat (the extracurricular theatre society), partly because it failed to attract the most talented undergraduates, partly because it was quite conventional in its choice of plays. But I frequently enjoyed the work done in the residential colleges, where dining halls, squash courts, and boiler rooms were spaces more appropriate to the level of performance than the vast reaches of the University Theatre. I scouted these productions—some of them quite adventurous and experimental—with a self-interested eye. I was looking for potential talent for the Drama School.

Partly for similar reasons, I started working behind the scenes to improve the undergraduate theatre program. The Drama School had theoretical jurisdiction over this program, since we made the faculty appointments. But since Yale College supplied very little money for undergraduate drama courses, they were usually taught by indigent graduate students (primarily our own) with only a rudimentary grasp of their subject. Conscious that the undergraduate major was not meeting Yale's academic standards, I told the dean of Yale College that he should either upgrade the undergraduate major with professional supervisors and qualified instructors or drop it entirely. If he would provide a reasonable budget, we would be prepared to recruit an appropriate department head and help design a sensible program. If not, we would no longer appoint graduate students as undergraduate instructors. This created an impression that I was trying to destroy undergraduate theatre when I was actually using a Draconian strategy to improve it. The bluff worked. Before too long, Yale supplied some money and the program was totally revamped.

I was running a graduate program, but I had a number of reasons for wanting to influence the quality and direction of the college courses. As an erstwhile professor of English, I retained a vestigial skepticism about the value of pure performance courses in a liberal arts curriculum unless they had a strong literary basis; but as a theatre man, I believed the best way to analyze a play was through performance. I was also eager to attract educated students to the School. I wanted people with cultural background; otherwise, they would be unable to understand their parts. Our experiment in admitting non-degree certificate students, some of them barely out of high school, had fizzled; most lacked the ability to play anything but characters close to themselves. For this reason, it was important for us to identify talented undergraduates, preferably from Yale, who combined some experience in acting with a good background in literature and the humanities.

Norma had started an undergraduate acting course in 1969. Although not offered for credit that year, it attracted some formidable talents, and when she repeated the course for credit in 1970, the same students registered. Almost all of these *Wunderkinder,* as she called them, ended up in professional theatre. Some, like Charles H. Levin and David Schweizer, went to the School and thence to the Rep; another, Stephanie Cotsirilos, joined the company upon graduating from the School of Music; others, like Peter Evans, Carol Potter, and Alison Mills, went to conservatories abroad before entering theatre and television. It was a splendid class, and it was splendidly taught. Members of this group appeared in a dazzling production of *Jacques Brel* in one of the residential colleges while they were still undergraduates, a show we featured at the Rep the following year, with the same undergraduate cast and director, in a sequence called *Repertory Holiday.* And they appeared at the Dramat in a production of Gorki's *Enemies* where Norma joined them onstage as an actress.

In spite of my insistence on keeping all but the most talented and dedicated undergraduates out of the professional acting classes of the school, therefore, our activities were nevertheless helping to stimulate a lot of theatre around Yale. One way to illustrate this is with statistics. There were, for example, a hundred plays produced on and off Broadway in the 1970–71 season; in New Haven during the same period, there were sixty-three. Such statistics become even more meaningful when you compare New York's population of eight million with New Haven's one hundred fifty thousand. The city had not only two full-fledged professional resident theatres in the Long Wharf and the Yale Rep but substantial amateur, undergraduate, and coffeehouse activity. I had always believed that theatre generated theatre—that rather than competing for audiences, professional companies excited the tastes and enlarged the appetites of theatregoers. The existence of a thriving theatrical life in the Yale and New Haven community seemed to me proof of this thesis.

While theatre activity was proliferating at Yale, we were trying to contract. That year the School was reduced to what I believed to be the size most appropriate for the facilities—one hundred forty students. When I arrived in 1966, the student body numbered over two hundred, of which seventy-five were students in playwriting. I doubted whether there were seventy-five working playwrights in the entire world at any given time, much less in a single institution; obviously, most of these students were there for degrees. Admitting only the most promising and dedicated of the numerous applicants, we reduced the total of playwriting students to between twelve and fifteen, which allowed us to provide more personal instruction and production opportunities. It was our ultimate aim to admit no students to the School who could not be promised sufficient attention, and none who could not promise us in return a seriousness of purpose. The reduced size of the School would inevitably result in a better quality of student; it would also result in more work for everybody. By this time I knew that drama students complained seriously about two things only —overwork and underwork—and only the latter was an authentic cause of discontent.

There was no underwork that year at the Repertory Theatre; the productions were rolling thick and fast. Following *The Revenger's Tragedy* came four more shows in quick succession, beginning with Terrence McNally's *Where Has Tommy Flowers Gone?*

I was attracted to this play because of McNally's sharp ear for dialogue and his control of comic character. There were those who said I chose it because in the opening scenes the hero blows up Lincoln Center. My own distaste for culture mausoleums was a matter of record, and I had been highly critical of the successive managements of the Vivian Beaumont Theatre. That McNally shared these feelings was consoling, but I thought the play also had the embryonic makings of an important social satire. Directed by Larry Arrick, with Robert Drivas in the title role, *Where Has Tommy Flowers Gone?* had a lot of nervous energy and some fine comic performances, particularly by Jeremy Geidt as a garrulous tramp who has seen everything on Broadway, Henry Winkler as a touching young boy, and a student named Katherine de Hetre as one of Tommy's pickups, but it fell short of realizing its potential. McNally was canny enough to recognize the theatrical possibilities of making his protagonist a kind of lighthearted Weatherman, but I didn't think he sufficiently investigated the implications of his subject. I found him a little too detached from the violent propensities of his hero, as if he were exploiting radicalism for its topical value rather than examining its human and social consequences. I was probably exposing my own obsession again when I suggested that he end the play with Tommy "blowing up" the young girl he has brought home by lacing her drink with LSD (as written, she has a psychotic reaction to marijuana); I thought that would be consistent with the central explosive metaphor, and would also show the darker side of the hero and his cause. But McNally demurred. He saw Tommy exclusively as a victim. This took the bite out of his play, and when it was restaged off-Broadway the following season, even the Lincoln Center scenes were gone.

Our fourth production that year was scheduled to be *The Tempest.* A graduate student at the School of Music had persuaded me that the score Henry Purcell had written for the seventeenth-century operatic version could be a lovely counterpoint to Shakespeare's play. I in turn was able to persuade Clifford Williams to undertake the project after he completed his all-male *As You Like It* with the Royal Shakespeare Company. When Williams arrived in town to begin rehearsals, however, he confessed that—excited as he had been by the idea in theory—he couldn't for the life of him figure out how to combine Baroque music with Jacobean verse. After two days of discussion he felt obliged to abandon the project and return to England.

Once again I found myself playing the role of an understudy director. I had just finished doing *The Revenger's Tragedy,* but no other directors were prepared to undertake a production on such short notice. Because our subscribers were expecting *The Tempest,* I thought we were compelled to offer a Shakespeare play in its place. Lee Richardson had already been contracted to play Prospero; since he was available, I decided to do *Macbeth.*

Persuading Richardson to undertake this role was none too easy. Like most actors, he was superstitious about the "Scottish play" (in the theatre, one is not even supposed to name it), fearing some divine retribution if he defied the legend. But like most actors, he eventually found the part too juicy to turn down. Betsy Parrish, who had been playing supporting roles, deserved a crack at something substantial, Lady Macbeth. And with Jeremy Geidt playing Duncan, David Ackroyd as Macduff, James Naughton as Malcolm, and Carmen de Lavallade as Lady Macduff, I thought we had the nucleus of a strong cast.

I decided to do *Macbeth* partly because I thought I had an exciting new concept for it. I had lately been reading a lot of science fiction, and after finishing Arthur C. Clarke's *Childhood's End,* I began to look at Macbeth's description of the weird sisters—"What are these/So withered, and so wild in their attire/That look not like th' inhabitants o' th' earth/And yet are on't"—with different eyes. Not like the inhabitants of the earth! What if (I thought) the weird sisters were *not* inhabitants of the earth but creatures from another world? What if they had come down to Earth from another planet—like the Overlords in *Childhood's End*—to influence the course of terrestrial history? The more I looked at the play in this context, the more excited I became. This interpretation, for example, provided solutions for some of the problems that have plagued commentators—like the identity of the third murderer. He could be one of the weird creatures, materializing in human form to save the life of Banquo's son in order to alter the line of Scottish succession. I decided to set the play in prehistoric times, when men wore the skins of animals and ate their meat raw. It would take place at Stonehenge in front of those mysterious dolmens, now transformed into alien spaceships, which the creatures inhabit and then abandon to Earth after the death of Macbeth. I didn't realize until later how difficult it would be to integrate the primitive setting with Shakespeare's sophisticated verse.

Once again I was trying to demonstrate that the theatre was an arena for myth-making. I was entranced with the creative possibilities of Clarke's theory that certain human myths—say, the idea of a red horned devil with a pitchfork tail—are actually primitive memories, activated by early encounters with alien beings, which then enter history in distorted form. This I was eager to synthesize with the notion that great works of art, such as Shakespeare's plays, are themselves a form of myth that must be revitalized in each succeeding age. One showed one's love for *Macbeth* by trying to see it freshly, in the light of contemporary thought.

What a concept! What a mistake! In the grip of an idea, I once again neglected to pay sufficient attention to the acting values which, particularly in American Shakespeare, require an enormous amount of support. And even assuming I had a workable concept, we simply did not have the technical means to execute it. To get the effect of the weird sisters materializing on the dolmens, we had to project movies on the surface of Leo Yoshimura's set, but the films we made were crude and overexposed. And our inadequate lighting system did not help us create the "beaming down" effect (stolen from *Star Trek*) that was necessary to turn the creatures into human figures. I began to long for the kind of technology I saw in Disney World—the holograms in the Haunted House exhibit, for example—thus betraying my own conviction that the stage is always more exciting when it uses its own simple means.

The production attracted some favorable local reviews, and for the first time in our history, we were playing to full capacity. But the divine retribution that Richardson feared came in the form of an angry notice from Clive Barnes, who called our production "inept" and accused me of putting myself forward on the level of Peter Brook. Barnes had always had a certain proprietary interest in our company. "I love the Yale Repertory Theatre," he wrote in his negative notice of *The Revenger's Tragedy*, "If I had a chance . . . to run a repertory theatre, Mr. Brustein's company is precisely the company I would run." In his review of *Macbeth,* he seemed to be doing precisely that. After praising my talents as a critic, he not only roasted the production but delivered a lengthy lecture to me on my conduct of the entire theatre, concluding: "I am certain that if he brought a critical rather than a paternal eye to this production its faults and fallacies would be instantly apparent to him."

It was the beginning of a long battle, which I couldn't possibly win. I dashed off a letter to Barnes, asking how he could be certain I was unaware of the faults of the production or that I brought a "proudly paternal eye" to the works of the Rep. Vas you dere, Cholly? Was unfounded speculation the province of *The New York Times?* I don't believe I was simply reacting to a negative notice. I thought he had exceeded the privileges of his position. When he panned our production of *Three Sisters* in 1968, I had written thanking him for his review because I thought his comments were helpful to our theatre. But this was something different, and I don't think I was being paranoid in suspecting that Barnes had now turned hostile. I had noticed lately that while lavishing praise on the most meretricious Broadway product, Barnes was also prone to savage anything with a little intellectual content, such as the plays of Bernard Shaw or the productions of Jonathan Miller. I thought it conceivable that his recent attacks on me were motivated by extratheatrical impulses.

I was in the vulnerable position of being an ex-critic who was now running a practical theatre. This had obvious advantages, but it also made me a mark for all my former colleagues. Being able to distinguish between honest assessments and opportunistic attacks was a subjective business at best, and I don't claim to be any better at speculation than others. All I can say is that certain reviews struck me as suspicious, especially when accompanied by large generalizations. I admit I was growing defensive—partly on behalf of my own reputation, but mostly on behalf of the Theatre, which was highly visible, uncertain of survival, relatively defenseless, often forced to take the rap for me.

But it wasn't hostile critics who threatened the survival of the theatre that year, it was our friend and benefactor, Joseph E. Levine. He had mailed us a check for $25,000 in September, then simply neglected to send the remaining $75,000. Levine didn't respond to my letters; he wasn't in for my phone calls.

I had heard that as a result of the failure of his last few pictures he was now in financial trouble. So were we. I sent him a letter thanking him for his generosity in the past and imploring him to honor his pledge, lest we lose our Theatre. No reply. Through the grapevine, I learned that he was dissatisfied with the kind of plays we did; after I had stupidly invited him to see *The Revenger's Tragedy,* he had complained to a mutual friend about "all those boring Greek plays." In a last, admittedly desperate move, I wrote him a totally outrageous letter designed to arouse his Jewish guilt—or shame. I told him of how proud I had been that among the Rockefellers, Mellons, and Fords identified as supporters of the Yale Repertory Theatre, there was the name of Joseph E. Levine. Would he be the only one of this distinguished roster to be guilty of reneging on a pledge?

I was not surprised to receive no reply to this letter either. Months later came a phone call. "That was some letter you wrote me," said Levine hoarsely. "That was some pickle you put us in," I replied. "The thing is," he said, "I never told you I was giving any money to a *theatre.* I thought that money was going to a *film school.*" I paused to relax my jaws. "Joe," I said, "We *have* no film school. It was always understood that your money was pledged to the Yale Repertory Theatre. Don't you remember our talk in Greenwich last fall about how I needed the funds to pay the salaries of the actors?" "Oh," he said. It was his turn to pause. "Well, whaddya need for a film school?" "Ten million dollars," I replied testily. "Oh," he said. "I'll call you back." He never did.

Through the loss of this anticipated $75,000, and through our own misman-agement, we were in the hole that year to the tune of $110,000. It was the first —and last—time we showed a deficit of any substance at the Yale Repertory Theatre, though the School was always authorized to lose between $200,000 and $300,000 annually, made up by General Appropriations to supplement the income from our meager $1 million endowment. Because everything at Yale was being cut back because of a growing financial crunch, I thought this deficit meant we were finished. It was always tacitly understood that the university tolerated the Theatre as long as it didn't cost anything, and here we were, with a nice hefty debt and no cushion to absorb our first plunge into insolvency. Brewster came to our rescue with some discretionary funds and paid our outstanding bills—warning that the university must never be called upon again to save our skin. I consented to this with sheepish gratitude, feeling a little like a careless teenager who had overdrawn his checking account and couldn't have a date with his girl on the weekend until the account was replenished.

Most of this season Alvin Epstein had been absent from the company. After playing in *Story Theatre Repertory* in the fall, he had taken a leave to join Millie Dunnock at Long Wharf in a Marguerite Duras play, *A Place Without Doors.* I was not too happy about this, and vainly tried to dissuade him from leaving. What gave our work its style was our actors, and this style was distinctly different from that of other theatres. For one of our leading actors to shuttle back and forth between the Rep and the Long Wharf was to muddy the genuine distinctions that had developed between us, like Nureyev bouncing between a modern dance company and the New York City Ballet. Alvin disagreed. He believed actors should have the opportunity to act with a variety of companies if the roles were good. I argued that the National Theatre and the Royal Shakespeare Company rarely shared the same performers; he argued that Israeli theatres did. He thought of actors more as free-lance artists; I thought of them more as contributing members of a close collective. It was selfish of me, no doubt, to suggest limits on an actor's freedom, but I was trying to maintain the identity of our theatre, and I knew of no other way than through a permanent company.

My fears regarding Epstein's temporary departure were exacerbated when Arvin Brown, director of the Long Wharf, offered James Naughton a role in his forthcoming New York production of *A Long Day's Journey Into Night.* At the time Naughton was not only performing in *Macbeth* but rehearsing our next production. We had certain contractual agreements with Naughton, but to exercise these would only have created bad feeling. Wasn't this a splendid opportunity for a newly graduated actor to further his career in New York? As the dean of a school, I could feel proud of Jimmy; as the director of a theatre, I felt raided. It was as difficult for me to reconcile these conflicting feelings as it was to integrate my different functions. I let Naughton go, grumpily, and asked Arvin Brown to please talk to me first before he dangled another juicy opportunity in front of one of our actors under contract. As an artistic director himself, he must have known how hard it was to bond a permanent company in the face of raids from the commercial theatre.

My anxieties were somewhat relieved when Epstein returned in the spring to play the title role in Büchner's *Woyzeck,* which we were producing on a double bill with Beckett's *Play.* More significant was his involvement, as director, in another twin bill that season, *The Seven Deadly Sins* and *The Little Mahagonny.* This was our first full-scale Brecht-Weill production. It was also our first collaboration with the School of Music that provided us with a conductor, an orchestra, and a few dollars with which to pay them. Michael Feingold had written a terse, biting translation of the eight songs that comprised *The Little Mahagonny,* which was directed by Michael Posnick; and Carmen de Lavallade worked closely with Epstein in devising the choreography for *The Seven Deadly Sins.* The latter was conceived in Story Theatre style, with Betsy Parrish playing the singing Anna and Carmen the dancing Anna, but a few days before the opening, Carmen developed appendicitis and went into surgery. Her role was filled by Stephanie Cotsirilos with grace and gallantry, but we revived this very successful production the following year so that Carmen could be given the opportunity to play it. This happy experience with Brecht and Weill—itself an outgrowth of the Epstein-Schlamme Cabaret —was the beginning of a long relationship that was to deepen over the subsequent years.

The final production of that year worth noting was a School presentation of Jerzy Kosinski's *Steps;* it was noteworthy primarily for the presence of the author. Kosinski had joined our faculty in September, teaching a course called "the dramatic and literary dimensions of a fictive event" in exchange for a very small salary and an apartment in Davenport College. After reading *The Painted Bird,* I had been most impressed by his powerful talent, and thought he might just have a play in him. Kosinski, in turn, had admired my stand during the Panther crisis, and expressed a desire to help improve the writing style of our students. I found him an enchanting but very mysterious human being, who seemed to pride himself most on being an escape artist. He used to keep a complete survival kit in the trunk of his battered car, including inflatable rafts, tents, canned food, and hardware, as if preparing himself for instant flight. If you visited him in his New York apartment, he would disappear somewhere in that very small area and challenge you to find him (no one has yet discovered his hiding place). His concentration on survival made him a most touching figure—shy and reticent, yet capable of overcoming muggers; fragile and sickly, yet with the eyes and beak of a predatory eagle. One never remembered that he was a tall man, so cadaverous was his appearance. When Norma and I would eat a meal with him and his friend, Kiki, all of us worried like parents over his appetite and his health, forcibly restraining an impulse to chew up his food for him like a mother bird.

Kosinski, as it turned out, was less interested in teaching playwriting than copyrighting. Aside from imparting a rigorous unsentimental prose style, his greatest contribution to our students was the secret of protecting literary works from plagiary and theft. Having escaped from an East European bureaucracy, he was an expert in bureaucratic procedures. He advised his students to stamp each page of their manuscripts with seals of copyright, and he himself designed his own certificates—complete with huge red seals with ribbons hanging from them—to show authorities. At this time Kosinski had no interest in seeing his books adapted for the stage or screen, but he did give permission to one of our most gifted doctoral students, Rocco Landesman, to try his hand at an adaptation of *Steps.* We decided to try this out in the University Theatre as a project for Richard Gilman.

Gilman had done a very crisp production of *Transformations* the previous season, but he had not gotten along very well with the actors or staff, some of whom were refusing to work with him again at the Rep. I thought by asking him to do *Steps* with a student cast at the University Theatre, I could help extend his directorial experience without bringing down the wrath of the company. I'm afraid that Gilman, a proud man, took this as a humiliation. Anyhow, it was a mistake. The production had some merit, but it was spasmodic and unfocused, partly no doubt because of the nature of the novel. Kosinski attended the opening night, in obvious agony, hunched down in his seat, his coat at the ready for instant flight.

I had completed a five-year term as dean of the School of Drama, and for the first time things were going well enough for me to contemplate renewing. The students were beginning to take real pride in the Repertory Theatre and helping to improve its quality. A new spirit of cooperation was taking the place of the old acrimonious atmosphere. I was convinced at last of forward movement, and I could see the fruits of development in the strong changing faces of the young and the old.

I thought I had reason to be proud. I also knew that the work was far from completed. I could either leave New Haven with my family, as originally planned, or take another five-year term, as Brewster wished. After considerable deliberation I decided to temporize. I went to Kingman and told him I was willing to serve another three years.

VI

Our Own Come into Their Own 1971-1972

Solness: Some day, the luck must turn, you see.
Dr. Herdal: Oh, nonsense, what should make it turn?
Solness: (*firm and sure*) It'll come from the younger generation.

—Ibsen, *The Master Builder*

I accepted the modified term only on the understanding that Brewster would help me find a substantial endowment over the next three years that would finally put the School and the Theatre on a firm financial footing. I wanted to make fund-raising a secondary concern rather than the prime demand of my daily routine. The system we called pump-priming—raising short-term grants each year to subsidize our work—was not a very sensible method of operation, and it was draining our energies. After our brush with extinction, none of us was eager to risk this danger again. By saving our skins at the last moment, Brewster had given me time to scratch up enough grants to last us maybe two or three years. Now I was asking the university to use this time to assume some continuing responsibility, finally, for this anomaly in its midst.

"I can say now," I wrote to Brewster, "that we have a training situation which is unique in the United States. It is continuing to blossom and bear fruit, and to spread its tendrils throughout the theatres of America. It has survived student unrest, faculty dissension, competing goals, logistical confusions, philosophical disagreements, and all the other troubles of our time to develop an essentially unified, productive, and creative direction. It now needs to be recognized by the University, and by the sons of the University, in the form of substantial and generous endowments. For the idea of this theatre has become a reality; it can be destroyed now only by indifference and neglect."

In my opening address to the School in September of 1971, I told them that the theme of this particular theatre season was . . . money. After the grants raised during my administrative leave were expended, we were going to be in trouble, and I was at a loss as to where to turn next. The Rockefeller Foundation—having given almost a million dollars to the School and the Rep—was advising me to ask for no more. And I was not having significant success either with government agencies, corporations, individual patrons, or other foundations. The private foundations were beginning to pull back on their funding of the arts, and the National Endowment for the Arts, on which many of us had pinned our hopes, was advancing too slowly to constitute an adequate alternative. Worse, it was gradually becoming politicized. I sat on the theatre panel for two years, and watched the professional panelists' concern for quality slowly being eroded by a competing concern on the part of the official functionaries for geographical distribution and representation by various political pressure groups, including unions and minority lobbies.

In addition to our other problems, we seemed to be hamstrung by our name; the word "Yale" in our title was a signal to lock up the cash register. The largest local grant-giving agency, the New Haven Foundation, gave the Long Wharf substantial subsidies each year, but continually rejected our applications because it considered us a Yale responsibility. The Connecticut Commission on the Arts—a state-funded agency—was also loath to support us, except in a token manner, for fear of arousing resentment from the citizenry and opposition from the legislature. As for local corporations, they saw no profit in giving money to a theatre associated with a university whose students burned flags and set fire to buildings. All of these agencies knew perfectly well that the Yale Repertory Theatre was a semiautonomous arts institution responsible for its own survival. It was how we were *perceived* that concerned them more than the reality. For the hundredth time, I contemplated changing our name.

Our university affiliation proved an obstacle of quite a different kind with the Ford Foundation. Traditionally the largest source of support for the arts, Ford had begun a process of generous subsidy to virtually every professional resident theatre in the country through its "cash reserve" program, designed to provide ready cash flow to financially besieged performing arts organizations. We were never able to qualify under the guidelines of this program because, we were told, we did not have a separate system of accounting. I suspected that this was a bureaucratic pretext to enforce the prejudice of McNeil Lowry, Ford's vice president in charge of the arts, toward university-sponsored theatre. During a speech made to graduate deans in 1963, Lowry had publicly declared his belief that the arts were incapable of functioning in an academic setting, largely because the university was devoted to amateur standards. I shared his anxieties over the university's relationship to the arts. This was one of my motives for trying to professionalize the Yale Drama School. It was also why I closed the acting classes to undergraduates. Instead of rewarding this effort, and helping to improve the situation, Lowry devised grants guidelines that were guaranteed to make his fears a self-fulfilling prophecy.

I paid repeated visits to his office, where I was always treated with great courtesy, and always came away empty-handed. (Joseph Papp and the New

York Shakespeare Festival received a similar treatment, though for different reasons.) For a few years, I accepted these rejections quietly, hoping the situation would change; finally persuaded I had nothing further to lose, I began to protest his decisions by letter. Our correspondence grew heated. At one point I began sending copies of our letters to McGeorge Bundy, then head of the foundation, and soon started writing Bundy directly. Thoroughly frustrated by what I perceived to be a bureaucratic smoke screen, I offered to set up an expensive separate accounting system for the Theatre, if that would satisfy the guidelines. Bundy courteously replied that the cash reserve grant was for "independent nonprofit artistic enterprises" with an "independently responsible budgetary and financial organization." Drowning in procedures, I started gasping for air. I had no way to appeal Bundy's decision, but I protested that it was shortsighted of him to talk about "independent" theatres as the only ones worthy of a Ford grant: "These theatres are no longer 'independent,' " I added. "They depend for their artists and personnel to a large extent on the training conservatories now functioning at the university." With the exception of the Rockefeller Foundation, no major foundation— including the National Endowment for the Arts—had yet recognized the relationship of these conservatories to the ongoing work of the resident theatres. And I couldn't even get Ford to recognize the value of our resident theatre until after Mr. Lowry retired, by which time it was too late to do me much good.

Despite our economic problems, we decided in the fall of 1971 to enter a system of rotating repertory. We had flirted with the system before, but never on a regular basis. Now we would finally earn the right to our name. This was an important decision, albeit a difficult one; every year we would question it, and every year we would reaffirm it. Rotating repertory is always more expensive than sequential production, not only because of the cost of changeover but also because of the need for a larger resident company. Then, our church theatre was not very appropriate for such a system, having no fly space, no storage space, and virtually no wings. Some actors don't like the system because it requires them to work on at least two roles at a time; playwrights resent it because it prevents them from having ideal casts; directors resist it because it divides their rehearsal time; designers are unhappy with it because it limits them to sets that are easily struck; the technical crew complains about it because they have to work twice as hard as usual, building, running, and changing the scenery; and the subscribers are confused by it because they are not always sure what they are going to see.

Why bother, then? Well, for one thing, rotating repertory keeps you honest. If you are performing three plays a week and rehearsing a fourth, it is impossible to dislodge a popular production from the season and produce it in New York. For another thing, the system keeps the company cooking, whatever its complaints. Playing a variety of roles in a short space of time is the way an actor stretches; it's impossible to grow lazy when you have to work up two or three characterizations in the course of a single week. Then, the audience learns there are other satisfactions in the theatre besides seeing hits—watching the progress of a theatre, for example, from play to play, or an actor's development from part to part. And finally, the system allows a stranger in the city to see as many as three different productions on a single weekend visit.

But perhaps the greatest advantage of the repertory system is an undefinable one, related to its very hardships and difficulties. Paul Sills had shown us that the most imaginative art was inspired by the most severe limitation; repertory taught us that as well. When a designer knows that he can only use a space in a particular way, that becomes a spur to the imagination. I am thoroughly convinced that the distinctive emblematic style of Yale designers—and their devotion to visual metaphor rather than representational settings—was a direct result of our limited stage and our restrictive repertory system. These virtually prohibited us from creating an illusionistic theatre, even if we had wanted to. For us, then, rotating repertory had the quality of a Jesuit discipline, toughening our sinews, sparking our spirits, giving us strength and inspiration and daring.

The initial works presented under this system were Ibsen's *When We Dead Awaken* and Lonnie Carter's farce *The Big House.* David Hurst and Nancy Wickwire, two veterans from our first season, were returning to play Rubek and Irene in the Ibsen play, which was directed by a young instructor from the acting and directing department named Tom Haas. I directed *The Big House* with a cast that included Jeremy Geidt, Betsy Parrish, and the comedian Dick Shawn.

Possibly because we were still working out the kinks in the system, neither production was particularly distinguished. In *When We Dead Awaken,* Haas decided to use a live string quartet to provide the bridge music, background accompaniment, and sound effects; it also substituted for the noise of the avalanche at the end. It was a nice idea in theory, but in practice the music made the proceedings seem more torpid than tempestuous; the dead never managed to awaken. Rubek and Irene should go out in thunder; instead, they went out to the accompaniment of two violins, a viola, and a cello sawing away on the upper stage at Beethoven's Fifteenth Quartet. Visually, the avalanche was represented by dropping a huge white sheet over the two central characters. It floated wistfully down to the concluding strains of the music while Norma muttered something in my ear about a *schmatta* (Yiddish for cheap rag).

The Big House ran into storms that were more political than aesthetic. With my ineffable sense of timing, I opened the play just after the prison riots began at Attica, and it was performed during the brutal weeks that followed—hardly the best background for a lighthearted jailhouse farce. The play was inspired by the Marx Brothers, but unfortunately, none of them was a member of the company that season. Jeremy Geidt decided to play the Italian character with a faint Cockney accent, and our Harpo ran around the stage shooting Silly String over his pursuers. Betsy Parrish did a fine rendition of a large-bosomed Margaret Dumont dowager, and Dick Shawn, as the Groucho figure, was outrageously funny in his inimitable way, beginning the second act with a fifteen-minute mime scene during which he washed his hair onstage. But the production was a bizarre mixture of Marx Brothers impersonations and modern farce procedures that never achieved the comic nostalgia I had envisioned.

Still, *The Big House* had a lot of pace and speed and energy, and it was generally enjoyed by those who didn't feel guilty laughing. Others believed we had committed a breach of taste by producing the play in the midst of the Attica uprising. One of these was Mel Gussow, who reviewed the production for *The New York Times*. His notice was essentially positive, but he concluded with a stern admonition: "While acknowledging Mr. Brustein's directorial contribution to the enterprise, one has to question his decision as an artistic director, to present a lighthearted prison spoof—especially today." This remark reminded me of something, which I couldn't quite recall for a while. Finally I remembered. It was my student, during the *Sidewinder* crisis, telling me to leave certain books on the shelf "until a better time." We had still not disengaged ourselves from the sixties, when certain subjects were politically taboo. Needless to say, I had no hint when we started rehearsing *The Big House* that Attica was going to blow up; but even had I known, I would not have considered dropping the show. I shared the general outrage over Governor Rockefeller's handling of the crisis. I also believed that laughter could be an effective, if temporary, antidote to the troubles of the times, even at the risk of wounding sensibilities.

Still, arguments with critics are never very productive, and this time, at least, I kept my trap shut. I kept it shut, too, after Clive Barnes in his review of *When We Dead Awaken* attacked Michael Feingold's "pedestrian" translation, and added these penetrating observations: "Admittedly this is a notoriously difficult play to translate—its very high-flown prose can easily degenerate into pseudo-poetic ramblings—but something more could be done, and has been done, than this almost stubbornly prosaic effort." Since almost everybody else had found Feingold's "stubbornly prosaic effort" to be a particularly lyrical rendering of the play, this comment struck us as a little odd. It seemed even more odd seven years later when Barnes reviewed a production of the same play in the same translation in Springfield, and wrote: "The translation, first commissioned by the Yale Drama School by Michael Feingold, is a distinct asset. Mr. Feingold contrives to make Ibsen sound like a contemporary playwright and yet manages to maintain a special historic perspective in the adaptation." Apparently, Mr. Barnes found variations in the quality of Feingold's translation according to where and by whom it was performed.

Mr. Barnes was entitled to his opinions, no matter how self-contradictory they may have been, but we usually breathed a sigh of relief when we heard that Mel Gussow was coming to review our work, not because we found him more perceptive, but because we believed him to be more disinterested. Obviously, our concern over newspaper reviews was growing. We had begun by discouraging the New York critics from coming to Yale. We soon learned that we needed them almost as much as the commercial theatre, though for different reasons. They had little effect on our box office, but they exerted a great deal of influence on the funding agencies. Most foundations did not have the staff to visit applicant theatres and evaluate their work, so they based their judgment on newspaper reviews! This meant that—as far as the press was concerned—we were still inside the system. We were forced to invite critics to our productions for the sake of our very survival.

As a critic myself, I could hardly denigrate the value of good criticism. But I had always regretted the powerful influence that the New York press exerted on the morale, not to mention the existence, of New York productions (this was the reason I once turned down an offer to become the theatre critic of *The New York Times*). I have never been able to shake the memory of watching someone climb on top of a table at Sardi's, after the opening of a Broadway play, to read aloud the *Times* review to everyone present. It was a pan, and one saw the pleasure drain from the faces of the producers and performers like fresh rainwater down a city sewer. Some of these people had spent months working on this production; in a moment, with a single notice, their labors had been rendered futile and their employment terminated.

Our own theatre had been conceived as an alternative to that wasteful system, and yet we could not manage to extricate ourselves entirely from its traps. Torn between my convictions and my obligations, I grew terribly divided about how and whether to use reviews in advertising our plays (my ambivalence used to drive our good-natured press officer, Jan Geidt, into spasms). It was our policy not to use critical quotes in our advertisements; but I would occasionally authorize republishing a favorable notice in its entirety to offset a particularly bad one. This was done primarily for reasons of morale —even in New Haven a dismissive review in a New York paper can affect the energy of the actors—but it was nevertheless an inconsistency. I knew that to reprint a good notice in an institutional ad was to validate, by implication, a bad notice. It was also to assign an importance to reviewers that permanent theatres shouldn't recognize. On the other hand, I had a duty to protect the members of my company whose careers were being affected—and I had a duty to protect my theatre too.

On this particular issue the DFA students were the conscience of the Rep. In training as critics themselves, they nevertheless argued vigorously against the use of any critical quotes, believing this demeaned the dignity of a serious theatre. Naturally, the actors took the opposite view. They believed that favorable quotes were the way to attract large audiences, and they were the ones who had to cope with half-filled houses. My own position was equivocal. I sympathized with the problems of the actors, but I disagreed about the power of reviews. Whatever their effect on the foundations, they seemed to have little influence with our audiences, who responded more to word of mouth. It was not an important issue, really, but it was one that reflected a larger problem.

Another symptom of this problem was the issue of billing, and here the DFA's, puristic about quotes, proved just as insistent as the actors. There was no difficulty about the company roster, which listed everybody in alphabetical order (in the program, the actors were listed in the order of their appearance). The difficulty had to do with our posters. These were handsome designs over which we all took a lot of trouble, their function being largely to act as a semipermanent souvenir of a woefully temporary event. Our custom was to identify the play, the playwright, the director, and the designers, accompanied by a graphic appropriate to the occasion. The actors complained, however, that if directors and designers were mentioned, then they should be mentioned too, and the dramaturges were also eager to see their names in print. There was some justice to these demands, but to concede them would have created a cumbersome poster. Soon the student actors would be asking for recognition too. The whole question of billing was an inheritance from the commercial theatre, where contracts often stipulate how large the actor's name is printed, whether or not it is boxed, and where it appears in relation to the title. I had little patience with the credit issue, and felt a little dejected that it arose at all. Finally I managed to settle the matter by removing everything from the poster but the name of the play, the playwright, and the theatre, a solution that seemed to satisfy the company. True, the inclusion of the playwright's name was a potential source of controversy, but it was one that, happily, never came up.

What, happily, did come up for our next production was a young actor named Christopher Walken. His performance in the title role of Albert Camus's *Caligula* was the acting highlight of the season. Walken actually was a replacement for Frank Langella, whom Alvin Epstein, the director, had originally cast in the part. When Langella walked out on the first day of rehearsal (he claimed that he had not been consulted about the translation), we learned of Walken's availability and interest, and cast him immediately. Both Alvin and I had been impressed by his performance in *A Lion in Winter,* where he transformed a relatively conventional character into a figure of mystery and depth, and both of us thought these were exactly the right qualities for Caligula. Walken's extraordinary physical beauty combined with a reticent touch of menace gave him the look of an angelic hood. His masked eyes and irresistible smile, his catlike grace and unexpected emotional swerves made him an actor you were always compelled to watch. He embodied the danger of the theatre, its unearthly reversals. He was simply incapable of making a graceless movement or a boring choice.

When *Caligula* opened, our students immediately sensed that something unusual was happening; so did a large number of Yale undergraduates who came to see Walken's performance as many as six and seven times. Like Marlon Brando's Stanley Kowalski, Walken's interpretation of Caligula had the power to change the style of an entire generation. Students, mesmerized, watched him pull this mercurial character through an endless variety of moods —and spied on him offstage as he loped along Chapel Street in his Napoleonic greatcoat and trailing scarf, peering inquisitively into the windows of New Haven's schlock stores. Walken was a totally dedicated performer who worked on his role night and day; he was willing to go anywhere for a good classical part. Having begun his career as a gypsy dancer in musical comedy—the source, no doubt, of his supple movement—he had had no opportunity for formal training. As an actor, Walken was an autodidact. He told me he had taught himself to speak verse by reading aloud through Shakespeare's collected works, one play a day, every morning of his adult life. Whatever the case, it was obvious we had an acting genius in our midst. After *Caligula,* I tried to bring him back to Yale in every subsequent year—unsuccessfully, until we collaborated in 1978, as director and actor, on a production of *The Wild Duck.*

After *Caligula,* the Rep exploded with activity. First came a *Repertory Holiday,* consisting of three separate programs in swift succession: a reprise of *The Seven Deadly Sins* and *The Little Mahagonny,* a double bill of two short plays by Robert Auletta and Edward Bond, and an evening of Jacques Brel songs, arranged and performed by Norma's talented undergraduates. Next came the American premiere of Natalia Ginzburg's domestic farce, *I Married You for the Fun of It,* in a fine new translation by John Hersey, followed by a sumptuous production of Calderón's metaphysical *Life Is a Dream.* Our final production of that year was the American premiere, twenty-three years after it was first written, of *Happy End,* a German play by Elizabeth Hauptmann with lyrics and music by Bertolt Brecht and Kurt Weill.

Happy End contained some of the most haunting songs in the Brecht-Weill canon, but it was rarely performed after its scandalous premiere in Berlin in 1929, partly because Brecht disowned it, partly because Lotte Lenya, who, as Weill's widow, controlled the music rights, thought the book too feeble to expose to the public. When Lenya visited Yale to see our production of *Seven Deadly Sins,* I capitalized on her enthusiasm for that production (and for Feingold's new translation of the songs in *The Little Mahagonny*) with a proposition. If we could come up with an adaptation of *Happy End* that satisfied her, would she permit us to stage the play? Lenya kindly consented, and Michael Feingold began to work on the book and the lyrics.

His adaptation proved entirely satisfactory to Lenya, who shared our enthusiasm for its terse, idiomatic Chicago flavor and Keystone Kop devices. Although the show never pretended to be anything more than a light entertainment, a kind of precursor to *Guys and Dolls,* I thought it was eminently worthy of production, if only for the sake of hearing its extraordinary songs (including "The Bilbao Song," "Surabaya Johnny," "Mandalay," and "The Sailor's Song"). The play was well directed by former student Michael Posnick and beautifully performed and sung by an amiable company; it extended our reach into the Brecht-Weill literature; and it helped restore a "lost" play to the American repertoire. It proved a happy end, indeed, to our entire season.

Happy End was very well reviewed, both locally and nationally—in the *Times* it was covered by both Walter Kerr and Mel Gussow. To our immense relief, Clive Barnes had not reviewed our work since the first production of the season, *When We Dead Awaken,* but he was very much on my mind, as he was on the minds of most people working in the theatre. Barnes was obviously an intelligent man, but something had grown seriously wrong with his critical posture. I suspect he was torn between a perception of the low quality of most American theatre and an awareness of his capacity to destroy it through the medium of a powerful newspaper. At any rate, he had apparently decided to abandon his former standards and indulge in manifestly insincere praise, with the result that his critical language had grown confused and contradictory, as if he were engaged in an internal argument over his own values. (Typical of this was his review of a play done in Washington as "precisely the kind of gorgeous mediocrity we need on Broadway"). I didn't think this was doing the American theatre much good; in fact, I believed it was destroying both his credibility and that of the plays he was praising.

Consequently, when invited to speak at Boston University that spring on the subject of freedom of expression, I decided—against all advice—to discuss the new permissiveness on the American stage in the context of its undiscriminating reception by American theatre critics, Mr. Barnes in particular. The speech cited some of the more flagrant examples of his hyperbolic prose, and documented a few of his many self-contradictions and inconsistencies. "Obviously," I commented, "no theatre can benefit in the long run from fake approval, partly because the critic becomes discredited, partly because the spectator grows disenchanted, partly because the theatre practitioner begins to lose faith in his craft. . . . The marriage that must exist in any art form between the mind that creates and the mind that responds has begun to dissolve in the theatre, with the result that the art form itself is in danger of losing its purpose and direction." I published this speech in *The New Republic* under the title "Freedom and Constraint in the American Theatre."

Coming little more than a year after Barnes's review of *Macbeth,* these remarks could have been construed as sour grapes; Barnes certainly so construed them. Perhaps there was an element of retaliation in my speech; if so, it was unconscious. The only indirect motive I can find in confronting Barnes in public was to bring our differences into the open, so that he might find it more difficult in future to review our productions. For I had become convinced, rightly or wrongly, that his attacks on the Yale Repertory company were really aimed at me, and I hoped, by challenging him directly, that he would turn his wrath on me instead of trying to hit me through the theatre. Anyhow, my plan failed. Instead of accepting my challenge (and thus disqualifying himself from reviewing the company), he began with renewed dedication to batter away at Yale productions, and at any Yale graduates that were working in New York. Which is not to say that I didn't get to throw a few punches myself.

My instinct for confrontation was exercised in other ways that year—both instances of antiwar activity. The first was theatrical, and followed the Mylai massacre in Vietnam. With Michael Feingold and Jeremy Geidt acting as dramaturgs, the company decided to stage a protest in the best way they knew how—through a production mounted on the day off. A theatre special was organized called *The War Show,* with the proceeds going to the children of Vietnam. Company members contributed speeches, poems, and dances to the occasion; Carmen de Lavallade, for example, gave her first showing of a stunning new work she had developed with her husband, Geoffrey Holder, called "The Creation." Alvin Epstein and Michael Feingold read some verse. Jeremy Geidt did "If the cause be not good" from *Henry V.* I did the Burgundy peace speech from the same play, along with a selection from Philip Roth's *Our Gang*—the first, but not the last, time I impersonated Richard Nixon.

My second opportunity for confrontation was political. I had received a call from a Yale colleague, around the time of *The War Show,* inviting me to participate in a Washington protest called "Redress." The idea was to deliver a petition for the redress of grievances to the halls of Congress. Since only Congress had the constitutional power to declare war, the Vietnam conflict was illegal; the petition asked Congress to stop the war through legislative action. Though undoubtedly fruitless, this plan seemed like a plausible and legitimate way to keep the pressure on our representatives to do something about the senseless, endless, brutal, and divisive Indochina conflict, and I had no hesitation about adding my name to the others on the list.

When I arrived in Washington, however, I discovered that the sponsors of the "Redress" movement had other things in mind. Robert Jay Lifton, addressing the meeting in a Washington hotel, informed us that we were to march to Congress en masse, deliver the petition, and then sit down in the congressional corridors until our demands were acted on. We received printed instructions regarding how to behave when arrested, what to bring to prison, and whom to call for legal advice; we were even advised to keep a dime handy for the telephone. I was sitting next to Joe Papp when this news was broken; we looked at each other wanly. I asked him if he had come there to get arrested; Papp merely shrugged.

I raised my hand to tell Bob Lifton that I for one had arrived in Washington under the impression that I was participating in a peaceful protest, not a sit-down strike. We were asking Congress to exercise its legitimate powers in regard to the war. It struck me as entirely inconsistent to follow this with an act of civil disobedience in public buildings. How could we dramatize the need for legal action when we were engaged in illegal action? I feared another good idea was about to be obscured by revolutionary theatre. Dr. Lifton then undertook to explain to me—calmly, moderately, rationally, as to one of his more thickheaded patients—that the "kids" had recently been getting arrested for their convictions and it was time now for the adults to confront the police as well.

The protest proceeded exactly as Dr. Lifton planned. Everybody walked up to the Hill, delivered the petition, and then sat down on their coats until the police pulled them out. (I left the group when the sit-down began, and flew back to New Haven.) They were arrested for a few minutes; the newspapers, as I feared, treated the whole affair as if it were another antiwar prank by some radical chic celebrities. In their eagerness to list the names of those arrested, the reporters didn't even bother to mention what "Redress" was all about. I trust Bob Lifton won a few brownie points with the "kids" as a result of his courageous confrontation with the Washington police.

Protest was gradually winding down that year—in the university as well. At the School, we experienced only one incident of student unrest in the form of a protest from the black students regarding their training and curriculum. These black students now constituted more than 13 percent of the student body. In an effort to increase these proportions, we had moved fast—too fast. Some of the students were not keeping up with the work, and two would be unable to graduate because of academic deficiencies. In April the black students delivered a new set of "demands," including one that insisted on our graduating the delinquent students regardless of their incompletes. This was no doubt the key issue, but corollary demands asked for more black faculty (we now had four), more black plays, and "an end to discrimination against Black students on an integrated stage." They threatened to boycott classes and productions if we didn't satisfy their demands.

This time we didn't hold any meetings. The administration and the faculty, as a body, sent a message to the black students reminding them of the first rule of the Theatre—promptness and attendance at rehearsals and performances— and the first rule of the School—promptness and attendance at classes and productions. If they broke these rules, we told them, they would be considered unprofessional and dismissed. The black students decided to meet their production requirements and returned to classes after a few days' absence. It was then that we sat down to discuss their grievances. We tried, but failed, to identify a single instance of "discrimination" in the casting of plays, and asked the students for clarification on this point. To their charge that blacks were sometimes cast as servants, prostitutes, prisoners, and retainers, we pointed out that white students often played these parts as well, reminding them of instances when blacks were also cast as kings and queens and nobles. It was regrettable that classical plays did not usually include characters of equal social class, but the development of talent would continue to be the sole criterion for casting at the School.

The two black students in academic difficulty failed to get their degrees that year, after being given repeated opportunities to satisfy the requirements, but they graduated after an additional semester when they completed their work. We had managed to adhere to our color-blind principles and standards and also to reaffirm that students do not determine the policies of the School. The whole dispute dissolved after the initial unpleasantness. Indeed, the protest never enjoyed much favor at the School, even among some of the black students. The third-year project—a production of Euripides' *Alcestis*—was distinguished by the participation of these students, who obviously enjoyed it despite some obligatory grumbling. One of the protesting students, an extremely gifted actress, later took a position in an academic theatre department in Utah, where she maintained a stubborn insistence on integrated casting in classical plays.

We had clearly come a long way from the agonies of 1969, and not only in our relations with the black students. The whole program, while it still had its problems, was proving successful in the one way that counted—results. Not only in New Haven but throughout the entire theatre world, the talents of our people were being recognized. Lonnie Carter and Robert Montgomery, two recent graduates in playwriting, received Guggenheim grants, Montgomery having just completed a highly acclaimed production of *Subject to Fits* at the Public Theatre, directed by another former student, A. J. Antoon. Susan Yankowitz's *Terminal* at the Open Theatre had gained considerable recognition, as did David Epstein's *Wanted* at the Judson Church. A. J. Antoon was highly praised for his production of *That Championship Season* (sets by Santo Loquasto), and Tom Moore moved his off-Broadway production of *Grease* to Broadway to begin a long commercial run. Ken Howard had just won a Tony for his performance in *Child's Play;* James Naughton was well received in *A Long Day's Journey Into Night;* Henry Winkler, Jill Eikenberry, and Leslie Roberts were ensconced at the Arena Theatre; Talia Shire was acting in movies. Our designers and technicians were desired by almost every theatre in the country. Our administration students were taking up important positions with major theatre and dance companies. Our DFA students were beginning to publish criticism and to take their places as literary managers with resident companies. A few former students were even starting theatres of their own, such as the Chelsea Theatre and, later, the Manhattan Theatre Club. People everywhere were beginning to look to Yale for the talent and new ideas that would help the American theatre move forward.

My pride was mitigated only by my fatigue. It was time for me to pause. Six years had gone by. On the seventh I took a sabbatical.

INTERMISSION

Abroad
1972-1973

For this relief, much thanks.

—Hamlet

In June of 1972, just following graduation, I drove wildly through the streets of New Haven with my head out the car window, shouting *"Free!"* Passing pedestrians regarded me as if I were mad. The season was over; the term was over. The whole next year would be spent in London. The Yale administration had approved my request for a sabbatical leave at half salary, and I had accepted an invitation to become the guest theatre critic for *The London Observer,* a well-regarded Sunday newspaper. I would be able to write on a regular basis again—something I had sorely missed for six years.

Norma and I also looked forward eagerly to a sustained sojourn in a real city—eating in a variety of restaurants, visiting fine museums, browsing in well-stocked bookshops, watching quality television, shopping in luxury department stores, listening to good music. New Haven was the scene of our work, and considering the circumstances, it was one of the few places in America where our work could have been accomplished in its developmental stages. But New Haven was not a happy place to live. Like many cities of its kind, it had deteriorated badly over the years. During that great progressive surge of social optimism called "urban renewal," the center of the town had been removed by city planners and replaced with a large shopping mall, which now served mainly as a refuge for addicts, pushers, and muggers. Even the main thoroughfares of New Haven were sites of danger. It was eerie wandering through this town in broad daylight without seeing a single solitary soul for two or three blocks. The spacious green where one found virtually the only architectural landmarks in the entire city (aside from New Haven's famous concrete parking facilities) was desolate and abandoned. It was like a city under siege.

The architecture of Yale also discouraged street life. Most of the residential colleges were designed in the style of Gothic castles with moats around them; these acted as confining walls, isolating town from gown. Extremely comfortable for students, the college system attracted people back inside the academic fortress for food and recreation instead of sending them into the city. And when the streets are deserted, something vital vanishes from urban life. Where were the jugglers and street musicians, the outdoor cafés and teeming pedestrian traffic? Not in the rundown neighborhoods of New Haven. A central commercial artery like College Street was becoming a shambles, unvisited by anyone from the college that gave it its name. The stately Taft Hotel was shut down and boarded up, a residence now for the neighborhood rats, and the Shubert Theatre was too inactive to attract many nighttime patrons. Instead of bakeries and bistros, College Street was filled with head shops, fast-food joints, and porno bookstores, a prime site for crime.

A few attractive shops, mostly on Chapel Street, occasionally made an effort to overcome this blight. But New Haven people were either uninterested in quality goods or too frightened to go out and buy them. None of these shops survived, and no new tenants occupied their deserted storefronts. Like many in the Yale community, Norma and I made our lives in our home and in the homes of friends, but this was not an opportunity our actors shared. Many of them lodged in a darkly lit hotel called the Duncan, often developing what our company doctor called the "Duncan syndrome"—depression, psychosomatic symptoms, alcoholism. These circumstances made it hard to attract good actors from New York, and those we did get were not happy with their environment. They were exposed to continual danger walking back from the theatre at night, and they found little hospitality in the homes of the Yale professoriate. Norma and I, and Jan and Jeremy Geidt, did what we could to warm up their lives with some hot meals, theatre gossip, and a homey atmosphere. But for the most part, they felt very lonely in a community that did not welcome them, and New Haven was a downer. It reminded us all of Taganrog, Chekhov's birthplace and the model for all those dreary provincial towns in his plays. And it stimulated arguments, like those between Vershinin and Tusenbach, over whether things would change or be the same in two or three hundred years.

We followed Chekhov's prescription, committing ourselves and others to work as an antidote for an unsatisfying daily life. For similar reasons, we tried to allow nothing to interfere with our summer vacations on the Vineyard and our winter vacations in the sun. Whenever we returned from these sojourns away from New Haven, Norma's moods would darken. While Danny and I unpacked the luggage and read the mail, she would spend hours watering the plants as if she were trying to re-create the natural harmony we had just left. Brewster's desire to have the university provide cultural compensations for what the city lacked encouraged concerts and recitals at the School of Music, interesting exhibits at the Art Gallery, and productions at the School of Drama and Repertory Theatre. But it was amazing to me that this university town had only two bookstores of any consequence, and no radio frequencies devoted to classical music—even the Yale station was dominated by rock and jazz, with classical programming restricted to a few hours on Sunday afternoon. If you wanted to see a first-run American film, you usually had to drive four miles to a movie supermarket in Orange, which reminded Norma of Kennedy Airport. And good dining (though this was later to improve) was limited to a Chinese restaurant—surrounded by a garage, a YMCA, and a vacant lot—and an Italian restaurant in a rundown neighborhood, where somebody once put a rock through the window of our car. As for shopping, you had the choice of an understocked Macy's near the Mall, or a Malley's that sold polyester suits and drip-dry shirts. In fact, about the only unique thing in New Haven, aside from the view from East Rock, was a really first-rate Jewish delicatessen.

Did we complain much about our lives? You bet we did, incessantly. Not usually at the same time, though—this would have made it harder for either of us to accuse the other of self-pity. I can still hear Norma's *"Yeccccccch"* when the New Haven "skyline" came into view on our way up Route 95; I can also hear her charging me with refusing to adapt to the city because I didn't share her familiarity with New Haven streets. She was doing her best to put down roots; I was doing my best to cheer her up when the roots failed to take. Both of us were ashamed of complaining, and tried to come to terms with the given reality.

But it should be obvious why we leaped at the chance to spend a year in London. Much remained to be accomplished at the School and the Theatre, and abandoning them for this lengthy period would be risky; but I knew I would soon be useless to both institutions if I didn't take some time to recover my energies. I needed time, too, to recover my good nature. Howard Stein had recently told me that the bickering in the acting and directing department may have been the result of my scratchy personality, which, he said, was also getting on his nerves. We had been working at close quarters for five years. He needed respite from me, and I needed rest and recreation from the battle. I appointed Stein as acting dean. As acting artistic director, I appointed Alvin Epstein. Epstein was a natural choice artistically, but he had no administrative experience or ambition—I used to kid him that he couldn't even organize his laundry. To give him support and advice in this area, I asked a recently graduated theatre administration student named Robert Orchard to be his assistant. I was confident that between them they could handle any crisis at the Rep, and any crisis at the School could be handled by communicating with me in London through letters and tapes.

I spent the summer preparing the ground for the interim administrators—appointing new faculty, organizing new courses, selecting an interesting season of plays. I felt carefree and relaxed and confident. This was one vacation that would not end in September. Our friends gave us a wonderful going-away party, which we left to board the ferry, waved off by Danny's friends in their Boston Whalers. We spent one day in New Haven, packing our bags, then set sail—first class—on the *France.*

I wanted to give Norma the best trip of her life in gratitude for all that she had given me; I think I succeeded. I have photos of the three of us—Norma and I in evening clothes, Danny in a velvet jacket with my red bow tie—raising champagne glasses in a toast, our table strewn with the remains of a seven-course gourmet dinner that started with a tureen of caviar. We were lolling in shameless luxury. During the day we swam in the large shipboard pool and took refreshing massages, or sat in the sun on deck chairs, bundled in blankets by courteous stewards whose sole purpose in life was to keep us warm and feed us beef bouillon. At night we spent hours gorging down those unforgettable dinners, or went to the movies, or danced up and down the carpeted stairs like Fred Astaire and Ginger Rogers, Norma looking ravishing in a flared polka-dot number we called her "Carioca" gown. We worked up fantasies about spending our old age on the *France,* coddled into oblivion by the uniformed staff, still trying to attack those delicious repasts with our few remaining teeth while cautioning each other not to gum the food. For five delightful days and nights, we pleasured ourselves into unconsciousness, convinced that after six long years in New Haven, we fully deserved every minute of this hedonistic orgy.

The rest of the year held pleasures of a similar nature. Having rented a spacious, comfortable house and garden in Notting Hill, we placed Danny in school and began making the rounds of restaurants, museums, Portobello antique shops, and department stores. I covered theatre four or five times a week in London and the provinces, writing a regular Sunday column for *The Observer.* Through an arrangement with *The New Republic,* most of these reviews were reprinted in the United States; I also published a monthly article, in *The New York Times,* on the state of English theatre. In London we discovered many old friends, among them the nuclear family of *Prometheus Bound*—Cal Lowell, Jonathan Miller, Irene Worth, and Kenneth Haigh, all of whom joined us for a nostalgic reunion lunch. We had also met Lionel and Diana Trilling again on the *France,* and visited them often in Oxford, where Lionel held a visiting professorship. Also in Oxford at the time were four former neighbors of ours from New Haven—Richard and Mary Ellmann, and Ronald and Betsy Dworkin—who invited us to high table at one of the Oxford colleges. There we were attended by uniformed guards, present (we were told) to make sure the Americans didn't pinch the silver; and when the meal was over, the gentlemen went off for cigars and coffee in the common room while the women were left to make conversation in the men's john. Norma had a few choice words for the master about this segregation of the sexes; she hadn't experienced anything like it since our first years in New Haven. But it was a rare life we led, with good friends, good food, and, always, the grand, handsome city of London. Later, Norma was to remember the year as if she had been living in a state of grace—"I thought I'd died," she told her friends, "and gone to heaven."

We traveled a lot, too, through England, Europe, and Africa. The latter trip took us to Kenya and Tanzania, where we photographed wildlife on the Serengeti, in the Ngorongoro Crater, and on Lake Manyara. Landing in Nairobi was like coming down on the craters of the Moon, and the soda lake of Manyara, all misted over in the early dawn, reminded me of Avalon—I half expected to see an arm break through the surface of the water, holding Arthur's sword. The eerie light, the strange topography, the Masai warriors in tribal dress, the lazy grace of the African lion, the herds of elephant, the cheetahs preying on the Grant gazelles—all left us dazzled by the riches of a continent at once the oldest and the newest in the world.

My travels took me to New Haven also. Returning in late fall to see what had been happening to the theatre and the school in my absence, I had the opportunity to enjoy the advantages of rotating repertory from the spectator's point of view. In three short days I was able to see three completed productions and watch another in the process of being rehearsed.

The most satisfying of these was Epstein's production of Molière's *The Bourgeois Gentleman,* performed in a colloquial, freewheeling adaptation by Michael Feingold. The response to this version was mixed, many people enjoying its audacity and impudence, others (including Mel Gussow) finding it mildly offensive. For me, the effect of the show was to reinforce my admiration for Epstein's originality. Clearly, his experience with the Rep was giving him the confidence and the imagination to attempt some daring new leaps.

It was ironic, though, that where I had previously been troubled by the relative conventionality of his approach to *The Rivals,* which many critics approved, the same critics were now complaining about the liberties he took with Molière, which delighted me. Gussow began his review by remarking that in the opening moments of the production, Molière's portrait is removed from the stage; he called this an act of discretion, considering what Alvin had done to Molière's play. But to me, Alvin's interpretation was truer to the spirit of Molière than the most faithful re-creation of the Comédie Française because it had the fragrance of a fresh experience instead of the musty odor of a museum replica. Epstein and Feingold had elected to dispense altogether with historical accuracy and dress the actors in a variety of costumes from a variety of periods, including our own. The idea was to comment on social climbing through the ages. Gags were stolen from the Marx Brothers and the Three Stooges, characters flounced about in T-shirts and long underwear, and the dramatis personae included a barbershop quartette singing "Jada." With a cast headed by Leonard Frey sporting a poodle wig as Monsieur Jourdain, and featuring such talented young comedians from the student body as Joe Grifasi, Michael Gross, and John Shea, the production took the play and whirled it about in a time-space machine. It was a welcome relief from all those flowery, well-mannered, ultimately deadly evenings which, I suspect, left the memory of Molière considerably more damaged than the Rep's impious but lively effort.

Alvin was a little shaken by the reception of his work in the *Times,* but he was nevertheless convinced that this was the most original work he had ever done. Something in his imagination had been liberated, and I was pleased to see how well he worked with some of the young actors we were developing. But as I had feared, Alvin's creative gifts were not matched by his administrative capacities; he had not yet learned how to concentrate on more than one project at a time. As a result, the second production of the season, in simultaneous rehearsal with *The Bourgeois Gentleman,* suffered considerably from his absentee artistic supervision.

This was *A Break in the Skin,* by Ronald Ribman, a play that had intrigued me greatly when I read it, but which was flat and disconnected on the stage. In a desire to accommodate the playwright, we had agreed to a director whose work was unknown to us, because Ribman had been closely associated with him at the Actors Studio. The trouble was that whereas *A Break in the Skin* is essentially surreal in style, the director's approach was essentially psychological, with the result that we managed to turn an unusual play into a largely conventional exercise.

Ribman had fashioned a powerful commentary on the effect technology has on ordinary lives, using science fiction devices and nonlinear forms; what we were offering was a realistic play about personal relationships. With a sinking heart I witnessed our commonplace production subvert a potentially original subject. Nothing depresses me more than watching our production apparatus fail a text, and we were failing this one badly. Inevitably, the critics blamed the playwright for the failure, but the fault was ours.

Our efforts to break free from the restrictions of American realism were often hampered for a variety of reasons, not the least of them being that realism was still the style most congenial to American theatre professionals. Most of the new playwrights, Ribman among them, had the capacity to create imaginative plays in a non-naturalistic vein, but when they needed a director or an actor, they still tended to call up the Actors Studio. We made no secret of our preference for poetic, nonillusionistic works over domestic plays or kitchen dramas, but we were still in the process of developing an appropriate production style. It was rather like trying to create a brand-new sculptural form using all the old molds, or achieve a breakthrough in architecture with a construction crew that only built ranch houses. That was the reason our training program was so important; the acting and directing style we needed would have to be developed at the School.

My own prejudice toward realistic drama did not prevent me from scheduling a social documentary as the third production of my leave year: Eric Bentley's study of the House Un-American Activities Committee's investigation of Communism in the entertainment industry, *Are You Now Or Have You Ever Been . . .?* Remembering George Orwell's attitude toward his own rules of prose style (break all of them rather than write something downright barbarous), I was prepared to overlook my own prejudices in regard to theatre style if a particular play attracted me. Bentley's work—a dramatic adaptation of his published transcript of the hearings—was not exactly a play, but it was certainly worthy of production. For some reason, many theatres had already turned it down as too controversial, including a few major groups in Los Angeles and New York. As an indictment of the whole inquisitorial system of government in the fifties, *Are You Now* could hardly have offended the liberal theatrical intelligentsia by virtue of its political posture. The problem, I suspect, lay in the way some of the witnesses in the investigation behaved at the trial.

For at the same time that the congressmen were revealing themselves as bullies and inquisitors, their victims from the prosperous world of culture and entertainment were hardly establishing models of exemplary behavior. A few conducted themselves with courage and dignity—Lillian Hellman's classical "I will not cut my conscience" speech was a highlight of the evening. But most of the others were busy either defending Stalinism or informing on their close associates in order to preserve their Hollywood income. The play told us more, by implication, about American opportunism in government and show business than any other document I know. And it was fascinating, too, for its almost Pirandellian qualities—American theatre celebrities enacting their own personal dramas on the stage of an American theatre, within the context of a congressional investigation.

The thin line separating theatrical illusion from reality was transgressed even further by the nature of the performance event. Under the direction of Michael Posnick, the Rep actors were depicting such personalities as Abe Burrows, Lionel Stander, Zero Mostel, Sterling Hayden, Larry Parks, and Paul Robeson—some attempting impersonations, some only borrowing mannerisms. It was unusual to see actors enacting the part of actors, but what really rescued the work from conventional courtroom realism was the electrical current that flowed between the stage and the audience (which was also cast in a part—that of spectators in the hearing room). On opening night, I am told, the Pirandellian implications of the evening almost led to a disturbance. Some of the people featured in *Are You Now* were actually in the theatre watching the play, and Zero Mostel created something of a scene in the lobby during intermission by loudly denouncing the author. I'm sorry I missed this event. It must have been a remarkable theatrical happening, which demonstrated the power of the stage to open wounds that were almost thirty years old.

My entire visit to Yale lasted eight days. In that time I not only was able to watch these three plays on a single weekend and sit in on a rehearsal of William Styron's *In the Clap Shack,* but managed to see a lot of work being done at the School. I took special note of a very beautiful and very talented first-year actress from Vassar named Meryl Streep; and I was able to look over a crop of first-year playwrights that included Christopher Durang, William Hauptman, and Albert Innaurato. Jules Feiffer—teaching playwriting that year—was very excited about his young charges, describing them to me, in a letter, as "real finds." The only thing that bothered him a little was their pessimism: "They are, most of them," he wrote, "hooked on isolation, meaninglessness and despair and I've decided that they are not yet old enough and beaten enough to have earned that philosophy, so, one way or another, I am going to try to subvert them into hope. Don't let this get around at risk to my reputation." I have kept Feiffer's secret for eight years, and only now am able to reveal that all this time he was really a closet optimist.

It was a curious experience to come to Yale as an outsider, but it permitted me, if only momentarily, a more impartial perspective, and not a little bit of pride. In comparison with the stylish and adroit productions I was seeing in England, our own performances were unpolished, but at the same time they seemed to me more adventurous. We were groping for something, and that fact alone gave our work an interesting dimension. I am referring now not only to Yale but to American theatre in general. By nature, we were stammerers—our language did not come fluently—but that disability resulted in a certain compensatory emotional power. Like his character Edmund Tyrone, Eugene O'-Neill has only the "makings of a poet" but his inarticulacy leads him into a more penetrating art, just as Billy Budd's inability to express himself issues in a highly charged physical act. It struck me that Americans had the opportunity to use their explosive tension to excavate new depths in the drama in the same way they once broke new geographical frontiers. I had nothing but admiration for the agile skills of English theatre companies; what I thought they often lacked was our intellectual daring and emotional force.

Like all my generalizations, this one got me into trouble, and when I expressed it in *The Observer* upon returning to England, my publisher, David Astor, was besieged with outraged letters. Not only had I committed a breach of hospitality, but I had divided the English theatre world on a subject in which it had invested passionate feelings. Some of this investment was economic— the London theatre was then becoming a prime tourist attraction, especially for visiting Americans, and any dissent from the prevailing opinions could unsettle the balance of trade. But it was also nationalistic. If there was one area in which the English could display their superiority to the barbarians across the sea, it was the theatre, and now this superiority was being questioned by one of that upstart number. Flower the skunk had returned in all his odorous glory. At a party we had been invited to, I arrived with Norma all gussied up for a good time, only to find the theatrical guests recoiling from me on both sides. I felt like Moses parting the Red Sea. Peter Cook, whose most recent show with Dudley Moore I had panned mildly for its parasitical relationship to *Beyond the Fringe,* turned his eyes to heaven when he saw me coming, and simulated a fainting fit.

My ungracious treatment of my English hosts continued throughout the year. I managed successfully to offend most of the leading figures in the London theatre. I exchanged public letters with the director Michael Blakemore regarding what I considered to be his overpraised productions of American plays at the National Theatre; I upset John Arden by calling his new Arthurian epic at the Royal Shakespeare Company polemical, pretentious, overwritten; I outraged John Osborne by finding his new play at the Royal Court a crude piece of conservative ventriloquism. Never one to take criticism lightly, Osborne sent me a postcard after this review, saying "Yank, do, please, go home," and he followed this with a telegram, offering to pay my passage: "INCREASING SYMPATHY FOR YOUR SAD WORSENING CONDITION. NOTWITH-STANDING ITS LACK OF INTEREST OR IMPORTANCE CAN HELP TO ARRANGE YOUR ASSISTED PASSAGE BACK TO UNFORTUNATE ENVIRONMENT AND SO ON WHERE YOU MIGHT BE CONSIDERED INSTEAD OF ALAS IGNORED. SHOULD CHEQUES OR GREEN STAMPS BE SENT TO YOU PERSONALLY OR DAVID ASTOR? GET WELL SOON OR NOT AS THE CASE MAY BE. EVER CHEERFULLY." Ever cheerfully, I responded with a telegram of my own: "FOUND YOUR CABLE AS WITTY AS YOUR LAST PLAY. I HAVE DECIDED TO STAY REGARDLESS. BUT SEND MONEY AND GREEN STAMPS REGARDLESS."

I was having a pretty good time, dodging the numerous brickbats thrown off by my reviews; along with my weekly notice, *The Observer* would usually publish a letter (naturally with a reply), assaulting my American ignorance and provincialism. I was developing a reputation in England, as I had in the United States, as a "controversial" figure; and David Astor received a lot of conflicting opinions about whether I was helping or hurting the English theatre. I didn't shun controversy, but I didn't seek it either. Although this probably sounds disingenuous, I never wrote anything purposely meant to hurt anybody's feelings. I enjoyed a good public quarrel, but I didn't consciously try to stir up strife. What I was trying to do, I thought, was speak the truth as I saw it without the usual fudging and flattery. Nevertheless, the word "controversial" stuck to me with the force of static electricity, and I haven't been able to shake it off to this day.

There was one time that year, I admit, when I purposely sought out a confrontation, and that was with my old antagonist Clive Barnes. Barnes's opinions in *The New York Times* were being reformulated regularly in the London *Times,* and his critical standards were continuing to give me dyspepsia. He had been typically condescending toward Styron's *In the Clap Shack* when it opened at the Rep, advising this poet laureate of military life to read David Rabe or David Storey "if he wants to hear what real men sound like in an all-male environment." But this dismissive review somehow bothered me less than his comments on Bertolucci's *Last Tango in Paris* and on Pauline Kael's admittedly hyperbolic review of that movie. Whatever one thought of Bertolucci, he deserved more than to be called "a sensationalist who will do anything for a quick laugh, a cheap thrill, and the fastest buck," and whatever one thought of Pauline Kael, she did not praise movies, as Mr. Barnes charged, because she thought they were "dirty." I was now more than ever convinced that the only thing capable of exciting Barnes's vituperation was the creative imagination—a sorry situation when he continued to write from the most powerful critical post in the theatre world. Consequently, when the British Broadcasting Company—having seen my *New Republic* references to Barnes republished in the English periodical, *Plays and Players*—invited me to debate him in a television studio, I accepted the offer with a degree of malicious pleasure.

The program, having turned into a general survey of the state of criticism, eventually included not only us two feuding critics, but critics of art, music, and film as well. I came to the studio armed with a collection of quotes from Barnes's reviews, all gathered from the theatre ads in a single issue of the Sunday *New York Times*. After expressing my conviction that Barnes was bankrupting the currency of criticism with his hyperbolic praise (according to another reviewer, Barnes would soon be carrying his rave reviews around in the same wheelbarrow used by the Weimar Germans to carry their inflated money), I then proceeded to read the evidence aloud to the rest of the panel. Barnes's careless use of superlatives ("best," "greatest," "finest") was a damning indictment of his critical standards—to which the unwary victim responded by crying "Foul." Having recovered his voice, he replied that the opinions of any critic would look silly out of context, and challenged me to subject my own reviews to the same sort of test. He looked so embarrassed over this unexpected confrontation that I felt a little sorry for him after. I was guilty of bad manners, but I hadn't been able to resist the temptation to hold a powerful critic accountable for his writings, and I believed I was striking a blow for all those in the theatre who had suffered from his reviews.

Barnes later made some reference to this encounter in *The New York Times,* expressing his anger over having been flown across the Atlantic (first class by his request) to be publicly insulted by "a remote and ineffectual Yale professor," as he called me without any further attempt at identification. He accused the BBC of trying to bushwhack him, and announced that he had foiled the plan by refusing to take offense. I had been foiled all right, but not on the BBC. By neglecting to identify me by name in his column, Barnes kept his quarrel with me from becoming public, and thereby reserved the right to revenge himself on my bad manners through other means.

Actually, Barnes had the courtesy not to review further Rep shows that year, and he didn't come up the next year either. But in 1974 he requested tickets again, so I wrote to him asking him to rethink the wisdom of his decision: "It is well known," I said, "that you and I have had serious personal and professional differences over the years, some of which have been aired in public. I have not spared you in print, and you have made slighting references to me as well. . . . I do not consider our public debates to have been either malign or unhealthy, and I do not question your right to say anything you wish about me personally. But I *am* apprehensive over the possibility that members of my company might become direct or indirect victims of what, after all, has been a personal matter between us. A few YRT actors have already begun to express some anxiety over the situation, and I have no way to allay their fears except to put the matter to you frankly, and to ask you to let a more disinterested observer, such as Mel Gussow, continue to cover our work."

Barnes never replied to my letter, but he did not visit our theatre again until 1978, for which I was grateful. Later he wrote in the *Times* that I had "barred" him from the theatre because I was piqued by his harsh reviews of my productions. This did not seem to be an entirely accurate interpretation of what had transpired. I had not "barred" Mr. Barnes—you can't bar a critic from a public performance. I had simply requested him to reconsider his relationship to the Yale Repertory Theatre in the light of our personal differences. And while I don't say I enjoyed his attacks on my own productions, I was more interested, I believe, in protecting some worried colleagues who lacked my means to defend themselves. Still, it was an unfortunate episode, and I'm not proud of my conduct in it. It gave me the reputation, partly deserved, of being a critic overly sensitive to criticism. People in the theatre will always be vulnerable to the vagaries of the press, but I still hadn't learned how to accept what I considered unfair or uninformed comments without making some effort at rebuttal.

In addition to critical wars that year, I was engaged in my usual battles over space and money—rather more difficult when waged long-distance. Since Yale had still not begun construction on the Mellon Gallery, we remained (precarious) tenants of the church. But the various bureaus of the City of New Haven —particularly the fire and building departments—were continually hassling us over our violations of their several codes. Each year we were threatened with eviction; and each year, we received a temporary last-minute stay of execution when we made another adjustment in the building. Something obviously needed to be done about bringing the church up to code, but since this required a significant outlay of money, it also required a genuine commitment from the university. I began hounding poor Kingman to guarantee the space to us for a minimum of three to five years, and to commit the funds needed for renovations to placate the various city bureaus. Brewster replied that he was analyzing the potential cost to the university, but lest I derive any comfort from this exercise, he was also looking for alternative sites for the theatre.

If there was still uncertainty about our physical home, there was better news that year regarding our finances. In 1973 we became the beneficiaries of a significant grant from the CBS Foundation to the playwriting program of the School and Theatre. The annual grant was $100,000—and it would last for the next five years. I had been negotiating this grant since 1971 with the president of the foundation—a gentle scholar of eighteenth-century history named Arthur Tourtellot. It was remarkable to find this learned antiquarian—a leading authority on the works of Ben Franklin—in charge of a large foundation funded by a mass communications medium; it was also very heartening. At the same time that the network was worrying about its ratings, Mr. Tourtellot was worrying about cultural standards—one of those rare times when a powerful corporation made some effort to repair a condition it had helped to create. Tourtellot and I met together several times, both in New York and in London, finally agreeing on a plan which, beginning in September 1973, was to have a far-reaching effect on the quality of American playwriting.

I think my proposal excited Mr. Tourtellot because it reminded him of the Nieman fellowships in journalism at Harvard (of which he was an alumnus). The plan was to invite four professional writers as CBS fellows each year to Yale, where they would spend a minimum of one day a week at the School tutoring student playwrights and developing new plays for the Theatre. Each fellow would receive $8,000 annually. Another $1,000 would constitute an annual CBS prize for the best play written by a student. And the remaining $67,000 of the grant would go toward new plays at the Theatre—which is to say, the production of works by the CBS fellows, or any other new American or European plays.

The beauty of this grant, to my mind, was its organic nature. It reminded me of an annual rotation of crops. The professional writers would teach the student writers, who, after graduation, would be eligible to become CBS fellows tutoring other students, and the CBS prize student play might very well find its way to the stage of the Rep. This strengthened our commitment to new American playwriting by providing subsidy for productions that were not usually very popular with audiences. It also reinforced our resolve to encourage nondramatic writers to experiment with plays. Each year one of the four fellows would be selected from a literary discipline other than the drama—a poet, a novelist, or even a critic.

One such writer—Isaac Bashevis Singer—was having his first play produced by the Yale Repertory Theatre at the very moment I was negotiating the grant in London. Mr. Singer had agreed to give us a play after he saw our Story Theatre version of *Gimpel the Fool* in 1970. I had approached him on the hunch that he had theatrical talents; it turned out he had once been a theatre critic for a Yiddish newspaper. I met this wonderfully engaging man in his New York apartment, on Eighty-sixth Street and Broadway, where he seemed to have barricaded himself behind a formidable array of protective devices. After I rang the doorbell, he spent a few minutes shooting various locks, and appeared before my eyes with a bird sitting on his bald head. Singer was extremely sensitive to the crime abroad in the neighborhood, which he seemed to associate with Nazism. He told me a story about the time when, without telling him, his wife had called a pest-control company to get rid of some roaches in his kitchen. The doorbell rang; Singer went to answer it. As he started to open the door he asked "Who is it?" and heard a large black man reply, "The exterminator." Singer quickly slammed the door and dove under the bed.

Following our meeting, Singer did send us a play, an adaptation of his short story "The Mirror." It was a charming folktale about a young girl who sees a demon in her mirror, falls in love with him, and follows him down to Hell —an erotic Yiddish version of *Through the Looking Glass.* With his first theatrical effort, Singer had not yet mastered dramatic form, and for all his experience as a theatre critic, he didn't know a great deal about the theatre. At the only rehearsal he attended he advised the actors to "speak loud like Shakespeare, not soft like Chekhov." The play was composed in a linear mode that was distinguished more by his sense of local color than by his control of character. Still, it was a better play than we produced, to judge from the performance I saw when I returned to New Haven in March. I'm afraid we made rather a mess of *The Mirror,* primarily because our largely Gentile company was unable to capture its full folk-herring flavor. It was amusing to see Jeremy Geidt and Betsy Parrish, cast as a Jewish mama and papa, applying upward inflections to their cultivated speech while hunching their shoulders in a vain attempt to simulate a Yiddish shrug.

We made an even bigger mess of another play I saw on that visit—Brecht's earliest dramatic effort, *Baal.* This production embarrassed me as much as anything we ever did at the Rep, partly because of the direction, partly because of the acting. Alvin, overwhelmed by administrative tasks, was getting a little careless in his casting that spring. The role of Baal—sensual, animal, appetitive—had been especially chosen for Christopher Walken. When he fell out, Alvin cast Bob Balaban, a gifted comic, but too diminutive to capture the mythic dimensions of the character. Other roles were cast with a similar carelessness, and the staging was flaccid and flat. It was the first time we had stubbed our collective toe on a play by Brecht, over whom we were developing an almost proprietary interest. The play had been assigned to an instructor from the acting/directing department who, whatever his gifts as a teacher, was not a professional director. When Alvin originally suggested him, I had demurred. Alvin thought the instructor needed credibility with his directing students, and he was eager to neutralize the sniping, common to many nonparticipants at the Rep, that was coming from the School. I thought it best if the instructor co-directed *Baal* with Richard Gilman, an authority on Brecht. The trouble was that Gilman and the instructor didn't get along, and Epstein didn't have enough confidence in Gilman's ability to direct it alone. Anyhow, the results of all this made me wince, and convinced me that henceforth the quality of production would have to assume more importance than relations between the theatre and the school.

I did not see the final two productions of the season. But by all accounts, Epstein's production of Ionesco's *Macbett,* directed in association with two Canadian cabaret-trained students from the third year, was a brilliant travesty of Shakespeare's *Macbeth,* which, I hope, partially redeemed my own unwitting travesty of the year before. As for our final production, Edward Bond's *Lear,* this had the unique distinction of virtually emptying the theatre every night it played, as well as losing us over a thousand subscribers the following year.

Like Ionesco's *Macbett,* Bond's *Lear* was a fantasia on a theme by Shakespeare, where an accomplished contemporary dramatist lets his imagination roam freely over a text that has almost assumed the status of a myth. But whereas Ionesco's fantasy was skittish and playful, Bond's was remorseless and cruel—not for that reason, I believed it to be the better work. Alvin and I had both been very moved by *Lear* when we first read it. It was for this reason that I fought so hard to keep the play when I heard that Bond was thinking of giving it to another theatre. The playwright had had a bad experience with the London production of *Lear* at the Royal Court, and he doubted that we could cast it properly. He proved right in this but not for the reasons he suspected. When I finally persuaded Bond to honor our stubborn fealty to his work and let us do the play, Alvin offered the leading part to over forty American actors before he found an actor willing to play it—the Canadian Donald Davis.

Finding a director for the production was almost as difficult. The task had been originally accepted by David Jones of the Royal Shakespeare Company, but he dropped out when he was unable to clear his schedule with Trevor Nunn. The play required a director with both classical background and modern sensibility—not easy to find in the American theatre. In the course of reviewing the Actors Company production of *'Tis Pity She's a Whore* in Cambridge (England), I had been very impressed by the directorial concept, which located the action in a near-contemporary Italy dominated by cold, ruthless assassins. The director was David Giles—someone, I thought, prepared to undertake the pitiless challenge of *Lear.* Giles readily accepted my invitation and, upon arriving in New Haven, impressed the company with his professional ease and workmanship. As it turned out, Giles's very fidelity to his remorseless mission was what proved too much for audiences. In a typical scene, Gloucester's eyes are gouged out onstage—as they are in Shakespeare —but here they were removed by a machine that also pumped out considerable amounts of blood from the sockets. Few spectators survived this appetizing scene to witness the carnage that followed. As Walter Kerr put it in his review, "The audience simply rose and fled."

Ill-fated from the start, the production never finished its run. Donald Davis came down sick with clots in his legs; the remaining performances were canceled. In their place, Alvin substituted additional performances of the popular *Macbett.* I had no way of evaluating our production of *Lear* because I never got to see it, but I persist in my stubborn conviction that it is an important play—perhaps one of the most important we had yet produced. It was true that Bond seemed to be fixated on cruelty and violence; it was also true that cruelty and violence were pervasive in contemporary life. I admired Bond's courage in refusing to flinch before the horrors of the modern world; I thought I perceived, behind his stoic reserve, the passionate convictions of a pacifist-poet. Later he would permit an ideological acid to etch into his cold, declarative art—his love of peace could not survive the appeal of revolutionary violence—but in *Lear* he was still a witness rather than an activist. Someday I hope to be able to redeem our faith in this play.

Speaking of violence, by this time the Vietnam tragedy had come to an ignoble end. In its place we were getting the comedy of Watergate. In a vaudeville produced the previous summer by the Committee to Reelect the President (CREEP), some low clowns had been arrested while trying to rifle the desk of the Democratic Party chairman. But to our astonishment, the primary backer of this bungled burlesque had been reelected President of the United States by the largest plurality in electoral history.

This outraged my political consciousness, but it excited my appetite for political entertainment. From the beginning, I was a confirmed Watergate junkie. I couldn't seem to get enough of Richard Nixon. In England I scoured the newspapers for new revelations about this fascinating scoundrel; I spent hours by the television in the hope of seeing one of his delicious press confer-ences. I loved his hunched shoulders, his Uriah Heep humility. I was wild about his Freudian slips, the way his inner demons were always threatening to pop out of his mouth and expose his secrets. I even liked the way he pronounced the word *"Warsh*ington." You could appreciate why Art Buch-wald called Nixon "the best President I ever had." It was impossible to resist a man who obviously knew so much better than any of his critics that he was morally unfit even to clean the lavatories in the West Wing of the White House, much less run the country.

Still keeping tabs on Nixon through precious issues of the Paris *Herald Tribune,* I took a holiday in Greece with Norma and Danny in the spring. We visited some of the most celebrated sites in ancient Greek drama—Delphi, Eleusis, Thebes, Epidaurus, Mycenae, old Corinth—and gained new insights not only into the old plays but also into their modern applications. Danny listened to the plots of Greek tragedies as if they were fairy tales, beginning to regard what at first seemed useless piles of rubble with new wonder and respect. At the Lion Gate in Mycenae we saw the very place where the Watchman had crouched "dog-like" awaiting word of Agamemnon's return from the Trojan wars; we thought we identified the very room where Clytem-nestra had lured her unwitting husband into the murderous net. We not only visited the sites where the Greek myths were originally created but examined the theatres where they were originally performed. Most tourists test the marvelous acoustics of these outdoor theatres by having someone drop a coin on the floor of the orchestra and listening to its ring from the topmost row of seats. We did it by sending Danny down to the stage to orate a line from *Oedipus the King:* "Be not stiffnecked and proud, O Tiresias." He discharged this duty with the embarrassment of any nine-year-old obliged to give a recita-tion.

It was on the way to Delphi, at the fork in the three roads where Oedipus unknowingly killed his father, that I was struck by the ironic parallel between the unfortunate Greek hero and our sleazy American President. Two leaders of state—Oedipus Tyrannos and Nixon Tyrannosaurus—are each responsible for a plague in their respective lands; but where one seeks to identify the culprit and discover the truth, the other seeks to hide the culprit and cover up the truth. I elaborated on this idea when I returned to London in an article called "Thebes and Watergate" which *The Observer* almost refused to publish. Like many English newspapermen, David Astor believed Nixon's accomplishments in foreign affairs to be far more important than our petty domestic squabbles. Wasn't Nixon opening up relations with China and starting a détente with the Soviet Union? Yes, I argued, but he was also bringing our country close to a serious constitutional crisis that would shake the confidence of many Ameri-cans in the honesty of our political leadership. Astor reluctantly published my article, but he obviously believed that theatre reviewers shouldn't concern themselves with politics. *The New York Times* indicated the same thing after I had turned my idea into a dramatic satire called *Oedipus Nix,* which was all prepared for publication in the "Arts and Leisure" section, until my editor was overruled by his superiors and the piece was returned.

One of the last things I reviewed during my stormy career on *The Observer* was Peter Daubeny's World Theatre Festival at the Aldwych. These visits of European and African companies were a welcome respite from my steady diet of English theatre production, and they provided some of the most exciting events of my year abroad. I was strongly impressed by Ingmar Bergman's visually threadbare but theatrically powerful version of Ibsen's *The Wild Duck,* and I was fascinated by productions from Spain and Belgium, and by a Zulu *Macbeth.* But the most stunning achievement of the festival was a production by the Cracow Stary Theatre of Poland of Dostoyevsky's *The Possessed,* as directed by Andrzej Wajda.

From the opening moment, when Stavrogin rattles off his confession at breakneck speed, to the final tableau, when a chorus of demons reveals Stavrogin's body hanging limply from a gallows, I was in thrall to this production. I was convinced we were in the confident hands of a major artist, whose control of scene design, lighting, and acting were, to my knowledge, unmatched by anyone else in the contemporary theatre. Wajda had the genius to create a vivid, unforgettable symbolic image by means of a few, well-selected scenic elements. And the setting of *The Possessed*—a floor of blistered mud, which caked on the shoes, trousers, and skirt hems of the characters—was a miracle of metaphorical economy.

Relatively familiar as a film-maker, Wajda was new to me as a theatre director; I felt a deep sense of respect and humility before his redoubtable gifts. I wrote an unequivocal, and quite uncharacteristic, rave review for *The Possessed.* The relative indifference of the English press and audience to this production (it was received with the same tepid praise as everything else) struck me as almost a personal affront. I was determined to persuade Wajda to direct at Yale; he had the potential power to transform the whole idea of American theatre. When Peter Daubeny kindly invited me to a reception for the Cracow company, I leaped at the opportunity to meet Wajda. I found him a gentle, modest, darkly handsome man with soft eyes. He understood English, but was reluctant to speak it; I knew not a word of Polish; we communicated haltingly in French. By the end of the afternoon I had won his agreement to come to Yale; the problem would be finding some time in his busy schedule.

In the journal I started to keep at that time, June 22 is identified on the top of the page as "the longest day of the year"—"and the saddest," I added mournfully in my illegible hand. It was the day we embarked at Southampton to return to the United States. I had gained twenty pounds that year from the marvelous food in England (and the starchy food in Greece); the return trip on the *France* was to add three pounds more. We would have to resume our Spartan ways, and not just in strenuous dieting. We had been gorging on more than food during this delightful year away, and we would be sacrificing more than dinners upon our return.

It is true I had not found the English theatre a source of unalloyed delight.

As compared with the glories I experienced during a visit in 1965, this London season struck me as falling off seriously in theatrical vision and power, and I had not been hesitant about recording my negative impressions at the very moment when multitudes of other Americans, at the behest of Robert Morley, were flying across the ocean on BOAC to sample the wares of the London stage. As a result, I imagine that not a few English theatre people were glad to see my back. David Astor wrote me a nice letter, after I left, saying that my reviews "came as a strong draught of oxygen—by which I mean they brought the stimulus of good sense, subtle perception, and a high sense of values." Harold Hobson of the Sunday *Times,* using a similar metaphor, wrote that I had "blown through the British theatre like a breath of fresh air from the North Pole. He has regained the other side of the Atlantic, but we are still shivering." Hobson had the charity to add: "He has not been very good to us but he has been very good for us. The English theatre is the spoiled child of the Western artistic world. . . . As a result of [his] visit, Britain is taking a smaller size in hats, and is beginning to get into its boots quite comfortably."

In spite of Mr. Hobson's kindness, I did not feel that my frigid presence, if that's what it was, had any noticeable effect on English theatre production. When I later collected some of my English reviews in a volume called *The Culture Watch,* for the first time I couldn't find a British publisher. I don't know what influence I had expected to have, but I felt as though I had dropped a stone down a deep hole and was still waiting to hear it hit bottom.

But we had had a wonderful time, and we returned to the United States with a renewed sense of purpose. Our trip abroad helped to tell us, if nothing else, who we were and what we wanted. For just a few moments, at the beginning of our visit, Norma and I had considered making our home in London. But like many other Americans who contemplate expatriation, we soon discovered the desire fading. We knew enough about how roots are formed to realize that we couldn't leave our country for very long without being cut off from a vital source of nourishment. For all its problems, the United States was where our destiny lay. Besides, Watergate was making the country interesting again, and it wasn't being covered very well in the British press. We looked forward eagerly to getting our *New York Times* again, so we could pull whole sections out of each other's grip at the breakfast table and read the complete transcripts aloud. The real drama was to be found at home.

Once we had determined to come to terms with being American, we also decided that we had to do something about the School and the Theatre. The acting department was still suffering from bickering and tumult, which, considering my absence, could not this time be blamed on my personality. The relationship of the students to the professional company was still not adequately defined. The criticism students were still isolated from the students in production. The playwriting students were still complaining about inadequate outlets for their plays. And the Repertory Theatre, despite an auspicious start, had still not managed to maintain a consistent quality throughout an entire season. I had my work cut out for me, and I also had to do something about winning back a large number of subscribers who had been alienated by some of the productions.

I would have to pay a price for my rest and recreation. Nevertheless, it had been worth it. And we still had a whole summer between the day we disembarked from the *France* and the day we had to pick up our duties in New Haven. This would help ease the reentry. We stopped at the house just long enough to drop off our trunks, and drove straight off to Martha's Vineyard to resume our carefree life.

VII

Actors!
1973-1974

The best in this kind are but shadows and the worst
are no worse, if imagination amend them.

—A Midsummer Night's Dream

During the summer of 1973 I was almost able to satisfy my insatiable craving
for Watergate: the Senate hearings had become a daily feature of television.
Sam Ervin headed a congenial cast of congressional investigators, with stunning guest appearances by such White House stars as John Ehrlichman, Bob
Haldeman, and John Mitchell—also, in a sensational debut, John Dean. President Richard Milhous Nixon, having totally displaced Erich von Stroheim in
the affections of his countrymen as The Man You Love to Hate, was rehearsing
some thrilling scenes with the Washington press corps. He even contributed
a few striking monologues of his own invention, one of which concluded with
the unforgettable exclamation "I'm not a crook!" Much of the script became
available later that summer, when some of the tape transcripts were released
to the public, and I had the chance to perform in the drama by reading parts
aloud to my friends on South Beach with all deleted expletives restored. I was
sharpening up my Nixon impersonation, delighted to find the country at last
developing some actors worthy of the name.

Other actors were not so dependable that summer—specifically those we
were trying to recruit for the company. Following his year as acting artistic
director, Alvin Epstein was now the associate director of the Rep; together we
shared the frustration of trying to cast significant classical roles in the season
offerings. The American actors didn't seem to want them, and the British
actors (who did) were still prevented from joining us by Equity's strict rules
prohibiting the employment of foreign performers by LORT theatres. Whenever we succeeded in catching one of the legal Equity fish, it usually fell off
the hook. A young American actress who had accepted an offer from us in late

July told us toward the end of August that she had contracted a bad virus and expected to be sick for six months. I was reminded of Strindberg, who once told Bernard Shaw that he intended to be ill at the very hour that Shaw wanted to visit him in Sweden. Unlike Strindberg, who was dying of stomach cancer, however, our actress must have made a speedy recovery because she appeared, just a month later, on a television game show.

My frustration over this sort of thing issued in impatience, my impatience in disappointment, my disappointment in despair over the conduct of the American acting profession; I believed such behavior was adversely affecting the serious American theatre. I recorded this impression, and some of these emotions, in a *Times* article called "The Profession Is Not Supporting the Profession," where I rebuked American actors for neglecting what presumably attracted them to the stage in the first place—namely, the great roles in the great plays. "After another season spent trying to cast a season," I grumbled, "and hearing the same set responses—the same 'Gee, I'd love to, but I can't afford it' or 'I'm waiting on a pilot' or 'I'm up for a movie . . . can I let you know in March?' or 'I'll come for a few weeks if you let me play Cyrano'—along with the same demands from agents that the actor have his name above the title or special songs written for him in the show, I still find it dispiriting that a performer could turn down a series of challenging roles in important plays . . . for a swipe at a TV series, or a small part in the musical version of *Valley of the Dolls.*"

I was generalizing again from my own disappointments, and like most of my generalizations, this one was unfair. Of course, every resident company, including our own, could count on the loyalty and devotion of a few versatile and talented actors. But there was a much larger group of gifted people in the profession who were capable of making these companies the envy of any in the world, and these were either showing no interest in the stage or breaking commitments when something more lucrative was offered or allowing their talents to atrophy while they waited for work not worthy of their time. It was wrong of me, however, to lay all the blame on the acting profession. Actors were simply part of a complicated and powerful machinery over which they had little control. What about the agents, for example, who usually regarded their clients less as developing artists than as objects for barter? Could these brokers of a commodity culture ever be expected to send actors to a theatre where the wages were substandard and the visibility low. I had always considered the agent to be one of the prime obstacles to the American actor's growth; but even the agent was not at the root of the problem. Fundamentally, the difficulty lay in the values of American society, as determined by our economic system.

For while the nonprofit theatre was collective and vaguely socialistic, the society at large was essentially anarchic and capitalistic. Like everyone else, the American actor was continually encouraged to be a free-lance individual in a culture of opportunity. Friends, family, and peers all pressured the poor actor to "make it" in the way that Americans respected, and that meant as a movie star or a television personality. In the face of these pressures, how could we ask such a person to give up his personal ambitions for the needs of the group? And what did we have to offer in return, besides the satisfactions of the work? The Gothic fortresses of Yale? The alluring city of New Haven? It was not enough to provide our company members with access to the library or privileges in the gym, or to have the university throw an annual party for them in the hope that an open bar and a few canapés might obscure, for a day, the fact that they were considered aliens in the community. It was difficult enough to persuade the actor of the advantages of permanent ensemble work. But it was virtually impossible to offer conditions attractive enough to compensate for the sacrifice of potential stardom and affluence. Even the most eager of our new recruits would soon be spending the day off making rounds in New York, sometimes leaving us for other jobs before the season came to an end.

This was not so true of the older actors who managed to make their homes in New Haven and enjoy domestic lives. But those without children or teaching assignments had very little to bind them to the area. What really alarmed me was how fast the infection was spreading among the students. It was not very difficult to sign a talented actor, fresh from the School, for a repertory season of plays, but it wouldn't take long before the hungry agents were buzzing around his head like flies around molasses. If it was hard losing actors one hardly knew, it was even harder watching our own—on whom we were depending to help reform the acting profession—take off so fast for Broadway and Hollywood. We considered Yale a part of a whole new system of noncommercial theatre; the typical Yale actor considered it a nest from which "to try my wings" (the recurrent phrase) in the commercial world.

In consequence, the casting we did each summer was always provisional. We never knew the actual composition of the company until the first reading of our first production—sometimes not even then. In the sixties, our theatre was hamstrung by those who wanted to make revolution, in the seventies by those who wanted to make careers. In trying to neutralize the endemic careerism of the American actor, we exposed our students to continual exhortations regarding the proper use of their gifts. We told them to be good caretakers of their talents (F. Scott Fitzgerald), to love the art in themselves rather than themselves in art (Konstantin Stanislavsky), to be themselves by slaying themselves (Henrik Ibsen), along with enough maxims of a similar nature to fill an *Oxford Encyclopedia of Moral Aphorisms.* Poor creatures. Their ears must have been humming with these gnatlike proverbialisms, so unwanted and troublesome, so easily slapped away. A few (very precious to us) were permanently affected by what they heard; a larger number paid lip service to our moral demands before proceeding blithely along the path of their original ambitions. It was naïve of me to expect otherwise. We were asking actors to fast when the banquet table was full, trying to influence the patterns of a lifetime through three short years at Yale. I soon realized I had been banking on something that was far from established—the idealistic instincts of young people who had grown up with Watergate and Vietnam.

Still, we always managed to fill the ranks of the company by the time we began rehearsals, though the quality of performance was inevitably affected by last-minute dropouts. That summer, we were trying to find a Prospero. Alvin Epstein had decided to undertake the Shakespeare-Purcell *Tempest*—the production that had baffled Clifford Williams in 1970. Epstein believed he had discovered how to blend a Jacobean text with Baroque music and Restoration lyrics; he would make the music an extension of Prospero's magic. Alvin took his cue from Caliban's line, "The isle is full of noises,/ Sounds and sweet airs, that give delight and hurt not." The island, the storm, the masque—all would be created by Purcell. To highlight the magic of the play, and its peripatetic nature, Epstein decided to cast not one but seven Ariels, encased in white elastic muslin that varied in shape according to the actors' gestures and postures. These Ariels would be led and choreographed by Carmen de Lavallade. In the concluding scene, Alvin planned to have Carmen wriggle out of her costume, to the lovely strains of Purcell's music, emerging like a butterfly from her cocoon in pristine nakedness after Prospero had set her free.

But where was the Prospero to set her free? We couldn't find him in the whole of *Players Guide*. We had assembled an accomplished cast (it included a beautiful third-year actress named Sigourney Weaver as Iris), but the crucial central role was going begging. Finally, Epstein decided he had no choice but to play the part himself, since his remaining energies were better spent in acting than in casting. The trouble was he was also directing. Alvin was putting a severe strain on his own capacities, but he expected to accomplish the task by working with a co-director.

The Equity contracts with the actors were drawn up and signed that year by a new managing director, Robert J. Orchard. One of my proudest appointments, a pure product of the School, Rob had prepared for this arduous job by acting as Alvin's administrator the previous year. He was golden-haired, blue-eyed, and innocent-looking. But despite his lack of guile and apparent youthfulness, he was a tough negotiator, whose rock-ribbed honesty compelled respect from even the most seasoned actors. I had not been happy with his predecessors in the job. They were, for the most part, professional functionaries without any particular aesthetic—which is to say, they could have performed the same duties in the same way for any other theatre. I had a secret name for technicians of this sort, who were beginning to crop up not only in administration but also in electrics, technical production, acting, directing, any area where people performed mechanically with no vision beyond the completion of the task itself. I called them "plumbers"—apologies to an honorable profession that the Watergate burglars had maligned in quite a different way. With Rob, we at last had a creative administrator—one who understood the needs of the artist and sympathized with the aesthetic of the Theatre, and thereby could always be expected to weigh artistic considerations against practical business judgments.

Another gifted young man joined our ranks that year from the student body —our resident designer, Michael Yeargan. Unfailingly cheerful, apparently tireless, Yeargan soon proved to be the ideal designer for a repertory theatre because he was capable of adapting his imagination to any directorial concept, to any space, to any style. It was not unusual for Yeargan to design the first two productions of the season while supervising the third, at the same time teaching a design course in the School—nor was it unusual for him to do both sets and costumes. He was so tireless, in fact, that he even found time to design outside of New Haven during the year, in collaboration with his close friend Larry King; together, they were very much in demand. Yeargan, though he grew restless if he stayed in one place too long, remained at Yale throughout my time and after—an important example to students of how designers grow through repertory theatre work. He also helped our theatre to grow through a form of collaboration more accurately described as co-direction, providing our work with a unique and imaginative visual identity.

My last important appointment that year was Bobby Lewis—returning to Yale as master teacher in the acting/directing department. I wanted Bobby Lewis because the department lacked a clear-cut aesthetic direction, and, worse, was still rife with factionalism, competitiveness, backbiting. The acting/directing department had always been the problem area of the School, perhaps reflecting the temperamental makeup of its constituents. I was now prepared to take the bit in my mouth and revamp the whole department; only this could justify my continuing at Yale. My resolve was strengthened when I discovered, soon after returning from England, that the actress who had impressed me so much the previous year, Meryl Streep, had been put on probation—and by the same instructor who, some years earlier, had ridiculed A. J. Antoon's Story Theatre production (Antoon left Yale in bitterness as a result). Was there another, more sinister meaning in the current phrase "Talent will out"?

Stella Adler had always struggled to keep the talent in. Whenever the plumbers plied their mechanical trade by trying to punish some gifted student for the infraction of some rigid rule, she would say in her most lofty manner, "We're here to serve talent." In my own student days at the School the really talented people were usually the ones who failed to finish the program—either by choice or by request. I realized, with a sinking heart, that with Stella gone the students were no longer insulated from the plumbers, and the School was in danger of reverting to its former glories as a military academy. Whatever one thought of Bobby Lewis's approach to theatre—and I couldn't argue with those who found it somewhat old-fashioned—he was one of the few teachers in the profession who respected acting talent. It was for that reason that I invited him back to the School, with the intention of grooming him as the head of the acting/directing department—over the strenuous objections of Howard Stein who, friendly with most of the existing staff, resisted this move from the start.

I was still oscillating between opposite poles—the need for discipline and the need for flexibility. I knew we needed rules; I always disliked having to enforce them. The regulations had been formulated as a deterrent to disruption during bad times; a few years later, when the climate had changed, they would no longer be necessary. At this point, however, still worried about vestigial eruptions from a few remaining radical students, we continued to hand out copies of the Drama Students Guide at the beginning of each year. The difficult thing was to discourage the faculty from using these rules in a way they weren't intended, or turning them into rigid unbreakable codes.

At the same time, it was necessary to persuade the soft-liners among the faculty to make judgments on the development of students; otherwise, we would be subject to Gresham's Law, letting the bad drive out the good. If we were here to serve talent, we were here to identify talent too. It was no help to the truly gifted to share a stage with those who were not moving forward; and it was no favor to those who clearly had no future in the theatre to encourage them in such a competitive profession. Trying to serve the needs of the group without penalizing the individual—at the same time guaranteeing individual rights without sacrificing the institution—was an important, if problematical, task at this particular moment in history. It meant trying to steer a course between permissiveness and autocracy, between rigid judgments and loose standards, between too many rules and no rules at all.

The perils of academic navigation were then occupying the attention of people in every university in the land. Some of these formed a group called the Committee on the University Emergency, which held its first meeting in Venice in October of 1973. This committee was organized by certain European and American professors who viewed the politicization of the university as a serious worldwide phenomenon. Just beginning to stick their heads over the ruins and assess the damage, they called this conference in order to share common experiences and devise protective strategies. I was invited to Venice by Charles Frankel of Columbia, and while I don't normally attend academic conventions, I was eager to join this one. It was an opportunity to communicate with like-minded people on an important subject; it was also an opportunity to revisit the lovely city where Norma and I had spent our honeymoon. Disembarking from the vaporetto, I was dismayed to find the place was sinking. The pavements were underwater; I could barely get into my hotel. Was this an omen for the university as well?

I enjoyed exchanging combat stories with colleagues who had had similar encounters with student radicals; it was consoling to be among war veterans. Nevertheless, I still managed to violate the general consensus. Some of the conferees—notably Richard Lowenthal of Germany—were just a shade too conservative for my taste, particularly in their conviction that it was the function of the university to develop "useful" citizens for society. I argued that the students were right in saying it was not the job of education to make people conform to a questionable social system. The university had value for society primarily as an *alternative* to society—something reflected in its clerical beginnings—and it could preserve this value best by remaining questing and critical, detached in its pursuit of truth. If this meant a return to the ivory tower, then so be it. The scholar's research was disinterested only when he was free from pressures to make his learning "useful." We all seemed to agree that the politicization of the classroom by radical students had had a malignant effect on learning. Wasn't it possible that the utilitarian demand on the modern university was just another, more subtle, form of politicization?

In retrospect, this debate showed the first signs of conservative academic backlash, a reaction inspired first by student radicalism and exacerbated later by the growing financial crisis. Academics had been working for government for years, in return for federal grants; soon they would be working for corporate interests as well, in return for fees and royalties. I had always believed that students were quite right in saying that Du Pont or Rand had no place on campus, though, for consistency's sake, I thought they should have objected to any kind of corporate or government recruitment. To me the issue was not so much political as functional. To treat the university as a superemployment agency, training young people for jobs, was really no different from using it as a center for industrial research, developing products and ideas for business. In both cases, education was being shifted away from its traditional function, which was to transmit a body of knowledge from one generation to another. How difficult it was to understand that society benefited as much through the preservation of learning as through its practical applications.

If there was a conservative form of academic utilitarianism, there was also a liberal version, which government agencies were now beginning to implement. In the sixties, students had pressured the university to solve the inequities of the social system; in the seventies, the federal government began applying pressure for this purpose as well, holding its grants as hostage. Under a program called "affirmative action," the Nixon administration was demanding that the university conform to certain hiring procedures regarding blacks, Hispanics, Indians, and women if it expected to receive further funding for research. Nobody could dispute the desirability of increasing the number of women and minorities on the faculty; what seemed arguable—and just a little suspicious, considering that the Nixon administration was hardly a model of egalitarian ideals—was the means. I always suspected that with "affirmative action," Nixon had found a shrewd way to confound his liberal intellectual enemies by hoisting them with their own petard. The academic community had become so captive to the government that it was in serious danger of losing its traditional autonomy along with the right to determine its own future.

"Affirmative action" virtually monopolized discussions at the deans' luncheons that Brewster held every month with his newly appointed provost, Hanna Gray. The federal government had delivered an ultimatum to private universities concerning what it called "goals and timetables" for achieving minority representation on the faculty; if these weren't met, all federal grants would be suspended. As a predominantly white and predominantly male institution for most of its history, Yale had undoubtedly been guilty of discrimination against women and minority groups in the past. Now it was expected to correct these inequities within a limited period of time. There was no argument over the need to improve Yale's hiring practices. The argument was over how, and whether this should be mandated by government agencies. For it was likely that in trying to make quick restitution to disadvantaged groups, universities like Yale would be required to hire unqualified people. The threat to the language was even more immediate—phrases like "goals and timetables" were really euphemisms for deadlines, while "affirmative action" was bureaucratic jargon for quotas.

Fortunately, I had to listen to such language only during these monthly deans' meetings. At other times I had the luxury of listening to Shakespeare's verse. For we were now into rehearsals of *The Tempest.* Epstein's keen ear for music had helped him solve the problem of integrating Purcell's score, but he had not yet solved the problem of staging Shakespeare's text. The music was exquisite, the performance was mundane and domestic. Alvin had become so involved with his own role as Prospero that he had virtually withdrawn from directing the play, leaving the task to his co-director, an Israeli movement expert whose first language was Hebrew. The actors' diction was sloppy, some scenes were inaudible, energy was low, the performance lacked unity. I thought we were headed for disaster. I engaged Alvin in a late-night session during which I persuaded him to take over the production and charge it with life. In less than two days, he managed to unify the disparate elements and give the cast some confidence. *The Tempest* was not an entirely successful production, but it had a few lovely, soaring performances, and the Purcell music worked its magic on the ears and minds of the audience. Most important of all, it represented an important advance for Epstein. He was gradually learning how to direct Shakespeare by investigating the rhythms of the verse. I regarded this production less as a final product than as a test run for what would prove to be Epstein's finest achievement—*A Midsummer Night's Dream.*

Two weeks after we opened *The Tempest* we put a new play into repertory by David Epstein; it was called *Darkroom.* Neither the play nor the production was particularly memorable, but *Darkroom* was the first play we produced under the auspices of the new CBS grant. Epstein, a former playwriting student at the School, was one of the CBS fellows that year, along with Adrienne Kennedy, Terrence McNally, and E. L. Doctorow. Each was committed to give a class or seminar with the playwriting students, as well as to write a play for the Theatre; only Doctorow would fail to deliver the play.

When I invited Ed Doctorow to Yale, he was teaching at Sarah Lawrence. He was a novelist and former book editor with no experience in theatre, but I had much admired his *Book of Daniel* for its lively dialogue and characterization. I thought he was a potential dramatist, and so did he; when I offered him the fellowship, he expressed some eagerness to try his hand at a play. What he had in mind was an epic drama about the abolitionist John Brown which, he told me, would revolutionize our sense of theatrical language. It sounded good, but it never arrived, despite repeated assurances that it was just on the verge of completion. Overly excited about the project, I very foolishly announced the play for the following season, even though the author hadn't provided so much as a cast of characters or a synopsis of the action. From time to time, I would follow Doctorow around his various speaking engagements in the hope of wresting something material from his hands. What I got were more assurances.

I have no doubt that Doctorow was entirely sincere about his desire to write a play. The problem was that when he accepted the assignment, he was just about to publish *Ragtime,* and the subsequent success of that book distracted his attention from other commitments. Soon he was preoccupied with writing the screenplay of *Ragtime* for Robert Altman (who never got to direct it); he also acted a role in Altman's film *Buffalo Bill and the Indians.* I waited two or three seasons for the John Brown play, bombarding Doctorow with letters, badgering him with phone calls, generally making a pest of myself in my embarrassment at having announced to our subscribers a nonexistent work. When I was finally willing to admit to myself that he wasn't going to deliver, I wrote him a letter, asking this newly wealthy writer if he wouldn't care to make a tax-free contribution to a financially hard-pressed theatre—namely, the portion of the fellowship he was paid for writing the play. He sent me a check for the amount, accompanied by an angry letter calling me an "asshole." I probably was, but we needed the money; I offered to accept another of his choice expletives provided it was accompanied by another check.

In spite of our failure with Doctorow, the CBS grant was a guarantee that there would always be a number of gifted playwrights on the grounds, not only producing their own plays but stimulating student plays as well. This promise was fulfilled in our next production of that year, *Watergate Classics.* Like many of our more successful ventures, *Watergate Classics* was a replacement for a canceled project, a new translation of *The Misanthrope,* which we lost to a Broadway producer. I wasn't unhappy. Here was a chance for the Rep to offer something on our favorite current subject, and our favorite political scoundrel. Jeremy Geidt and Jonathan Marks had written a satire on Nixon the previous year called *The Bug Stops Here.* Its warm reception in the cabaret suggested there was an enthusiastic audience primed to vent some steam over the Watergate affair. Why not take the opportunity to expand this into a full-length satirical evening?

The pattern of *Oedipus Nix,* which had used classical drama for the purpose of parodying contemporary political figures, struck us as a useful basis for the rest of the show. During a long conference, we discussed a number of plays that might be employed in a similar manner. Ideas and suggestions poured forth in abundance, which Michael Feingold incorporated into a lengthy memorandum. Lonnie Carter developed five short skits in as many days. Student playwrights began to submit material. Some of America's most trenchant satirists—Philip Roth, Jules Feiffer, Art Buchwald—gave us new or published material. Isaiah Sheffer, after agreeing to direct the work, contributed songs and sketches of his own.

From the first, the venture seemed perilous. We began rehearsals in a state of trepidation—uncertain about what shape the amorphous show would take, unsure about which writers would respond (and when) to our solicitations for material, uneasy about whether we would have enough. We soon received sufficient material for three or four such evenings. Some of the sketches were overtaken by events and discarded; some were strengthened by events; some were revised as the events continued to unfold. We combed the newspapers daily for fresh information and inspiration, our greatest anxiety being that history might betray us, rendering the whole undertaking obsolete by the time we opened. We told each other that Nixon's most criminal act would be to resign before we got our crack at him. As it turned out, Nixon decided to hang in for nine more months and permit our show to open; and since Congress was too sluggish to start impeachment proceedings until the following summer, the President managed to be our best press agent and contributor, adding Saturday-night massacres, eighteen-minute gaps, lost tapes, and new revelations of his finances whenever our show threatened to go stale.

The intention of *Watergate Classics* was simply to comment on recent history with the aid of relevant texts: in the first part, we did established classics linked by a Shakespearean Chorus borrowed from *Henry V;* in the second, modern classics introduced by a Citizen quoting from the Founding Fathers. Jeremy Geidt and Jonathan Marks contributed a *Samlet,* with Sam Ervin as Hamlet, Haldeman and Ehrlichman as Rosencrantz and Guildenstern, John Mitchell as Polonius ("Felonius"), and Uncle Sam as the Ghost of the murdered state, admonishing Samlet to "remember me!" Lonnie Carter wrote a version of Lucky's speech in *Waiting for Godot,* spoken at a feverish rate by Alvin Epstein (coincidentally, the original Lucky of the Broadway production), which invoked every Watergate phrase and reference in a nightmarish Joycean pastiche. Sheffer developed a parody of *The Wizard of Oz,* in which Julie Nixon, looking for her daddy, encounters Gordon Liddy (the Scarecrow), John Mitchell (the Tin Man), and finally her long-lost father (the Cowardly Lion), to whom she sings: "Daddy dirtied the rainbow/ Let's hope he won't for long."

I contributed *Oedipus Nix* and worked up a new sketch called *Dick's Last Tape*—which replaced the ancient Krapp with an aging Nixon—trying unsuccessfully to insert the phrase *"But it would be wrong!"* into a tape where he is heard saying that to give a million dollars in hush money to Howard Hunt "would be no problem." I also got my chance to impersonate Nixon again in what proved to be the most frightening sketch of the whole evening, Philip Roth's *The President Addresses the Nation.* Sitting in the Oval Office, with photographs of Lincoln, Eisenhower, and his family collected on his desk, Nixon first acknowledges the right of Congress to impeach him, and then refuses to go: "Richard Nixon is not going to be the first President in American history to be removed from office by the Legislative branch. I am sure that is not the kind of President that the American people elected me to be." Roth had caught perfectly Nixon's sleazy hypocrisy and cunning. We added a little terror: as Nixon waved good-bye to the audience his shoulders hunched and his two hands raised in the Victory sign, actors in the uniforms of the National Guard took their places in the aisles and in front of the stage, their bayonets drawn as the audience filed out.

It proved a sobering conclusion to a funny, purgative evening during which spectators sometimes became so intent on watching the proceedings that they forgot it was a show. During one performance, just as I was winding up Roth's Nixon sketch, a man in the third row yelled at me, *"Go to hell!"* It was a tribute to the moment, but it shook me a little too. I did not want to share the fate of a nineteenth-century actor in the Wild West who once played Iago so convincingly that a member of the audience shot him dead on the spot. (According to legend, the dead man's gravestone read, "Here lies the perfect actor," while the murderer's read, "Here lies the perfect spectator.")

Still, it was gratifying to discover that a collective creation by professionals and students had the power not just to entertain our audiences but to help express their tensions and anxieties over Watergate. During the run of *Watergate Classics* we were a unified community in New Haven, both backstage and in the auditorium. Naturally, there were dissenters—fewer from the right than from the left. One DFA student objected to the show both when it was performed and when it was later published in *yale/theatre,* on the grounds that by draining off anger against Nixon's criminality we were thereby blocking the public's desire for impeachment. It was an interesting demonstration of the conflict between cathartic (or Aristotelian) theatre and activist (or Brechtian) theatre. The student obviously believed in the capacity of the stage to help change the course of history. I entered this debate, more out of pedagogical obligation than pleasure, arguing that *Watergate Classics,* rather than having a soothing effect on audiences, left them aroused and shaken, perhaps even angrier than before. But I didn't have much stomach for this argument. The whole affair seemed too reminiscent of the old confrontations, complete with threats of disrupting the performance.

The Theatre had a strong season that year. Following *Watergate Classics,* we did a production of a new play by Terrence McNally, *The Tubs* (later called *The Ritz* when it was done on Broadway). We had some difficulty identifying a director for this witty farce about a homosexual steambath, perhaps because the subject matter was still a little explosive in those days. After a number of false turns, we settled on Anthony Holland, who was returning to our theatre for the first time since our initial season. Holland was not an experienced director, but he was a funny and intelligent actor, whose work with Paul Sills had taught him a good deal about improvisation and stage business. When we asked him to take an acting part in *The Tubs,* Holland had refused, saying that playing a queer onstage would not be good for his "identity crisis." (Two years earlier Holland had turned down another role with our company, pleading a "nervous breakdownette.") He was eager, however, to direct *The Tubs,* and so we had the pleasure of his amusing company again, along with that of a highly accomplished cast.

It was a sign, perhaps, of how fast history was overtaking us that *The Tubs* was not at all controversial in New Haven; our audiences accepted it with very little difficulty. McNally had not really come to grips with his subject matter,

I thought, except in a long coda at the end of the play in which the hero examines his experiences in the bathhouse, and discovers that he is attracted to men, in spite of his genuine love for his wife. This scene, however, was written almost in another style, and when the play was done on Broadway, it was cut, along with other references to the hero's sexual ambivalence. McNally was an extremely accomplished young playwright, and it was always a pleasure to do his plays. But something still prevented him from taking that extra step out of the realm of entertainment into more thicketed terrains.

The Tubs was followed by the most ambitious undertaking in our history to date, a full-scale production of Brecht and Weill's opera, *The Rise and Fall of the City of Mahagonny.* We approached this monumental music drama with fear and trembling, partly because it required an orchestra of forty-eight, a chorus of eighteen, and a singing cast of nine. We were not an opera company, we were a company of actors; even trained singers usually had problems realizing this difficult modern piece. Still, we had gained much confidence as a result of our successes with other Brecht-Weill works, and we thought we were suitably prepared. Our work with *Seven Deadly Sins* and *The Little Mahagonny* had brought us to *Happy End,* which, in turn, led directly to the big *Mahagonny.*

Alvin Epstein was assigned to direct the production, and Michael Feingold prepared a new adaptation. We engaged, as our conductor, Otto Werner-Mueller of the Yale Collegium, a towering German martinet, with a splendid affinity with the music of Kurt Weill. He was given the additional burden of teaching such bathroom warblers as Jeremy Geidt and Kurt Kasznar (playing Fatty the Bookkeeper and Trinity Moses) how to find their way through the incredibly intricate, often atonal score. Now that Lotte Lenya was too old for the part that had been written for her, Stephanie Cotsirilos was assigned to play Jenny. To play Jimmy and Widow Begbick, we brought in two professional singers—the dynamic Gilbert Price, a tenor capable of thrilling you with his high notes, and the good-natured, generously proportioned soprano Grace Keagy. Alvin, going from strength to strength, had commissioned a design that placed the action in Alaska during the Gold Rush. And after five short weeks of rehearsal, we opened the production for a straight run in the University Theatre.

Norma and I had courted over *Mahagonny.* One of the ways we learned we had mutual interests and affections was the love we shared for this opera. Norma's first present to me was a copy of the German album, with Lenya singing Jenny, and the more I listened to it, the more convinced I became that it was the finest musical work of the twentieth century. It had been a great disappointment to both of us that nobody had yet devised an appropriate production of *Mahagonny* in the United States. The Metropolitan Opera Company still considered it too avant-garde, and Carmen Capalbo's production, off-Broadway, had been a disaster. One of the great satisfactions of our time at Yale was the opportunity to fulfill this failed opportunity. Granted, some of the singing in our production was not fully professional. Still, the major arias were beautifully realized by Cotsirilos, Price, and Keagy, and the other cast members more than compensated for their musical limitations with acting performances of considerable power and ferocity. The production had grit, strength, savagery; it was tough and hard-bitten, qualities noticeably missing from the Met production of 1979. After a triumphant opening, it enjoyed a very successful run; we had vindicated *Mahagonny* for the theatre. On closing night I spoke the part of the Narrator, announcing the coming of the hurricane and the fateful time when God came to Mahagonny; I felt myself to be a part of a major artistic undertaking.

With our next production, we were in trouble again—trouble of my own making. Sam Shepard had given us a strong new play, *Geography of a Horse Dreamer,* perhaps to compensate us for the loss of *Operation Sidewinder* four years earlier. It was short, however, and I thought it could use a curtain raiser. I had other reasons for adding another play to the evening. I wanted to offer production to one of our CBS fellows, Adrienne Kennedy, who had a one-act piece called *An Evening With Dead Essex.* This play was not, as the title might suggest, about Elizabeth the Queen and her unfortunate English suitor. It was about the black revolutionary, Mark Essex, who had recently shot a number of people in New Orleans from the roof of a Howard Johnson's, before being gunned down himself by police. Normally a poetic, somewhat expressionistic writer, Adrienne Kennedy was here writing in an uncharacteristic vein. Her play took the shape of a rehearsal—a group of black actors preparing to reenact scenes from the life of the dead Essex, and recalling his history through slides. I can't, for the life of me, tell you why I wanted to do this particular play. Both in subject matter and treatment, it was far from the sort of thing I normally responded to. I was eager to have more CBS fellows represented in the season; I wanted to be responsive to students demanding more black theatre at the Rep; I assumed that *Dead Essex* would have some impact as a documentary about a significant recent event.

It was not long before I knew that I had made a bad mistake. In her own mind, Adrienne had written not a documentary but an activist piece with revolutionary implications, and the director she selected wanted to treat *Dead Essex* as a piece of racial propaganda. Instead of a symbol of violence, as I had perceived him, Essex was being turned into a symbol of martryrdom, a victim of a repressive white police state. The interpretation was not in the relatively neutral writing, but rather in the stage interpretation. In the script, for example, the action concluded with each of the characters quietly leaving the theatre for home. In rehearsal the play ended with everybody passing a gun from hand to hand, the implication being that they were preparing to take up Essex's dedication to violence.

I considered this inflammatory, especially in view of Patty Hearst's recent kidnapping by the Symbionese Army. I warned Adrienne that there might be a strong and unexpected reaction from the audience. I also said that I could not contribute to any work of theatre advocating revolutionary violence. Both Adrienne and her director kept assuring me that I was overreacting, but at the next rehearsal, when the gun came out again, I got very agitated. The director told me that the gun had no particular meaning; it was just a prop that the actors were bringing home from rehearsal. I had the impression I was being jived, and said so. I asked that the gun be removed from the production. Adrienne then charged me with trying to water down her play. Why, she asked, did I want to do it in the first place? For this I had no answer, except that this was not the play I thought I had accepted for production. It was perfectly all right, I said, to do a play about Mark Essex, but not in a production that so clearly sanctioned his actions. After much consultation, we agreed that the gun would be sheathed in the next rehearsal. It was, but now the sheathed gun was held up provocatively in the air.

We were at an impasse. I admired Adrienne, both personally and professionally, and, as a civil libertarian, was extremely reluctant to exercise any restraints on free expression, even the symbolic kind. Still, these were peculiar times, and, considering the feelings abroad, this kind of gesture struck me as tantamount to shouting "Fire" in a crowded room. I decided to place *Dead Essex* after rather than before *Geography of a Horse Dreamer* in the order of the evening. I also warned the director that if the gun came out onstage in a provocative manner at any time during the performance, I was prepared to circulate a letter to all the spectators present dissociating the Rep from the entire production, and remove it from the stage the following day. Adrienne and her director were both incensed at me, for perfectly understandable reasons, and the black students were questioning my motives in choosing the play in the first place. I wasn't behaving very rationally, I must confess. But perhaps the coincidental conjunction between a play by Sam Shepard and an act of black militancy had awakened in me some hibernating memories and resentments.

On the night of the Thursday preview the audience watched the Shepard play with interest and approval, but by the time the Kennedy play was over, sixty-six people had walked out on it. On opening night we lost forty-four, and there were nights during the run of this production when nobody at all was left in the theatre when the actors came out for their bows. It was odd to stand in the lobby and watch the audience hemorrhaging out of the theatre. It was reacting all right, but not quite in the way I had imagined. Virtually nobody liked this play, and I must confess that the acting was not of high quality. I had spent so much time worrying about the rifle that I had neglected to worry about the performance.

The seventh and final production of the subscription season that year was another new play by Isaac Bashevis Singer, amusingly entitled *Shlemiel the First*. Having forgiven us for the massacre of his first play, Singer had given us another, and I was determined to provide him with a better production. The trouble with *The Mirror* was that it had been performed by an essentially Gentile company. Hoping to avoid that in *Shlemiel*, I cast a lot of Jews, including a couple of Brusteins—Norma as Yente Pesha the matchmaker (a part she played to perfection with a lovely comic shrewishness) and Danny as one of Shlemiel's children. Norma had appeared once before with the Rep, playing Martha Mitchell in *Watergate Classics,* but this was Daniel Brustein's stage debut. In his program bio, he expressed the conviction that he was "the latest and best in a family of wonderful actors." Tony Holland was cast as Shlemiel, the holy fool, who leaves his village of Chelm on an errand, and through a series of misadventures, returns home convinced that he is in another town, the exact duplicate of his own, inhabited by people who look exactly like his wife, children, and neighbors. The wise men of Chelm, just as dumb as Shlemiel, are convinced as well, and much of the humor of the play derives from Shlemiel's effort to be faithful to his wife, in spite of the fact that he is very attracted to a lady who looks exactly like her. It was a charming evening—alas, still insufficiently Jewish. Concentrating on its fantastic folk flavor, the director and the designer left out its yeasty Yiddish seasoning.

It was the end of the year, and the company was tired. But as if everyone had not worked hard enough, I scheduled one more production following the conclusion of the subscription season—a one-week straight run of Aristophanes' *The Frogs* in the swimming pool of Yale's palatial Payne-Whitney gymnasium. This, admittedly, was the idea of a showman rather than an artistic director; I couldn't even claim it as my own. The production had been done before with undergraduate actors, some thirty or forty years earlier, when Burt Shevelove (who originally conceived it and who was to redirect it with our company) was a student at Yale. I had enjoyed a passing friendship with Shevelove over the years, and during my London stay I persuaded him to repeat his undergraduate triumph for the benefit of the Yale Repertory Theatre. I had much admired Shevelove's adaptation (with Larry Gelbart) of Plautine farces, *A Funny Thing Happened on the Way to the Forum.* I imagined that Shevelove might have as much fun with a comedy of Aristophanes. Not surprisingly, the Theatre was in need of money again. It occurred to me that this event might prove both a financial bonanza and a postseason lark for the company.

It was silly of me to think that we could confine the interest in this project to the local area: Shevelove was a very successful Broadway director. Although he had no commercial plans for his production of *The Frogs*—the Yale swimming pool is hardly portable—it inevitably took on the quality of a commercial property; it also took on a few commercial pressures. Shevelove was eager to have a star, Larry Blyden, in the leading role of Dionysus, though he agreed to use our resident company in all the other parts. It soon became obvious that not all of our people pleased him. He began grumbling, for example, about Anthony Holland and Jeremy Geidt ("your two geniuses," he called them), who were cast in the roles of Shaw and Shakespeare—the warring playwrights Shevelove had substituted for Euripides and Aeschylus in the debate scene. Shevelove suggested that we replace them, but they were members of our permanent company, and we were not accustomed to firing people in the midst of a season. Then, he wanted to rehearse the actors on Sunday, which was the company day off, and he demanded two consecutive twelve-hour days for technical rehearsals when the LORT contract strictly limited us to one.

Shevelove hadn't asked for more than he was accustomed to in the commercial theatre; it was simply that our two systems were very different, and these differences were causing conflict. And it was obvious now that we were getting involved in much more than we had bargained for. Shevelove had written a funny, racy, updated adaptation of *The Frogs,* but now he was beginning to insist on a musical score, which he wanted Stephen Sondheim to compose. Sondheim, in turn, was insisting that he could not do the job properly without the help of his orchestrator, Jonathan Tunick. And Tunick needed a large orchestra. Since all of these people were contributing their services for modest fees, it was difficult to deny their requests, but the additional expense of the musicians and the cost of copying—not to mention the funds required for improving the acoustics of the reverberant swimming pool—were adding significantly to the production budget. The small cast on which we had originally agreed in London had now swelled to include not only our eighteen-member company but also a singing and dancing chorus of twenty-eight, a swimming chorus of eighteen, an orchestra of twelve, and a support group backstage of thirty-five. With over a hundred people involved in this undertaking, the production had mushroomed into a spectacular extravaganza, indistinguishable in most respects from a Broadway show, and a musical at that.

In trying to satisfy Burt, I had lost control of the production. I was beginning to get a lot of wan, dour looks from the company, many of whom were puzzled by the presence of this juggernaut in our midst. I did my best to maintain an atmosphere of calm through frequent talks with the actors and crew, explaining the purpose of the production, thanking them for their patience and cooperation. After one of these meetings, Stephen Sondheim blew up at me; I had neglected to thank the chorus and orchestra. He said he knew I was contemptuous of his work, but I didn't have to take it out on his colleagues. It is true that I had criticized Sondheim's music for *A Funny Thing* when I reviewed the show in *The New Republic* (I thought the score was superfluous), but this was not meant as a fundamental judgment on the work of a gifted composer, about which I didn't know that much anyway. I replied awkwardly to Sondheim that I meant no slight either to him or to his musicians, and apologized the next day to the chorus and orchestra for my oversight. I don't think I ever managed to convince the offended Sondheim that I had considerable admiration for the score of *The Frogs.*

The New York critics arrived one night after we opened, and with them an enormous crowd bussed in from the city, including Harold Prince, Leonard Bernstein, and other Shevelove-Sondheim collaborators and friends. This accounted for much quarreling over seats before the show, and much backstage kissing afterward. One of our actors blew a song that had just been handed to him a few hours before; three days after the opening the play was still being rewritten and the score revised. We did our best under these conditions, but I imagine that Shevelove, Sondheim, and Larry Blyden considered us a bunch of amateurs who didn't know how to stage a musical. We, in turn, were surprised by all the last-minute hysteria being introduced into a single production—and a postseason holiday at that—after a year of seven regular offerings in repertory. Even the expected financial benefits failed to materialize. Despite the fact that every seat in the 1,700-seat swimming pool was sold out for the entire one-week run, the budget came in at $18,000 over its initial $25,000 estimate, and all we were able to realize was a modest $7,000 profit.

The critical response to *The Frogs* was wildly enthusiastic, which only helped to reinforce my lack of respect for New York critical standards. The show had some fine moments, to be sure, especially the thrilling first appearance of the swimming chorus of frogs, diving into the pool to the accompaniment of Sondheim's rousing music, but it failed to capture the anarchic spirit of Aristophanes the way I thought *A Funny Thing* had caught the spirit of Plautus. It was successful primarily as a stunt. Nevertheless, the critical ecstasy was unabated, and Martin Gottfried, then with *Women's Wear Daily,* used the occasion as an excuse for hectoring our theatre about its insufferable superior airs. Writing that Shevelove's "theatre intellect and know-how" was "a combination that every academic theatre in the country ought to observe attentively," he added, "It is especially good that an institution such as the Yale Repertory Theatre makes peace with the Broadway that it and theatres like it always met with an odd mixture of contempt, defensiveness, envy, and insecurity." He also claimed that we were hypocrites, after charging us (wrongly) with having invited the glossy opening-night crowd. "Even sorrier," he wrote, "was the Yale company's palpable reveling in the publicity and flash. This only betrayed the sham and hypocrisy that lies beneath our institutional theatres, crying for artistic purity and their decrying of the commercial theatre's pressure."

Gottfried had no way of knowing how bad I was feeling about having brought Broadway to Yale, or how bad our company was feeling about having been used for this purpose. He probably would have sneered at us if he did. The ill will that permeated his review was strong enough to stimulate my Pavlovian rebuttal glands. I therefore composed another letter in my Famous Critics Series, suggesting that he spend his professional time in future reviewing theatres more in sympathy with his own prejudices: "Honest men can differ," I wrote, "about individual plays and productions, but this review reveals you as so clearly unsympathetic, if not downright hostile, toward the very idea of a non-profit repertory theatre that you are, in my opinion, disqualified from reviewing its work. . . . Whatever its virtues, *The Frogs* was never more than a show, while *Mahagonny* [a production Gottfried had panned], whatever its failings, was never less than a work of art. Your inability to perceive this distinction says a lot about your critical standards but even more about your preference for the commercial theatre system. Nobody can bar you from a public theatre, but I was hoping, at least, that you might have the decency to recognize your prejudices and voluntarily stay away."

Gottfried replied—with some justice, I must confess—that I had always been a tough critic myself; why was I reacting this way to somebody else's tough criticism? But the point I think I was trying to make had less to do with his opinion of this or that production than with his critical predilections in general. Imagine a book reviewer fond of the novels of Irving Wallace bringing the same critical values to bear on experimental novels published by Grove Press. Only in the theatre are the products of two entirely different systems subject to review by the same individual. I had made the mistake of introducing the procedures of another world into the world of the Rep, but this error helped to prove my point about the misalliance between the resident theatre and Broadway—and between the resident theatre and Broadway critics. I longed for what I called a "repertory critic," someone who understood the nature of permanent theatres and felt a duty to remind them of their original ideals. But this would require an entirely different kind of theatre observer, one trained in dramatic literature and theatre history, with demanding critical standards. We were helping to change the system of theatre production; we had not been very successful in changing the system of theatre criticism. Our DFA program had been started to help train American theatre critics of learning and sensibility, but unlike our other students, the students in criticism were not making much impact on the profession. Many of the magazines were dropping their drama pages, and the newspapers were still recruiting their theatre reviewers from the sports, dining, dancing, and political sections. The kind of letters I was sending to Barnes and Gottfried was hardly going to improve the situation. But writing them made me feel a little better for a couple of hours at a time.

Critics of quite another sort were beginning to show up at *The Frogs,* who also gave me the opportunity to indulge my incorrigible penchant for correspondence. One irate neurologist from the Medical School wrote in high dudgeon to express his outrage over the "scanty" costumes of the undergraduate aquatic chorus which, he noticed, left a portion of "their buttocks exposed." Incensed by this, he continued: "Since when has Yale become so accustomed to public nudity that a production of this kind can be staged at commencement time without comment or caveat for the proud parents of graduates, alumni, faculty, children of faculty and the public at large?"

He had asked for the courtesy of a reply. I was glad to oblige. "In your outrage and embarrassment over the bare buttocks of the swimmers," I wrote, "you apparently failed to notice that the show also featured an exposed breast on one of the actresses. Whatever your preference for male behinds as opposed to female mammaries, I hope you will agree that, in this time of equal rights for women, your failure to take note of this fact is an insult to the opposite sex. I promise not to report you to the women's movement if you will promise not to report me to the Watch and Ward Society. Please feel free to be disgusted over all future productions of our theatre."

My reference to a reaction by the women's movement was meant to be frivolous; it actually proved prophetic. A day or so later, two female staffers of the Yale Women's Liberation Center (one of many such organizations springing up at the time) wrote to complain that *The Frogs* was "sexist" in limiting "the roles of women to sex objects and an ugly old hag. . . . The issues are too destructive of millions of people's lives to be treated as a joke." I treated their letter as a joke. Instead of referring them to Aristophanes for an appropriate answer, I thanked them for giving me a good laugh: "I think your satire on the humorlessness of the extremist elements of our society is priceless," I wrote, "and I'm going to recommend it to Dwight Macdonald for inclusion in his next book of parodies. If you do something in dialogue form, we would very much like to consider it for our next season at the Yale Rep, which we expect will have strong satirical overtones."

The nuts were multiplying, and I was getting pretty nutty myself. Add to the number of our customary problems the fact that foundations were not coming through with their usual grants and that Kingman had still not committed the church for permanent use, and you may begin to understand why I was starting to grow a little giddy. There was much fiscal disappointment in the spring of that year. Howard Klein, new arts director for the Rockefeller Foundation, had welcomed me warmly upon my return from London and virtually assured our theatre of a large gift, despite the stipulation in our last Rockefeller grant that it was to be the last. Soon after, however, he told me that Rockefeller was withdrawing from institutional giving and slicing its arts budget in half. The $300,000 we had been promised was first reduced to $75,000, then to zero, after Klein informed me of the change in foundation policy. We had built the grant into our next year's budget on Klein's assurances. After a visit to the foundation with Rob Orchard, during which I did a little shameless begging, Rockefeller awarded us an "orderly termination grant" (sounded like cancer to me) amounting to $35,000—and with this settlement, an important and valued relationship between the foundation and our theatre came to an end.

The Andrew Mellon Foundation was beginning to make a round of grants to institutional theatres that year, but to my chagrin, the Yale Rep was not among those being considered. I made an impassioned case for our quality and our need, and managed to persuade the officers of the foundation to include us in their plans. I had less success with the Noble Foundation, which had previously supported our theatre criticism and theatre administration programs. Its executive officer was refusing to reply to letters or phone calls, even refusing to talk to Kingman. There was something about us that was turning off the foundations. Was it only the academic word "Yale" in our title? Was it the high-culture nature of our enterprise? Was it me? Foundations don't usually say when they turn down your proposals or neglect to answer your calls.

Kingman, for his part, responded to our facility problem with what I regarded as an unacceptable proposal. He had decided to build an art history library on the site of our church theatre. What he offered to us, in return, was the university theatre with the promise of a million dollars for renovation purposes. There had been many plans, none of them very feasible, for expanding the old university theatre to accommodate more than one activity at a time.

Stella Adler teaching her first-year class (1966). Among those listening are Ken Howard and Talia Shire.

Kenneth Haigh, Irene Worth, and Jonathan Miller preparing for Robert Lowell's *Prometheus Bound* (1967), the triumph of the first year.

Having my picture taken with Joseph Heller (playwright) and Larry Arrick (director) during a lull in rehearsals for *We Bombed in New Haven* (1967). This is the happiest Heller ever looked at that time.

The Living Theatre in *Paradise Now* (1968), the production that got some of its members arrested on the streets of New Haven.

The wild chorus of *Bacchae* (1969) threatening Pentheus onstage as it sometimes threatened him off it. Henry Winkler is at left, on the shoulders of another student.

Location Theatre version of *The Sea Gull* on the Styron lawn (1969). Norma Brustein as Polina suspiciously eyeing her husband as Shamrayev.

Kingman Brewster trying to calm the storm growing over May Day, 1970.

May Day, 1970. Dave Hilliard, surrounded by his bodyguards, haranguing the students of Yale.

Don Juan (1970). Produced in relative tranquillity after May Day. Alvin Epstein in the title role pretending to ask forgiveness of his father (John Cromwell).

On the S.S. *France,* eating our way to London (1972).

Jeremy Geidt as the Cowardly Lion (Nixon), Stephanie Cotsirilos as Julie, and Jerome Dempsey as the Tin Man (Gordon Liddy) in the "Wizard of Oz" sequence from *Watergate Classics* (1973).

WILLIAM BAKER

Andrzej Wajda's striking production of *The Possessed* (1974). Christopher Lloyd as Stavrogin turns a deaf ear to the pleas of Meryl Streep as Lisa Drozdov.

WILLIAM BAKER

Durang and Innaurato's satirical *The Idiots Karamazov* (1974). Meryl Streep, transformed into the ancient translatrix, Constance Garnett, listens to the singing of Christopher Durang (Alyosha).

The gang from *Happy End* (1975)
—Jeremy Geidt, Alvin Epstein,
Paul Schierhorn, Charles H.
Levin, Ralph Drischell, Jerome
Dempsey—singing the Bilbao
Song.

Elsbieta Chezevska as Laura
being terrorized by Rip Torn as
Adolphe in *The Father*.

A Midsummer Night's Dream in Alvin Epstein's first production of it (1975). Christopher Lloyd, a reptilian Oberon, crawling down the scoop toward Carmen de Lavallade as the sleeping Titania.

The picnic scene from Andrzej Wajda's production of *White Marriage* (1977). Blanche Baker describes the mushroom she found to Stephen Rowe and Carol Williard (standing), and Alma Cuervo, Eugene Troobnick, Norma Brustein, Alvin Epstein, and Elsbieta Chezevska (sitting).

The Yale Repertory Theatre Company in a group portrait. Cast of *Ivanov* on the left; cast of *Puntila* on the right; support staff above.

The Andrei Serban production of Strindberg's *The Ghost Sonata* (1977). Max Wright as Hummel, hovering over Jeremy Geidt as the Colonel.

Serban's production of *Sganarelle* (1978). The Dumb Show, complete with explanatory placard. Left to right: (standing) David Marshall Grant, Mark Linn-Baker, Elizabeth Norment, Michael Gross, Marianne Owen, Richard Grusin, Jonathan Marks; (kneeling) William Roberts and Joyce Fideor; (supine) David Crombie.

Constance Cummings as Mrs. Stilson trying to express herself to Marianne Owen as the Nurse in Arthur Kopit's *Wings*.

The death of Hedvig in my camera-lens version of *The Wild Duck* (1978). Left to right: Eugene Troobnick, Lee Richardson, Marianne Owen, Blanche Baker (on the couch), William Roberts (behind chair), Jeremy Geidt, Christopher Walken. Photograph blowups show old Werle (Sheppard Strudwick) and Mrs. Sörby (Norma Brustein) on the left, and Gina (Marianne Owen) and Hedvig (Blanche Baker) on the right.

A. Bartlett Giamatti, new president of Yale, explaining that my dismissal is "an appointment matter, not a policy matter."

The Yale Repertory Theatre exterior—advertising "The Lucky Thirteenth."

Norma trying on one of her costumes for *The Sea Gull* (1979), a photograph taken to accompany her interview in the New Haven *Register*.

A scene from *The Sea Gull,* showing Norma as Arkadina, Caris Corfman as Nina, and Addison Powell as Dorn.

Our last production at Yale—Andrei Belgrader's *As You Like It* (1979). Harry Murphy as Charles the Wrestler frightens Jeremy Geidt as Duke Frederick, while Mark Linn-Baker reveals his disdain.

My surprise party at the theatre (1979). Embracing Ben Halley (class of '77) while Mark Linn-Baker (class of '79) looks on smilingly. In background on right is David Clennon (class of '68).

But even a million dollars would have been inadequate for a major undertaking of that kind. There seemed to be no way to turn the university theatre into a space acceptable to both the students and the company, and that meant that we would all have to endure the same cramped, irritating conditions that had caused the ugliness of 1969. I told Kingman I was ready to resign; I was not going to engage in a replay of all the old problems. My threat must have helped convince him that we were serious, and, at last, he agreed to find another site for the art history library. After five years of occupying the church on a precarious, temporary basis, we were now permanent tenants, and could begin to plan how to turn the building into a real theatre. With this, I agreed to another two years as dean which, by 1976, would bring me to the end of two five-year terms.

My duties were not over that year until I had attended a conference in Princeton called FACT, an acronym for the First Annual Congress on Theatre (it also proved to be the last). Attended by representatives of both the profit and nonprofit theatre communities, FACT had been organized by certain Broadway producers to provide a forum for discussing issues of common interest in an ecumenical spirit. Translated into colder prose, this meant simply that both systems were looking for some way to help each other avoid bankruptcy by pooling their resources. Broadway, recognizing that soaring costs were making it impossible to produce anything but surefire, pretested products, was looking to the resident theatre for potential properties; the resident theatre, recognizing that foundation support was threatening to disappear, was looking to Broadway for royalties. The FACT Congress, although occasionally disrupted by Richard Schechner of the Performance Group and other radical theatre types was, for the most part, a love feast between two previously wary but now hot and eager partners, ready to jump into bed together.

To my way of thinking, however, the relationship was a mismating—one that, whatever its short-range advantages, would seriously endanger the integrity of the nonprofit theatre movement. I did not believe that resident theatres could justify their private and public subsidies if they became out-of-town tryout houses for commercial New York interests. Such theatres, I believed, had been developed as *alternatives* to the existing system, not as conduits to it, and would inevitably suffer if they were treated, and treated themselves, as theatrical tributaries to Broadway.

I said this in an article for the *Times,* when I reported on the events of the meeting, and almost got myself excommunicated from the resident theatre movement as a result. I had expected to attract some hostility from the Broadway producers; what surprised me a little was the strength of the reaction from my own colleagues in the nonprofit sector. Judging from the published and unpublished outcries, I had apparently hit a nerve; since most theatre people (myself included) like to think of themselves as somewhat purer than ordinary mortals, my article had the effect of throwing back the covers on a surreptitious embrace. The response was not entirely critical. One who supported my views was Robert Kalfin, artistic director of the Chelsea Theatre (then in Brooklyn), who, having just transferred his successful production of *Candide* to Broadway, was in a position to give personal testimony concerning the internal and external pressures on his theatre to develop another commercial hit. This was my fear as well, that the formulaic thinking associated with the commercial stage would begin to seep through the corridors of permanent institutions, that project choices would be influenced by past financial successes. (Just a few years later, Joe Papp would start producing musicals like *The Umbrellas of Cherbourg* at the Public Theatre, and Gordon Davidson, at the Mark Taper, would be trying out Neil Simon's newest comedy.) I feared that the resident theatre movement was in danger of losing whatever chastity it still had left.

VIII

Ill Reports
1974-1975

Good my lord, will you see the players well bestowed?
Do you hear, let them be well used . . . After your
death you were better have a bad epitaph
than their ill report while you live.

—Hamlet

My own chastity was threatened in the summer of that year: I was offered
$50,000 and a free trip to Sweden to do a Volvo commercial. "Do it!" shrieked
Norma. "Do it!" whooped Danny. But how could I continue to exhort my
students to sacrifice if I showed up as a "thinking man" on a TV spot,
salivating over the padded interior of my automobile?

Juicy as the offer seemed, it was never a serious temptation. I didn't really
need the money, since my father had left me enough in his will to provide a
comfortable supplement to my academic salary. One of the reasons I am able
to maintain my insufferable moral posture, my intolerable high-mindedness
about financial matters, is my relative freedom from economic cares. It was
Aristotle, I believe, who wrote that the prime requisite for a virtuous life is
money. A sensible conclusion, with which I entirely agree, though I don't
think it makes the ideal of a virtuous life any the less meaningful.

I was involved in a more serious moral dilemma that summer, which resulted in a savage fight with my wife. Andrzej Wajda, unable to direct *The
Possessed* the previous spring as planned, had now agreed to direct it in the
fall, and Alvin and I were hunting around for a Stavrogin. As usual, we were
meeting with disappointment. Frank Langella accepted in early August—and
fell out in the middle of the month. Lawrence Luckinbill accepted in mid-
August—and fell out on August 30. Wajda was due in three days to begin
rehearsals, and the leading role in his production was still uncast. Alvin and
I faced each other in panic. Finally, out of desperation, we decided to save time
by making simultaneous offers to two actors, Christopher Lloyd and Philip
Kerr, confident (from past experience) that at least one of these actors would

refuse the role. To our surprise and consternation, both of them accepted, and I was left with the miserable task of informing Kerr—the son of close friends of mine in New Haven—that the role I had offered him firmly was no longer available.

Norma was in a fury. She found my conduct ruthless and unfeeling, the sort of thing we had pledged ourselves to avoid. She feared for the future of our theatre if our policies were now to be subject to expediency, and she feared for my character if I were to begin to treat actors as objects. "Mark this day," she said, her face red with anger. *"Mark this day!"* And I, infuriated by guilt, riddled with shame, screamed back, *"I will,"* at the same time grabbing a black felt marker and scrawling a crude large cross on our newly painted white wall.

I wrote to Phil Kerr, admitting this was "precisely the sort of thing I deplore in the theatre, and now I've gone and done it myself." I begged his forgiveness, and he very graciously told me to forget about it. Norma forgave me as well. But that cross still remains on my wall as a morbid reminder.

That summer had its amusements, along with its difficulties. One of these was the long-running Watergate show, which finally closed on August 8, when Nixon, having released his most incriminating tapes, decided to escape impeachment proceedings through resignation, and bid his staff a tearful goodbye the following day. I watched the resignation speech on television at Art Buchwald's house on the Vineyard, heartsick that I didn't have Richard Nixon to kick around anymore. I expressed hopes that the Justice Department might start criminal proceedings against him, but the columnist Joseph Alsop, also present that night, shook his head: "Not a chance." He proved to be right. Our new President, Gerald Ford, would pardon his predecessor less than a month later, thus depriving us of a sequel to the Nixon show and, worse, condemning us to two years of really dull presidential theatre and flat, mediocre acting.

After Wajda arrived in New Haven with his charming wife and collaborator, the very talented designer Krystyna Zachwatowicz, the first thing he did was to recast some of the roles. Wajda had mailed instructions to me describing the qualities he wanted in each of the parts, but with the barriers of language and oceans separating us, I had made some errors. Chief among them was my casting of Alvin as Peter Verkhovensky, a character whom Wajda had imagined to be very young (one of his aims in *The Possessed* was to reenact the war between the generations characteristic of the sixties). We soon shifted Alvin to the role of Kirilov, the suicidal nihilist, and gave Peter Verkhovensky, the ruthless revolutionary, to a young third-year actor, Steve Rowe. Other third-year actors in the youthful cast included Meryl Streep as Liza Drozdov (Stavrogin's hapless mistress), Charles ("Chuck") Levin as the Narrator, and Chris Durang (a playwriting student) as the Student, while the professional company included a beautiful, melancholy Polish actress, Elsbieta Chezevska, who had worked with Wajda in films; Norma played Stavrogin's mother.

We had an excellent company that year, including a few returning actors from previous seasons; and with Wajda in our midst, we had a genuine theatrical artist to guide us. Everyone took to him immediately, because he was also a splendid human being. He conducted rehearsals with a combination of sweet reasonableness and creative stimulation that made us feel we were participating in an experience that was at the same time artistic and spiritual. I had a small part—that of the priest Tikhon, who takes Stavrogin's confession—but I hung around the rehearsal hall a lot, just to absorb some of that marvelous atmosphere. Wajda insisted on communicating through a translator, though his English was a lot better than he modestly assumed, but the actors were soon picking up Polish words and phrases, and employing them in rehearsal to the director's amusement. The production included a mute "chorus of demons" —played mostly by Yale undergraduates—who were there to change the settings, provide transitions, and hover around the action like silent controls; Wajda gave this chorus almost as much attention as he gave the actors. And with the help of his wife, Krystyna—whose contribution amounted virtually to codirection—he recaptured the extraordinary look of the production I had seen in London, with its blistered mud floor, its doomful skies, its eerie luminosity.

Despite the excitement of the rehearsals, however, the dress and preview performances played to relatively unenthusiastic audiences. Traditionally, these were always our worst houses anyway, my theory being that people tend to value what they see according to what they pay for it, and such showings were always either free or discounted. Still, the reaction to *The Possessed* was surprising, considering our own high estimation of the production. None of us could say what was wrong. We decided to have the company do an "Italian rehearsal," or "speed-through," on the afternoon of the opening—rattling off lines at top speed while trying to preserve the acting values. This not only improved the pace of the opening performance, it also changed the tone: that night, we were astonished to hear howls of laughter greeting what we had all assumed to be a morbid tragedy. The audience was telling us something interesting about our production—that it had many of the qualities of a farce. Fast pacing, heightened characterizations, bizarre situations, these were key elements in Dostoyevsky's feverish story of nihilism and revolution; all we had to do was to recognize them. The result was a triumph. Jan Kott called the production the best thing he had ever seen in the United States, while Jack Kroll of *Newsweek* wrote that "the new season will be hard pressed to produce an event of greater interest." Just a day earlier, we had been in considerable distress about our progress. Now we were enjoying a great success. For the hundredth time, I reflected on the volatile and unpredictable nature of the theatrical event.

Our next production was designed to serve as a counterpoint to *The Possessed,* since it was a parody of Dostoyevsky, if not of all Western literature —*The Idiots Karamazov.* Christopher Durang, the young man who had played the Student in Wajda's production, and Albert Innaurato, another third-year playwright, had decided to collaborate on an epic spoof with cabaret overtones. Each had had productions the previous year in workshops where Durang had produced *Titanic,* and Innaurato *The Transfiguration of Benno Blimpie,* two short plays that were later to be seen on the New York stage. *The Idiots Karamazov,* under the title *The Brothers K.,* had first been produced the previous year in a student workshop, where it featured an extraordinary performance by Meryl Streep in the role of the ancient "translatrix," Constance Garnett—notorious to drama students for her early renderings of Chekhov and Dostoyevsky. In that production, Meryl whirled around the stage in an antique wheelchair pushed by her mute lover, Ernest Hemingway, badgering the other characters, chattering incessantly about the genteel marvels of literature, and finally transforming into Miss Havisham from *Great Expectations* in order to assail Alyosha (also transformed—into Pip) about his crude manners and lack of education. Meryl was totally disguised in this part. Her aquiline nose was turned into a witch's beak with a wart on the end, her lazy eyes were glazed with ooze, her lovely voice crackled with savage authority. This performance immediately suggested she was a major actress. Her behavior in the curtain call alone was worth the price of admission, as she rolled her wheelchair through the audience, brandishing her cane at the spectators and shouting "Go home . . . *go home!*" I was determined to see this performance of hers again on the stage of the Rep, and I was equally determined to see a full-scale production of this iconoclastic play.

The Rep version of *The Idiots Karamazov* was somewhat impeded by an inappropriate set design, for which I was to blame. It had occurred to me that a good setting for this satire on Russian drama would be a replication of those tacky interiors seen in photographs of Stanislavsky's Chekhov productions—the flowered wallpaper, the overstuffed furniture, the omnipresent samovar, etc. The trouble was that we were unable to exaggerate the tackiness of something already pretty old-fashioned, so all we got was the look of a badly designed box set. Finally, we decided to strip down the set to its basic components, removing everything but doors and windows, adding some comic portraits of the Karamazov family, and exposing the stage braces that held up the flats and doorframes (stenciled with such designations as *Three Sisters,* Act II). When this was done, it opened up the design, and freed the performance considerably.

The Rep's *Idiots Karamazov* never quite achieved the full manic hilarity of the workshop production, partly because the direction emphasized the farce at the expense of the satiric elements. Still, it was effective enough to stand as one of the high points of our season. From the very first scene, when the three Karamazov brothers leaped onto the stage like the Three Stooges and began to sing "Oh we gotta get to Moscow," through successive episodes featuring Djuna Barnes reading from *Nightwood,* Anaïs Nin seducing every available male, Father Zossima ogling a couple of choirboys, and Ernest Hemingway committing suicide with a shotgun, *The Idiots Karamazov* hammered away at the most beloved works and authors in literature, leaving Western culture in momentary ruins, like the detritus of a dead civilization. The impulse behind all this, like the impulse behind much satire, was essentially nihilistic. But the odd thing was that, however savage, the evening was somehow also very touching and sad. The younger generation was finding its voice through a form of dissent that simultaneously rejected—and confirmed—everything that had gone before, including (it amused me to see) our own production of *The Possessed,* which *The Idiots Karamazov* satirized remorselessly.

The production was heavy with students, which accounted for both its daring and its problems. The restive rehearsal period reflected some of the unpleasantness afflicting the acting program ever since Bobby Lewis came the previous year. Now that Bobby was officially the head of the program, the troubles, if anything, were multiplying. These troubles took a variety of forms. One I should mention occurred during the *Karamazov* rehearsals. A third-year actress in the cast was suddenly forced, as a result of her mother's serious illness, to leave the School for a while; I replaced her temporarily with a second-year actress named Christine Estabrook who, because she was taking the part on such short notice, was promised the opportunity to play it for a few performances. When the actress she had replaced returned soon after, following her mother's death, she demanded her role back, and, to my surprise, refused to let her understudy play it even once. Because she had been away, the woman was not fully prepared to open in the part and, anyway, I thought she owed her schoolmate a certain debt of gratitude for helping us all out under difficult circumstances. Despite my efforts to reason with her, however, she remained firm in her position. The part belonged to her, she said, and nobody else was going to have it. I failed to convince her that she was not yet sufficiently rehearsed to face the public in the play, and I couldn't shame her into an unselfish act. Finally, I said that whatever her expectations, she would have to accept my decision and let Christine perform for a week while she got more rehearsal under her belt. She reacted by raging out of the theatre and inciting some of her classmates in the production to freeze out Christine.

I'm sure the story is common enough in theatrical circles. It would not be worth retelling if it didn't point up something widespread in the atmosphere of the acting department. We were providing roles for students at the Rep, which constituted an important component of their training, but these professional opportunities were also generating a lot of petty malice. Whatever qualities this particular class of acting students enjoyed, generosity was not notable among them, and I was beginning to worry that the chance we were offering them to extend their talents was not doing very much for their characters. I had begun a policy the previous year of giving every graduating actor Equity status plus two weeks' salary at Equity minimum, as a way of rewarding them for their year at the Rep and initiating them into the profession. Now this was being regarded not as a gift but as a right. We were eager to encourage professionalism, but all we were managing to do was stimulate vanity and ambitiousness.

Troubles of another kind were afflicting the acting department. In taking over the program, Bobby Lewis had requested the right to choose his own staff, a reasonable enough demand, since it was now his responsibility to shape the training. Bobby had gone to a number of classes in movement and voice the previous year in order to evaluate the faculty, concluding that he wanted to replace some of the existing teachers with people of his own choosing (the customary practice in such cases was to give a full year's notice). Some of these decisions I agreed with; others caused me pain. Bobby was making his judgments not just on the basis of the instructor's teaching abilities, but also on his or her approach and methods. Still, Bobby had to have the chance to design his own program, and with that in mind, I sent letters of termination to three instructors—one in acting, one in voice, and one in movement—while informing another in voice that henceforth she would be working exclusively as a vocal coach with the company. Because some of these teachers were particular favorites of the acting students, this naturally caused resentment, especially among the second-year actors, who began to turn rude and surly in Bobby's class. The resistance to his work hurt Bobby deeply. Always a popular, well-beloved teacher, he was now being regarded as an ogre. One student offered to audition *him,* as he had auditioned the teachers being terminated; others grew delinquent about going to class. A notice was posted reminding the actors that attendance was mandatory. Somebody tore it down. Still disapproving of Bobby's appointment, Howard Stein was finding it difficult to give him the kind of support he needed with the other faculty members, many of whom (in their last year at the School) were not inclined to cooperate much anyway. The factionalism I had hoped to end with Bobby's new program was instead growing out of control.

Bobby, in turn, was not exactly embracing the responsibilities that went with running a department—making judgments on students, monitoring disciplinary problems, supervising the schedule and staff support. Accustomed to working in his own studio, perhaps with one or two associates, he was not prepared to undertake the burdens of a large and complicated program, and he was secretly opposed to students taking parts at the Rep. What he really expected was to be a master teacher with muscle; he had never pretended to be an administrator. As a result, he tended to duck the unpleasant decisions, leaving those tasks to Howard or to me. Neither of us objected, but deans were not the best people for minor disciplinary actions; the office was a little too threatening and heavy. For example, I had the distressing job of calling in Meryl Streep—then working up two major roles at the Theatre—and telling her that while I was aware how hard she was working, she would have to start attending Bobby's class more regularly if she wanted her degree. A simple request from him would have been much less oppressive.

There was restiveness also in the DFA program that year. Joe Papp had agreed to conduct a new course on the role of the artistic director, but he ran into such strong student criticism of his policies at the Vivian Beaumont that he left in distress before the end of the semester. Another instructor, Rocco Landesman, was experiencing difficulties of another sort. He was fresh out of the DFA program himself and his youthfulness was causing discontent among students, who were continually challenging his authority to teach them. In a doctoral seminar that Landesman and I held together, two students ridiculed his (quite brilliant) comments on a report under discussion, and I had to tell the class that Rocco was on the faculty because he was one of the brightest students who had ever passed through the School. It was not a pleasant year for him until he solved the problem himself by reminding his students that however close in age he was to them, he had one power they did not—the capacity to fail them if they didn't do their work. From that day on, he earned the respect of his peers, and he soon regained their affection too.

I had naïvely assumed that drama students would applaud the presence of their near-contemporaries on the faculty and in the company, if only because this held out the promise of similar opportunities in future for them. What I didn't realize was that, wanting their opportunities *now,* they resented anyone who seemed to be in the way. Jealousy and meanness of spirit were rife in the School. I think I preferred revolution. Kingman had recently referred to the "grim professionalism" he saw pervading the university. I was beginning to understand what he meant.

It wasn't just the students who were gripped by malaise that year; it was infecting the faculty and the administration as well. Petty rivalries and personality conflicts, admittedly always present in a place of this sort, were becoming even more conspicuous than usual. Some of the instructors put on notice by Bobby were, not surprisingly, bad-mouthing him with the students. One refused to teach her tutorials; another announced publicly that her new role as Rep vocal coach was a "demotion." I was making an effort to mediate these disputes and to support Bobby at the same time, not always an easy task in the vacuum of authority that was developing. The most hassled of all of us was Howard Stein, fending off petitioners in his glass-enclosed office at the storm center of the School. Subject to constant pressures, and always on a short fuse anyway, Stein was beginning to lose his temper with the students, and lecture them like a disappointed parent; he was also blowing up at faculty meetings, sometimes rebuking his colleagues for their lack of responsibility. At one point, he had a major flareup with a senior professor in the DFA department when that distinguished gentleman refused to hold tutorials with students during the January work month, choosing instead to spend the time on a Martinique beach.

Meanwhile we were performing a Story Theatre version of Joseph Conrad's novel *Victory.* It wasn't very good, and I was finally beginning to admit to myself that certain forms of literature, particularly those with some depth and texture, were not as appropriate to this technique as fairy tales and myths. *Victory* would be our last Story Theatre production; we had played out the form. Still, it was good to hear this beautiful novel spoken aloud. And its mood of isolation—of alienation, suspicion, and defeat—was pretty close to what Norma and I were feeling during that fall of 1974. One line at the end of the play seemed so apt that Norma always nudged me when she heard it spoken —Lena's dying words to her fastidious lover, Heyst: "Why don't you take me in your arms and carry me out of this lonely place?"

I took Norma in my arms in mid-December and carried her out of New Haven. We spent a two-week holiday on Virgin Gorda, renewing our strength and reviewing our lives at Yale. When we returned, we found a note pinned to our door by Rob Orchard, informing us that Bobby Lewis had suffered a serious heart attack.

The stressful pressures of the first semester had taken their toll on Bobby. He would need more than a month to recover. Adrift before, the acting department was now completely rudderless.

From his sickbed, Bobby gave instructions. The first- and third-year actors were engaged in projects for which supervisors were already assigned. For the problem second-year class, he wanted Norma. This seemed like a sensible idea: she had been functioning all year as his assistant anyway—over my initial objections. Although she had always assisted Stella in much the same way, I did not wish to subject her (or me, for that matter) to potential charges of nepotism in that grim atmosphere. Bobby, however, had insisted, saying that Norma was his choice, not mine, and that she should not be penalized just because she was the wife of the dean. If our marriage was in the way, he added jokingly, I could always divorce her.

I found it difficult to resist such a good-natured appeal, particularly since Norma was available, willing, and qualified. As Bobby's assistant in the second-year class, she was now the obvious person to replace him while he was away. There was a difficulty, however. Bobby—accustomed to scheduling and criticizing scenes by himself—had never given her a chance to function in the class. As a result, while Norma attended all the sessions, she made no conspicuous contribution to instruction, outside of taking attendance and scheduling actors for the playwrights workshop. Out of boredom, she began to participate in the class as an actress, doing some scenes with the students.

I mention this to explain why, although she was the logical choice to conduct Bobby's class while he was convalescing—as well as the logical choice to replace Bobby on the trip we took, with Alvin Epstein, to New Orleans, San Francisco, and Chicago, for the purpose of auditioning applicants in acting and directing—she did not seem the logical choice to the second-year acting students. When Norma was announced as their temporary teacher, members of this class sent a telegram to Bobby on his sickbed, expressing their "surprise" and "disappointment":"We are surprised," the telegram read, "because you led us to believe that Mrs. Brustein was a student in our class and disappointed because we were never consulted or, perhaps, even considered in this decision."

I was surprised and disappointed too—also stunned and appalled. I found this telegram to be profoundly callous, not so much because of the insult to Norma as because of the danger to Bobby. He had just suffered a serious coronary, and was at a very delicate stage in his recovery. To bother him over this problem at such a time—to complain about a failure to consult with them regarding what at most was a one- or two-month replacement—was to treat student governance as more important than a person's health. I had seen enough selfishness and insensitivity among the acting students this year, and

I was fed up. Furious and heartsick, I reacted to the situation rashly. I called the entire second-year acting class into the Experimental Theatre and, handing out blank withdrawal slips, informed the students that if they were dissatisfied with the School or any members of the faculty, they were free to fill out those forms and leave. All of them refused my angry offer, and left the room in a sullen manner.

The next day, word spread through the School that I had dismissed the entire second year. I thought I had better talk to the students in a calmer mood. I was calm, all right, but a little feverish; I had contracted the flu and my temperature was up to 102 degrees. At this meeting, I talked about the hard time they had been giving Bobby all year. I laid out Norma's credentials, describing her background as an actress, as Stella's assistant both at her Studio and at Yale, and as a very effective teacher of Yale undergraduate actors. I also tried to explain why I had handed out withdrawal slips—not to kick them out of School, which I had no power to do anyway, but rather to dramatize, through shock tactics, what it feels like to be rejected. I reminded them, in regard to their demands for participatory democracy, that in a conservatory situation, student governance was not feasible. They were there to absorb the training, not to vote on their teachers; if this condition was unacceptable, the option was departure. The students listened to me, grimly and quietly. The air was not too warm with friendly feeling. Norma then proceeded, in an angry, businesslike fashion, to outline what she intended to do in the course and what she expected of the students. After this, we dispersed, and I returned to my sickbed.

But by this time, the *Yale Daily News* had gotten hold of the story and was interviewing everybody available. The *News* had been planning a series of articles on drama at Yale for which I had already been interviewed regarding the Drama School. At that time I was under fire because of a speech I had given, a few months earlier at Sarah Lawrence, about what I thought to be the function of undergraduate theatre activity. There I expressed my belief that undergraduate theatre courses should be not professionally oriented but related to a liberal arts curriculum and grounded firmly in dramatic literature; it was for the professional schools and conservatories to provide intensive training in craft courses. This speech seemed to inflame the undergraduates at Yale, and the recent unpleasantness with the second year only helped to fan the fires. The drama issue of the *News* duly appeared, festooned with such headlines as DISSATISFACTION PERVADES CAMPUS DRAMA and BRUSTEIN'S PHILOSOPHY SPARKS HOT UNDERGRADUATE OPPOSITION. But the articles covered not only my "negative" attitude toward undergraduate theatre—a position they continued to misconstrue and distort—but also what they called "deep discontent in the School of Drama." This "discontent" was linked to my ill-advised confrontation with the second-year actors, which the *News* described as follows: "When acting Professor Robert (Bobby) Lewis suffered a heart attack during vacation, Drama Dean Robert Brustein appointed his own wife Norma, a lecturer in acting, to substitute as instructor of the second year acting class. The *News* has learned that some second year students wrote a letter to Lewis in the hospital, stating that they felt since the Dean's wife had been a member of the class during first semester, she should not be made its instructor. They also expressed a wish that they had been consulted in the search for Lewis' substitute. . . . The incident now seems to have blown over [but] second year students refused to talk about it. 'Whatever we say will backfire on us,' said one. . . . A drama student explained, 'We are all in a position where we can be removed. No one is free.' "

This story, and others like it that were later to appear, contained so many half-truths and inaccuracies that it would have been impossible to correct them all; nevertheless, I tried. My corrections became the occasion for further distortions. All I succeeded in doing was to settle down deeper into the mire. The conviction that I was hostile to undergraduates, or that I was a Genghis Khan presiding over a Stalinist tyranny, was just the sort of thing most likely to raise resentments during a period when the major issue arousing students was student governance. How could I describe the difference between a conservatory and a university to young journalists who didn't even know the difference between professional training and drama for credit in the liberal arts?

The most damaging charge was that I had appointed my own wife to the acting faculty, imposing her on an unwilling group of students; this was much too rich, in that particular atmosphere, to yield to facts or refutations. From his sickbed, Bobby Lewis wrote a letter to the *News* trying to correct the record, but his efforts were in vain. He did his best to deny that I had been responsible for Norma's appointment, declaring, "There was only one person I wanted for this many-faceted job and that was Norma Brustein, and she was appointed over Dean Brustein's objection." He also gave an account of her career as an actress and teacher—something one would have thought the *News* might have thought to research, since her undergraduate courses were legendary.

But all these efforts were futile. Anytime a faculty member or a drama student wrote a letter to challenge the outlandish charges that the Drama School opposed undergraduate theatre, or that drama students were in fear of their lives, or that Norma was a member of the class rather than a professional teacher, the *News* responded by "standing behind its study on problems in drama at Yale," and defending its decision to "rely on the students involved" rather than investigating more objective sources of information. Norma had always ridiculed my concern with the inaccuracies of the *Yale Daily News,* which she considered an organ of amateur journalism that nobody took seriously. Now, from painful personal experience, she was learning that even an undergraduate newspaper can have a serious influence on your life.

For the events had affected her deeply. She was having difficulty sleeping and she was full of remorse. She thought she had not only brought misfortune on me but ruined her own career. And in the claustral atmosphere of New Haven, she was vulnerable to a great deal of malice. One of her so-called friends, the wife of a Yale faculty member, upon meeting her on the street, remarked, "You're such a good decorator and housewife. Why do you want to meddle in your husband's profession?" Subsequent stories in various other student newspapers referred to my "warped narcissistic incestuous pedagogy" and suggested that I turn over the School to someone else, "one perhaps without a wife." A satire in the *News* pictured me becoming president of Yale and appointing Norma as provost. For a time, we felt trapped in quicksand, drowning in bad will. Norma's looks were eloquent. "Why don't you take me in your arms," they said, "and carry me out of this lonely place?"

There was a real issue buried under this rubble that few were then prepared to discuss—namely, whether a gifted and spirited woman should be prevented from practicing her profession because she was married to somebody on the same faculty. The women's movement had forced some adjustments in the University's traditional nepotism rule, which for years had limited the role of faculty wives to baking cookies and handing out tea. But it wasn't yet very effective in changing people's attitudes, and "the Sisters" had nothing to say in Norma's defense. In the minds of the outside world, I was both my wife's employer and her husband; and there were probably suspicions abroad that I was enriching myself through her appointment.

The fact is that I had long resisted giving Norma what she clearly deserved —namely, good roles at the Rep and teaching assignments at the School. She had held the title of "Lecturer" on our faculty since 1971 so that she could conduct her undergraduate and residential college classes, for which she had been recommended by various college masters and Yale faculty members. But her appointment form was signed by the university provost, not by me, and her salary was minimal. Norma complained about her low salary, as she complained about her small roles. But I was convinced that only by maintaining a low profile could she practice her profession without arousing accusations from the community. Today I know I was too cautious; the accusations would come anyway. I was trying to protect her, and all I succeeded in doing was deprive her of her rightful due. Only some years later, when the women faculty of the Drama School protested Norma's low rank and pitiful salary to the Yale administration, did she receive the portion she deserved, despite her misfortune in being my wife.

Bobby returned to the School in March, by which time Norma had won the admiration and the respect of her second-year class. He was not certain he wanted to come back to that atmosphere, and when he met the class for the first time, he told the students of the despair he was feeling over his failure to create a humane situation. It was obvious that the bad karma of the acting department had not disappeared during his convalescence. Students were refusing roles they had been assigned, or withdrawing from production in the middle of rehearsals. Attendance was still off, and those who came were often late. Everybody's tempers were frayed; soon after Bobby's return, a black actress withdrew from the School, claiming that Bobby had insulted her "personhood." As for Bobby himself—understandably worried about further stress—he had begun to shrink from controversy, eager to conserve his remaining strength and energy.

In short, the hopes I had had for a radical transformation of the acting training were all being dashed. I loved Bobby Lewis, and so did Norma, but it was obvious that he had lost the appetite, if he ever really had it, to be a chairman. I had no wish to expose Bobby to any further problems. On the other hand, I had a responsibility to the program and to the training of the students. Who was going to run the acting department now that Bobby had decided to limit his involvement to watching scenes? I discussed the situation with the students in the course of several meetings. I even discussed it with Chuck Levin and Meryl Streep during a Passover seder held at our house. And, of course, I discussed it daily with Bobby, who was now prone to palpitations whenever we touched on disagreeable subjects. As a temporary expedient, we agreed to hire an administrator for the acting department the following year who would assume the several tasks for which Bobby had no temperament, thus leaving him free to enjoy the authority of his position without the onerous responsibilities.

I was considering another solution, which was to admit defeat and disband the entire program. In eight years we had gone through four or five chairmen and six or seven master teachers—something seemed to be wrong with the whole system. I had a fantasy of dismissing the acting faculty and graduating out the remaining students, then combining the released salaries and scholarships into a single pool that would fund a junior company of recently graduated actors, its purpose being to service the directing and playwriting projects, and to perform in the Cabaret. The more I thought about this solution, the more I liked it. In one fell swoop we could put the Yale acting training out of its misery. No more would we have to worry about how much time the Rep took away from student preparation for classes, or how much time the classes took away from the Rep. No longer would we be subject to those wearisome quarrels and disputes. Why, the plan was worth trying if only to put an end to those boring semiannual disquisitions at my house with the department on the purpose and nature of acting. And it could have a very positive influence on the rest of the School, since young performers would now be available for the projects of student playwrights and directors without interference from other activities.

But it was a desperate notion, not a serious one, just something to keep my mind busy during sleepless nights. I played with the idea the way I often played with the idea of resignation, as a way of keeping alternatives open when things looked dark. Norma tolerated these fantasies, just as she tolerated my various efforts to draft a letter of resignation. Whenever it seemed as if I was getting serious, she would laugh at me and tell me to forget it. The letters of resignation she made me tear up.

My regard for the university was being tempered then not only by the problems in my School, and what I considered the irresponsibility of the undergraduate press, but also by the behavior of academic institutions in regard to the issue of free expression. Yale enjoyed a considerable reputation at this time as a center for higher learning; it did not enjoy a similar reputation as a center for free speech. This was partly because of its treatment of visiting lecturers whose opinions ran counter to the prevailing wisdom of students and faculty. In 1963, when Kingman Brewster was provost of the university, he succeeded in persuading the Political Union to withdraw its invitation to Governor George Wallace of Alabama because of what Brewster called "the damage which Governor Wallace's appearance would do to the confidence of the New Haven community in Yale and the feelings of the New Haven Negro population." This action, while arguably liberal in intention, established a principle and a pattern that would soon seriously threaten liberalism in the university. A few years later, for example, General William Westmoreland was forced to cancel a visit to Yale because of vociferous demonstrations by anti-war students who had seized the Law School auditorium where the general had been scheduled to speak. Secretary of State William Rogers had to postpone a visit to Yale as a result of threatened disruptions by radical students.

And in the worst such episode, the Stanford University physicist William Shockley was forcibly prevented from participating in a debate at Yale on the subject of genetics because of an organized disruption described as "open, determined, and menacing from the start." On this particular occasion, President Brewster urged not the cancellation of the visit but a boycott of the debate, saying that the invitation involved "the use of free speech as a game," which made "provocation rather than understanding . . . a basis for inviting speakers to a campus." Shockley's racial theories were unquestionably provocative, as well as highly insulting to black people; but the original invitation to debate these theories had been made at the suggestion of Roy Innis, black chairman of the Congress of Racial Equality. The issue was not whether these theories should be accepted but whether they should be heard. At this particular event, nothing was heard but the derisive shouts of black and white undergraduates who drowned out the speakers with applause, vocal insults, and obscenities the moment they appeared. President Brewster deplored the behavior of the disrupters, and expressed his opposition to what he called their "storm trooper tactics" in his baccalaureate address later that year. Twelve of the offending students were suspended for the next fall term, though the Executive Committee of Yale College (of Wright Hall fame) later ruled that they could be readmitted to the university if they expressed willingness "to abide by the conditions of General Conduct" in the undergraduate regulations. (Eleven of the twelve agreed, and returned in the fall, on disciplinary probation for one semester.)

The only positive thing to come out of "the Shockley affair" was the formation of a committee to study the deteriorating nature of free speech at Yale. It was chaired by the distinguished historian C. Vann Woodward. The committee's report, a model of clarity and forthrightness, reaffirmed the commitment of the university to the principles of free expression, even when the speaker was offensive to others and the speech defamatory or insulting. It was an important statement about First Amendment rights at Yale, the only embarrassing thing being that anyone should have been required to reaffirm these rights in an institution ostensibly devoted to free inquiry. To some it seemed that the chickens of May Day were coming home to roost.

The report was not uncritical of the Yale faculty and administration, among whose ranks it detected "instances of faltering, uncertainty, and failure in the defense of principle." These criticisms, however, were tempered by an understanding of the unusual historical circumstances we had all been living through. Inevitably, the report and the committee came under attack from various quarters of the student body and the faculty, and Vann Woodward suffered from considerable personal abuse.

It was not a pleasant time for Kingman, either, who was criticized in the report for failing to "assert the primacy of free expression over competing values." I felt bad for him, because I know he took these criticisms hard, but I was glad such things were finally being said in a clear, authoritative manner. It was a visible sign that the era of coercion was drawing to a close, and the university might once again be open to the expression of minority opinions.

All this time, in the midst of considerable tumult, the Rep was moving forward vigorously. A revival of *Happy End* was mounted, with most of the original cast intact, except that Chuck Levin had replaced Stephen Joyce as Bill Cracker and that Norma, following Nancy Wickwire's death, was playing the Major. The show was received with considerable enthusiasm. On one weekend, Stephanie Cotsirilos lost her voice and Meryl Streep, who had a small role in the production, played Lillian Holiday for three performances. I almost ruined her performance by sitting in the first row (the only seat available) wearing a red tie. She sent me a frantic message at intermission to get the hell out of there if I expected her to get through the afternoon. (Years later, she played the part on Broadway in the Chelsea Theatre production, with Christopher Lloyd as her leading man; on that occasion, my tie was blue.) Meryl was being worked very hard that year. She was also cast in our next production, playing Bertha in Strindberg's *The Father.*

The Father had not originally been scheduled for the season. What we had planned was a sequel to *Watergate Classics* to be called *American Patrol.* A few sketches were in hand, including a short Durang satire on David Rabe's *Sticks and Bones,* and a skit about American immigrants called *Wretched Refuse,* but this time we couldn't find sufficient material to make up an evening —the monotonous Ford administration was simply not generating enough outrage or interest to stimulate our writers. Persuaded by Norma to postpone this production until a more propitious historical occasion, I looked around for a new play for a few weeks before settling on a recent submission, Robert Patrick's *Kennedy's Children,* but the playwright withdrew the play from us when he was offered an off-Broadway production. Finally, Michael Feingold suggested that we do *The Father* and I agreed. I liked the play a lot, and it suddenly occurred to me that Rip Torn would be marvelous in the title role.

Torn immediately consented to play it, providing that he be allowed to contribute to the translation. This seemed a reasonable enough request, and it was acceptable to Jeff Bleckner who was returning to the Rep (after a five-year absence) to direct the play. But while Torn's work on the text went smoothly enough, his conduct in rehearsal was weird. One of the most intense human beings any of us had ever met, Torn had been involved a few years before in a fracas with Norman Mailer during the filming of one of the novelist's movies. In one of the scenes Torn had hit Mailer on the head with a toy hammer, and Mailer had bitten one of Torn's earlobes. None of this was very encouraging to us at the Rep. We never knew when he was going to interrupt rehearsals over some apparently insignificant provocation like a lost prop or a missing costume element. Everybody suffered from this behavior, but Bleckner bore the brunt of it. As director of the play, he was an authority figure to Torn, therefore a juicy target if he didn't watch himself carefully. (I stayed out of Torn's sight entirely, sensing that, as artistic director, my presence might be particularly provocative.) On the evening of dress rehearsal, Torn refused to perform unless an antique rifle on the wall of the set was immediately replaced by a flintlock, and after this was done, he walked through his entire part making no attempt to act it. Instead, he used up the time examining the props, refitting his costume, glaring at the other actors.

On the evening of the preview, when he faced his first audience, I learned the reason for this curious behavior. Torn had been getting used to the room, turning his costume into clothes, making the props his own possessions. That night he proceeded to give a performance that was so riveting in its realism, so honest and terrifying, that we feared he might, at any moment, do serious harm to Elsbieta Chezevska, playing Laura, his malevolent wife. As it was, she was a mass of bruises; and Torn tended to treat her offstage with the same cruel contempt with which he regarded her in the play. It was quite another matter with Meryl, playing his beloved daughter, Bertha; both on stage and off he was the doting father. Once, after Meryl had complained to me of overwork and I suggested that she let her understudy do her role in *The Father,* she rejected the idea with horror: "Impossible!" she said, "Rip would never stand for it. He really thinks I *am* his daughter. If anybody went on in my place, even if you told him about it beforehand, he would stop the show immediately and say, *'Where's Bertha!'* "

Torn never again achieved the full frightening power of that preview performance, but even at a lesser intensity, he gave an impressive display to audiences. By the time we opened, Jeff Bleckner had lost a good deal of weight and was pasty-faced. Any vestigial resentment I may have felt over his behavior during the *Sidewinder* affair was gone now; he had paid his dues in full. As for Torn, he became a pussycat as soon as we opened. A pleasant, intelligent dinner companion at home, he was a happy actor at the theatre, affirming every night that he had never before worked under such congenial conditions. I didn't tell him what his satisfaction had cost the company; but his rehearsal behavior may have accounted for Elsbieta's subdued performance in a role where we had all expected her to command the stage. At any rate, I had become convinced that we would have to have precisely the right part under precisely the right controlled conditions before I again subjected the company to Rip Torn's special brand of theatrical reality.

The Father was followed by *The Shaft of Love,* a play by CBS Fellow Charles Dizenzo satirizing television soap operas. This had some hilarious performances by Streep, Levin, Grifasi, Jerry Dempsey, and Norma as a female pyschiatrist, but it was not well received. Although Dizenzo knew this world intimately, having been a scriptwriter for CBS, the target was too easy, and the production failed to carry the play beyond facile media parody into what I thought to be its deeper intention: the sense that life itself was permeated with the conventions of soap opera. This was what had originally attracted me to the play, but since the playwright seemed not to be aware of it, I had to admit that I may have been fantasizing.

The disappointment of *The Shaft of Love* was soon alleviated, however, because now we were gearing up for a massive undertaking that would prove a hallmark in our history: Alvin Epstein's production of *A Midsummer Night's Dream.*

Having already succeeded in marrying Shakespeare's text with Purcell's music in his production of *The Tempest,* Alvin had done the exploratory work necessary to extend his investigations into *The Dream,* for which Purcell had kindly provided another score. Actually, the music was for a Restoration opera, named *The Faerie Queene,* based on Shakespeare's play, but it occurred to me that it could be adapted in much the same way. When I suggested this to Alvin, he requested a week off to read the play and listen to the score. He emerged from hibernation, his eyes glowing, to present us with a thrilling concept.

Alvin had made a discovery through his careful, methodical examination of Shakespeare's imagery—that *A Midsummer Night's Dream* was not the charming pastoral romance of nineteenth-century tradition, full of gossamer fairies and languorous lovers, or even the daytime circus world of Peter Brook's invention. It was rather a fractious and contentious play about conflict, packed with images of warfare and quarrel. Theseus wins Hippolyta in battle; the lovers quarrel incessantly; Oberon and Titania are engaged in a serious dispute over a changeling child; even the fairies are at each other's throats. In Alvin's mind, this play was less a dream than a nightmare—a battleground of lunatics and lovers—and it was as a dark, brooding nightscape that he proposed to do it.

For this purpose, he evolved with his designer, Tony Straiges, the brilliant student with whom he first collaborated on *Mahagonny,* an abstract wooden architectural setting, full of curves and slides and inclined planes, with the court scenes performed in front of a massive battle drop painting after Paolo Uccello, depicting knights with lances on horseback. When this rose, during the "transformation" into the fairy world, a huge wooden scoop was revealed on which the forest scenes were played before an enormous moon, textured by Straiges with popcorn. With a set of such magnitude, and with an orchestra of twenty-six, a chorus of sixteen, and a cast of twenty-four, this was obviously going to be an expensive undertaking—an expansive one, too, requiring the use of the more spacious University Theatre. Alvin's budget was larger than any approved at the Rep before, except the one for *The Frogs,* but he was reluctant to compromise on any details—the expense, he argued, was essential to realize his concept. We did some trimming, nevertheless, and we supplemented our own meager funds with a grant of $4,000 in support of the physical elements of the show from the Corbett Foundation of Cincinnati; we also persuaded the School of Music to contribute something toward the cost of the orchestra and chorus, since both units were peopled primarily with Music School students.

The music, by the way, was arranged and conducted by Otto Werner-Mueller, that Wagnerian giant who had beaten us into submission during *Mahagonny.* The acting company included Christopher Lloyd and Carmen de Lavallade as Oberon and Titania; Meryl Streep, Peter Schifter, Stephen Rowe, and Kate McGregor Stewart as the lovers; Jeremy Geidt and Franchelle Dorn as Theseus and Hippolyta; and, as the rustics, Chuck Levin, Joe Grifasi, Jerry Dempsey, Paul Schierhorn, and Fred Warriner. As Puck, Alvin decided to cast a woman—a third-year actress, Linda Atkinson, who, like Oberon, shaved her head for the part.

The magical settings, the sumptuous costumes, the lovely Baroque music, and, above all, the splendid performances resulted in a triumphant evening that represented, surely, the culmination of everything we had ever done. Certain images from the production remain fixed in the mind with the tenacity of dreams: Oberon, encrusted with cobwebs, slithering down the scoop toward the sleeping Titania like a luminescent reptile; Titania shuddering in her sleep in exquisite spasms; the four lovers, gradually reduced to their underwear, struggling on the stage like bumptious children; Bottom, awakening from his dream with the memory of having had the sexual equipment of an ass; Flute, passionate for onions, losing the two he had placed in his dress to serve as breasts at the moment he begins his "death scene"; and, finally, Puck delivering the melancholy epilogue to the concluding elevating strains of Purcell as the lights faded slowly on the moon.

It was one of those productions an artistic director has no problem whatever in monitoring. I saw it many times, and always with the same uplifting sense of delight. One Saturday matinee, as I popped out in the air during intermission, I came upon Bart Giamatti standing in front of the theatre engaged in conversation with another professor of English. I invited them both in to see the final act. I had encountered Giamatti seldom since the Wright Hall episode, usually during meetings of the Yale Dramat, where he and I both served as board members. It was known that he was not particularly friendly toward the Drama School or the Repertory Theatre, possibly because of his affiliation with the undergraduate Dramat, possibly because his wife was an alumna of the old Drama School. Since I had never seen him at any of our productions, I figured this might be an opportunity to introduce him to our work. We stood together in the back of the jampacked auditorium, watching the Pyramus and

Thisbe scene, listening to the laughter and applause of the excited audience. After the show he thanked me for having invited him in, saying that he had never expected to see anything like this. But if he ever came to the Rep again, I didn't know about it.

One spectator missed that raucous final act of *A Midsummer Night's Dream* —Walter Kerr of *The New York Times*. He left the play after the second intermission, informing Jan Geidt, our press officer, that although he found the production "magnificent," he had to leave early for another engagement. This premature departure didn't prevent him from reviewing us in the Sunday paper. His notice was appreciative but grudging. He called the settings "among the most beautiful I have ever seen on any stage," and decided that the Purcell music was "irrelevant but charming to listen to." He complained that "we rarely become interested in the characters as characters," and concluded by admitting that "an early morning call took me away after two and one half hours of the three hour-plus collage; but I'd found the collage seductive enough in its otherworldly way."

It was not the tepid nature of the review that dismayed us all. Mr. Kerr had a right to his opinion, which we were able to weigh against a large number of positive notices. It was rather that he had written his piece without having seen the most important part of the production—the act that summarized the entire concept. William Honan, editor of Arts and Leisure at the *Times*, invited me to reply to Kerr's review in his new "Backtalk" section, but I declined. By this time I was tired of quarreling with critics. Instead, Michael Feingold wrote a short piece rebuking Kerr for failing to mention the name of the director in his entire review, though Alvin's contribution was vital; for failing to understand the organic relationship between the music and the text; for failing to perceive the idea behind the whole production. Feingold concluded: "To attend a permanent theatre institution and single out 'elements' of production is as useless as isolating the production itself without reference to the other works in the repertory; it is to ignore the fact that each person's work, and each production, has value only in the service of a larger idea than itself, that it is merely a step in a company's life, another muscle tensed for an even greater leap in future. To praise or blame isolated 'elements' without reference to the whole is a brand of criticism that means nothing to a theatre dedicated to steady progress toward a long-range goal."

It was a presumptuous reply, for which we could be fairly chided for lacking manners. It was at the same time, I thought, an important statement. I was heartened that in Michael Feingold we might finally have developed that "repertory critic" I had been seeking for so many years, though when he began to practice criticism in *The Village Voice,* he disqualified himself, because of his previous association, from applying his perceptions to our own work.

A few days before the opening of *Midsummer,* on April 29, the Vietnam war officially ended, so the production became something of a celebration. Despite the long-awaited peace, despite the lift of the show, my own mood was hardly celebratory. Actors were now giving us a gorgeous theatrical experience. Actors had also given us considerable grief and pain, and were undermining my faith in the American stage. I had a meeting with the problematical second-year class in April, as I had met with it many times in preceding months, and tried to talk to the students about empathy. I said that if they did not feel for the suffering of others, they could never properly inhabit a character, they could not be true actors. Because they lacked empathy, I added, Norma had been badly hurt and Bobby's faith in his calling was shaken. Something crucial was missing from that class which had begun to affect the entire school.

From all outward signs, we had had a very successful year. Most of the productions were well performed and well received, and our subscribers had grown to four thousand, half of them students. But I felt tired and dejected, despite the refreshment of my recent year abroad. Norma's moods were darkening, and so were mine. In another year I would have completed two full terms as dean. I was feeling real satisfaction in the productions of the Rep, and real satisfaction in the accomplishment of our graduates, but I had still not managed to complete what I had first set out to do—integrate a training program with a professional theatre so that the young could help transform the ideals and artistry of our stage. Would I ever attain that increasingly distant goal? I was filled with doubts. The era of actors' egoism was threatening to accomplish what the years of radical tumult had not—kill my hopes for the future. Consequently, when I heard President Brewster mention, during the honorary-degree dinner in May, that Yale deans are appointed only for ten years, I went to the provost soon after and told her of my intention to leave my post in June of 1976, the final year of my current appointment.

IX

Losses
1975-1976

Musing upon the king my brother's wreck
And on the king my father's death before him.

—T. S. Eliot, *The Fire Sermon*

I was feeling nervous, brain-tired, a little washed out. I had just been fitted by my dentist with a device to keep me from grinding my teeth at night. I had agreed to write my customary quota of articles that summer; but even in the serene atmosphere of Martha's Vineyard, I was finding it hard to complete a sentence. I sat in my study, watching my neighbor's goats grazing in his meadow, pleasuring in the lush landscape over which a hawk circled lazily in the sky. But after these two uninterrupted months of relaxation were over, I didn't think I had very much to look forward to.

That summer, it took Norma and me considerably longer than usual to enter the rhythms of the Vineyard. There are periods when the exterior world seems to parallel and reinforce your internal feelings. At this time all our appliances decided to break down simultaneously. The pump was losing its prime at least once a week; the motor in the washing machine had frozen; the hot-water heater was blowing fuses; the boat wouldn't start. When Norma and I first took up housekeeping together and began accumulating possessions, I used to imagine that all our appliances would choose the same moment to complete their cycle of planned obsolescence. That summer, my fantasy was coming true, and I was reaching the end of some obsolescent cycle myself.

These deliberations were particularly self-indulgent in the light of what was happening to others. What a terrible year for illness and death! In June we heard that Larry Blyden had been killed in an automobile accident while driving through Morocco. Two weeks later we learned of the death of Yale's veteran teacher of scene design, Donald Oenslager, one of the two surviving figures from the George Pierce Baker days. At the end of the academic year the other survivor of that period also died—Constance Welch, the very first acting teacher at the School of Drama. That fall Susan Sontag contracted a virulent form of breast cancer. In December Hannah Arendt died, thus depleting the world of one of its few remaining intellectual giants. And at the end of the summer I learned that one of the greatest of these, Lionel Trilling, was in the hospital dying from cancer of the pancreas.

Trilling had been my intellectual father. My own father, who had died seven years earlier, used to say that every morning he would get up and read the obituary page of *The New York Times;* if his name wasn't on it, he would get dressed and go to work. He felt, he told me, as if he were in the front lines of a major war, with people dropping all around him. All this death and illness was telling me what he meant. Along with disease and death, there was considerable madness as well. Norma's mother came down ill that summer, and we had to go to Miami, where she lived, to place her in a hospital. We stayed at an overdecorated luxury hotel on the beach called the Deauville, advertised in the brochures as superior to its namesake in southern France because it had no "antique and mildewed castles." During our short visit, somebody, in an unusual use of the facilities, decided to shoot himself to death in the men's room. And a few days after our return the estranged husband of one of our faculty members invited me to a press conference in his New Haven hotel room, which he had called to announce that he was a candidate for the presidency of the United States.

With all this curious behavior, you might think the country was suffering some kind of internal convulsion. But as a matter of fact, our appointed President, Gerald Ford, was actually leading us through a period of bovine monotony. The most electrifying thing he was able to do, after pardoning Nixon, was bump his head a few times on plane doors and get shot at twice within a short period of time. Ford was hardly a convincing chief executive; even the assassination attempts were bungled.

Do I sound a little hysterical? I probably was. The tensions were getting to me. I usually have three ways of dealing with intolerable situations: to make a joke, to make a scene, to make a decision. I believed that I had taken the third course when I told Hanna Gray in June of my intention to leave the Drama School at the end of my second term, in compliance with what I assumed to be the new university regulations. But I wasn't feeling any relief, partly because Hanna had not conveyed my decision to Brewster. Norma took the occasion of his birthday party on the Vineyard in early summer to inform the president of my conversation with the provost. At first he looked startled, then waved the matter away, saying "Everything's negotiable." We made a date to discuss the situation, but for one reason or another the meeting kept getting postponed. Not until August did we finally sit down to discuss my future at Yale.

By that time something really encouraging had happened. The Ford Foundation—which, for nine years, had virtually ignored the existence of the Yale Repertory Theatre—wrote to inform me that it was considering a major grant of $500,000 as endowment for the Rep and the School, on the provision that it be matched (on a three-to-one basis) with another million and a half dollars from outside sources. McNeil Lowry had recently retired from the foundation, and with him had been retired his policy opposing support for the arts in universities. We were still ineligible for Ford's cash reserve plan because of our accounting procedures, but Marcia Thompson, who had taken over many of Lowry's responsibilities, was working out the terms of a special grant that was to be valuable not only in itself but also for the manner in which it acknowledged the inseparability of our training program and our professional theatre. Hitherto, foundations had either supported the School or the Rep. This grant supported both, and in such a substantial manner that when matched at three to one, it would triple our meager $1 million endowment. This was significant enough to make me reexamine my options. I still wanted to relinquish my position as dean of the School. But it occurred to me that if I remained as artistic director of the Theatre I might be able to enjoy the creative pleasures of the job without its administrative hassles.

When I proposed this plan to Kingman, he was not very keen on it. What he preferred was for me to accept a third five-year term as dean. The ten-year rule announced by him at the degree dinner, he confessed blushingly, was a subterfuge devised that year to encourage the departure of another dean. In my case, he told me, the "rule" didn't exist; I was welcome to remain as long as I liked. But, he hastened to say, Yale University was built on an administrative system of deans, who controlled the budgets of their respective schools and supervised faculty appointments. How could I drop the title and still keep the power? Even were it possible for me to remain at Yale only as a theatre director, was I prepared to tolerate another Drama School dean telling me whom I could hire and how much I could spend? He advised me to take some time to think it over.

I was already convinced that the decanal structure of a university was incompatible with the needs of a professional school. Deans made young people feel like graduate students pursuing degrees instead of conservatory artists developing their talents, and they caused faculty members to think in terms of tenure and course loads and "perks" instead of the consuming daily needs of the training. I had gotten pretty jaundiced about the traditional academic paraphernalia, which seemed to me a considerable obstacle, if not a threat, to the creative spirit. Maybe Lowry was right, after all, and universities *were* poor breeding grounds for the arts. Still, if universities didn't support the serious theatre, then who would? And without such support, how could the serious theatre avoid being absorbed by the commercial system? I couldn't make up my mind. I still hadn't lost my faith in Yale as a laboratory for our work. But I didn't want to dissipate my dwindling energies in such demanding academic matters as ceremony, discipline, and procedure, not to mention that trio of recent obsessions called "racism, sexism, and affirmative action." After considerable reflection, I returned to tell Kingman that I would remain no longer as dean; and he agreed to investigate how Yale might bend its traditions to accommodate my desires.

Kingman had always been a dependable source of moral support, but in recent months his support had also become material. Not only had he provided us with the permanent use of the church, but he had also committed $500,000 of Yale's precious (and shrinking) income with which to perform the necessary renovations. It was the first tangible sign that the university believed the Theatre to be an integral part of its regular operations; I considered it a significant endorsement of the performing arts. Brewster felt a deep personal pride, I knew, in what had happened at the School of Drama; more than once, he had referred to it as "the jewel in Yale's crown." The Theatre was attracting considerable good publicity to the university; as Kingman had hoped, it was also helping to attract scholars to New Haven who might otherwise have been repelled by the city's grim, featureless environment. Yale's growing commitment to our enterprise was obviously weighing heavily in my present deliberations.

It was our tenth anniversary season at the Rep. Could so many years have passed so fast? It was also the fiftieth anniversary of the School. I decided to celebrate the two birthdays by reviving three of our favorite past productions: *A Midsummer Night's Dream* from the ninth season, *Don Juan* from the fourth, and *Dynamite Tonite!* from the first. This would provide something of a historical perspective on what we had done, and it would provide an excuse for a reunion with some of our old associates. While the church was in the process of being renovated we would stage *Midsummer* in the University Theatre, and then have a grand opening of our proud new theatre with my production of *Don Juan.*

As usual, we supplemented the existing company with a number of recent graduates from the School, and once again these people filled positions in every area of the Theatre. As usual, we also suffered some losses. Our good friend Jerome Dempsey left us after two solid seasons at the Rep, and Meryl Streep couldn't be persuaded to spend a year with us following her recent graduation. Losing Meryl was a particular disappointment, and not just because she was so obviously destined for greatness. The company was in sore need of a leading lady with the capacity to transform into character parts, and from the moment I first saw her, I expected Meryl to fill this gap. In our impatience, we had compressed time; Meryl became our leading lady while she was still a student at the School. In her last year she appeared in six out of the seven Rep productions, performing as well in the third-year acting project, *Cock A Doodle Dandy.* She acted substantial parts in all these plays excepting *Happy End,* where she did a bit as a toothless derelict, but even there, as already mentioned, she had an opportunity to play the lead for three performances.

Meryl was worked very hard in her third year; perhaps we were unfair to feature her so prominently at the expense of her fellow students. She suffered, as a result, from considerable exhaustion, as well as from considerable envy and jealousy, which brought her close to an ulcer. Nevertheless, I am convinced that Meryl's experience in her third year at Yale was a key element in her future success. The range of her roles gave her the opportunity to stretch her talents greatly in a very short time, and her association with such gifted actors as Christopher Lloyd and Rip Torn, as well as with such imaginative directors as Andrzej Wajda and Alvin Epstein, gave her a confidence on stage which otherwise might have taken years to develop. It also gave her the courage to take right off for New York, without the customary postgraduate year at the Rep, but I believe she was as grateful to our theatre for what it had contributed to her development as we were to her for what she had contributed to the Theatre. She was kind enough to acknowledge this contribution in a letter she sent to me declining our offer to join the company: "The Rep is home, I'm no ingrate, and you've given me opportunities and encouragement that form the basis of my confidence in and commitment to the theatre." These sweet words were some compensation for the loss of her. But although she kept close links with the School as a member of the advisory committee, and often came to see our productions, she never again returned "home" in a professional capacity, enjoying instead a rapid rise to stardom on the New York stage and in Hollywood.

Still, a number of talented students did accept our invitations, and it was not proving so hard this year to cast the older company. In an odd historical repetition, we found ourselves again offering the same roles to Christopher Lloyd and Philip Kerr—though this time, thank heaven, the offers were not simultaneous. Alvin wanted Lloyd to play Oberon again in the revival of *Midsummer,* and I wanted him for *Don Juan,* since Alvin had grown just a mite too grizzled, in the intervening years, for that attractive seducer. Lloyd was advised by his agent not to repeat Oberon in New Haven (instead he urged him to repeat Kaspar in New York), and although he was eager to play Don Juan, our company policy discouraged hiring an actor for a single role if we could find another actor willing to commit for the season. For this reason, we offered both parts to Kerr, who immediately accepted. The following day, Lloyd's agent called to say that his client was now interested in playing both parts. I threw a wan eye toward that black cross on my wall, and told the agent the parts were no longer available.

While *Midsummer* was rehearsing, the renovation of the church was proceeding under Rob Orchard's careful scrutiny. Ming Cho Lee and Michael Yeargan had designed a new performance area that gave us wing space, a trap area, a Bayreuth-style orchestra pit (beneath the stage), and a light grid on which to hang frontal instruments; up till now, our light sources had all been on the sides. Most important, the new design raked the audience instead of the stage. For the first time in five years, our actors would have the luxury of walking upright instead of on a tilt, and our propman would be able to build furniture with symmetrical legs. We also had now a glass-enclosed light booth from which the stage manager could call the cues, an attractively decorated lounge area, and pleasant dressing rooms and showers. As for our audience, long accustomed to sitting through productions on hard-backed chairs, this long-suffering group would now enjoy roomy, comfortable, cushioned seats, with lots of leg room and excellent views of the stage. We were very proud of what we had accomplished for $500,000—a completely renovated modern theatre to equal that of any multimillion-dollar culture center. Unlike most of those concrete palaces, our theatre was designed for artists, not for conspicuous display, and built to the specifications of a working company by its own members, who knew, from long experience, precisely what was required for its needs.

While the workmen worked feverishly to complete the interior renovation in time for our second production, we made some changes in the exterior of the building as well—not without the inevitable collaboration of Kingman Brewster. Still profoundly interested in any architectural changes at Yale, Kingman wanted to be consulted about designs for the kiosks that advertised the plays, about the new railings, about the colors we were choosing for the exterior woodwork. When we were about to make a decision as to whether to steam or sandblast the brick façade, we were told to hold everything until Brewster had personally inspected samples of both processes. I could hardly complain about Kingman's need to involve himself in such petty details. When we started Yale Cabaret, I had myself insisted on choosing the design of the silverware, glassware, dishware, and tablecloths.

The reception of *A Midsummer Night's Dream* that fall was even more enthusiastic than it had been the previous spring; by the end of the run there were fistfights outside the theatre over seats. Still, Alvin was none too pleased with the results. Because so many of the roles had to be recast, he felt at times that he was directing a company of understudies. Having refused our offer to join the company after graduation, the student who had played Puck was replaced by Randy Kim, a lithe, sinewy, passionate Korean actor, who was perhaps a little too eager for audience approval to capture the full ferocity of Alvin's interpretation. Moreover, Philip Kerr was a touch too "classical" for the reptilian quality of Oberon, and the lovers, though more evenly matched than the previous quartet, were affected by the loss of Meryl's dreamy, lethargic Helena. Carmen's performance, however, deepened with repetition; and the rustics—relatively intact, except for the addition of Jeremy Geidt as Quince—were continually adding new farcical dimensions to their madcap scenes.

I was not very happy with my revival of *Don Juan* either. The production had originally been inspired by the fact that our theatre was a church; now that our church had been turned into a theatre, we had to recapture a lost condition. The church organ had been removed from the building many years before to create some storage space in the loft; now Richard Peaslee was obliged to tape his music for the ending, so much more harrowing when played live. Furthermore, the acting was not entirely satisfactory. Philip Kerr caught the coldness and the boredom of the character, but not his brutal sensualism; I was never successful in penetrating his emotional reserve. Gene Troobnick improved on his lisping Sganarelle, Carmen once again brought a terrifying beauty to the Specter, and Alma Cuervo and Christine Estabrook (from the student body) were lively as Maturina and Carlotta. But I had lost some of my conviction in the intervening years, and a little of my anomie must have communicated itself to the cast. The Black Mass was somber without being terrifying, the hooded celebrants confused the audience, the final transfiguration had lost its quality of transcendence. Between the first production of *Don Juan* in 1970 and its revival in 1975 a movie called *The Exorcist* had been released, which, I think, may have managed to take some of the novelty out of our diabolism.

The production was also plagued by bad vibrations. Randy Kim had consented to play the small part of Pedro, but I do not think he was happy with the size of his part. He moped and stewed, and, following the preview performance, while I was giving notes to the cast, chose that moment to attack me and the entire production. He accused me of destroying Molière on behalf of a meaningless concept that was particularly obscene at a time when people were starving. This emotional outburst, which vilified the efforts of the entire company, startled us all. It was obvious that he was very angry, but it was difficult to determine the reason. I asked him why he had waited to say these things until this delicate public moment, one day before our opening, when we had been working together for over four weeks. His only response was to stomp out of the theatre.

I was dismayed by Kim's outburst, and not just because it seemed so irrational. I worried about the effect it would have on the attitude of the students, not to mention the morale of the cast. It's difficult enough to work in the theatre, but at the Rep we worked under the glare of continual student observation. Anytime one of us had a fit of temperament, it became the subject of considerable greenroom conversation. Having to function as professional models of behavior both on stage and off made life more than a little uncomfortable at times, particularly because temperament is one of the motor faculties of an actor, and often helps to produce a spirited performance. On the other hand, Kim's angry speech had left me puzzled. Just a few weeks earlier he had taken me aside to say that he was enjoying his work with the company so much that he was turning down the opportunity to play Hamlet in Hawaii in order to be in our last two productions. I thought we had made another convert to the small ranks of our committed senior actors. "Beginning to feel the company is taking hold," I wrote that day in my journal. How many times had I recorded hopes of a similar kind before discovering they were premature?

Fortunately, the opening of the newly renovated theatre revived all our spirits; it also distracted attention from the deficiencies of my production. We celebrated the occasion with a huge revolving searchlight that cut through the smoky New Haven air, giving a momentary spark of life to the corner of York and Chapel. Quite a few theatre leaders, Joe Papp among them, came to pay their respects on opening night, providing what Gussow of the *Times* called "an ecumenical feeling" to the event. The audience was very happy with its new surroundings, and the show was much better reviewed than it deserved, Gussow writing that it had "lost none of its throbbing, ritualistic intensity." The opening was also the signal for the appearance of another old friend—our resident bat. At exactly the same moment as five years before—when Don Juan is turning to stone to the accompaniment of flashing lights and a booming organ—the bat flew out again above the heads of the spectators, apparently as delighted with the new space as everybody else.

Dynamite Tonite! was meant to be a gathering of old friends too. It was the first production ever staged by our theatre, after the visits of the Theatre of Living Arts and the Open Theatre in 1966, and the people associated with it had been responsible for much of the work we had done since. It had puzzled some of our audiences during the first production; I had hopes that at last it might be accepted. Paul Sills had agreed, during the summer, to return and restage the play, but he had done it three times already, and I don't believe that given his restless nature, he had much enthusiasm for the project. He procrastinated over the design, saying he didn't want to settle on anything until rehearsals began, and he wanted the performance to be something of an improvisation, too. For scheduling reasons, we were forced to change the production date, and Sills, who had a conflict, withdrew—not, I suspect, with much regret. Alvin and Walt Jones agreed to co-direct *Dynamite Tonite!* and Heidi Ettinger was assigned to do the design. Billy Redfield, who played Smiley in the original production, was dead, and George Gaynes, who played the Prisoner, was in a television series. Time, fate, and careers were playing havoc with our reunion. Linda Lavin, however, returned to play Tlimpattia again, and Alvin and Gene Troobnick were available to do the Sergeant and the Captain. The ranks were depleted, but the survivors had enough spirit to compensate for those we had lost.

The performance had a lot of dash and energy. Chuck Levin, now playing the blind Smiley, gave the character a contemporary Lenny Bruce twist by continually walking into walls. Bolcom's music was as fresh as ever, and the text had lost none of its goofy semantic innocence and gaiety. The setting was an accretion of boots, bombs, knees, shoes, elbows—the detritus of war. It was only after rehearsals had begun that I realized this was the first time we had done *Dynamite Tonite!* during peacetime. Would it have a meaning for anyone but us old-timers? It certainly brought back a lot of memories to me. When Alvin sang, in his high-pitched falsetto, about the bombing of his church— "Hello, God, be good to us, look at the fuss we make over you"—a flood of feeling came over me. How many years had passed and how much fuss. I wasn't the only one to be moved; although it still wasn't a popular success, the play seemed genuinely to involve our audiences. Malcolm Johnson of the Hartford *Courant*—an exacting reviewer who had seen every production in our ten-year history—called *Dynamite Tonite!* "a truly eloquent piece of American musical theatre whose time has come at last." We believed we had finally placed this idiosyncratic work in the permanent theatre repertory. Other companies, both American and foreign, began to produce it thereafter. For once, a little persistence had paid off.

We had launched the new theatre with two plays in repertory. Between the fall and the spring seasons there was a breather. I could now turn my attention back to the problems of the acting department. These had been suspended rather than resolved; the program was still something of a mess. Bobby was teaching well, but he had stopped taking any responsibility for the other classes, which, as a result, were going off in various directions like the several segments of a severed snake. It was time for me to admit that Howard Stein had been right, and that Bobby, for all his creative gifts and personal qualities, did not have the temperament to lead a large, ambitious acting program. It was not a lack of capacity so much as a lack of sympathy with the special needs of the place that was hampering his efforts. For one thing, he was no longer bothering to hide his disapproval of the participation of acting students at the Rep—something on which our whole system was based. Like virtually every master teacher who had preceded him, he believed that actors were trained best in classes, through scene work and supervised projects. The apprentice system we had devised to supplement the classes was, to his mind, not an advantage but an impediment, which prevented students from giving enough time to preparation for scenes.

I was obviously in disagreement with this position. To me, the work the student actors did on the stage of the Rep was the very taproot of their training. I had enough evidence now to know that what made Yale actors special was the assurance and versatility they gained through the resource of a professional theatre. I believed firmly in the importance of scene work, and voice and movement classes; I believed even more firmly in getting up on the stage and *doing* it. The School had originally been founded on a principle of combined theory and practice. Protecting that balance in the face of competing demands from classes and productions was difficult, but it was necessary. The hardest to convince were the teachers of acting, who sometimes reminded me of the experts in Molière's *The Bourgeois Gentleman*—each believed that his or her particular area of expertise contained the secret of life, and each believed that one could achieve perfection in art primarily through theoretical instruction. By placing his lips in the appropriate positions, Molière's Monsieur Jourdain learned how to utter sounds that he had spoken all his life; voice teachers were doing pretty much the same thing for acting students. There were undoubtedly important results to be obtained from vocal training—breath control, remedial work, dialects, etc. But Voice was too often presented as a mystery designed to exclude the uninitiated, full of secret code words and arcane physical exercises that functioned not as a supplement but rather as a rival acting training. Tyrone Guthrie had observed that the only really important things an actor could learn from voice classes were phonetics, and how to read eight lines of verse without taking a breath. He expressed a frustration I shared with people who sometimes tended to use their expertise as a method of establishing their influence in a competitive field.

Most American acting instructors were also obsessed with theory. I was impressed by how few "master teachers," including the best in the field, were associated any longer with working theatres. There was a significant historical reason for this. In the thirties the Group Theatre had functioned both as a stage for practice and as a theoretical laboratory—providing plays for its audiences and classes for its performers. When the Group Theatre disbanded in the early forties, the practical side of the training disappeared with it. Many former members of the Group, those that hadn't gone to Hollywood, set up acting classes in New York. And it was in those studios—working with Lee (Strasberg) or Sandy (Meisner) or Stella (Adler) or Bobby (Lewis)—that American actors received their training in the fifties, sixties, and seventies. They received something even more important in the studios that they could not get in the commercial theatre—a sense of worth. The American acting profession, with its meat-market mentality, did not provide actors with the conviction that their calling had any dignity or nobility. In the studios, on the other hand, they had the opportunity to regard themselves as artists. The same actor who was making the rounds of producers and casting agents in the afternoon, hoping for a small part in a Broadway play or a television commercial, in the morning might be doing a scene from *Three Sisters* in Stella Adler's Studio, having it carefully critiqued by an experienced guide and mentor.

In short, the New York acting teacher was important not just as a critical eye but also as a caring parental figure who provided a home for those who were serious about their work but had no serious theatre. At Yale, on the other hand, we had such a theatre. The dignity of the actor's calling was built into the very structure of our system; not only did Yale actors do Chekhov scenes in class, they performed Chekhov on the stage. For that reason the prevailing guru method of New York acting training was not appropriate for us, and neither was the spartan, self-denying, total immersion in the acting class rather than in the working theatre. We had experimented with the various methods of Studio training—including denying students the stage so they could devote their full energies to classwork—but this often produced an insecure and frightened actor for whom performance was an ordeal. Whatever the problems created by supplementing classroom work with Rep production—and this caused many scheduling difficulties and many tired people—no one could honestly quarrel with the results. Our actors were strong and accomplished, even to the point of arrogance. They lacked the passionate loyalty to us that the New York studios commanded, but they enjoyed a proud, independent spirit. Few of our successful graduates were willing to give much credit to our training—in contrast with Strasberg's movie stars, who were continually paying tribute to the Actors Studio—but the mark of the Yale actor was nonetheless unmistakable: a willingness to take risks on the stage and to look as if he or she belonged there.

And most important, the Yale actor was versatile. Every master teacher who came to us paid lip service to the idea of the "total actor," which is to say, an actor prepared for every kind of style, every kind of character, every kind of play. But in actuality, the classes were almost always devoted to scene work in realistic drama, usually from the contemporary American repertoire. I could not deny the value of this work, and I had respect for many of the plays from which the scenes were drawn; but since American realism was already very close to the actor's experience, it seemed to me superfluous to spend so much time on it. (I had the same resistance to black actors concentrating their energies exclusively on black plays. You don't have to be taught much about your own background; what you have to learn about is someone else's.) My personal disdain for domestic realism was hardly a secret. On the other hand, I had great admiration for realism of a deeper, more poetic kind—the plays of Ibsen and Chekhov, for example—and I considered the Stanislavsky technique to be a basic building block, if not the cornerstone, of American acting. But it was only a building block, not the whole architecture—a firm foundation on which to build castles in the air. There was a whole world of great drama waiting to be performed, a universe of major roles waiting to be interpreted, but the master teacher rarely brought the student beyond the initial step. It was as if the ground floor—the Stanislavsky approach to realism—had been carefully built to specifications but the doors to the numerous floors above were barred and bolted.

I also sensed a danger that the actor would never have the opportunity with the master teacher to develop beyond the scene class. It is not enough to do a scene from *Ghosts*; to build your character properly, it is essential to do the entire play. The usual procedure of the master teacher was to assign a scene, to criticize it, to reassign it, and to recriticize it. The training proceeded in fits and starts, deepening rather than extending an actor's range. Rarely did the student have the opportunity, in class, to examine a character from start to finish, in its relationship to the theme, form, and style of the play, as well as to the other characters.

It was for this reason that I insisted on performance for Yale actors, even when the teacher believed they were not yet prepared to appear on a stage. I was hedging my bets out of fear that training alone would not prove sufficient for their development. My insistence on casting students "prematurely" in plays was deplored by almost every acting teacher at Yale, including Bobby, and this disapproval sometimes created little battles within the department that made our faculty meetings tense. The master teachers claimed I was meddling in an area that was not my province, the implication being that I didn't know very much about acting training. They were right, if "acting training" meant only the teaching of circumstances, objectives, actions, intentions. But if I didn't know much about these mysteries, I knew what I didn't like—and that was the incompetence that Studio-trained American actors typically displayed when they untypically acted the classics. Stella's influence was unmistakable on such extraordinary performers as Robert de Niro, Al Pacino, and Marlon Brando. I was convinced, however, that if such stars had been able to supplement their work in her Studio with roles in a repertory theatre, they would all now be major classical actors, and not just charismatic movie personalities.

Norma, who knew a lot about acting training, nevertheless shared my belief in practice, though she herself had studied in Stella's Studio. She believed that student projects were the culmination of the classwork, and that Rep performances were the culmination of the training; for her, even a hastily rehearsed Cabaret production was a valuable opportunity for freeing the imagination. Bobby Lewis, on the other hand, was getting increasingly disturbed by the time that practice was taking away from theory; some of his students, overly involved at the Rep, were not preparing enough for class. He was, moreover, getting dissatisfied again with some of the other acting teachers, particularly those drawn from the company. Midway through the term he asked me to drop one of them from the program. I had appointed these teachers partly for the sake of economy, but primarily because I wanted to keep a tutorial connection between the Rep and the School. Although I agreed that the instructor in question was far from inspiring, I refused his request. I had already terminated a number of teachers in the acting department by his demand, causing considerable ferment in the School. To drop any more would have had an explosive effect on morale, and might have jeopardized the delicate relationship that was just beginning to develop between the company and the students. Bobby was not at all happy about my decision. He told me it had become clear to him that I, not he, was the head of the acting department, since I was denying him the power to hire and fire. Without autonomy over his staff he could not function effectively, and he was not sure he wanted to work at Yale anymore. He was even more worried about his health, because the situation was causing him stress. In a state of considerable agitation, he left the School for a month and returned to his home in Westchester.

By the time he felt strong enough to return we were both ready to acknowledge that things weren't working out. A basic division had arisen between us regarding the nature of acting training. If Bobby was dissatisfied with what his students were doing at the Rep, I was not very happy with what they were doing at the School. But a more serious matter was our disagreement about actors. Before Norma and I began accompanying him on auditions, Bobby had chosen an incoming class that, with three or four significant exceptions, was composed of student actors that we just couldn't cast in responsible parts at the Rep. And at the auditions we held in New Haven in the spring of 1976, Bobby had astonished me by rejecting Mark Linn-Baker, a young Yale undergraduate whose impressive work with the Dramat had persuaded us he was precisely the kind of acting student we wanted in the School. Hearing of this rejection, I asked Bobby the reason. "A college actor," he replied. I told Bobby to take him anyway, thus increasing the distance between us. Bobby finished out the year without much conviction. Before he left, I had determined on an entirely different course of training for actors at the School.

Bobby and I parted amicably, though he refused my offer to continue in the program as a teacher. For all our disagreements, there had never been anything but affection between us. I regretted that aesthetic conflicts should enter personal relationships, but I had chosen my course and I had to steer it. Bobby's half-joking references to me as head of the Acting Department had contained more than a grain of truth. It seemed as if an earlier dispute—between Larry Arrick and me regarding the company—was being reenacted between Bobby and me regarding the acting students. I had tried, and failed, to implement my policies through another. It was inevitable that this would cause friction. Gifted people had a right to freedom in artistic affairs; yet I still had an obligation to develop a unified program. The conclusion was obvious—if I wanted to achieve a goal, I would have to reach it myself. It was possible that this accumulation of responsibilities could be interpreted as an accumulation of powers, opening me to charges of being a monomaniac, spreading my tentacles over the entire School. But these were not powers I looked forward to exercising; to take them on, frankly, was a pain in the neck. I finally had to recognize, however, that the only unifying factor in this recalcitrant equation was my own leadership. If I was really serious about ending factionalism in the acting department, choosing the right talent for the Rep, and integrating the Theatre and the School, I would have to do the job myself.

By making this decision, I had clearly stopped temporizing over another term as dean. My summer resolve had melted before the circumstances of the winter. Still, some stubborn imp in my nature continued to block the way to full commitment. I wrote to Kingman, thanking him for his kind offer of another term, but saying, "I just can't bring myself to accept another five-year term and even three years presents some problems in my mind. Would you allow me to accept a two-year term, with the option of renewing for another three years in 1978? The two-year term is not entirely without precedent, since you invented it for me two years ago after I had invented the three-year decanal term five years ago. I think if we could agree to reverse the previous sequence, I would then be able happily and firmly to accept another period as dean."

I had stopped wavering, but I was still hedging. I didn't want to quit in the middle of a five-year term if the situation at the School became intolerable again, but I wanted the chance to continue my work if the new program worked out to my satisfaction. Kingman unhesitatingly agreed to the unusual request of letting me decide on the length of my own term. In reply to my letter, he wrote: "Delighted to acquiesce in the two-year idea with the possibility of renewal at the end of that time. Congratulations to US!" These two letters, Brewster's and mine, were to prove important documents in the peculiar events that lay ahead.

In my negotiations with Kingman, I was eager to determine not only the length of my stay at Yale but also his own. There had been rumors that the presidency was no longer challenging him, and without Brewster at the helm, our work at the School could be endangered. He was able to give no assurances that he would remain in his present position throughout the next five years, or even the next two. Later he hinted that he might be leaving the presidency in 1978, and, if so, would give a year's notice of his decision (he actually left in 1977). I could fully understand Kingman's desire to leave; it was clear enough, at our deans' meetings, that he had lost his appetite for the job. The report on free expression at Yale had wounded him in a way that Agnew's criticism and Old Blue scorn had not; and I suspect he was bored by the kind of issues the university was forced to deal with at that time—particularly the continuing preoccupation with federal regulations on affirmative action.

"The kind of deaning you love," he whispered to me when the subject came up for the hundredth time at another of our decanal lunches. He was right about my distaste for the whole issue, and I didn't help him very much in his efforts to bring the university into conformity. From the start, I believed affirmative action had unconstitutional implications. Like most people of my generation, I had always been taught that it was illegal and undemocratic to inquire into the racial or sexual background of potential employees or students. Now we were being told to use racial and sexual criteria as a basis both for hiring and for admissions. In the past, any inquiries into people's ethnic or religious background were invariably considered a secret method of discriminating against them; now such inquiries were being used for discrimination of an "affirmative" kind. Either way, it was still discrimination, and my head was spinning from the twists and turns of social-political fashion. One could sympathize with the goals of affirmative action, as I and others like me certainly did, without agreeing to reach these goals by suspending sensible laws and fair practices. Considering the pendulum swings of history, it was possible to foresee the day when (the mood of the country having reversed itself once more) the information we had been asked to gather for benevolent purposes might again be used for purposes of exclusion, discrimination, or worse.

Besides this, I worried about the psychological effect on any group—blacks, women, ethnic minorities—that had its status changed through a special dispensation. Our black students, for example, had been admitted to the Drama School because they had talents of a very high order. What would they think if other black students were admitted simply because they were black? And what would the less talented black students think about themselves? That they were a lower form of being and thereby subject to evaluation by different criteria of judgment? I knew all the arguments about the obligation to compensate women and minority groups for a history of repression and discrimination. But none of these arguments could overcome my fear that affirmative action was merely a new form of condescension that disguised, without repealing, the attitudes of superiority felt by white American males.

For these reasons, I refused to cooperate when asked by the Yale office of affirmative action to submit a breakdown of my faculty according to sex and race. The School of Drama had as many women on the staff, proportionately, and just as many black people, as any department at Yale—probably more. But something in me balked at supplying such information to the inquisitive bureaucracy. When I argued, somewhat disingenuously, that I had no way of gathering these statistics without invading people's privacy, I was told to apply a "visual scan" to determine the racial breakdown of the student body. What, I argued, if I mistook an American Indian for an Oriental, or a Sephardic Jew for a black? The whole business was getting ridiculous, I thought, and I didn't disguise my impatience with the poor functionaries who had been assigned to collect the information. I sensed there was a sensitive and complicated constitutional question at issue here, and I was refusing to commit what I thought might be an illegal act, even on orders of the government. It was inevitable that the question would eventually reach the Supreme Court, and I determined to wait until it was resolved by the appropriate judicial body. (Unfortunately, the Supreme Court's confused decision in the Bakke case only muddied the waters further.)

Naturally, my resistance to affirmative action exposed me, and others like me, to the usual charges of racism and sexism. I was getting pretty fed up with these reckless imputations by now, and I was getting fed up with the inquisitorial tactics of the accusers. Around this time, *Ms.* magazine sent a questionnaire around to several theatres, announcing that it was compiling information for a study and demanding to know, at the earliest opportunity, the answers to three questions: (1) How many plays written by women had been produced by our theatre? (2) How many plays about women had been produced by our theatre? and (3) How many women had directed plays at our theatre? I replied that we were compiling information for a study of our own, and, while we were preparing answers for *Ms.,* hoped that *Ms.* would supply some answers for us: (1) How many articles by men had been published by the magazine? (2) How many articles about men had been published by the magazine? and (3) How many male editors were employed by the magazine? To my knowledge, neither of these invaluable studies was ever produced.

I had been fully reinstated in the lists of radical-liberals following *Watergate Classics* (Robert Jay Lifton himself welcomed me back into the fold). Now I was reacquiring my old reputation as a cranky conservative. The political noun was wrong, but the descriptive adjective may have been apt. Feeling slightly overwhelmed by administrative, artistic, pedagogical, and fiscal problems, I was starting to get pretty short-tempered with my colleagues and friends. I'm always at my worst when I'm feeling hassled; then I can't suppress an impulse to hassle others. I'm not at all proud of this, and I've done my best to overcome it. But when too many events and needs start crowding in on me, I feel an irresistible urge to bark, which, from a position of authority, can be threatening to people. Norma pleaded with me countless times to maintain a courteous demeanor regardless of my mood, and countless times I pledged myself to change. But then my schedule filled up, my phone began ringing, my calendar got overbooked, my time contracted, and off I went again. It was a tribute to the good nature of my associates that they were willing to forgive me for this, and it was a tribute to Norma's love that she continued to tolerate my bad temper, even when it directly affected her.

But it gave me the reputation with not a few people of being something of an ogre. When my book *The Culture Watch* was reviewed in *The Village Voice,* it was characterized as the work of a middlebrow imperialist, manning the barricades against anything adventurous in art; the point was illustrated with a doctored photograph that showed me smoking a pipe and sporting a Roman toga around my open shirt. It was ironic, in view of the press we were receiving for our next three productions at the Rep, to find myself perceived as an enemy of new writing and techniques, a fuddy-duddy academic installed in a protected enclave from which he battled the imagination on behalf of traditional forms and concepts. For while *The Village Voice* was attacking us for conservatism, the New York reviewers were recoiling before a spring season devoted to new American and English plays, following our fall season of revivals.

We had begun this series with Robert Auletta's cryptic and powerful study of Midwestern fratricide and family strife, *Walk the Dog, Willie*. Auletta was a poet with a strong sense of the supernatural. The writing, and the acting of a particularly strong cast, created a throbbing atmosphere that some people found puzzling but compelling, and the second act, set in an animal surgery room, lent an air of cruelty that reinforced the central conflict of the play. I thought it was a genuine work of art, though it was well roasted in the Sunday New Haven *Register* and *The Village Voice,* the very newspaper that had chided me for my opposition to the new. As for our third new play in that series, Michael McClure's fantasy about comic-book superheroes, *General Gorgeous,* this seemed to please nobody except *The Village Voice,* though it was an entertaining enough soufflé, with no pretensions to deathless literature.

I chose *General Gorgeous* partly for the sake of my son and all like-minded eleven-year-olds, including myself. It featured a duel to the death between the eponymous hero and his mortal enemy, the Blue Mutant, who, in a climactic scene, transforms Gorgeous into a padded armchair. It also a featured a subplot involving General Gorgeous's parents—Roar (amusingly played by Gene Troobnick, even though he found the character beneath his dignity) and Mouse Woman (played by Norma with a middle-class Long Island accent, which offended her tennis partners)—two retired superheroes living in Miami, who are imprisoned by the Blue Mutant in a "dimensional sink." Danny had teethed on comic books, and when he and I wrestled on the floor of my bedroom, each of us used to assume a different super-identity—he was Godka man, so named because the red pajamas in which he conducted this struggle looked like long underwear, and I was Underarm man, felling my enemies with a well-placed whiff of body odor. In these combats, Danny usually conquered, after a few bad moments when he was almost overcome by my armpits, by muttering the obligatory imprecations ("Gotta get more strength") that increased his powers. *General Gorgeous* had much of the same simple childishness, and Danny and his friends loved it, particularly when Chuck Levin, as the Blue Mutant, went through a series of transformations that miraculously changed his color, appearance, and size, with the aid of nothing but his powers of concentration. But there were others in our theatre who found the whole event a mistake. "Is this the sort of thing the Yale Repertory Theatre should be producing?" asked our production supervisor on dress-rehearsal night, wrinkling his usually solemn features into an even more lugubrious scowl. Perhaps not. But it was fun, even though the production was plagued by misadventure, including one terrifying moment when Carmen de Lavallade fell through a trapdoor, and for a few awful seconds, we feared that she had broken one of her beautiful dancer's legs.

Between *Walk the Dog, Willie* and *General Gorgeous,* we produced another play by Edward Bond in its American premiere: *Bingo,* a fantasy about Shakespeare's life during his last years in Stratford. Eventually this spare, cold, uncompromising work got the reception it deserved, including the only Obie award ever given to a production outside of New York, but it opened to atrocious reviews, as well as to a double whammy in *The New York Times* by Gussow in the daily and by Walter Kerr on Sunday. My defenses were down, and I was discouraged. For a while we seemed to be drowning in bad criticism. To the Establishment press, we were too far-out; to the alternative newspapers, we were too far-in. This left precious few reviewers very sympathetic toward us, including those in our own bailiwick. That year a reviewer for the *Yale Daily News* announced that the real theatre for Yale (and New Haven) was the Long Wharf.

I respected the Long Wharf for its craft and competence, but—and I was hardly in a position to say this then (or now)—I didn't find it a very adventurous theatre. The basic style of the Long Wharf was domestic realism—plays in which people discuss their problems over hot meals—and this made it a congenial resting place for the middle-class New Haven population, lulled by the sight of familiar lives on the stage. It was consumer theatre at its best, relying principally on the proven American and English repertory, and including about one play a year that might be risky at the box office. It was admittedly hard to separate my standards as a critic from my feelings as a competitor, so these opinions should be taken with a grain of salt. But it didn't make me feel very good about the state of the American theatre when the comforting staples of the Long Wharf received such enthusiastic praise from critics, and it was even more discouraging to see them becoming models for Yale undergraduates, who had once done Sam Shepard and Alfred Jarry in the colleges, and now were producing Arthur Miller and Cole Porter.

One of the few things I ever truly admired at the Long Wharf was Ron Daniels's production of David Rudkin's *Afore Night Come.* Like our production of *Lear,* this usually lost about half its audience every night, and for much the same reasons. The play was remorseless, and the production did not flinch before its cold, cruel images. I wrote a letter to the cast after I had seen the show, praising its artistry and courage. Soon after, a member of the Long Wharf board asked me if my letter wasn't intended to be "facetious." Everyone down there thought the production a scandal, and suspected my motives in liking it.

I was not only entirely sincere in my letter, I immediately invited Ron Daniels to direct our production of *Bingo.* His meticulous, impressionistic handling of that haunting play had a powerful impact on our company, drawing from Alvin one of his most concentrated performances as the aging Shakespeare, and from Tom Hill a savage characterization of Ben Jonson, ravaged by drink and envy. But even more impressive was Daniels's influence on Jeremy Geidt, playing a demented, erotic old caretaker—a breakthrough performance for Jeremy, who, always a fine comedian, had now learned the secrets of minimalist acting. The play, however, was bound to upset the academic community, particularly the English department. Many resented Bond's imputation that Shakespeare in his last years was a grasping landlord who exploited his tenants and turned his back on human suffering; even more provocative was Bond's allegation that Shakespeare had died by committing suicide in a state of self-hating anomie.

Baffled by the gnomic Biblical intricacies of *Walk the Dog, Willie,* unamused by the playful comic-book drolleries of *General Gorgeous,* incensed by the literary irreverence of *Bingo,* audiences and critics alike were turning off our new plays. When Yale writers were produced in New York, they ran into similar troubles. Albert Innaurato's *Benno Blimpie* was an exception; produced in a crisp off-Broadway version by Robert Drivas, it won considerable praise and attention for its young author. But the off-Broadway production of Christopher Durang's *Titanic* drew some venom from the fangs of our old admirer Martin Gottfried, now writing for the New York *Post,* who used the occasion for another attack on our work: "Nearly everyone involved with the production is a graduate of the Yale Drama School. One might well wonder about the Yale Drama School," he wrote about a group that included Sigourney Weaver, Peter Mark Schifter, and Kate McGregor Stewart, not to mention the talented Durang.

I was wondering a little about the School myself, though for different reasons. The most popular figure to appear that year was Henry Winkler, fresh from his artistic triumph in the penetrating television series *Happy Days.* When Henry arrived, he was treated with awe not only by the entire student body, but by almost the entire faculty. The room in which he spoke to the School was so full of human bodies that people were gasping for air, whereas, for previous talks by Francis Fergusson, Irene Worth, Eric Bentley, Robert Penn Warren, Harold Clurman, Susan Sontag, and other distinguished people, we usually had to raid rehearsals and classes so the speaker would not be embarrassed by an empty room. Henry was obviously delighted to be back at Yale, and he hardly resented his sudden, inexplicable fame. But he spoke, too, of the pain he felt in being recognized everywhere as "the Fonz" instead of as Henry Winkler. He was losing his identity as an actor inside a profitable, superficial television image; there was some question about whether he would ever be able to do a classical role again. Very few people took note of his anguish, or the price he was paying for his celebrity. All they saw was a famous personality, whose career, I feared, would be the one they envied most.

I wanted recognition for artistry and intellect, not for celebrity. With a start, I realized that I also wanted recognition for myself. A friend of mine, celebrated in his field, had recently spoken to me of his desire for a Pulitzer Prize; he was getting older, dammit, and he wanted the tangible rewards of his society. A few years earlier I would have deprecated this notion. Now I was beginning to understand it, just as I was beginning to understand why Henrik Ibsen had grown so fond of collecting medals and honors toward the end of his life. I had built a minority theatre, knowing full well what that meant in a society that rewards majority success, and here I was, beginning to yearn for social recognition and critical approval, as if I had forgotten the consequences of my choice. I tried to hide from Norma my chagrin when other theatres won the Margo Jones Award for the production of new plays or other theatre people won the Brandeis Award for creative achievement. But I couldn't hide it from myself. Instead of getting thicker from critical blows and buffets, my skin was getting thinner—a dangerous condition for somebody in a toga, talking about high art, puffing on a pipe.

I was not the only one that year to feel unsettled by the sour response to our work. Members of the company were chafing too, and at the various meetings we held to discuss our progress and problems, they were severely critical of my season choices. One actress with a small role in *Bingo* took the occasion to deliver a scathing attack on me and the theatre for failing to do "women's plays"—by which she meant plays in which women played not just a central but an activating role. She had difficulty naming any titles after *Medea* and *Phaedra*; the classical dramatists, unfortunately, did not have the foresight to anticipate the feminist movement. One of our veteran actors then complained about my attraction to classics and new American plays; what he preferred was an entire season of American revivals, from *The Great Divide* to *Death of a Salesman.* Gene Troobnick took the floor to observe that every play we did that year had at least one corpse onstage by the end of the evening. It was a theatre fit only for undertakers. Was I in love with death or something? Couldn't we affirm life as well? He may have had a point. The 1975–76 season probably reflected my own dejection during that period, my sense of finality and completion when so many good people were dying.

Our final offering of the season, *Troilus and Cressida,* also left a few cadavers strewn about the stage by the end, but it was nevertheless a powerful interpretation by Alvin Epstein, who had now evolved a persuasive American style for Shakespeare. With a striking setting by Tony Straiges which located the entire action before a peeling, parched Trojan wall, the production had some lacerating performances, particularly by Chuck Levin as a vitriolic Thersites, Tom Hill as a fatigued Ulysses, and Jeremy Geidt as a lubricious Pandarus. A courageous challenge of a difficult text, it made a fitting conclusion to a problem season. Stella Adler took what was for her an arduous drive up from New York to see it, and cried on the way home, so affected was she by the dedication of the company. Generous as always, she wrote a letter to Alvin about the production, praising the performers for their "total sense of giving us all they had—all their richness and spirit. And by the time they lined up to bow, I understood that there is no more noble man in the world than the actor."

Be that as it may, we were still having our usual difficulty in keeping some of these noble people committed to the cause of great drama. Andrzej Wajda, also riveted by the performances in *Troilus and Cressida,* was visiting us with the purpose of settling on a production for the next season. Both of us agreed that Chuck Levin would be ideal to play the lead in *Peer Gynt,* one of the projects under consideration. I was reluctant to propose this to Chuck, since he had already expressed a desire to try his "wings" in New York that season, and had asked me to find an agent that might help him expand his wingspread. Still, it was hard to imagine that the opportunity to play one of the greatest roles in the literature under one of the greatest living theatre directors was something he would turn down lightly. When Wajda and I put the proposition to him in his dressing room following the matinee, Chuck began to stammer. "Gee, well, you know I've already decided to go to New York and all. Well . . . I really don't know what to say." We dropped the idea immediately, and began to discuss a project more suited to the available talent.

Graduation came and went, and Norma, Alvin, Danny, and I celebrated by going down the Colorado River on a raft. It was a glorious adventure, battling the white-water rapids, exploring the geology of the canyon, camping in sleeping bags under cloudless skies, devouring delicious grub cooked over an open fire. The marvelous river water, so fresh you could drink it, was too cold for more than a momentary dip. Norma washed her clothes in it, furious at me when I took photographs of her laying her handkerchiefs out on a boulder because of the retrograde effect of this action on the cause of women's lib. Most fascinating of all were the continual changes in the rock formations as our raft swept through the canyon; each new stratum was composed of the organic matter of another million years. During that trip, Alvin was the perfect companion; everything took on an extra dimension when seen through his inquiring eyes. The experience convinced us that nothing had been created by man that was not first conceived by Nature—in the rock formations could be seen sculptures by Moore, paintings by Braque and Picasso, even the figure of Snoopy the dog. Through the perspective of the Grand Canyon, we gained a new sense of our insignificance in the order of things, and in that awe-inspiring environment, I also gained a more humbling sense of the meaning of "permanence" in a place where human ambition counts as nothing in the context of infinite time.

Upon my return, I attended a conference of "permanent" theatres, held in New Haven under the auspices of the Theatre Communications Group. TCG was a service organization, directed by one of the founders of the Guthrie Theatre, Peter Zeisler, for the purpose of servicing America's resident theatres. This particular conference was a "purified" version of the FACT conference previously held in Princeton—"purified" in the sense that it excluded representatives of the commercial theatre. Zeisler had convened the representatives of the nonprofit theatres in order to discuss certain common problems. The one problem that interested everyone was the "fiscal crisis." Subsidies were shrinking, and theatres were trying to develop practical methods of unearthing new sources of unearned income. This meant learning new techniques of "advocacy," or how to put pressure on legislators, corporations, individuals, and private foundations through carefully organized campaigns.

The Rep shared financial problems with its sister theatres. But there was another problem I expected to hear discussed at this conference—namely, whether the nonprofit movement was living up to its original promise and goals. After Brewster had warmly welcomed the participants to Yale, and I had made a brief speech acknowledging Kingman's contribution to the performing arts, the cordial atmosphere soon dissolved in a welter of acrimonious controversy, for which I was partly responsible.

The question I kept nagging the conference members to consider was "Do we *deserve* to be funded?"—admittedly a touchy issue at a convention devoted to "advocacy." I was disturbed by how many panels were devoted to questions of lobbying and fund-raising, how few to artistic and philosophical questions. How could we persuade the money sources we were worthy institutions if we refused to define ourselves? McNeil Lowry, now retired as vice president of the Ford Foundation, suggested the same thing in his keynote address, where he warned against the growing tendency of nonprofit theatres to ally themselves with Broadway ("It is very difficult to be just half commercial," he said, with an obvious glance at the theatres that were sending shows to New York). But his remarks went largely unheeded in the panel discussions that followed, dominated as they were by such profound creative subjects as techniques of increasing subscriptions, methods of approaching corporations, and ways of establishing public action networks. Other panels dealt with Outreach programs and with minority companies—valuable for "turning on young people to their own creativity," as well as for extracting social welfare funds from the government. I was depressed to find so many talented theatre artists collected together in one place in order to learn how to behave like bureaucrats and functionaries when they had so many more important things to teach each other. And so, when a panel on which I had been asked to serve ("Defining the Statement a Theatre Makes") was canceled abruptly to leave more time for discussion of fund-raising, I led a mini-revolt that resulted in getting the panel reinstated.

I was feeling edgy as hell. When I finally got my chance to speak, I made a provocative statement about the primary importance of the art we serve, and the secondary importance of the material means. My trip down the Colorado had taught me how ephemeral were our monuments and achievements. If our theatres were not destined to last, then at least we could leave behind a record of struggle. To survive was less important than to survive with honor; otherwise, defeat was a preferable alternative. I was upset over how many of our best theatres had sold their birthrights for a mess of royalties. Did we start this movement with the intention of producing plays for the commercial theatre? Had we made this effort in order to reproduce the same system we were pledged to reform? I had believed in the permanent-theatre ideal, I had trained my students for it. It was now beginning to look as if very few of the resident theatres were worthy any longer of their time and sacrifice.

I didn't say all this at the time, but I said enough to upset Michael Feingold, who had become a member of the board of TCG. Depressed by what he called my "pessimism," he canceled out of a panel on which he was scheduled to appear in the afternoon, and took to bed. My remarks also brought a visit in my office from Peter Zeisler, who had learned that I had been invited to write an article on the conference for the *Times*. Speaking, he said, on behalf of his entire board, he asked me to drop the assignment. I had the "wrong ideas" about the conference, he told me. It would be better to let a more "disinterested" reporter—he suggested Michael Feingold, also a member of the TCG board—report on the events of the panels. Noting the astonishment on my face, he offered further explanation. Producers have the right, Zeisler said, to ban critics from their shows; he was requesting the same privilege in regard to me. As one who had also tried to challenge unfriendly reviewers, I could understand his position, but not his procedure. And so I replied that although nobody is obliged to give free tickets away to critics, you can't ban them from a public performance, and you certainly can't ask them to withhold reviews if you suspect they haven't liked your show. But the discussion was moot. Although Zeisler attempted to have me replaced on this assignment, the *Times* published my piece anyway under the title "Art versus Advocacy." It contained the remarks of a lobbyist who, in addressing the conference, told this group of artistic directors and managers that "Basically the game you're involved in is creating truth." Naturally, the *Times* received outraged letters, protesting my "distortion" of the facts, from almost all the board members, including one who hadn't even shown up at the conference.

Once again I had managed to isolate myself from my colleagues through spiky behavior. The Yale students observing the conference shared my sense of alarm over the proceedings and what it boded for the nonprofit theatre movement. This was some comfort to me, but I had also alienated one of my oldest students, Michael Feingold. The year had begun with death and illness; it was ending in controversy and contention. My state of aloneness, largely of my own creation, was soon intensified by an event over which I had no control. Alvin informed me that the Guthrie Theatre had offered him a position as artistic director, and he was thinking of accepting. I was about to lose one of my most valuable and beloved associates.

X

Definitions
1976-1977

The errors of a wise man make your rule,
Rather than the perfections of a fool.

—William Blake

Alvin visited us on the Vineyard that summer, and we spent a week together, weighing the pros and cons of the Guthrie offer. I tried to be as dispassionate as was possible to me in evaluating the advantages to him as against the disadvantages to the Rep. I had to recognize that for Alvin this was becoming an offer he couldn't refuse. He had reached a certain stage in his career where he deserved to have a theatre of his own, along with the freedom and independence to realize his own aesthetic. It was also encouraging that the Guthrie, which had grown so hidebound and unadventurous in recent years, was apparently now willing to change its conservative policies. On the other hand, I wasn't convinced, from what Alvin told me about his meetings with the Guthrie management, that he was going to have the autonomy necessary to implement his own program. Alvin was being offered the job of artistic director, but the final decision-making power remained in the hands of the executive director and the board. Who would prevail if there was an artistic disagreement? I wasn't persuaded by Alvin's conviction that the Guthrie management would back him down the line. Could he navigate the dangerous political shoals of this oversized, compartmentalized institution? Alvin was an artist, not a functionary. He had no experience whatever in bureaucratic infighting, and little interest in practical business matters. I was apprehensive that we would be losing a brilliant actor and director while the Guthrie might be gaining an indifferent administrator.

But my arguments were nothing against the blandishments of the Guthrie. Alvin took a trip in August to Minneapolis, where the warm reception he received quickly overcame whatever reservations he may have still retained about leaving Yale. He was offered a munificent salary (more than double what we had been able to provide), free housing, and the exclusive use of a new Oldsmobile. And he was given considerable lead time—always an important factor in Alvin's thinking—to plan for the future and to put his affairs in order. He would stay with us for a final year, acting and directing, and he would have an additional year in residence in Minneapolis developing his first season. His initial production would not take the stage until the summer of 1978 (it was now the summer of 1976)—a leisurely period of preparation, which Alvin found irresistible. He accepted the Guthrie offer, and immediately set about developing his last Shakespeare production at the Rep—*Julius Caesar*—with which we had decided to open our 1976–77 season.

Alvin's decision made me happy for him, but it put me in a meditative mood. Ten years had passed. The period of trial and error was over. It was time to take stock. Our various resident artists had helped to shape the identity of our theatre. Now it was important to fix that identity so that the theatre could have a character independent of the people who were coming and going through its doors. Play selection over the last ten years had been partly a matter of my own taste, partly a result of historical circumstance, partly a reflection of the talents of the company. I felt a compulsion now to define precisely what the Yale Repertory Theatre stood for, and what distinguished it from other institutions of a similar nature. This meant defining the style of our theatre, its relationship to the audience, its place in the university, its purpose in the social system, its organic connection to training, and its choice of repertory, in order to make deliberate and programmatic what, before, had been improvised and unconscious.

I had another reason for making these definitions: I was about to introduce a major change in the acting program. My ruminations about the position of the master teacher in American acting training had issued in a firm conclusion —that henceforth we would dispense with this system at Yale. In place of the single individual who followed the progress of the student through three years and served as the primary mentor, we were now prepared to substitute the Theatre itself. From now on, the Yale Repertory Company would be the master teacher, insofar as the aesthetic of the Theatre would determine precisely what would be taught, and the example of our acting would determine how.

But what had this collective master teacher been exemplifying over this ten-year period? Pouring over the repertory, I was able to distinguish three distinct styles of plays. The first style was essentially realistic in a very special meaning of that word, as embodied in works by the major contemporary theatre artists—Ibsen, Strindberg, and Chekhov. Although these were key playwrights in my study of modern drama, *The Theatre of Revolt,* we had not done many of their plays, largely because most of them were already too familiar from performances by other companies to justify production in a theatre devoted to uncovering neglected dramas and developing new production approaches. Nevertheless, these were central writers in any modern theatre, and their spirits hovered over ours—either through the example of their own work, or through their influence on their successors. We had already done one play by Ibsen, two by Strindberg, and one by Chekhov; we intended to do many more when we discovered the way to make them fresh and contemporary. All three were seminal writers in a form of realism that penetrated the documentary surface to a poetic core beneath—this probing realism would be the basic building block of the new acting training.

The second style indigenous to our theatre was suggested in our productions of Shakespeare and the Jacobeans. Under Alvin's direction, we were developing a peculiarly American approach to verse drama which, like the nation itself in 1776, had declared its independence of British rule. This was partially a matter of rhythm, partially a matter of gesture, but essentially it meant investigating the American experience instead of exploiting familiar stage conventions. Our first season had featured experimental approaches to Ben Jonson and Aeschylus, and almost every season thereafter had included at least one production of a play written in verse by a classical author that we tried to explore in a contemporary manner without recourse to facile updating. This process of renovating the classics would also find its way into the new acting training we were devising at the School.

The third style of our theatre was a little more difficult to define because it was based on all the new plays, both European and American, produced by the Rep. How can you identify a quality common to writers as diverse as Sam Shepard, Robert Auletta, Lonnie Carter, Christopher Durang, Albert Innaurato, Edward Bond, Jules Feiffer, Arnold Weinstein, Samuel Beckett, Eugène Ionesco, and dozens of others, each working out of a distinct, inimitable personality? There was, however, one thing that each of these writers shared —a postmodern sensibility. Each, however unconsciously, was trying to devise a response to modern realism that would reflect the special nonlinear, phantasmagorical quality of the age. This theatre had its earliest roots in the dream plays of Strindberg and the intellectual conundrums of Pirandello, but the unifying writer among them was a figure against whom some of them were rebelling—the German Marxist playwright Bertolt Brecht. Brecht's early plays contained many of the fevered germs of postmodernism, and his work with Kurt Weill laid the foundation for the more lyrical side of this movement, if movement it was. Our own work with Brecht and Weill had been continuous and intense. Their collaboration would be the cornerstone of the most advanced aspect of the acting program.

Poetic realism, verse drama, and postmodernism—these were the styles of our master teacher, the Rep. They would also form the basis of the acting training. Each class in each of the three years would devote itself totally to one of these forms of theatre, meanwhile taking different, increasingly responsible assignments with the professional company. The incoming class of students would play walk-ons and small roles at the Theatre while training at the School in basic Stanislavsky techniques and the plays of the poetic realists. Voice and movement would be essentially remedial and corrective, including phonetics, voice placement, fencing, and acrobatics. And a new script breakdown course, given by an instructor from the DFA program, would introduce these students to modern realistic plays from the actor's point of view. Having applied itself to this style for a full year, the first-year class would complete its training with an acting project drawn from the "poetic realist" repertory—*Three Sisters* or *The Sea Gull,* for example—directed by one of its instructors, cast to give everybody in the class a chance to play against type, and performed two or three times in the Experimental Theatre before a School audience.

In the second year of the program the class would proceed to verse drama. Voice classes would now be devoted to scansion and verse speaking, while movement would deal with period dance and stage combat—the core techniques for performing in Renaissance plays. A mask class would complement the acting classes, geared to improvisations based on commedia dell'arte characters or Shakespeare's clowns, and culminating in a rowdy, obscene mask show in the Cabaret directed by Jeremy Geidt. Second-year students would also take singing classes, studying the music of Dowland and his contemporaries, while their script-breakdown course would introduce them to Elizabethan and Jacobean plays, one of which would be chosen as the final acting project. At the Rep, second-year students would understudy featured roles with the professional company, and—in order to provide serious motivation for these assignments—would have the opportunity to play the understudy role at least once, usually during a matinee.

In their final year the acting students were prepared to play important roles at the Rep (though they occasionally performed these roles in the second year as well, if they proved qualified and the parts were appropriate). As members of the company, these third-year students had more obligations to the Theatre than to the School, so they had fewer class hours. Nevertheless, the classwork —in "postmodernism"—was designed to be concentrated and intense. Voice work included singing, primarily the music of Kurt Weill, and movement introduced the students to aikido, a nonviolent form of Japanese combat. Script breakdown was offered in the plays of Brecht, Beckett, Handke, Shepard, and others; and the final acting project would be a highly experimental free-form exercise directed by their acting teacher—either Lee Breuer of Mabou Mines, who the first year of the program took the class through a fascinating shadowgraph version of Wedekind's *Earth Spirit,* or Andrei Serban who directed his third-year class later in a version of Shepard's *Mad Dog Blues,* performed outdoors on the beach at West Haven. As if this advanced class did not have enough to do, its members would also form a cabaret company, performing skits, songs, and satires at Yale Cabaret when they managed to find a few idle hours.

The purpose of this three-layered program was to develop a versatile, transforming actor. I was convinced that any student trained in the three styles employed at the Rep would be capable of performing in any play ever written. And the various script-breakdown courses would make certain that the actor was familiar with the entire literature of the field, so as to bring not only skill to the profession but also knowledge and cultural background. The new acting program accepted the preeminence, as a training method, of the Stanislavsky technique, but did not adopt it as an exclusive procedure. In the Yale program, Stanislavsky was a basic building block, not the entire scaffolding, in an architecture that aspired toward the classic literature and experimental drama from a platform of honesty, truth, and imagination.

I was proud of this program—not least because it had the potential to forge powerful links between the School and the Theatre. To reinforce these links, the senior company actors were established as tutors to the students, advising them, following their progress, helping them onstage, and discussing their personal problems over lunch and dinner. The major disadvantage of the program was the absence of a single figure who could stay with the student over all three years; but I believed that I might be able to fulfill this particular function myself as the one person who had seen all of his or her performances —whether at the Repertory Theatre, on the Main Stage, in the Experimental Theatre, the Studio Theatre, or the Cabaret—meeting with the student briefly after each role, and offering a longer evaluation at the end of each year. Anyway, the advantages far outweighed the disadvantages, I thought, for although in theory the master teacher had the potential to monitor the student's progress over a period of time and provide supervisory continuity, he couldn't give the student anywhere near the breadth of training provided by this program, even in the unlikely event he stayed for the whole three years. It was a chance I was willing to take because I knew the experiment would work. We had evolved it, through trial and error, over a long period of time, just as we had developed the physical improvements at the church out of the knowledge of our own special needs. The new program was a success from the day it was initiated, and it had a very salutary effect on the spirit of the whole enterprise. It put an end to rivalries among the faculty, it unified the students, it turned the Rep into an acknowledged training resource, and it made the acting department into a progressive functioning unit instead of a morass of seething discontent.

My welcoming speech that year reflected my pride in the new training plan. It dealt with the potential of an institution as a work of art. People had been suspicious of institutions—understandably—for such a long time that it was hard to recognize that institutions could be a source of satisfaction and creativeness. We had also begun to forget that institutions were composed of human beings, not inanimate particles; it was people who provided the quality and substance of a place. I reminded the students that they *were* the institution, and therefore partly responsible for its welfare. Warning them that they were going to work very hard this year, I urged them to marshal their time and watch their health. I cautioned them against *Schadenfreude,* enjoying the pain of others, and begged them to recognize their involvement with the progress of all their fellows. "This is another way of saying," my speech concluded, "that you are in the inside of this place, not the outside; what happens to it should be of moment to every one of you; and the performance of any of its members, whether they be your fellow students, your faculty, your tutors, or your supervisors, is of ultimate importance to the whole. If we can join together as a creative unit with generosity toward each other, then we will all have something to believe in again, and this institution may indeed become a work of art—not just in the artists it develops, but in the very vitality, amplitude, and life of the School."

I was accustomed to making Bar Mitzvah speeches of this sort every time the School convened for the year, but this fall I was feeling more positive about things, and my exhortation had a ring of hope. Norma and I had handpicked the incoming class of actors and directors during a three-city audition tour and after exhaustive auditions in New Haven; we were convinced we had a sparkling class. I liked the look of the new students. They seemed ready to work, ready to learn. It was not just that their faces were fresh with expectation—incoming students always looked like that. This class seemed prepared to give as much as it received. Since the new program was still untested, we needed that sense of commitment beforehand, and these students were more than willing to provide it. From the very beginning, they were a genial, hardworking, talented lot who cared about each other in a way that augured well for the future of a harmonious acting ensemble. And during their entire training at the School they were a pleasure to teach, a pleasure to rehearse, a pleasure to chat with in the greenroom at the Rep. Years later, they would prove to be wonderful professional colleagues as well.

One week before School officially started, indeed before they had the time to find apartments or register for classes, the new students were in rehearsal with *Julius Caesar*. One of the obligations of the first-year class was to serve as supernumeraries in repertory theatre productions, and this group assumed those tasks from the very start. Our professional season, by design, included plays by the three key figures in their acting training: Chekhov, Brecht, and Shakespeare. And while Norma was introducing them to Stanislavsky technique in the acting class, Alvin was drilling them in verse and choral work at the Rep. It was a lot to throw at a group of people still unfamiliar with their surroundings, but it proved to be the best way possible to ease their way into a strange new world. It also had the advantage of immediately establishing our special pace. Naturally, there was some grumbling about how little time was reserved for eating or sleeping, but in general the new students undertook their duties with good nature and goodwill, creating an immediate rapport with the members of the professional company.

The pleasant atmosphere persisted throughout the rehearsal period, even though *Julius Caesar* did not prove to be one of our more effective productions. Casting it had been a problem as usual. Bobby Drivas had agreed to play Marc Antony, Ron Leibman was returning to play Cassius, and Tom Hill was set as Caesar. But for a while it seemed as if nobody in the American theatre was willing to take the part of Brutus, one of the plummiest roles in all of Shakespeare. Late in summer, Norma suggested that we shift Tom Hill into Brutus and ask Alvin Epstein to play Caesar. Alvin wisely refused, no doubt remembering the mistake he had made in doing double duty with *The Tempest.* Finally, we cast Jeremy Geidt as Caesar. Although he didn't have the physical stature for the part, he nevertheless performed it with authority, continuing to grow in artistry (if not in height) with every character he played. We were trying, whenever possible, to stretch the members of the resident company, even if we had doubts about their suitability for certain roles. For company reasons, we also decided to alternate Carmen and Norma in the parts of Calpurnia and Portia, thus giving each actress the opportunity to play a different character each night as compensation for their relatively small roles.

The problem with the production, however, was not so much the acting as the concept, though this naturally had an effect on the acting. Alvin's interpretation was inspired by the supernatural happenings following the murder of Caesar. He saw a world in chaos, turned upside down by violent events—an idea that could have potentially added an interesting dark color to the classical Roman atmosphere. For this purpose he wanted a score of "natural sounds" —provided by the advanced composer Kirk Nurock—to be produced by the chorus. But what was meant to be frightening more often proved absurd—a cacophony of annoying clicks and rattles and groans emanating loudly from human throats. The actors dealt with this tumult good-naturedly at first, then with mounting irritation. But although Alvin reduced it considerably, he could not be persuaded to cut the caterwauling, even when it was obvious it was ruining the performance.

Instead, he spent a good deal of the time he normally gave to actors in trying to make the "natural sound" work. As a result, the evening did not have the unity of Alvin's previous Shakespeare productions. Drivas created an epicene Antony with a mean streak in a galvanic display of acting that drew cheers, but Tom Hill's Brutus often fell into Romantic postures reminiscent of Edmund Kean's Hamlet portrait, and Ron Leibman's Cassius was a weird refugee from a mental institution who screamed when he was crossed and sniffed when in repose. Like many of Leibman's characterizations, this one was always on the edge of something brilliantly original, but it fell over the other side into caricature. He took a bad drubbing from the reviewers and, perhaps in consequence of this disappointing reception, turned his back on the audience during one of the curtain calls. He also decided, two days before the production closed, to abandon the show for Hollywood, thus giving us an opportunity to test our understudy policy for second-year students, which worked beautifully in the emergency.

All in all, *Julius Caesar* was not one of the Rep's finest hours. It marked for Alvin a temporary break in his growing mastery of Shakespeare; and for us it represented a lost opportunity to relate this tragedy of assassination to America's recent past. The production was successful primarily in exhuming the more unconscious, phantasmagoric elements of a play that is usually produced in clear daylight, and exposing some of its qualities as a dream.

That whole year my own unconscious life was very active; I seemed to be dreaming every night. During this time I dreamed that Alvin and Bobby

Drivas were planting explosives in an army camp, an act that implicated me. I was showing apprehensions about the effect of *Julius Caesar* on our season; but the shrapnel from that dream explosion was fortunately deflected by another production we opened soon after—Sam Shepard's *Suicide in B-Flat.* This fascinating and bizarre play helped consolidate Shepard's growing reputation as America's most original young playwright, one who entered new territory with each succeeding work, preserving a distinctive style without ever repeating himself.

Suicide in B-Flat is an effort to break down the boundaries between artistic forms—specifically, to permit the drama to approach the condition of music. A musician as well as a playwright, Shepard was inspired by progressive jazz; his play is a loose improvisation, though it also uses the conventions of pulp fiction. Jazz, in fact, is played throughout the evening, by a pianist who accompanies the words of the actors with his back to the audience. Shepard said he wrote the play to be performed as a musical set in one long sitting— "a kind of suicidal ordeal," as he described it to me in a letter, "of marathon intensity," an idea he got after "having sat through several sets of Cecil Taylor's quintet and listening to his nonstop explosions of 'free-form' jazz."

Not only does the play take the form of music, it is about musicians. The hero is Niles, a celebrated jazz composer, whose corpse has been found in his room. Was his death a murder or a suicide? The two investigating detectives cannot decide, and the chalked outline of his body on the floor reveals no secrets. When these two conventional gumshoes are joined by a suicidal female bass player and a skinny spaced-out saxophonist who blows soundless music (Niles's jazz is so advanced that even dogs can't hear it), things begin to go haywire. One of the detectives starts wrestling with his own hand, which has developed a life of its own and is trying to stab him. The other gets hypnotized by the sax player, who sits on his lap and tortures him with his protruding bones.

Niles appears, invisible to all except his companion, a drugged-out young groupie. He may be dead or—perhaps the same thing—he may have gone over into another space-time dimension; Shepard never tells us. But before Niles can rest, he must annihilate a series of identities that prevent him from achieving his authenticity. By the end of the play, Niles has walked through the walls of his room to accept the guilt for his own death. As the detectives lead him away in handcuffs, the upstage pianist concludes with the haunting strains of his own jazz.

Like much of Shepard's work, the play is a hallucination, and therefore not available to logical analysis. With this play, it seemed to me, the American theatre took a step beyond the familiar causal Newtonian universe, where every action has an equal and opposite reaction, into a world of dream, myth, and inner space. It was our happy obligation to find a production style to match. Under the faithful direction of Walton Jones, and with an accomplished cast, an atmosphere was created that evoked Shepard's bizarre world more effectively than anything we had previously done—in a production which, characteristically, the hermetic playwright never saw.

With our first two productions launched in repertory, I was able to give some time to administrative affairs. These included the monthly deans' lunches with Kingman and their continuing preoccupation with affirmative action. The demands on the university were escalating. Now the benefits of affirmative action had been extended to the handicapped, which would have been praiseworthy were it not that the definition of "handicapped" had recently been widened to include anybody suffering from alcoholism or drug addiction. This meant that every time a job opened in the university the employer was obliged to interview not only all the applicant women, blacks, Chicanos, and other eligible "minority groups"—and not only those suffering from physical disabilities—but also any drug addict or alcoholic sober enough to fill out a form. Of course, the federal government had devised the usual "goals and timetables" to monitor our progress, with the usual implication that it was ready to cancel grants if we failed to meet the deadlines. W. B. Yeats had written about "the mad intellect of democracy" before affirmative action was even invented; what would he have written of America in the 1970's? When President Brewster asked us if we had any response to the new regulations, I replied that an appropriate response had already been formulated about two hundred years ago, beginning, "When in the course of human events . . ."

Once again I found myself taking issue with what, in theory, was a piece of compassionate legislation. My objections had nothing to do with the principle guiding the rules; obviously, the handicapped, like many members of minority groups, had been victimized by prior prejudice. I was opposed, rather, to the absurd interpretations of the legislation and to the implications of blackmail behind the federal enforcement. I was also irritated by the intervention of the government in the affairs of a private institution. As it happened, a crucial member of our staff was a paraplegic, but we didn't need federal bureaucracies to tell us how valuable he was or how well he could work. This was Arthur Pepine, an old friend of mine from Group 20, who had joined us at Yale in 1966 as resident stage manager. Pepine had had a dreadful accident in the summer of 1967 when he dived into a backyard swimming pool of insufficient depth and broke his neck; this left him totally paralyzed, except for the push muscles in his hands. After a long period of rehabilitation, Pepine learned to navigate a mechanical wheelchair, and, with the aid of a compressed air device, could hold a pencil, dial a phone, and even use the typewriter. He returned to us soon after, acting as Financial Aids officer and producer of Yale Cabaret—two positions he discharged with effectiveness and authority. Despite his recurrent infections and his miserable confinement, Pepine never uttered a word of complaint; in fact, his unfailing cheerfulness was a continual contrast (and rebuke) to our own propensity to whine. The best tribute to Arthur's equanimity was the fact that, in his presence, students invariably ignored his disability and let him have the full force of their disappointment over the size of their loans or scholarships.

While my war with the government was continuing, my war with the critics was abating. In October I received a call from the *Times* to tell me Clive Barnes was ready for a reconciliation. A resolution of this conflict would have been good for the theatre, but I couldn't quite trust the news. Barnes had recently written a scathing attack on Robert Lowell's dramatic trilogy, *The Old Glory,* when it was produced at the American Place Theatre, calling it "poetaster stuff—dull and gray, trying, with a certain intellectual arrogance" by an author he called "a tiresome and obvious bore" whose "writing is often dead and deadly." Not only was Robert Lowell our leading poet at the time, *The Old Glory* was one of his most inspired works. As a matter of fact, Barnes himself had previously praised very highly at least two of the plays in this trilogy—*Benito Cereno* in the introduction to an anthology of best plays that he selected and edited in 1967, and *Endecott and the Red Cross* in a review he wrote in 1968. To reverse these opinions without acknowledgment signified that Barnes was still continuing to dance what John Simon once called his "jesuitical two-step," but it also may have signified something else. I had very recently published a strong appreciation of *The Old Glory* in *The New York Times Magazine;* it was conceivable that my praise had triggered Barnes's disdain. Wynn Handman of the American Place Theatre was also noticing something strange about Barnes's reviews. Whenever his theatre produced a play by a Yale-trained playwright, Barnes invariably employed his most vituperative vocabulary. We commiserated together about our common problem, and its potential consequences to the playwrights we were both trying to help.

My suspicions of Barnes were also aroused by an article he had written recently about Connecticut theatres in the Connecticut section of the *Times.* Praising the artistic quality of all those institutions, he added, "I must here attach a rider because I have not seen the Yale Repertory Company for some years at the express request of Mr. Brustein, himself a critic and dean of the Yale Drama School, who did not approve of my previous reviews. As I did not appear to be missing much, I acceded to his request in the better interest of his seemingly fragile equanimity and mine." This was hardly the whole truth, but it was the spirit behind the remarks that worried me more than his interpretation of the facts. Would Barnes continue to carry this spirit into our theatre under the guise of "reconciliation"?

Three weeks later Barnes's equanimity was further shattered: the *Times* had decided to fire him. I thought it was time for us to pull the hatchets out of each other's skulls, and try to bury them. I therefore submitted to Barnes's request for press tickets to our production of *Mr. Puntila and His Chauffeur Matti*—and not just because he told me the *Times* would never review us again if I didn't. I had unfamiliar feelings of compassion for him in his present distress and even sent him a letter of sympathy. The *Times* was absolutely right to drop him from its theatre pages, but the circumstances were painful. Although he was invited to remain with the paper as dance critic (a position he dropped upon becoming drama critic for the New York *Post*), his abrupt dismissal was, from all reports, a considerable humiliation. Whatever our personal quarrels, I didn't like to see him suffer. In any other position, Barnes would have been harmless enough; it was only when his criticism was endorsed by the enormous influence of the *Times* that he constituted a danger to the theatre. Who was to blame? The man—or a system that gave to one newspaper the power to dictate cultural opinion?

At this time we were in rehearsal with *Ivanov*, our first production of Chekhov since the ill-fated *Three Sisters* in 1968. I loved Chekhov above all other playwrights, which may explain why we did his plays so seldom. I had endured so much bad Chekhov production that I had vowed not to do his works unless we could rescue them from the customary atmospheric malaise. Ron Daniels had developed such a crisp and simple style with *Bingo* that I was convinced he could lead the company through an innovative production of *Ivanov*. His concept preserved the melancholy of the play without scanting its wit, vigor, and liveliness. Michael Yeargan contributed an imagistic setting that suggested interiors and exteriors through the barest of means (doorframes, drapes, platforms), and the cast included Alvin in the title role, Elsbieta Chezevska as Anna Petrovna, Jeremy Geidt as Borkin, and Norma as Zina-eeda. Also in the cast were a number of first-year actors in small roles, and me as Count Shabyelsky.

I was making one of my rare stage appearances with this play, and I was worried that I might have grown stale in the interim. It was difficult working my way back into performing, but Daniels was a great help. He had the same influence on my acting as he did on Jeremy's during *Bingo*, cutting away everything mannered or external to expose the inner core of character. As a Marxist, Daniels felt obliged to find political justifications for every play he directed. *Ivanov* was hardly a Marxist play, nor was Chekhov a Marxist playwright, but there were undeniable social implications underlying the action, which Daniels did much to uncover. At the early rehearsals he made us read a lot of historical material, and a lot of Trotsky, regarding the oppression of the serfs and the tyranny of the Czars. Not much of this was very relevant to Chekhov's study of anomie and exhaustion among the middle classes, but it did rescue the play from being a mere psychological study. We did our homework dutifully, then got down to the more interesting business of exploring the characters and their relationships—the source of the farcical currents in the play. It was an entirely engaging rehearsal process conducted by an entirely charming director.

After we had been working on the play for about two weeks, I received a call one night at my house from Daniels. He told me, in a voice that sounded alternately amused and pained, that he had just been run down by a car while riding his bicycle home on Whitney Avenue. "Are you badly hurt?" I asked. "Dunno," he replied, "perhaps." I rushed to the firehouse where he had been taken following the accident, and found him bundled in a blanket, bleeding profusely from various wounds. His front teeth were broken, he had severe lacerations on his nose and forehead, and a bloody contusion on his right leg. He described the accident in a tone he might have used in talking about someone else. I'd never seen such a cool reaction. The only thing that seemed to worry him about the incident was the fact that his glasses were broken. I accompanied him in an ambulance to the Yale–New Haven Hospital, where he had his bones X-rayed and his wounds sutured, then took him to our house, where Norma fed him chicken soup and tucked him into bed.

After two days of this treatment Ron was recovered; the shock had worn off and his spirits were high. He returned to rehearsals looking as if he had just emerged from a brawl, with two black eyes and two missing teeth, but he proceeded to shame us all with a display of raw energy that galvanized us into a performance of considerable strength and power. From Daniels I learned as much about directing as about acting, particularly the secret of how to persuade a company to do your bidding while appearing to conduct a free and open rehearsal. With the actors he was always the supreme diplomat, extracting precisely the performance he wanted while flattering us into thinking we were making our own discoveries. His most commonly used phrase was "Yes . . . but." *Yes* was his acknowledgement of our contribution; *but* was a prologue to where he wanted us to carry it. "Yes . . . but" was his carrot and his stick, the goad to prod us just one step further. Only once did he lose his temper—during the tech-dress rehearsal. The run-through was dreadful, he told us, a disgrace—we had lost everything we had developed. If it didn't improve drastically, he added, the production would be worthy only of Broadway (a remark greeted by one of our more ambitious first-year actresses with a very shrewd grin). All of us were eager to please him, so we proceeded to give the next dress rehearsal the size and confidence he wanted. He rewarded us with a gap-toothed smile. The play belonged to us now, he said; he could return to England a happy man. On opening night the response of the house told us what we really already knew—that with *Ivanov* we had finally discovered our way into Chekhov's plays.

Daniels had agreed to return in the spring to direct our production of Brecht's *Puntila.* Also scheduled for the spring season were two new plays by former students and current CBS fellows, Christopher Durang and William Hauptman, and Tadeusz Rozewicz's *White Marriage,* directed by Andrzej Wajda. Two new American works and two unfamiliar European plays—I knew we were testing the tolerance of the audiences, if not taxing the patience of the critics. My choices had run into difficulty in the last year; they were beginning to cause troubles again. Just recently we had received a bunch of outraged letters from current subscribers, protesting our cancellation of *Macbeth* (which Wajda had planned to direct before deciding he didn't know enough about the English language); there were others complaining about our policy of new plays. Even some of the staff were expressing reservations about the play submitted by Durang, a savage satire (which I found priceless) called *The Vietnamization of New Jersey.*

My dreams at that time were full of foreboding and defiance regarding our position as a minority theatre. One night (months before we produced it), I dreamed that two thirds of the audience walked out of *Vietnamization* and I told those remaining, "All right, we've established our community; let's get on with the play." In another dream, Durang, a lapsed Catholic, offered to pray for my soul. A few weeks later I dreamed that fires were breaking out in the basement of the theatre and I tried to board up the windows against the arsonists. Soon after, I dreamed that, having given Wajda our house, I had to ask for it back, since we had no place to stay. All this testified to my uncertainty and fear in what was at best a risky business. I wasn't losing any conviction about the value of our work, but I was obviously feeling we were on shaky ground. My sense of instability even provoked me to formulate a haiku in my dreams: "This is a climbing century, one must rise fast merely in order to stand still."

Along with these dreams, I recorded dreams in my journal about invalid passports and flights across the sea. My unconscious was testifying to my desire to flee—and also to my desire to stay. Staying was the new element; departure had been in my thoughts since the very beginning. It is true that we were continuing to alienate a lot of people; we were also developing a number of faithful supporters. The acting company was still plagued by constant defections, but the young people in the acting program were giving us renewed hope. Still vulnerable to vitriolic attack from time to time, the theatre was also starting to attract genuine understanding from certain critics. Funding was always a problem, but we were to end the current season with a surplus of $60,000. And finally, though I never ceased to despair over channeling talented people into the commercial system, I also never lost the hope that we were doing something to help change it.

Without that hope the whole task was futile. The very Yale-trained stars who attracted press attention to the School—often making it easier to recruit new talent—were a sign that we were failing in some essential purpose of our work. I could never explain this adequately to the journalists who interviewed me—they only wanted to hear about Henry Winkler and Ken Howard—but it was the uncelebrated ones who validated the quality of our program because it was they who were devoted to artistic development rather than to careers. Those who had caught the message of the training were now working in Louisville, in Minneapolis, in Houston, in Washington, not in Hollywood or New York. These were the people who were our best examples, rather than those who appeared in the feature pages of the *Times* or *People* magazine. If we were no more than a star factory, a ladder to commercial success, then our work was a mockery and we were all hypocrites. Yet here I was, becoming something of a celebrity myself while preaching once a week about the pitfalls of fame. Wasn't *this* hypocritical? And weren't my ideals for the theatre just a hidden form of pride?

I examined these problems incessantly without being able to frame an adequate answer. The fault was in our stars; it was also in myself. My one defense was that if I had achieved a certain measure of fame, it had not been consciously sought. And since my public persona was virtually inseparable from the institution with which I was associated, whatever reputation I enjoyed belonged to the School and the Theatre. I never ceased to believe, moreover, that however we might be perceived, we were still devoted to resisting the system, a task that never lost its urgency. At the funeral of a friend of ours in January we were startled, along with the other mourners, to hear the memorial loudly interrupted by a CB radio blaring its "Breaker Eight" language over the PA system of the chapel. Our sound system in the Theatre was frequently host to similar intrusions, often right in the middle of a very delicate scene. I considered this symbolic. No place was safe from invasion by the majority culture.

Therefore, we started the spring repertory with a new plan, designed to form a common front with some of our most gifted associates. We wanted to bond them to the Theatre in a manner that might encourage their continuing loyalty and commitment. The plan was to form an organization called the Yale Repertory Theatre Associate Artists (YRTAA), made up of twenty-five creative people from the acting, directing, playwriting, and design areas who met the requirements of membership—a minimum number of seasons acting with the company or a minimum number of plays written, directed, or designed for the Theatre. Each year we planned to add new people to this nuclear body as they became eligible, until the ranks were swelled with the most talented people we had developed. We gave everybody a gold YRT lapel button, and we met at regular intervals to discuss our past, our present, and our future. I was really hoping that by joining the YRTAA, these artists would be persuaded to continue working with us, or to come back again at some future time, much as members of the Comédie Française remained affiliated with that parent body during their entire lifetime. "In this manner," I wrote in a program note describing the new organization, "we hope to provide continued stability, permanence, and continuity for our theatre, and to dramatize how a theatrical institution can continue to draw strength and nourishment from the people who have helped to establish its identity."

The plan worked, at least temporarily, in attracting back one actor whom we thought we had lost—Chuck Levin, playing a role in *The Vietnamization of New Jersey*. Chuck returned over the strenuous objections of his agent, who wanted him to stay in New York during the TV-pilot season. But he had been rusticating for many months now, living on promises, and he wanted to get on a stage again. Levin was already familiar with this play, having rehearsed an earlier (one-act) version in 1975, when it was called *A American Tragedy*. This was the Durang satire we had originally considered for inclusion in *American Patrol,* now expanded into a two-act assault on the American family, with side shots at guilty liberals, antiwar plays, and mealymouthed priests.

The Vietnamization of New Jersey is set in an American suburban living room, piled to the ceiling with the garbage of our consumer culture: two hair dryers, three television sets, an outsized roto grill, sculptured ducks in flight over the fireplace. Seated at the breakfast table is a family borrowed from David Rabe's play *Sticks and Bones,* now renamed Ozzie Ann (instead of Harriet), Harry (instead of Ozzie), and Et (instead of Rickie). Also included in this parodic dramatis personae are David, a blinded veteran of the Vietnam war, and Liat, his Vietnamese wife, who later turns out to be a girl named Maureen O'Hara from Schenectady (she changed her name because she wanted to break into musicals like *The King and I*). What Durang wanted to satirize was the cut-rate merchandising of guilt that permeates so much contemporary American drama—the heavy-handed symbolism, the piety, the self-satisfied indignation, the clumsy confrontations—at the same time that he was attacking the clichés about the Vietnam war being formulated both by the political left and the political right. With this play, Durang declared a separate peace, and, as far as American theatre was concerned, finally managed to bring the Vietnam war to an end.

This was a play with which our young actors had a special affinity, and under the direction of Walt Jones, the rehearsal was a delight and the production enjoyed a scandalous success. It was much more popular with audiences than any of us expected, considering the strong reaction it had inspired earlier from our own staff. Audiences did not walk out on it as I had feared in my dreams; they stayed and laughed. Durang went on to greater notoriety that year with a first in resident-theatre history: back-to-back productions of *A History of American Film* at the Arena Stage, the Hartford Stage Company, and the Mark Taper Theatre. For a while, our spoiled priest, our dark blasphemer—this deadly piranha with the manners of an Etonian and the innocence of a choirboy—was enjoying something of a vogue in the American theatre.

Our next new play was much more problematical; for the first and only time at the Rep, I canceled a production before it reached the end of its scheduled run. *The Durango Flash,* by William Hauptman, was a study, relatively realistic in style, of aspiring Western movie actors, with more nerve than talent, trying to make a go of it in Hollywood. The play had many strong qualities; like all of Hauptman's writing, it contained much that was powerful and persuasive. On the other hand, it had not yet been entirely formulated, and the man we chose to direct it—one experienced mostly with domestic dramas—was able neither to guide the revisions properly nor to charge the text with an imaginative physical life. The tech week was mostly patchwork as each of us tried to find some way to energize the show—the designer suggested stripping the set, the lighting man suggested slides, I suggested cuts—but no one could devise a successful strategy. The play lay there onstage like an expiring fish, demoralizing the cast, frightening the director, paralyzing the playwright, depressing me. I had great faith in Hauptman's talent, and I knew he needed encouragement and reinforcement, having just completed another bad experience at the American Place Theatre, where his sensitive play *Domino Courts* was savaged by Clive Barnes. But I did not believe that this new play was ready, or that our production was adequate. *The Durango Flash* opened to moderate reviews, and played to tolerant audiences, but I really disliked what we had on the stage and made the decision to curtail the run. Out of aesthetic fastidiousness, I failed a gifted playwright who needed support; I hope he has managed to forgive me.

With our production of Brecht's *Puntila* we had a grand success. Ron Daniels's spectacular concept utilized the entire stage area, including the wings and auditorium, with the performance continuing during intermission in the downstairs lounge. Daniels staged *Puntila* like a carnival, with peddlers hawking popcorn and balloons before the show, and jugglers, acrobats, and mimes performing in the lounge during the interval (one booth had two large cutouts, where spectators had their photographs taken either as Puntila kicking Matti or as Matti being kicked). William Bolcom's boisterous score provided the show with just the right touch of carny pizazz, and the performances, particularly Tom Hill's mercurial Puntila, were full of punch and vigor.

Still, *Puntila* did not prove an entirely satisfying experience for the company, whatever joy it brought to audiences. Many of the actors felt they were there only to dress up the stage effects. *Puntila* had chaser lights, toy cars, saunas, and a wonderfully jazzy lighting design by Tom Skelton, but for all the production glitz, the director rarely got his teeth into the meat of the play. This was odd, considering that Daniels, whose political leanings were leftist, was staging a work with a strong Marxist theme; but as far as the political aspect of our production was concerned, we might have been doing *The Sound of Music.* Most of the actors, being uninterested in the anticapitalist message of *Puntila,* didn't resent the obscuring of the theme. What bothered them was a feeling that they had been abandoned during the rehearsal period, especially after the expectations aroused by their relationship with Daniels during *Ivanov.* They played with gusto but without enjoyment. A key element was missing. It seemed to them that Daniels had lost in penetration what he had gained in inventiveness, as if he had decided to dazzle the audience rather than challenge it.

Nevertheless, this production was instrumental in a key respect: it taught us how to use our theatre. Daniels followed Brecht in avoiding all stage illusion. Everything was exposed, including the gridwork, the scaffolding, and the lights, and the source of all the effects was revealed. No tricks, no stratagems. The stage was a stage, and nothing else. Extending the action into the audience and lounge areas also utilized a feature unique to the theatre—the capacity to break down boundaries between the reality of the spectator and the reality of the stage. I think this production would have delighted Brecht in every respect but one: the loss of the human element in technical razzle-dazzle.

Soon after the opening of *Puntila,* Kingman Brewster was appointed United States ambassador to the Court of St. James's. President of Yale since 1963, he was to leave the university not, as expected, in June of 1978, but a year earlier, in May of 1977. This clarified Kingman's immediate future, but it clouded mine. Would the new president support the policies developed at the Drama School over the past eleven years? Would the university continue to accept this anomaly in its midst? Would the silent opposition finally discover its voice? Clearly, the choice of Kingman's successor was going to be a very important decision not just for the future of Yale but for the future of the

Theatre and the School as well. At that time, no one had a clue as to who this would be.

A number of us at the university, however, were currently being consulted on the question of succession. In early April I received a visit from William Bundy, a key corporation member acting in his capacity as head of the newly formed Presidential Search Committee. Following what I considered to be an obligatory question regarding whether I was interested in the position, Bundy responded to my negative answer by showing me a list of those people who had been nominated, inviting my comments. On this list was the name of Hanna Gray, Kingman's provost, and, to my own mind, the person best qualified to be Yale's next president. None of the others under consideration could equal her in experience, fairness, or probity, but I suspected that Yale was not yet ready to consider a woman at its helm. I added my comments on the other names Bundy showed me. Only one brought me up short—that of A. Bartlett Giamatti from the English department. I spoke frankly to Bundy about my doubts regarding Professor Giamatti's qualifications for the post. I gave two principal reasons, admitting that one of them was selfish. There was reason to believe that Giamatti was not very sympathetic to the present policies of the Drama School, and might therefore prove unsupportive of our work. But more than this, I said, there was evidence to suspect that Giamatti did not have the character to be the next president of Yale. I cited Giamatti's behavior during the Wright Hall incident, when he had privately supported an unpopular position regarding student disruptions and then had publicly voted with the majority. Bundy thanked me, and the interview was over.

It may seem odd that a single incident should have influenced my impressions so strongly, but one of the interesting things about the days of radical tumult was the way a crisis of action could force a crisis of character. We learned in those days that no matter how long you might have known someone, you could never anticipate how he would behave in an extreme situation. Old friends sometimes discovered more about each other in two hours than they had in twenty years. This was particularly fascinating to me because it confirmed the whole nature of the drama. What we know about Oedipus or Lear, or Mrs. Alving or Mother Courage, we learn when they are engaged in crisis. Action is like a yeast that brings our best and worst qualities to the surface. And in the normally actionless, contemplative university, the events of the late sixties and early seventies were a testing time that provided more insight into the academic character than virtually any other period in recent history.

I was engaged in candidacies of quite a different sort that spring—namely, casting Wajda's production of *White Marriage*. This play, an extremely powerful examination of the development of two adolescent girls into sexual awareness, demanded not only great delicacy of interpretation, but also great care in the selection of the two female protagonists. Casting it was particularly difficult because Wajda was abroad, and again had to send instructions by mail in his Polish version of French. It was difficult also because the girls were required to play some key scenes in the nude. We could have easily cast the parts from the School, but I was hesitant to ask my own students to bare their bodies onstage. Perhaps I was too scrupulous; for many, this would not have been a difficulty. Still, I had no way of knowing what influence the opportunity to play a major role would have on somebody's instinctual disinclinations. Since I couldn't be certain which of them actually had no embarrassment about nakedness, I feared that asking a student to play a nude scene would have violated some unspoken covenant between us.

Wajda had described to me the quality he wanted for one of the girls—the sensual, outgoing Pauline—by saying she was a "baby doll," referring to the character played by Carroll Baker in Elia Kazan's film. A lively actress named Blanche Baker showed up in New York to read for the part. Because she fitted Wajda's specifications perfectly, we cast her on the spot. She was also, by an odd coincidence, Carroll Baker's daughter. When Wajda arrived, he was delighted to have the beautiful offspring of the original Baby Doll in his production, but he was not at all delighted with the actress we had chosen for the other girl, Bianca. She was too ripe, too womanly, for what he had imagined to be a delicate, waiflike, almost wasted character. Rehearsals were held up while we continued to audition until we were finally able to find someone closer to the concept in his head.

Rehearsing *White Marriage* was just as pleasant and inspiring as rehearsing *The Possessed,* and the company continued to feel warmed by the creative humanity of this unusual man. About three weeks into rehearsals I received a call from Wajda; he was in a panic. He had just had his first (private) rehearsal of Bianca's nude scene—the final moment of the play when she appears before her new husband and tells him "I am your brother"—only to discover, to his dismay, that one of the actress's breasts was considerably smaller than the other. This normally insignificant birth defect plunged Wajda into despair. A deformation of this kind might confuse the audience about the meaning of the play. Was this the reason why Bianca seemed so reticent about her sexuality? Was this the source of her strange erotic fantasies? Humane to the marrow of his bones, Wajda couldn't bring himself to tell a sensitive actress she was being discharged for such a reason, but as an artist, he knew he had no choice. We deliberated over the problem late into the night. Finally I agreed to inform the actress of Wajda's decision, telling her, as a pretext, that she was too young-looking for the part. The role was recast quickly with someone more physically appropriate.

Zachwatowicz's setting was one of the most compelling designs ever to appear on our stage—a false proscenium in the shape of a huge egg through which one peered into a bizarre world of erotic imagery. The forest was made up of penises instead of trees, a huge erection sprang out of the pants of the old grandfather while he was fondling one of the girls, the very mushrooms had a phallic design. Krystyna and her husband virtually forced the audience to look at the world of material objects through the eyes of uninformed adolescent girls—a subjective experience that had the power to rearrange one's consciousness.

Alvin played the Grandfather with a jerky pelvic walk and a cackling voice that made him look and sound like an old turkey-cock with a waddle; Norma watched this performance nightly from the wings, returning home each night to remind me how much we were going to miss this rare transforming artist when he left for Minneapolis. Norma herself played the Aunt, with a mustache and a lubricious leer. Blanche Baker and Carol Williard (as Bianca) were fetching and innocent as the two young girls, and Steve Rowe was endearing as the shy, scholarly Fiancé. Playing the parents were Elsbieta Chezevska as the dotty Mother, and Gene Troobnick as the powerful Father, transforming at will into a rampaging bull. As for the staging, it was simply exquisite. The only problems Wajda had were with the transitions between the scenes. These were eventually solved by "Baby Doll" herself—Carroll Baker, present to advise her daughter on her performance—who suggested that we accompany the silent-cinema titles Wajda had devised with pianola movie music.

Not everybody liked this production. Mel Gussow wrote that *White Marriage,* in his opinion, was considerably less "substantial" than *The Possessed.* A few of the local reviewers tried to disguise their shock through the familiar device of announcing their boredom. And one of our retired faculty members loudly declared during the opening-night party that the playwright was "impotent" and "deserved to be castrated." Still, many people in the community, a number of them women, wrote to express their gratitude for our production of this play. It was not just thanks for an entertaining evening in the theatre; *White Marriage* was profoundly affecting their waking and dreaming lives. One woman member of the Long Wharf board wrote Norma to tell her she didn't think she would ever be the same again. And Jack Kroll of *Newsweek* called *White Marriage* "the best new play and best production I've seen this season." I thought it quite possibly the best new play and best production we had ever done.

Within the next few weeks, activity increased considerably at the School, perhaps in reaction to the activity at the Rep. Lee Breuer's production of *Earth Spirit* with the third-year class galvanized that flagging group with a final project of which they could be proud—Breuer put the audience on the stage of the University Theatre with the actors, and used the empty auditorium as a playing space with the comically lighted seats treated as another character in the play. Around the same time the fine first-year acting class, which had been working all year at the Rep, did twin productions of *The Sea Gull,* each with a different cast, both of them demonstrating how much they had all benefited from the initial year of the new training, and particularly from Norma's acting class. From now on, Norma would not only teach the first-year, she would have a great deal to say about their casting, keeping a careful eye on what each student needed in the way of parts for the sake of continuing development.

At the final acting-department meeting of the year—over which I was continuing to preside—everyone declared the new program an unqualified success. For once, we had tangible evidence, in the form of talented, versatile students, of what we were accomplishing, and for once, the meetings were devoted not to wrangling over what direction we should take but to discussing how to improve the one we had chosen. Only the second-year final project had failed our expectations—my fault, I had chosen the wrong director—but if I continued to make mistakes, I at least knew now how to rectify them. I had taken full personal charge of the acting training—determining policy, holding regular meetings with students, teaching some classes, hiring and firing faculty. What I didn't know about the procedures of day-to-day training I could learn, and my ignorance of the mysteries could be partially compensated for, I thought, by the fact that one voice—at last—was speaking for both the Theatre and the School. The troublesome problem of integration—a problem that had plagued us for ten thorny years, setting friend against friend, actor against director, administration against faculty, School against Rep—was finally now being resolved.

It was Kingman Brewster's last graduation ceremony at Yale. As he marched in front of the procession in his colorful ceremonial roles to the rhythms of William Walton's traditional *Crown Imperial,* I thought about how many commencements I had experienced with this elegant and witty man. By this time he had permanently alienated many Old Blues, and he was soon to be severely criticized for his handling of Yale's endowment and expenditures; but it was hard to imagine that anyone watching that slightly stooped figure walk toward the platform could fail to feel a pang over his imminent departure. He and I had had disagreements over the years—far fewer, actually, than I normally have with figures of authority. But we shared a mutual respect that strengthened our relationship and kept our association fruitful. At our last deans' luncheon—realizing with a bit of a shock that I was now the senior dean —I had expressed appreciation to Kingman, on the part of all those present, for what he had given us in the way of style and spirit. I risked his embarrassment (and my own), but I was reluctant to let the occasion pass without recording our genuine gratitude. At graduation, Kingman pretended for the last time to stumble over his Latin address to the doctoral candidates, and, for the last time, got his annual laugh over the explosive way he pronounced the word *Nunc.* For the last time, he read the citations for the honorary degrees, and, for the first time, received an honorary from Yale himself. Also receiving one that year was the English playwright, Edward Bond, a writer who was hardly honored in New Haven. I took this as a final parting gift from my departing president.

Other farewells were also made that year. Rocco Landesman was leaving us to start his own investment firm in New York—the only faculty member we ever lost to Wall Street. Chuck Levin went back to New York to wait for that chimerical TV pilot; Tom Hill went to Broadway; others left to "try their wings." The last farewell was the most painful. I had to say good-bye to Alvin Epstein. He, Danny, and I took another white-water raft trip before he left for Minneapolis—this one down the Salmon River in Idaho. Norma had wisely decided to go to Japan with a woman friend rather than brave the rapids again. I missed her badly (those two weeks apart were the longest separation of our marriage), but once again Alvin proved to be the most delightful of companions. The river trip, however, was a hardship because the weather was cold and rainy, and we were continually being soaked under threatening skies. Still, we had a lovely week in Wyoming, camping, fishing, and sightseeing under the shadow of the Grand Tetons, and we spent a few days in San Francisco, eating well and going to junk movies. We parted at San Francisco Airport, Alvin shuttling back to the Guthrie, Danny and I returning to New Haven, and found ourselves speaking more intimately about things than in all the eleven years of our association. An era was coming to an end; another was beginning. The School had found its definition. The Theatre we had nursed into birth—and nurtured through drought and blight—had finally taken root and flowered. Alvin was leaving us, perhaps forever. But his work in Minneapolis I considered a graft or voluntary of this developing plant, and strong enough proof that it would continue to grow.

XI

Year of the Ax
1977-1978

Beware the ivy. It has the power to crumble stone.

—Old saying

This climactic year began with an auspicious appointment—that of Andrei Serban as associate director of the Yale Repertory Theatre. This slender, youthful Rumanian artist, with his steel-rimmed glasses and soft blond beard, had the appearance of a student revolutionary and the manner of a sophisticated intellectual. By the time he reached thirty he had already transformed the American theatre with his audacious new methods. After seeing his stunning directorial essays on three classical Greek plays, *Fragments of a Trilogy*, I had been especially impressed by the visual and aural imagery Serban invented for *The Trojan Women*, performed in a language composed of ancient and modern Greek, Sanskrit, and Swahili, and distinguished by moments of startling beauty and power. What was particularly attractive about Serban's work was the way he entered a play and transfigured it. His company at La Mama was the only performance group I knew that actually illuminated classical texts. It didn't take long for us to discover that we shared many of the same theatrical values, and after a few meetings in the winter of 1976, Serban had agreed to direct some plays and teach some courses at Yale. He arrived a year later than planned. Joseph Papp needed him first to rescue Lincoln Center.

When Papp called to tell me of his desire to take Serban away for a year, he was very apologetic. He knew about our agreement; he hoped I would understand; he gave his word that Serban would come to Yale the following season. At the Vivian Beaumont, Serban staged his controversial productions of *The Cherry Orchard* and *Agamemnon*, both of which brought him significant press attention. The next spring (1977), Papp called to say that he was delivering to us "an international star." With Serban's productions, and with Richard Foreman's *Threepenny Opera,* Papp had finally developed a strategy for Lincoln Center—doing experimental versions of established texts. But within a few months he had resigned from the theatre, complaining that it was draining his resources. The income from *A Chorus Line,* with which he had been supporting his presentations at Lincoln Center, would now be used for his work at the New York Public Theatre.

I had been following Papp's fortunes closely while preparing an article on funding for the performing arts, later published in *The New York Times Magazine* under the title "Can the Show Go On?" I was convinced that the financial difficulties he was experiencing were common to most nonprofit arts institutions. Private foundations were reducing their support, and federal and state endowments were not taking up the slack; neither, for that matter, were corporations or individual philanthropists. I repeated the information, previously published in the press, that both Ford and Rockefeller were preparing to make drastic cutbacks in their annual subsidies to the performing arts. For some reason, my remarks enraged the current president of the Rockefeller Foundation, who denied that his trustees had authorized any reduction in arts funding—despite the published statement of his own arts director, Howard Klein. He demanded that I "correct" my story, but failed to provide any basis for correction other than the fact that Rockefeller had recently increased its budget for the humanities. Two years later I learned through a letter from the new arts director at Ford that he too had been insulted by my article. Didn't I realize what he had done to help get the American Literary Classics publications off the ground? This was another humanities project. I was beginning to perceive that—at least in the world of the private foundations—the arts tended to get confused with the humanities, and that helpful policies for indigent institutions were sometimes of less importance than "good ink" for the officers.

I was assuredly guilty of biting the hand that fed me, even if the food was getting rather meager. I must have known that this would bring retaliation, but I was either too dumb or too cocky to worry about it at the time. I figured I might as well make a scene—better to be hanged for a sheep as for a goat. If I could do something to expose the capricious nature of foundation giving, I might just possibly have some positive effect on future policy; if not, I might help induce the public sector to recognize a real emergency. In urging state patronage for theatre, opera, and dance companies, I was accused by some critics of demanding handouts for artists, but the collective nature of performing-arts institutions left them helpless without it. Moreover, significant "unearned income," as distinct from the box office, was the only way to keep these companies honest. It was hard enough for the nonprofit movement to withstand the allures of the commercial world. With foundation support declining, the profit-making alternatives were bound to become irresistible.

We still had our large Ford grant, which, when matched, would bring in $67,000 each year in interest. The trouble was that it wasn't being matched. Bogged down in a slow-moving capital campaign, Yale was not yet prepared to commit any new funds to the arts, and the School of Drama would not receive any proceeds from this grant until after I left in 1979. We were, moreover, reaching the end of our invaluable CBS grant. The gentle Arthur Tourtellot had died that summer and his successors had changed CBS policy: only arts groups in cities with large numbers of television viewers would now be beneficiaries of CBS largesse. I was beginning to see small advantage in remaining in New Haven. The Connecticut State Council was slowly increasing its annual budget, after years of making disgracefully small contributions to local professional groups, but we—as part of Yale—were still considered a political liability. We weren't performing enough community services, and half of our audience were students from out of state. If I was still naïve enough to believe that artistic excellence was a criterion for state support, I was quickly learning that a more important standard was public service.

Still, after years of experience at fund-raising, we were proving adept at discovering new springs of money as the old wells dried up. That, combined with our ever-increasing audiences, helped us to finish each season without falling into debt. By this time we had developed a splendid organization, led by Rob Orchard, which was significantly reducing the fund-raising pressures on me. To their eternal credit, none of the staff ever rebuked me for making their jobs more difficult by scolding the foundations in the pages of *The New York Times.*

And, as a matter of fact, the Rockefeller Foundation repaid my ingratitude by providing a portion of Andrei Serban's salary at Yale. Other new appointments that year included Walt Jones as co-associate director at the Rep, and the celebrated classics scholar, William Arrowsmith, in the DFA department. These two different personalities from entirely different fields were to work together on a School production of Aristophanes' *Thesmophoriazusae,* translated by Arrowsmith under the title *Euripides at Bay.* And the last fellows at the School under the expiring CBS grant would include—along with Derek Walcott, Charles Ludlam, and Dwight Macdonald—a recently graduated student named Ted Tally, whose *Terra Nova* would be the third production of our new season.

The appointment of Macdonald raised a few eyebrows that year, since he had no background—or apparent interest, for that matter—in the theatre, and he was unlikely ever to write a play. His experience, aside from the movies, was in politics. Still, he qualified under our prior agreement with CBS to invite at least one writer each year from outside the field of drama. I had recently learned that this lively intellectual, so influential in the forties and fifties, was down on his luck and extremely dejected. He had been hospitalized some months before, and had suffered from a serious writer's block for at least ten years. I didn't often find myself in agreement with his political or aesthetic judgments when he was writing freely, but I believed that our students might benefit from contact with a dedicated professional journalist. And, anyway, I was in a position to offer some help and encouragement to a valuable American on whom society had turned its back.

That summer—the summer of 1977—New York was in flames, following a blackout that brought considerable looting and burning. The Son of Sam was finally apprehended, after having wantonly murdered a large number of innocent people; the Bakke case was being argued before the Supreme Court, in an effort to determine if benign racial quotas were not a form of reverse discrimination; some women at Yale were preparing a brief against the university charging sexual harassment by professors who, they said, traded good grades for sexual favors; and the cultural world was further depleted by the deaths, in quick succession, of the poet Robert Lowell, the conductor Leopold Stokowksi, and the singer Maria Callas. Also that summer, Lillian Hellman and Diana Trilling—two close friends of ours and of each other—were locked in an unpleasant public quarrel about censorship and suppression, which made me fear for a while that intellectuals might soon be remembered more for their arguments than for their achievements.

In other words, it was your typically mild, uneventful summer, complete with the usual flares and eruptions, but despite these, my mood was relatively sanguine. I still continued to vacillate, however, over my future at Yale. Not knowing who was to be the next president or what that appointment would portend for the Drama School, I decided to tread water during the summer months before deciding on the length of my next term. I was feeling proud of the work and considerably less exhausted than usual; that was on the positive side. But one night toward the end of summer I dreamed that at a revival of *Ivanov* I had forgotten my lines and misplaced my costume and decided not to go onstage. This dream suggested that however confident I may have been in my waking life, my unconscious was still unsettled. For that reason, I told Acting President Hanna Gray in the fall that I was willing to accept a trial year as dean until June of 1979, keeping my options open on the final two years until I learned more about the situation at Yale.

Like Brewster before her, Hanna Gray was very supportive of our work and forbearing about my indecision. More than Brewster, she had a feeling for the theatre and took genuine pleasure in the productions of the Rep. Not just for that, or because she praised my achievements, I liked her a lot, and I wished I could have helped her more in her time of trouble. For this was not an easy year for Hanna. She was acting both as president and as her own provost, an impossible task even in normal times. This year she was facing stringent economic problems caused by a badly invested endowment portfolio, as well as a long-drawn-out strike by the maintenance workers. Coping with the deficit brought her abuse from the faculty; managing the strike subjected her to ridicule from the students. She was continually depicted in the *Yale Daily News* as an uptight schoolmarm, always looking severely into the camera with her arms folded, whose vocabulary consisted of a single word: "No." Hanna had determined to get rid of the deficit and hold fast against inflation—popular positions neither with faculty who wanted perks nor with employees who wanted raises. As a result, the strike went on for months, and there was considerable muttering around the university about the "extravagances" of the Brewster years.

Like all Yale departments, we were required to cut our budget by 20 percent. We had survived similar cuts in previous years without having to reduce our faculty, largely through supplementary grants. Now that these were becoming scarce, the only alternative to reducing the staff was to increase the student body, thus generating more income through tuition. We were always willing to cooperate in helping to reduce the university's growing deficit, but some of the economies seemed to me a little petty. That fall, for example, the heat was not turned on in our buildings until the temperature dropped to 50 degrees. We spent many days in October and November wrapped up in our coats, huddled around electric heaters, our noses turning blue. Then we were asked to hire somebody to turn out lights when a room was not in use, which cost more in salary than it saved in energy. And at our deans' meetings, still being held monthly for the same boring purpose, there was no longer any lunch.

I never ate lunch anyway, so I didn't miss the cardboard chicken or the soggy salad, but it was amusing to watch all those heavyweight administrators sitting around an empty table at lunchtime discussing affirmative action with plastic cups of coffee in their hands. At one of these meetings the dean of the Law School, my good friend, leaned over to me miserably and whispered, "This is boring at best, but without a drink it's intolerable." There was no disputing the monotony of these discussions. I decided to make a little scene: one day I brought Danny's Snoopy lunchbox into the Corporation Room— a sumptuous chamber in Woodbridge Hall with a highly polished mahogany table and sober portraits of all the Yale presidents—and while the deans were listening to the the newest version of the plans to bring more women and minority groups into the university, I solemnly extracted from the orange lunchbox a peanut-butter-and-jelly sandwich on Wonder bread, an illustrated thermos filled with homogenized milk, and three Twinkies. I laid these neatly on the table, and offered a Twinkie to Hanna. Nobody laughed. Instead, one of the deans asked me questions about the nutritional value of peanut butter.

We didn't have too many laughs that fall; even our productions were a little gloomy. *The Ghost Sonata* was currently in rehearsal, along with a production of David Mamet's *Reunion* and *Dark Pony;* waiting in the wings was Ted Tally's *Terra Nova,* a play about Scott's ill-fated expedition to Antarctica. Serban had insisted on casting Norma, over her protests, in the role of the Fiancée in the Strindberg play. It was a wordless part, requiring her to wear pasty old-age makeup and a costume that appeared to be disintegrating on her body. As if this were not enough, Serban had instructed Norma to play the role as if she were looking into her grave. She gave a harrowing performance, her features fixed in a haunted expression of total despair, which may have reflected her mood, since she hated the part. It was not just that she preferred to look glamorous onstage; it was rather that the living corpse she was enacting had put her into a morbid depression, which she carried back daily from rehearsal and nightly from performance. When Stella Adler came up later to see the production, she rebuked me for letting Norma do the role. Didn't I realize how the psychic poise of an actress could be affected by playing a part of this kind? But Norma did it—cursing me all the way. She never allowed herself to be photographed in the production.

The Ghost Sonata provided an eerily beautiful experience, concluding with a projection of Boecklin's painting "Island of the Dead," which was gradually blurred in focus until it became a haunting abstract image. The only scene that failed to realize itself was the last, which the Student and the Hyacinth Girl played before an enormous statue of the Buddha in a slow-motion version of tai-chi. In a fever of inspiration, Michael Yeargan had designed three metallic and transparent boxes, which functioned as exteriors and interiors both, and the acting—particularly that of Priscilla Smith as a squawking Parrot and Max Wright as a batlike Hummel—was ferocious and intense. Serban's imagistic imagination was perfectly suited to Strindberg's hallucinatory vision. In the euphoria of the opening-night success, I tried to talk him into doing *A Dream Play* as his next project, but he, always restless, wanted to go on to something new.

The production of *The Ghost Sonata* was a distinguished addition to our repertory. But although Serban was very pleased with the results—and seemed to enjoy his working conditions—some of the actors were not as happy. They were a little miffed by a rehearsal process in which the director asked them to work on their parts alone while he, apparently ignoring them, pored over a model of the set. It's a mystery how Serban gets his results. He doesn't work closely with actors in the manner of American directors but, rather, focuses his energies on style, concept, visual images. An extremely authoritative artist whom some people find authoritarian, he demands invention from the actors, then edits out much of their contribution. As a result, those unwilling to submit to his controlling hand begin to complain that they are being manipulated onstage like puppets. On the other hand, the actor without vanity can learn a lot from Serban: Jeremy Geidt, for example, felt he had been initiated into a whole new world of performance.

The production was generally well received by the local and national press, but it generated a sour review from Richard Eder, the new critic for the *Times* and hitherto one of Serban's most ardent admirers. Just a few weeks earlier I had had lunch with Eder at his request; he wanted my advice about the resident theatre. Although admittedly untrained as a theatre critic (he was a foreign political commentator with the *Times*), Eder had impressed me as a prudent, intelligent reporter, with a decent writing style and a reputation for probity. He also seemed to have some sense of the power of his position. During the course of our lunch he asked me whether bad reviews in the *Times* could have the same killing influence on nonprofit theatres as they did on Broadway shows. I assured him that resident theatres had the capacity to survive a bad New York press, though we were not invulnerable. Persistent attacks on the work of a single theatre—such as Barnes's treatment of the American Place Theatre—were capable of influencing foundations, which, without adequate staffs, still tended to base their grant giving on New York reviews. My reference to Barnes brought an inquiry from Eder about his predecessor's relationship with the Yale Repertory Theatre, which I answered frankly. "You mean you *banned* him?" Eder asked, raising his eyebrows. In his mind, I had apparently broken some sacred journalistic code. I tried to explain that Barnes had not been banned from our theatre; rather, he had been asked to stay away voluntarily in recognition of the fact that our quarrels were influencing his judgments. This distinction was lost on Eder; perhaps it was so subtle that only I could understand it. At any rate, I had committed a blunder, and if I didn't realize this at the time, Norma let me know it later in no uncertain terms.

Eder's review of *The Ghost Sonata* was a disappointment, not because it was unfavorable but because it was dense. He surprised us by expressing his dissatisfaction with what we all believed to be the most original performance in the production—Max Wright's Hummel. Wright's acting was not conventional, but then neither was the play. In his *Newsweek* review, Jack Kroll had been among those to recognize Wright's contribution, writing that "he gives a demonstration of expressionist acting that would have caused Fritz Lang's monocle to mist over with delight." For Eder, on the other hand, Wright's Hummel represented "the production's chief failure." I didn't think the problem could be explained as a mere difference of opinion. Those are common enough among reviewers. What worried us about Eder's notice—as we watched him take his first steps as the critic of the New York *Times*—was his curious failure to recognize a performance so clearly out of the ordinary.

But I couldn't complain about the press we were getting that year. Both reviewers and feature writers were finally beginning to praise the quality of the Yale Repertory Theatre. Serban was inevitably a source of great interest and curiosity, even though the headline on his interview in the New Haven *Register* read, LOVE HIM OR LEAVE HIM (not untypical of the paper's attitude toward artists). But it wasn't just Serban who attracted attention that year, it was also the work of the Theatre and the School. The previous spring, *Camera Three* had done a comprehensive two-part television examination of our program; *Horizon* magazine had just published an extremely flattering article; and now *The New York Times* had informed me that it was planning a feature on the Rep in its Arts and Leisure section. The curious thing was the difficulty Bill Honan, the editor, was experiencing in finding the right reporter. Two or three writers submitted manuscripts that Honan found unacceptable; then Mel Gussow tried his hand at a piece—also rejected; later, Margaret Croyden spent weeks at Yale collecting information and holding interviews, but also failed to satisfy the editors. It was either that the articles on the Rep were too favorable or too unfavorable—the *Times* couldn't get a balanced assessment. Finally I was told that the article would come out in the spring, preceding a tour we were planning to the New York Public Theatre, but the writer would remain "anonymous" until the piece appeared.

I admit to being much too interested, around this time, in external opinion, especially considering how I used to scorn it. But I had reached the point where I desperately wanted some recognition for what the Theatre had accomplished over the intervening years. Everyone has at least one deadly sin. Mine is the deadliest—pride. My identity had somehow gotten so totally wrapped up with the Theatre and the School that when either of these institutions or their members were attacked, I took it as a personal affront. If somebody had the generosity to tell me he enjoyed a particular play or performance, a warm glow would suffuse my limbs. If somebody abused our work, I would stiffen. I remember one particular Yale party in New Haven where a guest took the occasion to attack our penchant for experimentation—particularly what he graciously referred to as "the schmucky Black Mass" in *Don Juan.* I felt my veins turn molten. On the same occasion the host made an effort to soothe my wounded feelings, saying, "The Yale Repertory Theatre is good for what it attempts, the Long Wharf for what it does." Why couldn't I accept this as a compliment? Everything seemed to increase my sense of alienation. We had designed our Theatre for an intellectual community, but at times we felt we were living in Siberia.

When I attended the Long Wharf opening that year for its revival of that Lancashire English romance *Hobson's Choice,* I looked the audience over with envy and dejection. We had never had more than six thousand subscribers, of whom half were usually students on discount passes; Long Wharf had fourteen thousand, including most of the Yale faculty. To me, this was a confirmation of the remark in the *Yale Daily News* that Yale's real theatre was the Long Wharf, not the Rep. I had come to New Haven believing that the university was the ideal place to do classical and experimental plays. Now the majority of Yale students and faculty often seemed to me as cautious in their tastes as New Haven's bankers and businessmen. Even more disappointing were the tastes of my colleagues in the English department who during the day taught Blake and Yeats and Joyce, and at night went to the theatre to watch Lancashire comedies and Irish romances. It was odd that most of our mature audiences came from the hospital and the School of Medicine—internists, cardiologists, epidemiologists, psychiatrists, nurses—but then Chekhov and Ibsen had already discovered that the true humanists were doctors. I had to remind myself frequently that we had elected to be a minority theatre. I should have had the strength not to care, but in my twelfth year at Yale I was feeling singularly unappreciated in my own hometown.

Norma had no patience with my whining. Every time I came whimpering home with a fresh complaint, she shrugged her shoulders and said "Quit." Danny was telling me to quit, too. He had picked up my feeling of entrapment in New Haven. On the other hand, whenever I spoke seriously about resignation, I would notice a certain glaze in Norma's eyes. She always used to kid me about my "obsession," as she called the work at Yale, but both of us knew that she was more obsessed than I was. Norma preferred that I stop complaining and improve our conditions. She said I was failing to communicate to the company the fact that our work was *important.* How could I ask for commitment when I was still so full of doubt myself? She had a point. In bemoaning my own fate, I was failing to give the Theatre a strong spine. I resolved to stop wincing over every disappointment and try to provide the place with cheerful, positive leadership.

One opportunity presented itself when Andrei Serban and I held meetings to decide on his second project at the Rep. He had agreed, tentatively, to direct *The Wild Duck*. Now he decided the play was too cerebral for his imagistic style. What he wanted instead was the chance to make a new departure. In the course of the next few weeks we discussed, agreed on, and rejected dozens of possible projects, including *Ghosts, Tales From the Vienna Woods, The Imaginary Invalid, The Master and Margarita, The Wood Demon, 'Tis Pity She's a Whore*, and *Six Characters in Search of an Author*. Finally, just at the moment when I was beginning to despair that Serban would ever make up his mind, he told me he had found his project: *A Cabal of Hypocrites* (sometimes called *Monsieur de Molière*), by the modern Russian playwright Bulgakov.

I knew the play—we had featured it some years before in our Sunday play-reading series—but I couldn't say I liked it very much. The form of it seemed to me old-fashioned, and the language was riddled with fustian and rodomontade, like a Russian version of *Cyrano de Bergerac*. On the other hand, I had great respect for Serban's instinct. And the designs he had in mind —a massive re-creation of the Palais Royal with the actors costumed like Molière's comedians—were bound to be visually impressive. They were also bound to start a revolt among our irritated technical staff, since Serban's procrastination had left very little time for construction. This problem I was willing to face, so relieved was I that he had finally decided on a project. I still had doubts about the play, but by this time I probably would have agreed to a Serban production of *Our Town* or *All My Sons*.

Serban came into my office a few days later, his eyes glowing. He was obviously excited by a new idea. Why not do *The Imaginary Invalid* as a curtain raiser to *A Cabal of Hypocrites*? A play *by* Molière preceding a play *about* Molière. I had only one objection to this proposal—the evening would last six hours. Would he consider substituting a short Molière farce from among those recently translated by Albert Bermel? I suggested one of the Sganarelle plays. Molière had played that part himself, and the actor playing him could enter from one play into the other, wiping the makeup from his features. Serban agreed almost too quickly. Too late I realized that we hadn't narrowed the choices, we had multiplied them, since now we had to make a decision on which Sganarelle farce to choose from among the seven or eight in the Bermel volume.

Serban suggested that we make our selection by reading through the entire collection aloud, using whatever actors were available to play the various parts. These turned out to be Norma, Jeremy, me, and the second- and third-year actors. The readings were fun; all of the farces had a simple vitality that delighted us. While Serban was deliberating on his choice, however, he was trying to cast the all-important role of Molière in *A Cabal of Hypocrites*. We interviewed or auditioned many actors, none of whom was available or interested or appropriate to Serban's concept. Finally, Serban asked me about Chuck Levin. He had heard he was a good actor; why not audition him? Chuck, who was in his twenties, was clearly too young for the aging Molière, but Andrei waved away my doubts. Much could be done with costume and makeup.

Chuck arrived the next day on a train from New York; Serban's tight schedule allowed the actor less than thirty minutes to look over the script. He gave a spirited and funny reading, but, as I feared, was much too youthful for the part. When I turned to Serban to see if he agreed with me, I noticed that he was sitting with his head in his hands, staring at his feet. "What's the matter?" I asked, my mouth getting dry. "We can't do this play!" he whispered fiercely. "It's *terrible*—a melodrama." "But . . . but"—my confusion made me stammer—"you liked it when you read it, didn't you?" "Yes," he replied, "but I hadn't *heard* it yet. It sounds *awful*. It's out of the question."

Meanwhile there was Chuck, standing on the stage under the impression we were discussing his talent, and waiting to be told the part was his. Serban didn't pay him the slightest bit of attention. Instead, he kept leafing through the pages of the script morosely. Chuck has a bit of a temper, and I could see the situation was getting to him. At last I took Chuck to the side and apologized to him. He had read well, I told him, but we were now involved with a serious production problem that was occupying Serban's attention. Would he mind if we called him? Chuck was furious. He had come all this way from New York, against the advice of his agent, and now the director wouldn't even favor him with the courtesy of a reaction. He couldn't wait any longer, either; the next train to New York was about to leave. I did my best to soothe Chuck's wounded feelings, and got him out of the room before he got around to physicalizing his anger.

During this time, Serban was pulling pensively on his jaw. He had decided, he told me, to hold his decision on the Bulgakov play until he could hear it read in its entirety by actors. Could we get some people together the next day? I was convinced that Serban had already made up his mind, and feared that another reading would not only waste our precious time but put a strain on the patience of everybody involved. Remembering my resolution about cheerful leadership, however, I scheduled the new reading and promised the actors it would probably be the last. We spent a good portion of the next day reading through the Bulgakov text before Serban announced that he couldn't possibly do the play. "Too heavy," he announced. "No style."

Now Serban had a new idea. Why not do the Molière farces we had been reading through all week? Why not, indeed? We could select three or four Sganarelle pieces, and call the evening *Sganarelle*. I was interested to see how Serban would work as a director of farce. But now we had the same old problem—choosing the plays. By this time I had enough experience with Serban to know that we had to read through all the potential candidates three or four times, and let him make his choice.

But this was not a waste of time. While Serban was deliberating on the plays, he was also deciding on his actors. Mark Linn-Baker, then a second-year student, gave such an inspired reading of *The Flying Doctor* that Serban cast him on the spot, though he intended at first to stage this play in the lounge during the intermission. After hearing me read the part of Sganarelle in *The Forced Marriage,* he chose that play, too, insisting that I play the role. He also decided on a third selection, the verse play called *Sganarelle,* because he thought its rhymed couplets would make an interesting formal contrast to the rough prose of the other farces. We had three plays now. Did we have our show? Not yet. Serban wanted to continue reading through all the plays.

Exhausted as we were by this play-reading marathon, we were also aware that it was helping to stimulate Serban's imagination. He was already developing a fascinating concept for the evening. Serban had originally been attracted to these farces because for him they had the directness and simplicity of street theatre. He decided that the company would play them as if it were a traveling troupe, performing wherever there was a space and a commission. His first idea was to stage the plays in every corner of the theatre, including the lobby and the lounge. When the audience entered, one of them might be playing in the street. Serban welcomed my suggestion that since the plays came from every period of Molière's career, we have a different Sganarelle for every farce, representing the development of this stock figure from vigorous youth to manhood to old age—also representing stages in Molière's life. Mark Baker and I were cast as the young and old Sganarelles. We had no actor in the company to play him middle-aged.

By the time I had persuaded Bob Dishy to read for that part, Serban was leaning toward an evening composed of five farces, two of them played during intermission in the lounge. I feared the production was in danger of losing its form. These fears grew when Dishy, whose reading Serban admired, told us that the Molière play he really wanted to do was *The Doctor in Spite of Himself.* Sganarelle was the hero of that play, too, but it was long enough to make an evening by itself. I started worrying again over the length of the production. Serban was worrying that if we didn't do the play that Dishy wanted, he wouldn't play the part that Serban wanted.

I tried to persuade Serban to offer Dishy the part we had proposed, and if it wasn't satisfactory to him, to cast someone else. Otherwise, *Sganarelle* would turn into an accretion of too many conflicting demands. If Dishy played two of the Sganarelles and two other actors played the others, the audience would be confused about the intention. I thought, for the sake of unity, we ought to have either five different comedians or one. But by this time Serban had become so enchanted with Dishy's comic talent that he was willing to do anything to keep him. I suggested another solution. Let Dishy play *all* the Sganarelles, except for the one Mark Baker would do in the lounge.

At our first reading it was quite obvious that Dishy was not happy watching two other actors play Sganarelle. Part of me looked forward to acting in *The Forced Marriage;* the more sensible part knew I would have little time to rehearse or perform it. Therefore it was no great sacrifice to offer my role to

Dishy. When I did, his doleful countenance brightened a bit. Now he had three Sganarelles to play—in *The Forced Marriage,* in *Sganarelle,* and in *The Doctor in Spite of Himself.* I was still dissatisfied with the shape of the production, however, particularly with *The Doctor in Spite of Himself.* It was out of balance with the other plays, not only because it was longer but because, unlike the others, it was a familiar, sophisticated classic. Besides, Bermel had not adapted it for his volume, and none of us was satisfied with the extant translations. At one session when the smile I was trying to keep on my face kept crumpling along the edges, Serban, Dishy, and the rest of the cast began a collective translation of the play—proposing phrases, quarreling over words, transposing lines. After a whole morning of this, they had agreed only on the opening speech.

Somehow Serban was able to begin rehearsals—with only three weeks left before opening night. Rehearsal was an odd process. Instead of working on scenes, he asked the actors to try on various costumes from the stock wardrobe, thinking that finding the right physical elements would help them find their characters. Only Dishy refused to participate in this three-day costume party. While the others traded hats, cloaks, doublets, and breeches, he sat quietly to one side, reading his script. It was clear from his melancholy demeanor that he didn't think much of Serban's rehearsal procedures. And when the director suggested that the actors improvise nonsense dialogue for *The Doctor in Spite of Himself,* Dishy registered a protest. Why waste time when there was so little left? Dishy had begun his career as a Second City improviser, but he apparently wanted the classics to be treated with more respect.

I left town, a little later, for a day of fund-raising in New York. When I returned that night, I was told that Serban had quit the show. The conflict brewing between him and Dishy had finally erupted into open warfare. When I eventually located Serban on the telephone, he told me that since Dishy had such strong opinions, Dishy should direct the show. He couldn't work with recalcitrant people. I sensed other reasons for Serban's decision—he was clearly unhappy with the way rehearsals were proceeding. Finally he confessed to me that he had lost his inspiration. He was not a machine punching out productions. He could not create under the pressure of time. I reminded him that we had chosen these plays in order to give him the opportunity to explore a new style, not in order to feature Bob Dishy's admittedly fine comic talents. We had compromised enough on the original idea. Now it was time to recapture it. We must let Dishy go, recast the plays, and postpone the opening, if necessary, until the show was completed to Serban's satisfaction.

This seemed to calm Serban. With some regret, I told Dishy that things had simply not worked out as planned. He readily agreed, relieved to be shut of this crazy Rumanian who rehearsed in such a weird way. We wondered together why the postmodernist improvisations of performance groups should be incompatible with the Stanislavsky-oriented improvisations of the Second City; I continued to hope these different traditions could be united. As for Serban, the whole experience confirmed his hatred of Stanislavsky and his suspicion of those with Stanislavsky training. When he recast the plays with the younger members of the company, he felt considerably more hopeful, considerably less threatened; I didn't bother to tell him that all of these actors had been grounded in Stanislavsky. After some initial resistance, he agreed to accept Gene Troobnick in *The Forced Marriage,* even though Troobnick also came from the Second City. In *Sganarelle*—the verse play—he cast Michael Gross, an athletic acting graduate with dance training, who delighted him, though Gross was a little too young to play opposite Norma. For the role of Sganarelle in *The Doctor in Spite of Himself* (which he was continuing to rehearse despite the departure of the actor for whom it had been chosen) he cast a second-year actor named Richard Grusin.

In the midst of all these hassles, *Terra Nova* had opened to considerable acclaim, with Arthur Hill, Lindsay Crouse, and Michael Higgins in the leading roles, and Max Wright, Michael Gross, Steve Rowe, and Jeremy Geidt stealing the play in lesser parts. *Terra Nova* had been originally performed in a student workshop. We cast as understudies in the Rep production the same students who had first played the roles, and had the pleasure of seeing them perform the play at a matinee before a house full of cheering schoolchildren. The understudy program was continuing to work; so was the rest of the program. The second- and third-year actors had another triumph that year in a holiday show first performed in the Cabaret—*The 1940's Radio Hour,* as devised and directed by Walt Jones. And Jeremy Geidt supervised the second-year actors in a hilarious mask show, using a loose scenario padded out with outrageous puns and obscene double entendres.

In short, the new training was continuing to demonstrate its viability in the only way that really mattered—in the quality of student performance and the professional manner with which these students went about their tasks. I was still having a bit of trouble, however, with the DFA program. Perhaps reflecting the aloofness of some of their instructors, the doctoral students in criticism continued to be a little isolated from the School, behaving like aisle-sitting critics instead of engaging in supportive performance tasks. We had made some steps toward integration by assigning these students roles as literary managers, jobs that they performed with pleasure and effectiveness. I was struck by the fact that while a few of the DFA students had become professional critics, more of them had gone into teaching. Lately they were also being employed as dramaturges by major resident companies. It was time to admit that the critics program was a failure and to redirect it toward a practical theatrical goal.

I therefore decided to accept incoming students not into a program offering a DFA in criticism and dramatic literature but into an MFA program in dramaturgy. We would concentrate our three-year training on literary management, and those who displayed talent as critics could *then* go on for a doctorate at the School, having earned their way in the practical theatre. When I proposed this change to Richard Gilman and Stanley Kauffmann, they raised no objection so long as their own courses were unaffected. Kauffmann had some anxiety that the DFA students, sensing a loss in status, would withdraw from the School, but although a few of them grumbled, nobody actually left. Within months the other students had accepted them totally as fellow practitioners, and our alienated critics had been transformed into helpful and creative associates.

Two productions were in performance, two were in rehearsal. Things were running smoothly enough to allow Norma and me to enjoy a brief vacation in the Virgin Islands. Three days after we arrived in Virgin Gorda, on December 20, I received a terse telegram from my secretary, Penny Pigott, which read: GIAMATTI PRESIDENT: STRIKE OVER.

Hanna Gray, having removed herself from a competition she stood little chance of winning, had already accepted the presidency of the University of Chicago. Henry Rosovsky, dean of the Faculty of Arts and Sciences at Harvard, had been offered the presidency of Yale and—to the embarrassment of the university—had turned it down. Giamatti had then accepted it.

Before all this happened, I had been invited along with the other deans and department chairmen to a meeting at the president's house on 43 Hillhouse Avenue to share with members of the corporation our opinions of the ten people being considered for the job. The most popular name on the list was obviously that of Giamatti, who—it was argued by some of his colleagues—had the advantage of being a homegrown product, a well-liked campus figure, a former college master, a participant in numerous university committees, and someone who wanted the job. One of his supporters noted—for those who might think his Italian background was inappropriate to a Wasp institution —that but for an accident of birth, his name might have been A. Giamatti Bartlett.

And now the corporation had made its choice: Giamatti was president of Yale. Under the sun of Virgin Gorda, Norma and I lay on the beach and took stock. Neither of us was very sanguine about the future. Aside from Giamatti's fervent advocacy of the undergraduate drama society, there were other reasons to suspect we might be in trouble. For one thing, his wife was a graduate of the old Drama School; for another, they were both strong supporters of the Long Wharf. These considerations—along with certain rumors we had been hearing about Giamatti's attitude toward the Rep—made it seem highly unlikely that the new administration would give us the same kind of endorsement we had enjoyed under Kingman Brewster and Hanna Gray. Before the vacation ended, I had decided to develop some guarantees against the future. We would take the Yale Repertory Theatre on tour, visiting Cambridge and New York at the conclusion of our current season. If Giamatti didn't try to influence our program or threaten my job, the tour to New York would help raise funds for the YRT from private foundations. In the event that I found it necessary to leave Yale, the tour to Cambridge would expose our work to another university—and another city.

Returning to New Haven in late December, I learned that Giamatti had attempted to call on me at the Drama School while I was away. I took this as a hopeful sign. Less encouraging was the peculiar headline used by the New Haven *Register* in announcing Giamatti's appointment after months of speculation: GIAMATTI'S ASCENSION ENDS YALE DRAMA. This gave the office a few giggles, but I wondered if it wasn't prophetic. I decided to find out as soon as possible. Calling Giamatti to congratulate him, and to express regret that I had been away when he visited, I asked him for an appointment. He replied that he was so busy with the burdens of preparing for his new job that he couldn't possibly see me until the spring.

Soon after, however, Giamatti's office called to schedule an appointment in late February. I had a couple of months to study the ground. During this time, we finally completed work on *Sganarelle* to Serban's satisfaction and were able to schedule the opening. When the New Haven Fire Department refused to collaborate, Serban had been forced to abandon his plans for staging two of the plays in the lounge. This helped to fix the content of the evening. Not the order, though—the director wanted to stay flexible. The show would consist of *The Flying Doctor, Sganarelle,* and *The Forced Marriage,* with two intermissions. Serban was still experimenting with nonsense syllables for *The Doctor in Spite of Himself,* and one day he brought in a text, invented by Elizabeth Swados and himself, which he asked the cast to memorize. It was a weird compound of primitive grunts and Slavic-sounding neologisms to which we gave the name "Neo-Siberian."

Soon after, Serban arranged a run-through for me; he was eager to get my impressions of this linguistic experiment. What I saw, though crude and unfinished, was intriguing—a wild knockdown farce featuring some Paleolithic cretins who beat each other about the ears while shouting fierce imprecations (these were later to be translated into English on placards revealed on the upper stage). It was called *Dumb Show,* an apt title in every sense of the phrase, and it bore only the slightest resemblance to *The Doctor in Spite of Himself.* But it was clearly possessed of a genuine Molièrian spirit. My first instinct was to treat this as a work-in-progress, offering it to the audience after the conclusion of the other three plays as a sample of something that would join the repertory when finished. But the actors worked so well and so hard on the piece that within a few days it not only was ready for audiences but, without doubt, was the highpoint of the evening. By the time we opened—in a blizzard!—it was an essential component of *Sganarelle,* and the most innovative play of them all.

In preparation at this time were the fifth and sixth productions of that season: Brecht's *Man Is Man,* with a rousing new score by William Bolcom, and Arthur Kopit's new play, *Wings. Wings* had originally been commissioned for National Public Radio. I had had the good fortune to hear a tape of the program at Kopit's house in Martha's Vineyard the previous summer, in company with John Madden, the gifted young Englishman who had directed it for *Earplay.* It occurred to me later that *Wings* might play very well onstage, an idea with which Kopit and Madden enthusiastically agreed. I chose *Wings* for the season because I found it an extremely moving, poetic work. I was also interested in the project because I thought the central part of Mrs. Stilson might be a lovely opportunity for Norma after years of playing thankless roles. Although Norma was about twenty-five years too young for Mrs. Stilson, she was acceptable, at first, to Kopit and Madden; soon after, however, both men developed second thoughts about the age gap. I had always experienced difficulty trying to persuade directors and playwrights to cast members of our company they thought wrong for roles; it was even more difficult in the case of my own wife. I couldn't force Norma into the production over the objections of Madden and Kopit, so to my great regret and Norma's considerable disappointment, I agreed to the casting of an older actress as Mrs. Stilson.

The playwright and the director both wanted Mildred Dunnock, who had played the role for *Earplay,* but Millie, suffering from exhaustion, wanted to take six months off from any stage activity. It was then John Madden's idea to offer the part to Constance Cummings, a splendid American actress who had spent most of her acting career in England. She was both available and interested, but she had another short professional commitment in May that she couldn't break. This gave Norma—who had agreed to understudy Mrs. Stilson —the chance to play the role for at least two performances while Constance was away.

The difficulty with *Man Is Man* was not so much in the casting as in the concept. Estelle Parsons, returning to the company after a ten-year absence, had agreed to play Widow Begbick, and our former students, Joe Grifasi, John Shea, and Michael Gross were cast in other important roles. But Ron Daniels, who was directing, seemed a little distracted during the rehearsal period. Recently, he had become artistic director of The Other Place, the experimental arm of the Royal Shakespeare Company, and his thoughts still seemed to be overseas when he arrived in New Haven for his fourth production with our company. Although *Man Is Man* was written years before Brecht had turned to Communism, Daniels elected to treat it as a revolutionary work, concluding with an entirely gratuitous melodic finale called "Fuck the War." Another revolutionary song that he interpolated for Estelle Parsons she flatly refused to sing. It seemed that Daniels was still having trouble with our actors, and these were not relieved by his newfound passion for spectacular scenic effects. *Man Is Man* had a massive setting which, as in *Puntila,* exposed every corner of our stage, and it featured a huge cannon that spit fire and brimstone into the faces of the audience. It was a generally well-received production, but the actors remained unsatisfied. Some of the performances were unfleshed; the theme was buried in epic devices; the show lacked an inner commitment. I kept waiting for the director to deliver the kind of speech we remembered so well from *Ivanov* that would fire up the company like a losing football team at half time. But he didn't even try a speedthrough. The time when our company was ready to break their thumbs for him was only a wistful memory. He sailed back to England the day after the opening, leaving the cast aground.

During rehearsals for these productions, Norma, Walt Jones, and I went off on our annual audition tour. Instead of including Chicago this year, we decided to audition applicants in Minneapolis so we could include a visit with Alvin Epstein. He seemed in wonderful spirits, preparing his first season for the Guthrie. He had scheduled a bracing year of adventurous productions for this Establishment theatre, starting with Ibsen's epic work *The Pretenders,* including a new play about incest by the Canadian playwright Tremblay, and an experimental version of Gogol's *The Marriage* by the Russian director Efros. As a sop to audiences unfamiliar with such risky scheduling, he had also included a couple of chestnuts—*A Christmas Carol* and *Boy Meets Girl*—but I wondered how the Guthrie management and subscribers would react to Alvin's season. At the time he seemed quite secure in his position. It was I who was getting pangs of insecurity, especially when I learned—with mixed feelings of pride and apprehension—that Alvin was trying to recruit large numbers of Yale people for his theatre, including some important members of our company and staff. Michael Feingold, moonlighting from *The Village Voice* as his literary manager, was no longer affiliated with the Rep, but many others were crucial to our season. I knew it was only natural for Alvin to recruit the people with whom he had worked so closely for eleven years, but if it hadn't been for the forbiddingly cold winters in Minneapolis—and possibly its distance from New York—our ranks would have been seriously depleted by his friendly depredations.

Around the same time, rumors began to circulate in the New York press that I was getting ready to leave Yale and return to theatre criticism. Liz Smith had an item in her column saying I was about to become the critic for a major New York newspaper. Investigating this unfounded rumor, the New Haven *Register* obtained denials from every paper but the New York *Post* (which refused to comment), thus leading it to conclude that I was about to replace Clive Barnes. The *Post,* in turn, ran an item in a gossip column called "Page Six" alleging that I would soon be replacing Walter Kerr as Sunday critic for *The New York Times,* and adding the encouraging news that Yale would not be sorry to lose me because my last few shows were "bombs."

We were, as a matter of fact, enjoying the most successful season in our history from every point of view. But somebody, obviously, was in a mood for mischief. A. L. Rosenthal, the editor of the *Times,* called to apologize for any problems these rumors might be causing me, and, in an action rare for that newspaper, published a strong denial. I wrote to Walter Kerr, expressing sympathy over the embarrassment to him. His reply was bemused—and quizzical. Malice afoot somewhere. Who could be responsible?

This was the winter of the Great Blizzard, which dumped almost three feet of snow on poor New England and plunged New Haven into a three-day emergency. Fortunately, it didn't cause us to cancel any performances, since we had already decided to go dark in order to clear some evening rehearsals for *Man Is Man* and *Wings.* Classes were canceled at Yale, however, and all automobiles were banned from the streets while the National Guard tried to clear away the mountainous drifts. Sitting at home one night watching the snow rise above my window, I received a call from Howard Stein. Dwight

Macdonald had just arrived in town at eight in the evening after spending the entire day on a train from New York, and now was looking around for his 11 A.M. class!

A few weeks later I was involved in another snowstorm. It was my scheduled meeting—the first of three—with President-designate Giamatti.

Giamatti received me affably in the new office he had improvised out of a room in Brewster's old house on 43 Hillhouse Avenue. This meeting was being held at my request, for I wanted to sound him out about his attitude toward the Drama School. We exchanged a few pleasantries, then proceeded to business. I asked his permission to be forthright, and requested the same frankness from him. I told him there was a perception abroad, possibly erroneous, that he was not entirely in favor of the directions the School had been taking over the past eleven and a half years. Drama School faculty members who had served with him on the board of the Yale Dramat had heard him make disparaging remarks about some of our programs and express the opinion that we should have been developing teachers for university theatre departments instead of professionals for the American theatre.

Giamatti conceded that he did think the School had lost some of its "academic justification." He regretted what he called "a loss of continuity," by which he meant a permanent and stable faculty; he also questioned Brewster's wisdom in putting an end to tenure at the School. What particularly concerned him was the turnover in the acting and directing faculty over the years, and he was disturbed by what he perceived to be our indifference to theatre history.

To my defense that we were still offering a traditional theatre-history course, which was open to all interested undergraduates, Giamatti replied he meant that Alois Nagler had never been replaced, upon his retirement, by an equally distinguished scholar. Perhaps Giamatti was unaware, I responded, that Professor Nagler had held his appointment jointly with the Graduate School, and that the Graduate School had terminated the PhD program in theatre history because of its low enrollment. We had no way to replace Professor Nagler without the help of the university. On the other hand, we *had* saved his course in the Drama School by giving it to one of Professor Nagler's former students who also served as our literary manager. I had to admit, however, that theatre history was no longer a priority concern of the School. We were more interested at present in a program of dramatic literature and dramaturgy, which had added more than a dozen new courses to the curriculum. He asked me whether those courses were being taught in a "historical" manner. I answered that our emphasis was primarily cultural and analytical. That, he said, is what he meant by "historical."

I tried to defend the School against his charge that the acting/directing program lacked "continuity" by explaining that we had been trying to evolve a whole new institution. I told him of my conviction that acting, like all professional disciplines, was taught better by practitioners than by college teachers, and professionals tended to be nomadic. Aside from this, the professionals we had been hiring for the program had often had a different aesthetic from the one we were trying to develop, and it wasn't until very recently that we had learned how to use the strengths of the Yale Repertory Theatre rather than the weaknesses of Broadway. The new acting program did have continuity now; it was provided by the structure of the three-year training and by my personal supervision.

Giamatti seemed to be satisfied by this explanation. He admitted that he had been talking about a situation that obtained five or six years ago, but added that this was the way most of his colleagues still perceived us today.

It occurred to me that the kind of worries Giamatti was having—over "continuity" and "academic justification"—reflected the fact that his university experience had been limited exclusively to the College and the Graduate School. These were not troublesome problems in the professional schools. I suggested that he consider the School of Drama as parallel with schools of law and medicine, instead of comparing it with programs in the humanities. He acknowledged the analogy, but then asked me how I would justify a professional conservatory in a university. I said it was always hard to justify anything —but how would he justify the School of Law or the School of Medicine? "They don't have deficits," he replied.

I tried another tack. Kingman Brewster, I told him, had often said that the School and the Rep were essential to Yale because they helped make life more attractive to students and faculty. Giamatti dismissed this with a brusque wave of his hand: "That's just ornamental," he said. When he spoke again of the desirability of tenure, I reminded him of the dangers of too much stability in an art form. I refrained from characterizing the tenured Drama School faculty, many of whom had been his wife's teachers. Instead, I called his attention to the Moscow Art Theatre, frozen into conventionality as a result of a tenure policy that gave actors permanent holds on their roles—one such actress, now in her sixties, was still playing the young Anya in *The Cherry Orchard.* If it came to a choice between continuity and quality, wouldn't he choose quality? Giamatti replied that a loss of continuity could result in a loss of quality.

Our conversation then turned to the financial situation, and I filled him in on the terms of our Ford grant. He seemed very interested in this, and quite eager to help the School find the matching funds. I also told him of our coming tour of Cambridge and New York and, when he expressed his approval of this kind of exposure, asked him whether Yale would help finance the trip: he advised me to speak to Hanna Gray. I then informed him that the Theatre would have a surplus for 1977–78 and that the School had not exceeded its approved deficit. He advised me to apply this money toward the tour.

In parting, Giamatti expressed a desire to have an informal meeting with our faculty "not to give a speech but perhaps to answer questions over a cup of coffee." He was eager, he added, to put to rest any fears that he might not be sympathetic to the Drama School. I invited him to attend a faculty meeting in April. His manner grew more relaxed, more expansive, at this point in our meeting. I noticed that he had been smoking a lot more than usual; although we had been talking only forty minutes, there were already five cigarette butts in the ashtray. He assured me that he loved the theatre above all other arts, which may have been the reason why he was perceived to be passionate on the wrong side of the issue. I replied that his passion was evident enough, but it seemed to be more for college theatre, and undergraduate instruction, than for a professional theatre and conservatory. He denied this, but returned to a subject that seemed to trouble him: How does such a conservatory fit into a university structure? All I could do was repeat my analogy with the Medical School and the Yale–New Haven Hospital. This time, however, he found a distinction—professors of medicine were permanent officers, he said, and they were engaged in basic research. But, I countered, wasn't the training we were doing at the School a form of laboratory work, and the experimentation at the Rep a kind of basic research? Giamatti smiled but didn't answer. Instead, he remarked that he and I were very much alike. On that puzzling note we parted.

I came away feeling that we had had a good meeting; our differences had been exposed to fresh air. It was true that most of Giamatti's questions had had an adversary ring about them, but I had been warned he had a combative nature, and this was probably the way he elicited information. Norma was of another mind entirely. "You *dummy,*" she said. "Don't you realize that this was a *terrible* meeting?" I was surprised by the strength of her reaction, and that evening, when I typed up the notes I took of the meeting, I still believed that things had gone well.

Giamatti had requested another meeting with me in April, and I looked forward to the opportunity to explain our policies further. In the meantime some of the "continuity" I had defended at the School was beginning to evaporate: Richard Gilman announced his intention to accept a much better paid position at the City University of New York, and Carmen de Lavallade asked to extend her current leave of absence in order to work up a new dance piece. Carmen agreed to do a master class in movement one day a week while on leave, but I couldn't persuade Gilman to reserve a day at the School for playwriting classes. A grant from the Educational Foundation of America had replaced the CBS grant for playwriting fellows, so we were still in a position to invite some professional tutors to the School. But we badly needed some-body to guide the students through the three-year training program. Gilman's participation at the School had not been full-time, since he never moved to New Haven, but what he lacked in supervisory attention, he more than made up for in critical perspective. His departure meant that we had to find a full-time playwriting instructor to replace him, but it gave me the chance to restructure the whole program.

One prime candidate for Gilman's position was the author of the play we had opened in early March—Arthur Kopit. I had not been an ardent admirer of Kopit's other plays, but *Wings* was a work of considerable intensity and feeling: I thought it might be his artistic breakthrough. It was also an extraor-dinary success with its audiences and with every critic except Clive Barnes, who panned the play as "a self-indulgent exercise in language with hopeful pretensions to a kind of poetry," though he characteristically reversed this judgment later. This time I couldn't interpret his remarks as a smack at me, since he flattered me shamelessly in the same review as "a pragmatic artist," capable of calling on "the most interesting talent in the English-speaking world," and as "a theatre director [who] reveals a kind of genius" (the notice wasn't entirely made of sugar—he also called me "an extremely ill-disciplined and pretentious critic" and repeated his allegation that I had banned him from my theatre as a result of an unfavorable notice). This was a puzzling turn-around, which left me more bewildered than flattered, but it infuriated Kopit, who apparently had future plans for the play which Barnes's review had momentarily dashed.

I was soon engaged in preparation for the final production of the year: Ibsen's *The Wild Duck.* My participation as director of this play was another understudy assignment, since all the directors we had approached had fallen through, but it was a chore I attacked with pleasure. The year 1978 was the sesquicentennial anniversary of Ibsen's birth. He had always been one of my favorite playwrights, and I was eager to demonstrate onstage what Ibsen had said about himself: "I have been more of a poet and less of a social philosopher than is commonly believed." There was a poem embedded in *The Wild Duck* beneath the realistic dramaturgy and declarative speeches, and I wanted to see if I could unearth it.

To realize this intention, I held a number of fascinating sessions with our resident designer, Michael Yeargan, who had recently been making some significant advances through his collaboration with Serban on *The Ghost Sonata* and *Sganarelle.* At the same time I was rereading the text I had also been reading Susan Sontag's monograph *On Photography,* and it struck me with considerable force that the central metaphor of *The Wild Duck* was the camera. The self-deluded Hjalmar Ekdal was by profession a photographer, one who touched up his photographs as he touched up reality. And Ibsen himself, following the critical failure of *Ghosts,* had angrily announced his intention to give up playwriting for photography. The kind of realism he had invented for his "modern" plays was itself a form of photography in that it imposed a documentary surface over an essentially poetic vision. The wobbly flats, the shaky doorframes, the painted view of the fjords, the prose dialogue, the very use of the "peephole" proscenium, were all Ibsen's attempts to suppress his poetic imagination for the sake of a more contemporary mode of documentation, though he was always too much of an artist not to "touch up" his own theatrical photographs as well.

We decided to take this metaphor literally and look at the play as if it were a gigantic black-and-white photograph; our perspective would be the lens of a camera. This lens would replace the curtain, opening and closing on the scenes, and catching the characters in candid still poses. The initial opening of the lens—at the beginning of the play—would be accompanied by a blinding light and an electronic musical sting: It would reveal Hjalmar taking a flashpot picture of the Werle dinner party to which he had been invited by his friend Gregers. This same photograph would then be enlarged and mounted on the wall of Ekdal's studio, changing form and symbolic meaning in each of the succeeding acts. In its first appearance it would be an enlargement of old Werle and Mrs. Sörby in evening clothes. In the next scene it would be joined by a close-up of old Werle's head. And finally, it would become a huge blowup of old Werle's eyes—so central to a play about hereditary blindness (and *seeing*), so emblematic of the way the Werle family was taking over the Ekdal household.

For the part of Gregers Werle, I succeeded in enticing Christopher Walken back to the Rep; we soon developed a warm working relationship. The way he transformed himself, from a loose-limbed, handsome young man to the ugly, morose, fanatical destroyer of the Ekdals, was a course in acting by itself; it was fascinating to watch his histrionic imagination at work. I spent a full week with the cast reading and rereading the text, both to make the translation more actable and to explore the inner meaning of the play. It was remarkable to discover how much Ibsen had hidden in his work. By the time we had the play on its feet the actors were already performing it with clarity and power. Walken's commitment was total. Any new piece of business that helped him reveal character was treated as "a piece of pure gold." He had a way of wrestling with a difficult scene through a process he called "mushing"— paraphrasing, improvising, dancing, toying with props, until he discovered exactly the right tone and attitude. One scene, which we called the "Daddy, Daddy" sequence because it involved Blanche Baker as Hedvig trying to keep her father from walking out of the house, was giving us particular trouble because it seemed so melodramatic. "Mushing" through this scene revealed its comic values, as everyone onstage joined Hedvig in a chorus of caterwauling.

Walken came to dinner a number of times during the rehearsal period, and fascinated Danny with his special charisma. There was something silken and coiled about his manner—like a cobra about to strike—much that was hidden and dangerous. He talked about the movies he wanted to make (*The Deer Hunter* had then been completed but not yet released), and he talked about the differences he noted between films and theatre. It was clear he was attracted to movie acting; it was equally clear that he would never forsake the stage. He liked the immediacy of live theatre, the sense of risk, the feeling of power over an audience. Each conversation increased my respect for him as a man and as an artist. In any other country he would have been playing all the great roles.

The Wild Duck had its problems. I had miscast a crucial role in order to satisfy a member of the company, and much of the rehearsal air was taken up trying to coach this actor into the performance I wanted. Still, from the very first reading, we knew we were on to something. Not until the tech, however, did I work out the final image of the production. It would be the wild duck itself. After Gregers, standing in the center of the lens, speaks the final words of the play, saying it is his fate always to be thirteenth at table, and Dr. Relling spits in disgust, the same blinding light that began the play would go off, leaving an afterimage of a blue duck rising from the depths of the sea—held for fifteen seconds as the image faded, the stage went black, and the camera lens closed. It was the only spot of color in the whole dramatic photograph, suggesting the transcendent release that Hedvig found in death, suggesting also the underwater quality of the play.

By the time we opened I was feeling rather pleased with myself. Rehearsals had been creative and untroubled, and we were all sharing that special une-qualed pleasure that comes from helping to create a work of art. I was con-vinced we had found a way into Ibsen's secret world that preserved the surface integrity of the play while exhuming its hidden depths. We had managed to capture the action, character, and tragicomic tone of this "crazy bag of tricks" (as Ibsen called it) while probing its unearthly, otherworldly values.

The opening was triumphant. Walken, with side whiskers and slicked-down hair, wearing a pince-nez on a false pointed nose, was riveting; Norma, as Mrs. Sörby, was radiant; Lee Richardson was bitter and sardonic as Dr. Relling; and Jeremy Geidt, as old Ekdal, gave a shambling, drunken, touching character performance. On the whole, the reviews were enthusiastic, the local New Haven paper calling *The Wild Duck* "easily the Rep's most powerful and most artistic production of the year," the Hartford *Courant* saying it "excitingly breathes new life into a classic play," and *Newsweek* affirming that "the beautifully controlled intelligence of this production makes it the best staging of a rarely seen masterpiece that we're likely to get for a long time." I cite these opinions not out of vanity but rather to contrast them with the odd reception the production received at the hands of Richard Eder of the *Times. The Wild Duck* incensed him. He attacked not only the one admittedly weak perform-ance in the production but virtually the entire cast, including (to our shock and dismay) Christopher Walken, who, he wrote, played Gregers like "a prissy madman." He was even more dismissive about my contribution, declaring that I should never have stepped in to direct the play and calling the production "all strategy and slight achievement; a kind of high-minded quackery."

High-mindedness I had been accused of before—but quackery?!! Once again, I appeared to be rubbing the fur of a *New York Times* reviewer the wrong way. The company—confident in the production—received this bad notice with equanimity. I also tried to shrug it off. After all, Eder had been very positive about our season thus far—aside from his sour notice for *The Ghost Sonata* —giving *Reunion, Terra Nova, Sganarelle, Man Is Man,* and *Wings* nothing but the highest praise. Still— I was getting the notion, possibly paranoid, that if I didn't write for the *Times* myself, I might have received somewhat better treatment at the hands of its reviewers.

One piece I did for the *Times* that year had interesting consequences—my article on the future of the national endowments for the arts and humanities. Both were receiving new leadership from the Carter administration, and I went down to Washington to see if this might lead to policy changes. I spent a few days interviewing Livingstone Biddle, about to be named chairman of the Arts Endowment, and Joseph Duffey, already appointed as chairman of the Humanities Endowment; I also met with a number of movers and shakers on the Hill. The conclusion I reached was that Carter's populist position was influencing his new appointments, and that grants would soon begin to be distributed more on a representative and geographical basis than on a basis of quality. The politicization of the arts and humanities had advanced another step. Social utilitarianism was beginning to replace excellence as the prime criterion of value.

As a result of this article, I was invited to the Yale Law School, at Joseph Duffey's request, to debate him, along with Michael Straight and Mary Norton, on a subject called "The Elitism Flap." On the morning before that debate took place, I had my second meeting with President-designate Giamatti.

The time was April 25, and the scene once again was 43 Hillhouse Avenue. The theme was whether a drama school that did not serve undergraduates was viable in the university. Giamatti remarked that both the School of Music and the School of Art had large numbers of Yale College students enrolled in their courses. Why was the School of Drama refusing to do the same?

I did my best to describe our contribution to the undergraduate theatre major, but Giamatti wasn't very interested in that. What interested him mainly was undergraduate participation at the Drama School. I told him that wherever it was possible to admit undergraduates into our courses we did so; they were only excluded from acting and directing. When he asked why, I told him that these were very intensive programs offered only to highly qualified students. Each year we chose fourteen acting candidates out of more than four hundred applicants, and four directing candidates out of more than a hundred. The classes, furthermore, represented only a small part of their activities; some of them were working as many as sixty hours a week. Professional students in training would undoubtedly perceive the presence of undergraduates in their classes as a form of "dabbling." I offered to provide special undergraduate courses in acting and directing at the Drama School, but for this we would need additional funding from the university. Giamatti observed that this was not likely.

Once again he repeated that we needed more academic courses at the School, and this time I realized he was talking about the acting program. When I asked him for an example of what he meant, he mentioned a course in the history of costume, which had been a staple of the acting curriculum when his wife was a student. I implored him to trust us. We had developed our current program over many years through a process of trial and error; we now knew what worked and what didn't. We had offered academic courses to actors in the past—I myself had tried to give them surveys in modern and classical dramatic literature—but we had finally had to recognize that actors thought about plays differently than literature majors. The script breakdown courses we had recently introduced were much more appropriate to people in training because they approached the text in a manner that actors could understand.

Giamatti raised an eyebrow. I was beginning to get a little desperate. Wasn't the success of our students in the profession sufficient proof that the program was working? To my astonishment, he replied that he wasn't aware our students were doing any better than those in the old program. I couldn't believe my ears. So many of the old graduates, including his wife, had given up the theatre profession to teach in high schools and colleges. When I started to reel off the names of our playwrights, actors, directors, and others who were now firmly established in the American theatre, he indicated that he knew about them all right; he just didn't admire them very much. "Okay," I countered. "Name somebody you admire from the old School who managed to complete the program." He mentioned Sam Waterston and Austin Pendleton. "But," I sputtered, "neither of these actors went to the Drama School. They were undergraduates from the College." "Ah," said Giamatti, "that's just what I mean. They hung around the Drama School and were allowed to take the classes." I didn't have the wit to ask him why neither of these good actors had shown any desire to apply to the old School after they graduated from Yale.

Giamatti then turned the conversation around to me. He was interested to know what I planned to do with my future. Grateful for the opportunity to explain my checkered contract history, I told him how Brewster had offered me a third five-year term in 1976, and how I had hedged on this, accepting a two-year term with three more years available to me at my option, and then another one-year term until 1979. I admitted that this showed ambivalence about the job, but lately this ambivalence had been evaporating. The Rep was at its peak; the School was in high gear; certain things still remained to be done. I was now prepared to take the last two years of the term that Brewster had offered to me, and end my time as dean on June 30, 1981.

Giamatti seemed startled. Collecting himself, he said, rather quickly, that if I wished to stay on, "there would have to be a review—and I don't think you'd care for that." I asked him why a review was necessary at this time. All of Yale's programs were being reviewed, he answered, as a result of the financial crisis. My dim wits had finally begun to grasp the fact that his questions were not being asked just for the purpose of collecting information; they reflected a fundamental opposition to our work. "It's becoming clear to me," I said, "that the present conduct of the Drama School is not impressing you particularly." Giamatti denied this, saying that it was his responsibility now to review every aspect of the university. "Do you intend to review the Rep?" I asked him. "Is the Theatre in any danger?" No, he replied, he approved of the Rep, though he assumed that what he heard was true—it wasn't costing the university anything. "Not at the moment," I replied, "but I have to raise funds for it every year."

Since Giamatti had dropped his guard for a moment, I decided to drop mine. "I'm beginning to realize," I said, "that our School is in danger. If you're serious about the thing you've been discussing, you may pull apart a delicate mechanism that has taken years to construct. I recognize that you are in a position to do anything you want with any school of the University. But rather than watch our program be dismantled, I would have to consider very seriously moving it somewhere else." Giamatti regarded me skeptically. "Move the Yale School of Drama?" he asked. "No, not the physical School. That is the property of Yale," I answered. "But the *idea* of the institution, as embodied in the Theatre I founded and the School programs I developed, that is certainly movable. And move it I will if I think its existence is threatened." Giamatti's response to this was icy. "That shows that the present institution is not essential to the university," he said. "Maybe it isn't from your point of view," I replied with a little heat. "But there are some people here who believe it *is* important to the university."

Giamatti smiled. He has a winning smile, which dimples his cheeks and wrinkles his eyes. Once again, he remarked on how alike he thought we were.

The atmosphere had lightened a bit, so I took the opportunity to explain my position a little more coolly. I had come to Yale originally, I told him, after eleven years as an English professor. I, too, had once believed in academic courses for actors. But after serving twelve years as dean of a professional school, I had to conclude that such courses as the history of costume were not very helpful to an actor's development. "But what if the student eventually wants to teach?" Giamatti asked. I replied that we were not training teachers, we were training for the profession. The Yale School of Drama was not designed for educational theatre. "You and I didn't train to be teachers," I reminded him. "We trained as scholars of English literature. Then if we were passionate enough and learned enough about our subject, we were somehow prepared to teach it." Giamatti conceded my point about English literature, but he couldn't accept the analogy with acting.

At our parting he reminded me that he was coming to visit the faculty on the afternoon of the next day; he would mention his plans for a review process at that time. He didn't wish to alarm the faculty, he told me; he simply wanted to make himself available to their questions. "They would appreciate that," I said. "There is a certain amount of nervousness in the air which, I am afraid, is shared by me." "No need to be nervous," he said with his good smile as he accompanied me to the door.

That night, Michael Straight and I debated Joseph Duffey and Mary Norton on the subject of elitism versus populism. Straight had recently been in the news with his accusation that President Carter had politicized the two endowments by appointing Biddle (who was a close associate of Claiborne Pell) and Duffey (who had worked in the Carter campaign). During his presentation, he elaborated on the consequences of politicizing the arts and humanities, and offered a brief history of elitism, defending it as "a concern for the best." Duffey responded by saying that the emphasis on "excellence" was simply a way of preserving the grip of an Establishment he saw centered exclusively in the Northeast; and Mary Norton, an instructor in women's history at Cornell, questioned whether it was even possible to measure excellence: "Excellence was really in the eye of the beholder; change the beholder and excellence changes too."

I read my own remarks from a prepared text. "The Elitism Flap," I said, "is the result of confusing politics with culture in the area of federal power; the use of the word 'elitism' in such a context signifies one of the causes of the flap—namely, the corruption of artistic and intellectual values in the name of electoral democracy. . . . Previously, both endowments generally accepted their responsibility to support and stimulate quality in the culture, regardless of its origin. Now there is considerable basis for believing that quality is no longer the first consideration at the endowments, that it is being subordinated to social and political concerns, and that the artist and scholar will soon be expected to be accountable to the consumer, as the politician is accountable to the voter, and the endowments to the politicians."

I then went on to quote from an interview with Duffey I had found in *U.S. News & World Report:* "Those who accuse the Endowments of elitism," said Duffey, describing a position with which he agreed, "are saying that humanist scholars need to realize they must listen more to the public. The people of this country are participants in the shaping of our culture and shouldn't be treated as passive recipients of wisdom dispensed by experts. Some of the talk about quality smacks of the worst kind of academic snobbism. All excellence isn't in Eastern, Ivy League universities. . . ."

This struck me as populist demagoguery and I said so. "Of course wisdom and quality and excellence are not to be found exclusively in Ivy League institutions," I said. "Nobody ever said they were. But it does not follow that you must make a *policy* of supporting inferior humanistic activities, simply because they are not in the East; you support the best *wherever* it appears. Nor is it accurate to say that the mass of Americans should be engaged in 'shaping the culture' and passing on quality because we all contribute tax dollars to the Endowments (enough, I am told, to run the Pentagon for eight hours). . . . A democratic culture is not synonymous, nor can it be, with a democratic politics. It is not only the function, it is the duty and the obligation, of the Endowments to support and identify excellence, and this means taking responsibility for judgments of quality, based on standards and not geographical distribution."

I concluded my remarks by drawing a parallel with ancient Greece, and asking my opponents to consider two Greek city-states: Athens and Sparta. The one was identified with philosophy, culture, and the arts; the other with militarism. Would a Greek Council on the Arts and Humanities distribute its grants equally between these two cities, regardless of the fact that Athens had most of the talent?

The argument I was trying to make—and Michael Straight made it better —was that "elitism," which formerly meant simply leadership, had now been freighted with so much pejorative meaning that the whole idea of qualitative judgments was being discredited. For our pains in trying to restore some meaning to the word, both of us were branded "elitists." Debate on these issues was going to be difficult when perfectly honorable terms were being transformed into expletives, and the debate was also difficult for me because I had other matters on my mind. I was on a short fuse, which didn't contrast very well with Duffey's smiling urbanity, and I didn't help things much by making disparaging remarks about what I assumed to be the low incidence of cultural activity in Montana.

The next day I met Giamatti on his way to join us at our faculty meeting.

"I hear you argued with Joe Duffey last night," he said with a half-smile. "You don't make my job any easier."

His job wasn't too easy at the faculty meeting, either, though he tried to lighten the atmosphere by expressing his strong feelings about the arts. The emphasis of the university would be on the College for the next five years, he admitted, but he couldn't imagine Yale without its four distinguished art schools. Nevertheless, all programs would be subject to review as a routine procedure of the new administration; the School of Drama, in fact, could expect to be visited soon by an external committee. "There are no secret plans to change the Drama School," he said, "but the capacity to engage a differing shape is fundamental to institutions."

Howard Stein then asked the question on everybody's mind: What were Giamatti's feelings toward the Repertory Theatre? "The symbiosis between the Rep and the School," he answered, "is not indefensible or unknown. But Yale, as a university, can no longer do everything it would like because of its financial problems, and the reviews of the various programs will be conducted with this in mind." When asked by Ming Cho Lee (head of the design program) what areas might be investigated in such a review, Giamatti replied that among the questions asked might be: How are the energies of the staff used? How does the program of the School compare with that of other institutions? How does the School function in relation to things around it?

I joined in by saying I would welcome such a review, but I hoped it would be public because the whole question of professional training in a university could be the basis for a valuable national debate. But would Mr. Giamatti care to speculate about what kind of "alternative models," as he called them, a review committee might propose? "No," he answered. Then perhaps in order to appear more forthcoming to a worried faculty, he reconsidered. "Well," he said, "a committee of this kind might conclude that the Drama School could be more responsive to undergraduate needs, or that it might pay more attention to academic subjects." Upon this, Ming Cho Lee addressed the president-designate with considerable intensity: "Mr. Giamatti," he said, "we are artists, and artists are always nervous. I have worked in many design departments in many universities, and I know that mixing professional students with under-graduates is a bad thing. It doesn't work and it affects the quality. Here we have an excellent department because the program is fully professional. It would lose quality like all the others if it began to accept amateurs." Giamatti replied that this was precisely the sort of thing that a review committee would be asked to consider. And after having charmed a segment of the faculty—and alarmed another—he bade us good-bye.

On the face of it, this meeting was an opportunity for a new president to introduce himself to the faculty of a school and respond to its questions. For me, however, having already had two encounters with Giamatti, it had a more ominous overtone. I had succeeded in drawing Giamatti out, in front of the faculty, on an important issue that was dividing us in private. And although he would never make any public admission of the criticism he directed at the

School, he was now on record in the faculty minutes about some of the changes being contemplated. By this time I no longer doubted that my position was in jeopardy and that the status of the School was shaky. Once considered "the jewel in Yale's crown," we were now "just ornamental"—costume jewelry of no particular value unless we adorned the undergraduate curriculum.

In the middle of May, Norma performed the role of Mrs. Stilson twice while Constance Cummings was away in London. *Wings* is virtually a monologue; it is written in an extremely involuted, poetic gibberish representing the speech patterns of a stroke victim; and Norma had to play it before an audience after only two rehearsals in the theatre with the stage manager. She had worked alone on the part for months, recording her lines into a cassette, which she played back continually. For all that time, our conversation, our meals, our bedtime, were preoccupied entirely with discussions of her character. She performed it the first time to cheers from the audience, with a delicate, vulnerable strength that exposed an entirely new side of a role for which Constance Cummings later won awards. And after she had been literally dragged onstage by the rest of the cast to take a bow—looking more reticent and frightened than I had ever seen her—she removed her costume and makeup, and went off to see a midnight performance of a Chekhov project by her first-year class. Exhausted, exhilarated, fulfilling simultaneously the obligations of the performer and the teacher, she had become the very embodiment of our vision for the School.

Around the same time, I was invited to give the keynote address during Connecticut Arts Week, an event sponsored by the Connecticut Commission on the Arts and attended by Governor Ella Grasso. I chose for my topic the distinction between the artist and the citizen, between the claims of the imagination and the claims of the community. Henrik Ibsen, on my mind a lot during the year of his one hundred and fiftieth birthday, was once again my model and mentor; I cited his conviction that the artist must remain aloof from the state, lest the state use him for ignoble purposes. "The State," Ibsen wrote, "still sees in science, in art, and in literature only the decorations, not the pillars and the beams, of the edifice. I think it is time this humiliating state of affairs came to an end." When I finished making these and other remarks regarding the government's insensitivity to excellence, half of the audience rose to its feet and applauded; the other half remained seated and booed. I was elated. Never before had I divided a house so evenly. I took this as an encouraging sign that—at least in this assembly—what had once been minority views were becoming more generally accepted.

Meanwhile I continued my efforts to persuade Giamatti that if the School and the Rep were not the "pillars and beams" of Yale, they were at least somewhat more than mere "decorations." I sent him a list of our numerous academic courses; I enumerated our services to undergraduates; I described in detail the contributions of our graduates to the American theatre. Each time he responded courteously, thanking me for my letters. On the night before graduation I dreamed that I had forgotten my cap and gown and failed to bring along my speech. Kingman Brewster—still president in my dream—invited me to sit beside him during the ceremony, but when I took my place on the platform I discovered I was sitting on a whoopee cushion.

My final meeting with President-designate Giamatti took place on May 24, and this time I really sat on a whoopee cushion. It was one day before the company was to go to Cambridge on the first leg of the tour. By habit, I had knocked on the door of 43 Hillhouse Avenue, only to learn that the meeting had been scheduled in Giamatti's office in Woodbridge Hall. Apparently, I was in for something official. When I arrived, Giamatti signaled me into the same easy chair where Kingman used to hypnotize me with his soothing voice, turning his wedding ring on his finger while the pendulum clock languorously ticked away the minutes. Giamatti was not hypnotic or soothing; he was, in fact, quite businesslike. "Hell, Bob," he began with no preamble, "I think you ought to know that next year will be your last as dean of the Drama School. Kingman initiated a ten-year limit on Yale deans, and I think that was sensible. I know he made an exception in your case, but I think it's better to be consistent about these matters. I'll be talking next to the dean of the Divinity School and telling him the same thing. His ten years are up next June." He paused for a moment to measure the effect on me. I think I managed to remain impassive. "Now, let's not have any tensions between us over this."

I assured him there would be none. As president of Yale, he had a perfect right to make any decisions he thought right. As a matter of fact, I told him, I felt relieved; he had lifted a great burden from my shoulders. I had been searching for years for a successor, and one of the reasons I had stayed so long was that I couldn't identify an appropriate person for both the School and the Rep. Did he have anybody in mind?

He replied that he was planning to form a search committee over the summer that would make a recommendation; he welcomed suggestions from me and any member of the faculty about its composition. Giamatti volunteered that he had been impressed at our faculty meeting by four people: two were in the technical area (he knew them also from the Yale Dramat, where they served with him on the board); one was our literary manager Jonathan Marks; and the fourth was "a sandy-haired fellow with a receding hairline" whom neither of us could identify at the time, though he later turned out to be our stage manager. He also wanted "outside" people on the committee—he mentioned Arvin Brown, director of the Long Wharf. I perceived, but did not comment on, a possible conflict of interest.

"Do you want any suggestions from me about your new dean?" I asked. "Yes, of course," he replied, "I would be interested in your suggestions, though I don't think it proper for you to be on the search committee." I agreed, but said I couldn't be very helpful until he told me what kind of School he had in mind for the future.

His reply was emphatic. "I want three things essentially. More undergraduates in the School, and especially in the acting program—not to flood the place, you understand, but I do think the School should be more responsive to undergraduate needs. I would also like to see tenure restored to a core faculty so the School can have more continuity. And finally, I would like to see more academic courses in the curriculum, particularly for actors and directors. In this way, I think the Drama School could be more of a resource for Yale and for the nation."

I acknowledged that these changes would undoubtedly make the School a resource for the College; I expressed skepticism over whether it would continue to be a resource for the nation. When he asked me why, I responded that the kind of things he had in mind for the Drama School would have the effect of "deprofessionalizing" it. Once again I affirmed that we had already tried most of the things he was contemplating, and had to conclude, after twelve difficult years, that they didn't work. Though he obviously didn't agree, we had finally evolved an effective program, but it would lose its effectiveness once it was academicized. Giamatti said he had every expectation of maintaining the high level we had achieved, but he did want to abide by Brewster's ten-year rule for deans.

"What procedures do you want to follow for announcing the news?" I asked. He replied that after appointing the search committee in the summer, he would meet with the faculty in the fall. "At that time, of course," he added, "I will have more to say about your accomplishments. I also want to take that opportunity to assure the faculty you haven't been fired." I looked at him quizzically. "How would you characterize your action, then?" I asked. He answered, "I'm just applying Yale's ten-year rule for deans."

I asked Giamatti if he would postpone his announcement regarding the search committee. It would be unpleasant for the faculty to learn of his plans through the rumor mill and demoralizing for the company to hear the news at the start of a tour. Giamatti readily agreed; he was under the impression that the tour was already over. I asked him the obvious question: "Do you intend to keep the Rep?" "Yes, indeed," he replied. "The Rep is a valuable facility for training student actors." "But will it still be run by the same person who leads the School?" I asked. "Absolutely," he replied. "I don't believe in two popes." I was interested in the nature of this one pope—would he be a professional or an academic? Giamatti answered that he had been very impressed by Dan Selzer of Princeton—an academic, but one with experience in the theatre. We both knew that Selzer had recently suffered a heart attack, and would probably be unavailable for such an arduous job (he died from the disease two years later). I urged Giamatti to consider a young man for the position; it required a great deal of physical and emotional stamina. Giamatti was more interested in learning what I intended to do. "I don't know yet," I answered. "I would have to examine my options." One of these was to keep my tenured position in the English department. Another was to take a sabbatical, following my final year as dean. He said he would grant me the sabbatical, and the meeting ended soberly.

I left Woodbridge Hall with conflicting emotions, among them a genuine feeling of liberation. The ambivalence I had experienced for so long was now resolved; my vacillation was over. Legally, I thought, I could have demanded two more years as dean, but I hadn't reminded Giamatti of my option because contractual rights are meaningless without support from the administration. Now I could extricate myself from this demanding position without guilt or remorse; I was effectively relieved of responsibility. Many good people were dependent on me, but I had great confidence in their abilities, I knew they could make their own way. I was anxious only about Arthur Pepine, imprisoned in his wheelchair; but Giamatti had promised me that Pepine would keep his job. I was at last free to contemplate all those pleasures I had always felt denied me at Yale—chief among them an extended period for writing, but also time for friends, travel, research, meditation. The more I thought about it, the more I was convinced that Giamatti had unwittingly done me a great favor.

It was therefore with a light step that I returned home to tell Norma of the news. She received it gently, lovingly, comfortingly, but also with what I perceived to be a growing melancholy. When I began to discuss with her our future options, I saw her mind wander. She had always been impatient with my "obsession" and just that morning had responded to my bitching by telling me to leave Yale. Now that leaving was real, she was revealing her true feelings. It was becoming obvious, if it wasn't obvious before, that this turn of events would be considerably more difficult for her than it was for me.

The next day, in a driving rain, we left for Cambridge to join the company. We had both determined, for morale reasons, to reveal nothing of what had transpired. We arrived at the Loeb Drama Center to find our technical and stage management crews, having worked through the night, already finished with the setup of *Sganarelle.* The performances were scheduled for Memorial Day weekend; with so many people from the Boston area on the Cape, we had been warned to expect small houses. But our pre-opening press coverage was excellent, and to our delight, we were beginning to sell a lot of seats. That night, *Sganarelle* opened to a full house and a standing ovation. At the opening-night party, we received more compliments for our work from Harvard than we got in all our years at Yale.

At bedtime Norma was very quiet, very gentle. She wasn't depressed yet, but she was possessed by a great sadness. "He did it to us at our peak," she kept repeating. *"At our peak."* The next morning the Boston press was uniformly good for the show, and Norma told me to send Elliot Norton's review to Giamatti. For what purpose? I asked her. Was she still preserving hopes? The next evening *The 1940's Radio Hour* opened—to more cheers. The company was given a magnificent party at an elegant mansion on Beacon Hill where people from the Boston cultural world assembled to toast our success. Jeremy Geidt, proud as a turkey-cock, started reflecting on the talents of the students in the company and the uniqueness of our Theatre. All of the actors asked me in turn: Why don't we move to Cambridge?

During the next day, I ambled through town, admiring the openness of the Harvard campus, marveling at the vitality and variety of Harvard Square. People walking in the *streets,* by God, not huddling behind moated walls.

Musicians, jugglers, lovers. Restaurants! I was seized by a great yearning. Wandering into the Brattle Theatre—once a place for plays, now a movie house—I idly checked its dimensions (too small!).

The reviews for *The 1940's Radio Hour* were just as enthusiastic as those for *Sganarelle,* and by the end of our short run we had played to 90 percent of capacity. To help support the tour, I had managed to wangle $5,000 from Hanna Gray of Yale, and equivalent amounts from Henry Rosovsky of Harvard and Jerome Wiesner of MIT. Financially, we were in the black; artistically, we were successful with press and audiences alike. The more enthusiastic our reception, however, the more Norma's despondency grew. "At our peak," she repeated, shaking her head. It had become a litany.

One night she had a very bad anxiety attack. She had awakened from a dream of cars crashing, ceilings falling, windshields shattering, and for the rest of the night she was unable to sleep. She crawled into my bed, holding me close for security and warmth, like a child. The future she foresaw was bleak—a future of packing boxes, isolation, uncertainty. I tried to reason with her, but she was not rational. Her father had died when she was seven, leaving the family penniless. Her mother was forced to take a job in a factory; Norma went to work first as a waitress, then as an elevator operator. Her education was broken off after one year of college, and until she was able to leave New Bedford, she and her two sisters were always moving, moving. For Norma, leaving a house dredged up irrational fears. In the past the very thought of pulling up roots was traumatic to her. Now it was assuming the magnitude of a major upheaval.

When we dressed the next morning, Norma showed me my horoscope in a women's magazine. It warned that it was impossible for the present month to bring good fortune: "The show is over. It's time to pull down the curtain." The imagery startled us both. Nevertheless, we tried our best to enjoy ourselves. The day was spent with Danny, wandering through Quincy Market and Faneuil Hall, visiting the Pompeii exhibit at the Museum of Fine Arts, playing with the gadgets at the Museum of Science. We drove through the streets of Cambridge while listening to good music on three different FM stations— admiring and envying the recreational languor of the Charles River, the beautiful colored domes of the Harvard houses, the mansard homes on Brattle Street. On one corner we saw the place where George Pierce Baker had lived while teaching his famous 47 Workshop at Harvard. Lacking support for his program from the university administration, he had gone to Yale to start the department that later became the School of Drama. Life had not been easy for him there either because of his conflict with the Yale Dramat and the English department, which was not resolved until Monty Woolley left Yale for Broadway and Hollywood. My God, I thought, Woolley has had his revenge, fifty years after the fact.

The more depressed Norma became, the more I was galvanized toward the future. I was getting excited by the prospects, and planning always made me feel better. I had assumed that upon leaving Yale I would return to teaching and criticism. Now, to my utter astonishment, I found myself thinking about founding another theatre. Both of us had gotten infatuated with the life we saw in Cambridge and Boston. Was this the Promised Land we had been told not to expect in New Haven? Driving down to New York to prepare the way for our Public Theatre residency, I began to speculate about what it would cost to run a theatre and conservatory in Cambridge along the lines of the School and the Rep. With a little cost-cutting, and by sharing expenses among a number of academic institutions, we could budget the whole operation, I guessed, for little more than a million dollars annually.

Our visit to the Public Theatre lasted four weeks—two weeks of *Sganarelle,* followed by two weeks of *Wings.* The pre-opening press in New York was somewhat less warm than it had been in Boston. The "anonymous" reporter assigned by Bill Honan to write about our Theatre turned out to be Richard Eder. Eder had praised almost every show the Rep did that season, but he used a lot of space to chew over his animosity toward *The Wild Duck* and to criticize what he called the "cliquishness" of the Yale training. Despite this equivocal welcome, the reviews for our plays in New York were even more enthusiastic than they had been in New Haven. John Simon of *New York* magazine wrote glowing notices of both *Sganarelle* and *Wings* that were quite extraordinary, considering his celebrated acerbity. And Clive Barnes, reviewing *Sganarelle,* once again anointed us with the distinction (shared, I'm afraid, with quite a few other companies) of being "one of the finest ensembles in the English-speaking theatre." I had been harsh about both these writers in articles of my own, but the knives we had been sharpening on each other were now apparently being sheathed in the atmosphere of goodwill being generated by this tour. The audiences at the Public were responsive too, although, unlike the audiences at the Loeb, they waited for the reviews before they came to the shows.

During this time, Norma was showing the strain of trying to be cheerful backstage with the company, and both of us were having difficulty sitting on the news of my dismissal. Rob Orchard and Penny Pigott were told the secret before we went to New York; I intended to tell the company and the faculty right after the run of *Sganarelle.* My timing was based on the fact that whereas *Wings* was not so dependent on the morale of Yale actors, the Molière production required a certain degree of high spirits, which might be dashed if the news leaked out too early. I worked up a statement that I planned to distribute to the faculty. It went through many drafts before I hit on the right tone.

The statement said that the president and I had agreed to terminate my contract as dean on June 30, 1979, since it is "university policy that ten years is sufficient for the term of any Yale dean, and, when I complete my present appointment at the end of next year, I will have exceeded this limit by three years." I added that there were certain "practical considerations, besides the length of my term," that made it sensible for Giamatti to choose another dean at the present time. His personal interest in drama at Yale, "influenced by his experience as a member of the board of the undergraduate dramatic society and consolidated by the nature of Yale's current financial crisis . . . have encouraged him to think of the professional Repertory Theatre and the graduate-professional School of Drama—designed by us as a resource for the national theatre movement—more as an educational resource for the Yale community, including larger numbers of undergraduate liberal arts majors than we have been prepared to accommodate. He has told me of certain changes he would like to see in the present system, which will most likely create a different set of conditions at the School and the Theatre. For this reason, and because of the unusual length of my deanship, I support Mr. Giamatti's decision to seek a new dean at the end of next year, wishing him and the new Drama School administration the best of luck and success, and pledging my full cooperation during the coming transitional year." I expressed gratitude to Kingman Brewster, and, mentioning how much I would miss my friends, my students, my fellow artists, and the work we did together, mailed the letter off on Friday, June 16, in the expectation it would be received the day after I spoke to the company. Giamatti was sent a copy.

It was as gracious a message as I could manage at the time, because the more I thought about the matter—and the effect it was having on my wife—the more I believed that something precious was being destroyed. Giamatti had the right to do anything he wanted with Yale; but the history of the Yale Repertory Theatre had been written in a lot of people's blood. We were nursing a fragile and vulnerable idea that was not likely to survive the kind of changes Giamatti was contemplating. I believed it was important to make the transition as painless as possible for my successor; I thought it was equally important to get the reasons for my dismissal on record. I didn't want to make a scene, but I didn't want the issue fudged either. It was a choice between loyalty to the institution and loyalty to the idea. Never being much of a company man, I wasn't very tempted to slink away in silence. Thus I ignored the chance Giamatti gave me to make a dignified exit on the basis of a bureaucratic ruling and, instead, revealed the nature of our disagreement in my letter. (Giamatti responded briefly a few days later, saying only "I was interested to see your statement" and thanking me for sending him a copy; soon after, he sent a letter to the faculty saying that he and I had "recently agreed" that my contract would terminate in June 1979.)

Another TCG conference was being held in Princeton that Saturday, which I attended with a heavy heart. I was not consoled by the fact that the same views that had so enraged those in the resident theatre a few years earlier were now more readily accepted. The Long Wharf had just received a Tony Award for its contributions to the Broadway theatre; in accepting it, Arvin Brown shared a platform with the producers of the "I Love New York" TV commercial. This and many other similar manifestations were creating doubt in the minds of some conference members over whether the nonprofit institutions were adhering to their original goals. Others, like Bernard Gersten of the New York Public Theatre, were more concerned with devising some strategy whereby the nonprofit theatres could have a bigger portion of the commercial pie, perhaps by producing on Broadway themselves. The central problem was still the inadequacy of support for the arts from funding agencies, and Livingstone Biddle gave us no confidence, in his address to the conference, that the National Endowment for the Arts would do much to improve things. As for me, I expressed my own sense of disillusionment—I didn't mention the reason —with the university as a haven for the performing arts.

Returning to New York on Sunday for the final performance of *Sganarelle,* I gathered the company together in the greenroom of Joe Papp's Newman Theatre and told them of Giamatti's decision. Jeremy Geidt wept; Gene Troobnick hugged me; the students thanked me for having been present at "the golden years." We talked about the past for a while, and then disbanded. I took Norma out for a soda, both of us relieved to have dropped this burden from our chests. We then went off for our first good night's sleep in weeks.

The following week I was invited to a "culture lunch" at *The New York Times*—a weekly event attended by editors and reviewers. I had been asked to talk about the state of American theatre to a group that included Richard Eder, but as soon as I arrived, there were inquiries about a rumor in the air, that Yale was getting ready to drop the Rep. It was a direct question that I probably could have dodged. Instead, I denied the rumor, but admitted that next year would be my last as dean. The whole table reacted in a manner that astonished me. Seymour Peck went into the composing room to look for a reporter, and Arthur Gelb began clearing the space for a major story.

I tried to cooperate with the reporter without causing trouble at Yale—a difficult feat, considering my tendency to generalize. I kept my remarks as factual and neutral as possible, letting slip only one sentence that might be interpreted as tendentious or self-serving: "If these policies are put into effect, it could constitute a serious loss to the American theatre. But I think as president of Yale, Mr. Giamatti is understandably more interested in Yale University than in the American theatre." The next morning, an item on the front page of the *Times* called attention to a story in the theatre section with the headline YALE DRAMA SCHOOL DROPPING BRUSTEIN. (By contrast, my appointment to Yale in 1966 had brought a two-line mention on the television page.) The article provided relatively accurate details, along with a flattering account of the accomplishments of the School under my auspices. To me the most interesting thing about the report was Giamatti's response—or lack of it. According to the paper, he was in Cleveland at the time and thus "unavailable for comment." Through a spokesman, however, he affirmed that the termination of my contract was "an appointment matter, not a policy matter." This kept the whole issue purely procedural, though I thought it fairly obvious that my contractual option to serve two more years in the deanship rendered this explanation "inoperative."

Was Giamatti going to deny that he had spoken to me of changes in policy? Apparently so. In a follow-up story citing the apprehensions of several distinguished graduates over the future of the School, Giamatti was quoted as "reiterating through a spokesman that informing Brustein his contract would not be renewed did not necessarily portend a change in policy for the Drama School. The spokesman added that any new policy would come only as a result of study over the coming year." I was getting aroused. I had no wish to join in public dispute with the president of Yale, but aside from the doubts being cast on my own veracity, there were going to be consequences affecting the School. If Giamatti had strong ideas about theatre training in a university, then he ought to stand by them—a debate on these issues might even be healthy. Now he was insinuating that if any changes were contemplated, they were not in his hands, and that my own version of our conversations was inaccurate.

This strategy became more obvious in the succeeding weeks after other organs of the press got interested in the matter. I had already told my story to the *Times;* my response to reporters from other media was simply to send them a copy of my statement to the faculty. I was genuinely surprised about the scene I had made, and I didn't see much profit in causing more fuss. A reporter for *The Village Voice,* however, after vainly trying to get me to elaborate on the published reports, told me that Giamatti's office was calling my story a "fabrication." This triggered my deadly sin. A lot of people had complained about my personality before, but this was the first time anybody questioned my honesty.

Consequently, when Jack Kroll asked to interview me for *Newsweek,* I agreed, expecting he would write a fair and balanced piece. I was not disappointed. Giamatti's position remained unchanged—my dismissal was simply a routine termination of a deanship after its normal life span. Still speaking through a spokesman, however, he now began to deny my charges openly, saying that " 'deprofessionalization' was not a word I ever used or a concept I have ever entertained. Obviously not. Nor do I see any grand shift in policy." Despite his disclaimers, this statement gave me some hope that by publicizing our differences I had perhaps embarrassed Giamatti into suspending—or at least postponing—his plans for changing the School. But Kroll was not convinced. He assumed that the situation at Yale reflected a shift in the nature of American theatre at large, beginning with the attack on "elitism" at the National Endowment for the Arts. In support of this view, he quoted the apprehensions of Alan Schneider, then head of the theatre center at Juilliard, whose dismissal the next year would further confirm it.

Kroll concluded his story by describing the move of George Pierce Baker from Harvard to Yale, adding, "Perhaps it's time for a transplant of this flourishing organism to another body—maybe even back to theatre-starved Boston." In this prophetic article, and in other pieces written around the same time, we were finally beginning to receive the kind of recognition I had always desired for the place—not exactly for the reasons I would have chosen. Letters were pouring in daily from friends, well-wishers, and former students, all expressing outrage and chagrin over Giamatti's action. At the university itself the reaction was mixed. Some support was forthcoming from outside the Drama School, mostly from loyal friends, and one or two of my fellow deans were willing to shake my hand in public. But for the most part the university community found the controversy very bad for Yale, and I was shunned. I was beginning to feel a little like Dr. Stockmann in Ibsen's *An Enemy of the People;* one day I even found myself wearing a pair of torn trousers.

Normally my wife would have ridiculed this tendency to self-dramatization. But Norma was having troubles of her own. Her depression had deepened, and she remained full of anxieties. She began to see our fate as a kind of retribution for all the times we had been short with people, or failed to extend ourselves socially. She had also begun to lose her faith in life. If this was the result of self-sacrifice and hard work, then what was the use of suffering? If this was the reward for achievement, then where was the sense in striving? I tried to excite her about the future, which seemed to me full of possibility, but some delicate string in her nature had broken, beyond my power to repair. That June she visited a psychiatrist in New Haven who prescribed a regimen of antidepressant drugs.

It was a bad month for Danny, too. On a trip to a skateboard park with one of his school chums, he was attacked on the corner of Church and Chapel, right smack in the center of town, by some kids who ripped off his skateboard and wallet and pushed him into the incoming traffic, where he was almost hit by a bus. Later that week he was chased down the street by a few toughs and had to take refuge in a store. A month later, some other kids held him up at gunpoint in the Mall. Danny was full of impotent rage. I knew these incidents were only a part of it.

We had all been mugged in New Haven. Any thought of remaining at Yale had long since vanished. Norma had built up my will during the early years at the Drama School. I was now determined to demonstrate to this languishing, damaged woman what the will could actually accomplish. I wanted to show Danny, too, lest he grow into manhood maimed and sullen, believing life was ruled by accident and caprice. It was not yet time to retire into a contemplative middle age. If the idea was worth developing, then it was worth preserving. That summer, I made up my mind that I would have to find a way to move it to Harvard.

XII

Exits
1978-1979

Touch her soft mouth, and march.

—Henry V

The publicity for the 1978–79 subscription drive—a campaign begun the previous spring—identified the coming season as "The Lucky Thirteenth." Posters proclaiming our happy state festooned the Theatre with unintended irony. People were telling me it would be wretched spending the year as a lame duck, so I was prepared for difficulties. But I also looked forward to a period relieved of worries about the future of the Theatre and the School. Norma and I could relax a bit and enjoy a little pleasure. For this purpose—and perhaps to protect us against any unforeseen personal difficulties—I scheduled a number of vacations throughout the year in pleasant places: Grenada, the Bahamas, Vail. At least we would go out healthy and tanned.

Norma wanted to leave Yale as soon as possible, and when a distinguished chair in the English department of NYU was offered that summer, starting either in 1978 or 1979, she pleaded with me to take it immediately, instead of considering it for the following academic year. For one thing, she was eager to resume her old life in New York, but I think she was also convinced that New Haven would be even more unpleasant now that we were preparing to leave it. In her heart she knew that we couldn't abandon the students, the faculty, or the company—or disrupt Danny, who was finishing his last year at Foote School. She also knew how necessary it was to prepare for the transition. But she was fighting a powerful impulse toward flight. It was lucky that our Vineyard summer began so soon after my dismissal from Yale.

Norma spent the first few weeks of that summer in the hammock, reading. Some time passed before I could get her to socialize. Her health had begun to fail; she was always coughing and wheezing and fighting for breath. The doctors diagnosed bronchitis and urged her to stop smoking. But Norma could no more give up her Trues than her evening martini. If she awoke in the middle of the night and discovered she was out of cigarettes, she would panic, and try to wheedle me into finding some all-night roadhouse with a cigarette machine. Against such a catastrophe, she used to secrete a number of emergency packs in the house, like a squirrel storing nuts, and then forget where she had put them. As for her depression, it stabilized when she took her pills, but she hated to be dependent on medication for her moods. When she went off the pills or misplaced them for a day, her depression invariably returned. Norma's condition was creating a dilemma. The pills were dangerous, especially if certain dietary restrictions weren't observed (Norma was careless about these), but the depression was dangerous too.

Friends were a huge consolation to both of us at this time. Letters of support continued to pour in, and although these were beginning to read a little like obituaries, we took strength from the testimonies of many old students, including some of the revolutionaries from the sixties, concerning the value of their Drama School experience. Our Vineyard pals were also very tender during that summer. Most of them, being writers, advised me to return to criticism; John Marquand urged me to become a matinee idol ("like Freddy March"). Art Buchwald counseled me, whatever I did, to avoid any further "fuss" in the press. That was my instinct as well. The issues were clear; I had spoken my piece; there was no more to add. When some Washington *Post* reporter (visiting Katharine Graham) told me over dinner my flap with Giamatti was the greatest "cause célèbre" of the year and asked to hear more, I smiled my Giaconda smile and kept my mouth shut. If Giamatti had created any doubts about my veracity, I would have to trust that time would dispel them.

I was happy when Norma began to entertain again. Her dinners were always joyous, funny, relaxed affairs, the tables loaded with good food, the room light with good cheer. At a party she threw for the Wallaces when Mike had to leave the Vineyard and return to work, Buchwald introduced a new game. Everyone was asked to put a penny down and then say "I have never . . ."—naming something he or she had never done that was assumed to be habitual for the others. Art won a few cents right off the bat when he said, "I have never smoked pot." Styron won even more when he swore, "I have never been to a shrink." I won some money from the women, saying, "I have never been kissed by Bill Styron." But Norma won the whole pot when she said, "I have never cheated on my current life partner." All the guests rose up in mock disgust, threw their pennies in her lap, and made for the door.

Those parties gave her pleasure, and before too long, her carefree mood returned, if only for brief periods. Norma continued to feel as upset by uncertainty as I was exhilarated by it. I bet her that by the end of the summer I would receive twenty job offers or feelers (I lost the bet—I got only eighteen), and tried to describe to her the excitements of unemployment. Why, anything was possible. Pope Paul had just died; another job was open. I felt the same sense of liberation I had experienced when we took our leave in England—

relieved of worries, cleansed of responsibilities. Why couldn't Norma share those feelings with me?

We were soon to learn we weren't entirely free. Problems still were nagging. *Wings,* for example, following its success at the Public Theatre, had attracted a Broadway producer, and Kopit now wanted to use not only the Yale physical production and sound effects but all the Yale actors as well. Since the cast included four matriculating students, this request put me in a painful dilemma. Our exclusive hold on the play gave us the legal right to prevent other productions until August 31, when the students would be returning to School. But Kopit wanted me to suspend those rights so he could open the play in July, offering to replace the students with professionals when their term began.

On the face of it, this was a reasonable enough request, but we had brought *Wings* to the Public Theatre as an example of our work, not to try it out for Broadway. And the students had performed in it as members of our company. I knew there was a danger in coming to New York. Still, I hoped the briefness of our visit and our rights over the play might protect us from the depredations of the producers, agents, and starmakers. Most of these students had already signed up with summer theatres. To offer them a role in a Broadway production was to tempt them into breaking contracts, with us participating in an unethical act. It was not that I wanted to prevent Kopit from enjoying the fruits of his labors, but there were plenty of good actors looking for work. Why insist on casting people with other obligations?

There was also the question of my personal pride. For twelve years we had managed to avoid the use of our Theatre as a Broadway tryout house, and I had hardly been reticent about my opposition to the practice by other resident companies. A Broadway transfer of our production of *Wings* would be a direct contradiction of my public position. It would make me look like a hypocrite, regardless of my attitude toward it. This was my final year at Yale. I had no wish to compromise the last moments of my administration.

On the other hand, I didn't want to make a decision purely on the basis of my pride. Other people were involved who might suffer pain or disappointment. Kopit had already informed the students in the play that they now had a chance at a Broadway credit—this made it inevitable they would think I was blocking an important career opportunity out of a ridiculous principle clear only to me. What to do?

I tried to reason with Kopit. I asked him to postpone his Broadway production till fall, when the students would be back in School. He was eager, however, to take advantage of the recent critical acclaim and open the show immediately. When I resisted, he offered to compromise. He really wanted only one student anyway, the second-year actress playing Mrs. Stilson's therapist; he would recast the other parts if he could have her. I found his compromise even less appealing than his first request, but he argued that Constance Cummings had become so dependent on this young actress that she couldn't play the part without her. Constance called from London the next day to confirm this, and I felt the pressures growing. Kopit was even beginning to question whether our rights over the play would hold up in a court of law.

I consulted with Norma on the question. I even consulted with Danny, who had not yet turned fifteen. He told me, "If people don't hold to their ideals, nobody will ever have them." His reinforcement of my position made me beam. Then he added, "But if the ideals are stupid, don't keep them." My smile faded. His wisdom was preternatural. But the hard thing to determine was whether my ideals *were* stupid.

I called the two students who had already signed summer contracts. I wanted to discuss the matter with them, and try to explain my position. The one relieved my mind by telling me he had no intention of going back on his first offer. The other accepted my decision, but sadly. She needed the money to get through the School year. I promised to get her the equivalent in scholarship funds, but knew this was only part of the problem. I was blocking something that meant a great deal to others, because it didn't mean much to me.

So I told Kopit that if he insisted on going ahead with his production in July, we would exercise no legal constraint. The Broadway *Wings* could take place, but without the cooperation of the Yale Repertory Theatre. In fact, we would drop our (small) financial interest in the show. But I would regard it as a pirated production that was proceeding over our protest. I hoped that Kopit would respond to these moral pressures and postpone his gratifications until the School year began. Kopit asked for time to think about it. He said he would probably hire the student he wanted anyway, and do the show immediately. He also offered to resign his appointment as playwriting instructor, a possibility I considered—and rejected.

Whatever Kopit decided, I thought, at least a little bit of the Theatre's honor was saved without imposing hardships on the students. But then, I thought, the hell with it. The whole issue was getting so entangled and ensnared in theoretical principles that I was ignoring Danny's warning about stupid ideals. I decided to withdraw my opposition to the production altogether—on the proviso that Kopit offer roles to *all* the students, and not just the woman he wanted. He was greatly relieved; so were John Madden and Constance Cummings; and so, I guess, were a few of the students.

As for me, I felt like a cork bobbing on a fickle current, incapable of maintaining a consistent position, too stubborn and yet too flaccid, hobbled and crippled by events beyond my control. Finally, the honor of the Theatre *was* saved, through no effort of my own. The producers couldn't get a theatre in the summer, so the production was postponed until fall. It opened with only one student in the cast (he had already graduated) to rave reviews by practically everyone, including the previously dissenting Clive Barnes; and it enjoyed a brief run before a small audience, those willing to pay top box-office prices without complaining, as others did, about "spending good money to see a play about a stroke."

I was still absorbed with the problems of Yale, but this didn't prevent me from examining future options. Offers continued to come in at the rate of two or three a week, and early in the summer I had my interview with NYU. Having obtained Norma's reluctant agreement, I told the president and chairman I couldn't possibly start any new position until the fall of 1979 and I would appreciate the time to consider my decision until September 30. Around the same time, Herman Krawitz called to ask if I was interested in starting a company at the Vivian Beaumont. I told him I was considering any and all offers, and Norma I began to discuss the possibility of combining teaching English at NYU with running a resident theatre at Lincoln Center.

This would put us in New York, where Norma wanted to be. I still had my eye on Boston. Boston, apparently, was also looking at me because, in mid-July, Mayor Kevin White's office called to set up a meeting regarding the future of Boston theatre. I attended this meeting accompanied by Elliot Norton, dean of Boston's theatre critics, who had befriended us during our Cambridge tour. He was very eager to see a resident company in his beloved Wilbur Theatre, now threatened with demolition. Kevin White received us with a pleasant lunch in the gracious Parkman House on the edge of Boston Common. He had read about me in *Newsweek,* and suspected I might be the person to administer the Boston theatre district for the city. He had interesting plans to improve the area architecturally, along the lines of what he had already done with Faneuil Hall and Quincy Market. What he wanted to hear from me was some idea of how the various conflicting cultural activities in the area could be unified and supervised.

I was flattered by his interest in me, but from the start I knew that I wasn't suited for the position. What he needed was a Joe Papp—somebody with entrepreneurial talents and strong civic interests who was devoted to myriad projects in various areas. I was more interested in finding a Boston theatre to which I could move the company. The Wilbur wasn't right, being a small-proscenium house with no facilities for changeovers, but perhaps there was another theatre in the neighborhood that might suit our needs. Mayor White preferred to table my needs for the moment. What concerned him during this meeting was a large scheme for improving a blighted area of Boston, and he seemed to have the will and means to do it. I was impressed by the man. It was not often one met a politician with such a genuine interest in the arts—not just because they were tourist attractions, but because they were important to the very life of the city.

Norton drove me around the theatre district following this meeting, pointing out various landmarks while discoursing on the history of each of the play-houses. He knew more about Boston theatres than any man living because he loved them more than any man living; his devotion to the stage was rare and refreshing in a theatre critic. During the course of our ride, he showed me the Boston University theatre, the only one in Boston built expressly for a repertory company. I told him of my interest in Harvard, but Norton seriously doubted whether Harvard would ever accept a professional theatre or a conservatory. Why, the university didn't have an undergraduate drama program; it didn't, for that matter, even offer credit courses in theatre. He reminded me that it was precisely this kind of indifference to the performing arts at Harvard that had been responsible for George Pierce Baker's defection to Yale.

Despite Norton's discouraging comments, when I returned to the Vineyard I composed a letter to Henry Rosovsky—dean of the Faculty of Arts and Sciences at Harvard—requesting an appointment. He had been very forthcoming when asked to help support the Rep's trip to Cambridge, and, although I had yet to meet him, seemed like the appropriate person to talk to about what my letter described as "an interesting proposal." When we held our meeting, in mid-August, I submitted to him a written plan for starting a professional theatre and training institute at the Loeb. What I offered was to move to Cambridge—in September of 1980—the core structure of what had hitherto been known as the Yale Repertory Theatre, along with a School of Theatre staffed by members of the company. This institution could function under the auspices of Harvard, or if Harvard was unwilling to accept the sole responsibility, it could be a joint undertaking of Harvard and other universities in the area, acting as a semiautonomous conservatory.

In the body of my proposal, I acknowledged "a potential obstacle to the successful fulfillment of this plan." Harvard undergraduates, having always enjoyed full access to the Loeb, might resent what they perceived to be a reduced role in their own facility. But I was convinced, I wrote, that once the plan were explained in sufficient detail, they would begin to recognize the considerable benefits of having such a resource in their midst—access to theatre courses, professional services, expert supervision, discounted tickets to the plays. It was my claim that the plan would cost Harvard no more than it was currently giving to the Loeb for student activities, energy, maintenance, and staffing (I had no idea what that figure was, but I hoped it was over $500,000). The rest we expected to raise through vigorous fund-raising and a potentially larger audience.

I concluded this brash statement by confessing my strong desire to come to Harvard. "At 51," I wrote, "I still possess the energy and the will to create another institution of a kind that has already proved its effectiveness over a long period of time. Because I believe passionately in the importance of such an institution, I am prepared not only to organize it and administer it again, but to advocate it and help raise its funds, as I have in the past at Yale. . . . I believe I have the talent; I have the experience; and I have the support and encouragement of many well-wishers, including the national and Boston press. I would be extremely honored to become a member of the Harvard faculty. I have always been convinced that Cambridge in general, and Harvard in particular, are the ideal locations in America for the kind of serious intellectual-professional activity I have been describing. I have devoted the last twelve years of my life to realizing this kind of institution, and my previous years to preparing for it. I have no doubt whatever that by combining our resources and yours, we could together, and quickly, build a School and a Theatre that are unique and unparalleled not only in the country but throughout the entire theatrical world. And no one with an aesthetic sense could resist the symmetry of the idea—returning it all to the university from which it first came."

It was no time to be modest, it was no time to be coy. Since my cards were all on the table, I wasn't in a position to bargain. I was the suppliant, and all I had to offer was the attractiveness of the proposal. When we met soon after, Dean Rosovsky surprised me by the warmth of his interest. He had, he told me, followed my writings, and was particularly grateful to me for speaking out during the difficult days of the student disruptions. He knew the Loeb needed a new direction, but he had to say he foresaw many obstacles to my plan. One of them was money; he was not persuaded it would not be costly to Harvard, especially since the subvention to the Loeb was closer to $200,000 than $500,000. Anyway, he concluded, it was not he but the president of the university who should have been consulted on the matter, and he offered to make an appointment for me to present my proposal to Derek Bok.

It was evident from this meeting, cordial though it was, that I had omitted a very important component from my plan, one I should have anticipated after my experience at Yale: the direct benefit to undergraduates. My proposal was for a professional institute, but the Loeb was under the jurisdiction of the Faculty of Arts and Sciences, which was primarily dedicated to undergraduate programs in the liberal arts. I wanted to preserve the professional nature of the conservatory; yet it was important to provide for undergraduate instruction as well. How could I do this without compromising the School or resurrecting the issue that had divided me and Giamatti?

Our managing director, Rob Orchard, provided an answer. He suggested a two-year "institute" program—the first year devoted to college seniors majoring in liberal arts at various Boston universities, the second year involving the same students after they had graduated. The institute could administer their undergraduate theatre major in the first year, with their home universities awarding them degrees, and the institute could take them over wholly in the second year, offering a certificate or MA at the completion of the course of study. I liked this plan because it enabled us to choose students from among the most talented undergraduates in the area, including those from Harvard, while preserving the independent and professional status of the conservatory.

It was this idea that I worked up in a supplement to my first proposal and presented to President Bok during our meeting on August 25. Bok is an extremely courteous man and so is Rosovsky, but they form a fascinating contrast. The dean is outgoing, expansive, emphatic; the president is reserved, deliberate, understated. While the relationship between the two men is warm and mutually respectful, their backgrounds are totally divergent. It is amusing to hear Rosovsky studding his speech with Middle European anecdotes and Yiddish phrases, which Bok has difficulty understanding ("Don't be so ethnic, Henry"). That Rosovsky could have achieved so high a place in Bok's administration I took as testimony to the president's openness and judgment, and it gave me heart.

But Bok's opening remarks, though friendly enough, were discouraging. Personally, he told me, he had a high regard for the arts—his grandmother had founded the Curtis Institute in Philadelphia. But he doubted whether Harvard was the proper place for professional arts training. He recognized the excellence of our theatre, but he had an obligation to undergraduate interests; he was eager to find some way of improving their extracurricular productions by providing them with a better grasp of the literature of the theatre. He respected my commitment to training, but did not believe that Harvard was now in a position to get "into" theatre.

I replied that Harvard was already "into" theatre, whether it knew it or not, by having originally accepted a gift in 1959 from the New York financier John Loeb to put up a building. The Loeb was a first-class facility, sitting prominently on Brattle Street, therefore vulnerable to judgment and criticism. Did he know that Harvard was generally perceived to be lagging behind other universities in only one area—the arts? With one bold stroke the university could not only overcome its retrograde reputation in this regard but become a leader in the field as well. For a split second, I thought I saw something light up in his eyes. He asked me to continue. I spoke of a professional theatre as a university resource comparable to a library. Just as no one would dream of teaching Dostoyevsky or Hegel without access to their books in Widener, so no one could properly teach Sophocles or Shakespeare without access to their plays on the stage. A classical repertory company was a living library, delivering dramatic literature in the way it was meant to be experienced, as a theatrical rather than a literary expression. I said that, contrary to the common opinion, I had a genuine interest in theatre courses for undergraduates, if only to develop better-informed audiences for the theatre; I informed him of my part in helping to build the undergraduate theatre program at Yale. But there were also great reserves of talent at Harvard that deserved to be encouraged. I named a few of the gifted Harvard graduates who had gone through our program at Yale.

President Bok then expressed his concern about finances. It was Rosovsky's impression that my plan was going to cost Harvard a lot of money, and the university was about to embark on a major capital campaign in anticipation of future deficits. I remarked again that the Theatre would pay for itself, especially if it managed to attract financial support from participating institutions. Bok then asked me why we needed any partners. It was the first hint of something I had not dared to hope for—that Harvard might be prepared to take this on alone. But again he grew guarded: he was aware of how Brewster had justified the existence of arts schools at Yale, but unlike New Haven, Boston was already a fine cultural resource for students and faculty. Not in the theatre, I reminded him, and Bok was forced to agree.

It occurred to me that certain members of the Harvard faculty might feel threatened by this proposal. I was eager to put these fears to rest. The university already had some expert people in the field of dramatic literature, including the present director of the Loeb Drama Center, Robert Chapman, who, for almost two decades, had been supervising undergraduate theatre activities, inviting visiting troupes such as our own, and teaching courses in theatrical texts. It was my desire not to displace anybody but to supplement, wherever possible, the existing resources. When I had first come to Yale, I told him, I was younger, brasher. Impatient to move quickly, I had broken some eggs in the process of implementing my programs. I was older now and, I hoped, less rude. But in one thing I still felt rushed—the timing of Harvard's decision. I had other offers pending, particularly the one from NYU, which had asked for an answer by the end of September. Bok replied that he expected to have something to tell me by that time, but September would be too soon to know everything. The term was not yet in session; he would have only two weeks to consult with faculty and students. He suggested that we proceed in stages, answering two questions: (1) Is the plan feasible? (2) Is the plan fundable? He promised an answer to the first question by the end of September.

In leaving, I thanked him for his courtesy and remarked that he now seemed more open to the idea than at the beginning of our conversation. He replied that he had been resistant at first because he wanted to know all the problems. But, he added encouragingly, proposals like this one were the way Harvard moved forward.

When I spoke to Rosovsky again, he told me the chances were fifty–fifty—considerably better odds than I had any right to expect at this stage. This cheered Norma immensely, and so did some feelers from Boston University that were now being made through the good offices of William Phillips, who had just moved up there with *Partisan Review.* Hope was returning to her heart; I was also glad to see the return of her old anger. Instead of feeling victimized by Giamatti's decision, she was beginning to feel enraged by it. The blood was coursing through her veins again. She pored over news stories about Yale's president, looking for fuel to feed her rage. It wasn't hard to find. In a speech to Yale alumni in Boston that summer, Giamatti told the assembled bankers and brokers that private universities had much in common with private enterprise. After all, each was devoted to freedom—the one in the classroom, the other in the marketplace. The equivalence he made between free enterprise and free expression was no doubt a strategy to attract back the support of Yale alumni alienated by Brewster's "radical" administration. But it also marked a significant change in the political atmosphere of the university. A few months later Giamatti would announce that academic institutions were "tributaries" of society, designed to service its needs and demands—the utilitarian definition of the university I had tried to dispute in Venice. No wonder William Buckley, conservative columnist and author of *God and Man at Yale,* remarked, soon after Giamatti's inauguration, that he was the Yale president with whom Buckley felt the closest ideological affinity. It was no secret, either, that Giamatti had voted for Richard Nixon in the presidential elections—both times.

Norma had other reasons, late that summer, to externalize her feelings about the new president in strong salty terms. First we heard that Giamatti, when questioned about the Drama School by Yale alumni, was telling them I had lied to the press about the fact that he had discussed policy changes with me.

And then we learned the makeup of the president's Drama School search committee.

We had expected this committee to be a reflection of the new president's personal preferences; what we hadn't expected was such a blatant rejection of the past twelve years. Appointed to the search committee were three faculty members from the School, all from the technical and stage management area; two of these, including the chairman of the committee, were old Drama School alumni who also sat with Giamatti on the board of the Yale Dramat. Other committee members included Arvin Brown of the Long Wharf; Maynard Mack of the English department; Edith Oliver, off-Broadway critic of *The New Yorker* (perhaps the only theatre reviewer in New York who had never seen the Rep at Yale); Bart Teusch, head of the undergraduate theatre program; Carrie Nye, an actress who had gone to the old School and was now married to Giamatti's former roommate, Dick Cavett; George White of the O'Neill Theatre Center, another graduate of the old School and college friend of the president; Peter Zeisler of TCG; and Peggy Clark, president of the Executive Committee of Drama School alumni.

It was not just that so many of these committee members were hostile to what had happened at the Drama School under my administration (Peggy Clark, for example, had persistently attacked our policies from a position she once described as "to the right of Goldwater"). But conspicuously absent from the ranks of the search committee were any representatives of playwriting or design or directing or acting or, for that matter, anyone who might be characterized as an artist or intellectual of the theatre. Also absent was anybody who had graduated from the School during the twelve years of my administration, or anybody presently matriculating. Some of my staff—particularly those who wanted to believe Giamatti's assurances about continuing present policies— were in a state bordering on shock.

It was not impossible that a committee such as this one would be able to identify an attractive candidate for dean. It was simply very unlikely that it would be in a position to understand the aesthetic of the Rep or the purpose of the School. Norma and I were no doubt oversensitive in regarding the choice of this committee as a personal insult, but unquestionably it was, whether deliberate or not, an insult to the institution. I had never doubted that the School would survive the comings and goings of deans. What was threatened was the Idea of the place and its relationship to future generations of students. If this search committee reflected Giamatti's plans, I could have little hope that the Idea would outlast my own departure.

In my welcoming speech that year I spoke to the students about the precarious condition of this Idea, and also about the uncertainty we all were sharing. "Every year," I told them, "it is my custom to welcome the incoming students and to greet the returning students—but this year, for the first time in thirteen years, I don't know what to say. You are all aware, I believe, that my deanship will be coming to an end in June of next year, and that a search committee has recently been formed to choose a new dean. I have every reason to believe that my successor will be someone of distinction, and I continue to hope that this distinction will have been earned in the profession of theatre."

It was natural, I warned the students, that they should be nervous until the new dean was named, and my own uncertainty was making me rather speechless on the subject of the future. I was able, however, to talk with some confidence about the past and how the students could contribute to perpetuating what had already been accomplished. "The Idea has been to serve the American theatre, as the Medical School serves the medical profession, and the Law School the judicial system. But we have had another Idea besides service, which is to advance and strengthen the American theatre as well." This effort at reform was to have been achieved through the energy and idealism of young people, with the Rep and the School providing standards and models. It was not an easy task in a university "which insists on continuity in order to protect the past," especially since a theatre "insists on change in order to guarantee the future." But our efforts had been supported for almost thirteen years, and that was "a pretty good run for any show."

It was only fitting, I added, in an institution built on the principle of change, "that I should respond to the need for change and accept the end of my own participation at Yale without remorse. This will be a relatively simple task as soon as I am convinced that this healthy but fragile organism is assured of a continuing existence. One of the most valuable achievements of anyone's life is the creation of a good Idea, and I think this has been a damned good Idea, which countless people have helped to create. Plato has told us that an Idea —being of the mind and spirit—can outlive any institution, because an institution is physical and therefore fleeting. If the Idea of theatre we have developed at Yale is any good, then it is assured of life despite its current institutional status, and all of you will find ways to preserve it. For this obligatory task, I ask for your patience on behalf of the School, your hard work on behalf of yourselves, and your vigilance on behalf of the Idea. We can begin by making this year one of the most productive periods we have ever experienced."

I was trying to be positive in an essentially unstable situation. I was also making an effort at salvage. Giamatti had changed the administration of the School in the same way he would have rotated the chairman of an academic department—without realizing there was a theatre attached that was not simply administered but also led and informed by a strong point of view. I had been appointed dean of an already existing school, but I had founded, funded, and developed the Theatre. I realized you couldn't patent an artistic institution as you would a formula or an invention, and I was reconciled to having it taken from my hands. But not having even been consulted on the choice of who would shape its policies in future, I was looking for other ways to preserve the animating spirit behind it. If we couldn't move it elsewhere, I wanted to keep the hope somehow that the Idea would not be destroyed at Yale.

As it turned out, I really didn't have to tell this to the students—the more creative ones already understood it. A group of them organized a letter to the *Yale Daily News,* which was framed and signed by a talented playwriting student named Mark Leib, urging the university to preserve the Idea: "If in the next few years," it read, "the Yale School of Drama becomes merely the best Drama School in the nation, I fear that we will one day find ourselves struggling to trace, for future graduates, the lineaments of a dead dream. If, on the other hand, the Drama School retains the uncompromising vigor and courageous arrogance which now render all comparisons superfluous, we may yet see the flowering of the American theatre." Even the traditionally adversary *Yale Daily News* issued an editorial warning that "the spirit of innovation and experimentation" should be the first order of consideration in the Committee's selection process," though it requested "a Drama School Dean more openly cordial to the undergraduate program than Brustein has been."

Another group of drama students denounced the makeup of the search committee and asked Giamatti for an explanation of the principles on which the committee was chosen. They also demanded some form of student participation in the coming deliberations. Giamatti had the good sense to meet with these representatives a number of times, but he firmly refused to let them enter the deliberations of a committee that he defended as representing "a high level of distinction and variety." Instead, he suggested that the students submit their own list of recommendations to the search committee, and promised they would be taken seriously. Following a great deal of consultation with other students at the School, this group finally did submit such a list. On it were the names of Peter Brook, Peter Hall, and Harold Pinter, with Joseph Papp and Gordon Davidson excluded for being insufficiently visionary. I was both flattered and amused. My students apparently had a much more exalted view of this position than I would have imagined—and a much less realistic sense of just who might be willing to leave fulfilling work and comfortable homes in London, Paris, and New York for the dubious attractions of Yale and New Haven.

Meanwhile the *Yale Drama Alumni Newsletter* had a new editor. This was a periodical produced two or three times a year at the School, usually by one of the DFA students, to inform alumni of Drama School activities and to chronicle the professional accomplishments of our graduates. It had now been taken over by the wife of one of the faculty members on the search committee, herself a disaffected graduate of the old School. The first issue she edited was devoted almost entirely to praising the committee, announcing memorial funds for dead and retiring faculty, listing the academic promotions of old School alumni, and congratulating Toni Smith Giamatti ("class of '60") on the inauguration of her husband as president of Yale. The most interesting feature, however, was a brief editorial by the new editor that explained why she was preempting some space previously reserved for a statement by the ad hoc student search committee. In her editorial judgment, the statement was "scurrilous," so she was making what she called "a more constructive appeal on behalf of the student body" for contributions to the Endowment Fund.

The rejected "scurrilous" statement was, nevertheless, mailed by the students to all living Drama School alumni. It said simply that students were "alarmed at the constitution of the President's Search Committee," and quoted from a letter written by Rocco Landesman to the *Yale Daily News* protesting the absence of appropriate representation: "If, as President Giamatti stated, this change is an appointment rather than a policy matter, why has he chosen for the Search Committee not a single student from the thirteen years of Dean Brustein's administration? For that matter, there are no persons on the Committee under forty, no Drama School students, no Drama School junior faculty." The students concluded: "We believe the Drama School and the Repertory Theatre hold a unique position in the American theatre, and that it is our responsibility to preserve that status."

This time it was the students who were making a scene; needless to say, I enjoyed it. I was very proud of them and their efforts to keep the School vital. Nevertheless, I did not take part in their discussions or offer any advice. I was trying, for obvious reasons, to maintain a neutral demeanor in regard to their various recommendations for a new dean, but I was also trying, unobtrusively, to get Giamatti to define his intentions. For this purpose, I wrote him a letter on September 22, asking if he would "kindly clear up a confusing situation that has now developed among the students and the faculty." In our three conversations together, I reminded him, "you had made it quite clear to me that you were contemplating significantly different policies for the School. Since you were unwilling to let me complete the five-year term that President Brewster had offered me in June of 1976, I naturally concluded that the premature termination of my contract was part of a plan to introduce these new policies under the administration of a dean more willing to implement them." I then tried to refresh his memory about the three things he had told me he wanted changed at the School: more undergraduates in the acting/directing department, the restoration of tenure to a core faculty, the introduction of more academic courses. I also reminded him of a conversation in which he had said that we should train more drama teachers and play more of a role in the educational theatre movement.

I then reminded him of his public comments following my dismissal, adding: "If indeed you have changed your mind about making this shift in policy, then it would be wise to so inform the Search Committee, the faculty, and the students. If, on the other hand, these policy changes are to be the mandate of the new dean, then it would be equally wise to declare them openly for the sake of drama students who applied, and were admitted, under entirely different expectations. The present situation—in which your public statements seem to be at odds with our private conversations—is not a very happy one, insofar as it is beginning to cause considerable dismay and alarm. . . . Anything you can do to clear up this confusion will be greatly appreciated by everyone concerned, not least of all by me."

If I expected to draw Giamatti into a confrontation, I was mistaken. His reply was swift and terse: "As you know," he wrote, "I have met with the Search Committee and I am confident that they will seek to identify a group of people who would maintain the highest possible professional standards in the School of Drama and Yale Repertory Theatre. I see no purpose in going back over conversations about which we clearly have differing recollections. I am puzzled, however, by your reference to the 'five-year term that President Brewster offered me in June of 1976' and its 'premature termination.' It is apparent from the records of the University that if any such offer was made, it was never accepted. The records of the Corporation show that you accepted a term of five years (July 1, 1966–June 30, 1971), a term of three years (July 1, 1971–June 30, 1974), a term of two years (July 1, 1974–June 30, 1976), a term of two years (July 1, 1976–June 30, 1978), and a term of one year (July 1, 1978–June 30, 1979).''

So that was to be the strategy, I thought grimly, a strategy of differing recollections. It sounded vaguely familiar to me from another recent historical context. But if I didn't have any tape transcripts in my possession, I certainly had the evidence that I had the option of staying on as dean until 1981: my letter to Brewster ("Would you allow me to accept a two-year term, with the option of renewing for another three years in 1978?") and Brewster's reply to me ("Delighted to acquiesce in the two-year idea, with the possibility of renewal at the end of that time"). I xeroxed these two items and mailed them off to Giamatti (with copies to the provost and the members of the corporation). Naturally, I couldn't resist the temptation to reply: "I am sorry that we seem to have such differing recollections of our various meetings. I took careful and extensive notes after each of these meetings and should be glad to show them to you upon request. I'm sorry also that you seem to be ignorant about my contract history with President Brewster. This is odd because I informed you of this history during our meeting of April 25, 1978, when you asked me about my future plans."

"It is possible," I concluded, dropping any remaining pretense of academic formality, "for two people present at the same accident to have differing impressions of it. But in the case of this particular accident the facts, I believe, are clear and irrefutable. Obviously, it makes no sense to serve another two years under the administration of a president who has expressed such fundamental differences with the present direction of the School. I mention this only for the sake of a clear and accurate record."

Perhaps I should not have been surprised to receive no reply whatever to this letter, either from Giamatti or from any of the fourteen other university officers who received it.

This exchange put my hands deeply into what Maureen Howard has called the "soiled bandages and bloody sutures" of academic politics. I didn't hope to gain anything except perhaps the satisfaction of keeping the record straight, and I obviously had no desire to agitate over my two remaining years. I wouldn't have served another day as dean after the conclusion of the present term; I had mentioned the two years only to prove that the "appointments matter" statement was a sham. Actually, I had little else to do during my lame-duck year but make mischief. While I was engaging in these futile episto-lary exercises, I was also trying to amuse myself by sitting in on Giamatti's deans' luncheons. My presence apparently made him uneasy enough to start chain-smoking again; his ashtray was overflowing by the time we concluded our coffee. The other deans should have felt uneasy, too, because the very first thing the new president wanted to discuss was how to punish a professor of philosophy who had been discovered taking a course of study at the Law School—the dean of Law had to explain that courses in legal theory were essential to the teaching of philosophy of law. Next, Giamatti told us of his desire to reconstitute a disciplinary committee, abandoned since the days of serious radical disruptions, for trying student and faculty offenses. And finally, he announced his determination to have the Advisory Committees of the various schools and departments selected by the President's office rather than by the Deans and faculties involved. I watched this new concern over watch-dog committees and punitive agencies with interest; it suggested a growing centralization of power in the hands of the President of Yale.

At the same time that I was trying to ensure the preservation of the Idea at Yale, I was doing my best to establish it elsewhere. This meant investigating other sites for the company, and one of these was at Lincoln Center. In late September, Rob Orchard and I met with the new board of the Vivian Beaumont, and while Richmond Crinkley asked us questions and John Mazzola doodled abstractedly on a scratch pad, we discussed the possibility of moving the Rep intact to New York. I was very hesitant about a future commitment —so, indeed, was the board—but I made a plea for a resident company at Lincoln Center that would be a model for the entire resident theatre move-ment, *"primus inter pares."* I wasn't convinced that New York City could ever be in a position to support a developing theatre organism, especially one devoted to process and adventure, and when Rob and I looked over the facilities of the Beaumont with a member of our technical staff, we were instantly persuaded that, whatever its promise for others, it wouldn't work for us. The dressing rooms and administrative offices were in an airless subterra-nean corridor in the bowels of the building; the theatre contained no rehearsal rooms or shop spaces or costume-construction areas; nothing seemed to have been designed for the people who would work there. As for the auditorium, it was a comfortable, handsomely designed house, but with faulty sight lines, and the stage was under a huge flyspace, which played havoc with acoustics and wasted enormous amounts of energy. We could understand why Joe Papp had abandoned this white elephant, complaining about the drain on his own resources, after having vainly tried to modify the existing stage. Although originally conceived for a repertory company, the Beaumont had been de-signed by people whose experience of the theatre was limited to Broadway— which meant rehearsing away from the theatre, sending designs out for bid, making the audience comfortable while ignoring the performers. It reflected all the waste and impersonality of the commercial system.

Norma, however, was still pressing for New York, and when a call from Alvin Epstein gave us our first hint of his dissatisfaction with the Guthrie, she took this as a signal that all of us should move to Lincoln Center. There had been some earlier feelers from the Beaumont about a year before my dismissal, but at that time she was the one who had rejected the idea. To move the company to such a glittering showcase, she argued, was to deny everything we stood for—it was also to deny much of what I had said in print. When I reminded her of this, she revealed something of her panic and desperation. In New Haven, she now felt like an "unperson"—the sense of ostracism, both real and imagined, was unsettling her. She wanted to go back where we once had been respected and loved. I held out for Boston; she insisted on New York. We argued about this constantly, and at all times of the day. Also at night. Once, when we had just finished making love, Norma responded to my expression of satisfaction by turning to me with a smile and saying, "Then it's settled. We're going to Lincoln Center."

But it wasn't settled, and I continued to travel to Boston and Cambridge in the hope that something might be decided. While President Bok and Dean Rosovsky were weighing the potential costs of my proposal and its academic implications for Harvard, I received an invitation from Boston University to discuss a possible affiliation with its School of Drama. My meeting with President John Silber made me wonder how much independence was possible under his interventionist administration. There were certain undeniable advantages to such a move. One was the Boston University Theatre, already fitted out for repertory; the other was the School of Drama, already organized for training. The attraction of the theatre was its location in downtown Boston; I liked the idea of a gritty, urban neighborhood. The disadvantage of the school was its large tenured faculty; I didn't have the strength to wait out any more retirements. Also, although BU had some graduate students in theatre, it catered primarily to undergraduates. I told Silber that I might be willing to take charge of the small graduate program if I could move it to the Boston University Theatre and turn it into a conservatory for a professional company. That way, the School of Drama could keep its programs and faculty intact.

Silber said he was willing to consider this suggestion, and I returned to tell Norma that if Harvard failed to accept us, we still had a chance to establish our company in the Boston area. She liked having a fail-safe position, but she had genuine anxieties about the proposed alternative. Silber's image in the press was hardly that of a warm, supportive administrator, and an article in *Esquire* about his imperious behavior had scared her. She asked me to take her along on my next trip to Boston so that she could size up the situation for herself—especially the character of President John Silber.

Silber had us to lunch with the retiring dean of the School of Fine Arts and the vice president in charge of the arts. It was a most peculiar meeting. With Norma watching like a hawk, Silber and I fenced with each other on the subject of how much independence I might expect. Not much apparently. The first thing Silber wanted was a controlling board. I expressed my suspicion of such boards, even when they helped to raise money for a theatre. Almost all of them wanted to help determine artistic policy, and they invariably counseled safe, conventional choices. We had managed to survive for twelve years at Yale without a board—that is, until the advent of a one-man board named Giamatti. Since I wasn't bargaining from strength, I told Silber I was willing to consider some control from his administration, but I wanted assurances that the theatre would not be subject to capricious decisions. Could he guarantee a minimum of ten years for the company? "I'd like some guarantees from you, too," retorted Silber. "For example, what guarantee would I have that you'd stay here?"

I was taken aback. "But why would I want to leave?" I asked him. "To take a better job," he replied. I remarked that if I decided to come to BU, it would be because I believed it was the best place for our theatre; I reminded him that by June I would have spent thirteen years in New Haven. "But what guarantee would I have that you wouldn't go crazy?" Silber asked. I had to admit there was nothing absolute to be promised on that subject, though I hoped it was nothing he would ever have to worry about. Another point of contention between us was the name of the institution. Silber wanted to call it the Boston University Repertory Theatre while I, remembering the problems caused by the name of Yale, held out for some nonacademic designation.

What finally shook me, and started Norma moving around noisily in her chair, was Silber's response when I told him that we had to reach some final agreement by September 30 because of the NYU deadline. He advised me to accept the NYU offer, and then drop it when the BU agreement was concluded.

Leaving the luncheon meeting, Norma surveyed me grimly. "For*get* it," she said. I couldn't really argue. I had been impressed by Silber's desire to improve the arts at BU, and I had a reluctant admiration for the man, despite his obviously autocratic nature. But I couldn't determine whether his interest in me was dictated by an interest in theatre or by the publicity my coming might generate for Boston University. He was also much too concerned, I thought, about our repertory (he had expressed his hope that we would stage some Broadway musicals), and I couldn't shake off the suspicion that hiring me was at least partly a way of stealing a march on Harvard, toward which he obviously felt very competitive. I had had my share of problems already with university presidents. Working with this one was only asking for trouble.

It was a dark period. All our possibilities were evaporating. Henry Rosovsky had raised the odds to sixty–forty after a meeting I had with his financial officer, but Harvard still had made no commitment. NYU's September 30 deadline had come and gone. I had managed to get an extension until October 30, but I didn't really expect to know anything by then either. What I did learn a few days later after a call from Dean Rosovsky was that President Bok had definitely ruled out the idea of a graduate institute. He was willing to consider an undergraduate program, but the decision, finally, was not his to make, and the cost to Harvard was still a factor. I agreed to table my plans for a professional school, and work up a proposal for undergraduates. There was need for undergraduate theatre courses at Harvard, and the untapped talent there was prodigious. I wanted a conservatory eventually, but it was not immediately essential. We could call on the talent we had already developed for about five years, and getting the Theatre started would be easier if we didn't have to worry at the same time about starting a school. But was there any guarantee that Harvard's decision would be positive if I made this new proposal? Rosovsky told me he could guarantee nothing, and cautioned me against giving up other offers in anticipation of Harvard.

Despite this discouraging advice, I decided to take a gamble. With Norma's reluctant agreement, I declined NYU's offer and laid all my chips on Harvard. If the decision proved to be negative, I would wait a year, write my memoirs on a Yale sabbatical, and look for some way to start a theatre in Boston. Under no circumstances would I remain in the English department at Yale. I was even beginning to reconsider the sabbatical.

The last thing Norma needed for her psychic stability was a state of indecision. I tried to keep from her my own sense that events were crushing us. Showing a new company actress around the Rep, Norma broke into tears. How many times had I told her that the building was only bricks and mortar? But it was hard to be convincing when the Theatre was about to lose its home. So were we; my disordered dreams during this period were full of traveling. In one, I dreamed that I had settled in a foreign city to which my checks were forwarded—and lost. That was easy enough to interpret, but another one had me puzzled. I dreamed that every room in my house was crowded with family, friends, and students; they stood around talking while Danny went down the hall stairs on a skateboard.

We were feeling quite unsettled, not to mention unwanted and unloved. We had almost a year more to spend in this lonely place, and my flap with Giamatti was not guaranteed to make it easy. That month an article appeared in the *Yale Daily News Magazine* by a female undergraduate which accused me of "manipulating the press" and "making a big splash with charges he has not attempted to back." The writer, assuming that I had lied to the press, claimed that I had chosen to make my "accusation" (regarding Giamatti's plans for policy changes) at a time when I knew that "Giamatti was out of town and unable to defend himself." The only question was why: "Perhaps the only reason to 'why' " the writer speculated, "is that Brustein used his charges to make himself look like a martyr, or to sling mud at Giamatti—whom he is reputed to dislike—or to make it hard for his successor, or to make it impossible for the Drama School to grow and change. None of these alternatives reflects well on the Dean, nor on the press he manipulated to achieve his ends."

I don't know how *The New York Times* felt upon learning that I had manipulated that newspaper for sinister ends; I know how I was feeling. After the initial storm in the press, I had been quite careful not to add fuel to the fires with any further public comment. While I was more than willing to defend myself against the imputations of lying suggested by Giamatti's denials, through letters to the president and the corporation, I had decided—for the sake of the School and for myself—to keep my evidentiary documents private, at least until the proper moment. Now the war was escalating. I had little doubt that Giamatti had contributed to this story. I knew the reporter had interviewed him, and she had repeated the claim he was making in private that I had chosen to attack him when he was defenseless in Cleveland(!). I found it interesting that she had made no effort to interview me. True, I would probably have refused to comment. Aside from my recent vow not to publicize the issue further, it had been my policy not to speak with the *Yale Daily News* ever since its attack on Norma. Still, it was hardly common journalistic practice, even for a student newspaper, to make such charges without at least attempting to hear the other side.

My pride was urging me to respond to this story; yet, Buchwald's counsel against making further fuss was still fundamentally sound. Finally I decided on a middle course. I requested a meeting with the officers of the *Yale Daily News* and asked them for a retraction. I said I had no wish to blow this fracas up into a major scandal, but the article was irresponsible, misleading, damaging, and false in almost every particular. To prove this, I would have to show them materials I had no desire to make public. This was not the time for an academic mini-Watergate. On the other hand, the *News* editors had been unwitting parties to a cover-up of which I was the victim. I requested, and received, their promise that my materials would be considered for background only and strictly off the record. I told them I was making that request out of an appeal to their sense of justice, fair play, and respect for the truth, which I hoped was stronger than their desire for a scoop or a scandal. Young journalists though they were, they were still obliged to observe journalistic ethics.

I then asked them, before reading the documents, to consider the following questions:

If my dismissal was not "unusual"—just another routine appointments matter—why was I let go when I still had two more years to serve as dean at my option?

What did I have to gain from lying about Mr. Giamatti's plans for the Drama School?

Did anyone believe I could have fabricated my notes on the three meetings with the president?

Why—if my version of these meetings was false—didn't Giamatti dispute it when he first saw it in my letter of resignation?

And finally, if some of my statements could be substantiated, wasn't it at least possible that all of them might be true?

Having been promised that they would neither be published nor mentioned, I then showed the materials to the editors—my notes of the three meetings with Giamatti, the Brewster-Brustein letters on my options as dean, the letters exchanged between Giamatti and me.

The students examined the documents soberly and quietly. A few days later the *Yale Daily News,* not particularly known for its readiness to admit error, published a correction and an apology. Alluding to recently received "confidential information," the editors wrote that some of the charges and particulars in the story "were incorrect and that substantial policy differences do indeed exist between President A. Bartlett Giamatti and Dean Brustein concerning the future of the School of Drama and Repertory Theatre." I felt vindicated—momentarily. Not long after, another *News* reporter accused me again of "manipulating the press" because I wouldn't divulge the contents of my materials to the readers of the paper.

I was jousting with critics again—and undergraduates at that—long after I had vowed to take my lumps in silence. And what a parochial issue to make a fuss over—who said what to whom and when. But I was a journalist too, and for reasons both professional and personal, my reputation for honesty was important to me. Also, I have to confess, I still enjoyed the smell of combat. I didn't have Nixon anymore. Now, at last, I thought I had found a surrogate.

On October 18, Dean Rosovsky phoned to say he was planning to bring "other people" into our deliberations; by this, he meant selected members of the Harvard faculty, particularly from the English department. I was also invited to a lunch with him and President Bok where I had the opportunity to present a proposal for fourteen undergraduate courses in theatre—to be taught by members of the company and myself—along with a schedule that allowed more time on the stage of the Loeb for the Harvard-Radcliffe Drama Club (HRDC). That same day I learned that Robert Chapman had just submitted his resignation as director of the Loeb Drama Center effective the following year—a personal decision reached entirely independently as a result of his attitudes toward the job. Through a peculiarly fortunate coincidence, my Harvard chances had improved immeasurably. It was one of the few occasions in my life when my timing wasn't off; I was lucky enough to be in the right place at the right moment. At the conclusion of that luncheon, Dean Rosovsky told me that the odds were now considerably better than sixty–forty. When I pressed him to post the new odds, he said they were seventy–thirty. First I had to clear the English department, which would decide on my appointment, and I would also have to deal with the anxieties of the HRDC.

When Norma picked me up at the New Haven airport that afternoon, she could hardly believe her ears. I don't think she ever considered Harvard a real possibility, which explained her fixation on New York. Now she was elated. The future, at last, was beginning to hold out some promise. And at last, I was in a position to hold out some promise to my stranded colleagues. Five key people were primed to leave Yale the moment a Harvard offer came through: Rob Orchard as managing director, Jonathan Miller as production supervisor, Jan Geidt as press officer, Jeremy Geidt as senior actor, Penny Pigott as executive secretary. The solid core of our theatre was formed. Later, large numbers of actors, directors, designers, and administrators would commit themselves as well.

A few days later, having learned that I was being considered for director of the Loeb, the *Harvard Crimson* erupted with a story telling of strong opposition to my appointment from members of the Harvard-Radcliffe Drama Club. These students were suspicious of my commitment to undergraduate theatre and unhappy about the potential loss of stage time in a facility they considered their own; they further objected to the theatre courses as being meaningless without credit, and expressed a belief that Chapman's resignation was linked to me. One member of the Club was quoted as saying that I would be acceptable only if I didn't bring along a company—mixing students and professionals, he added, was like mixing oil and water. On the other hand, other Harvard students, including some dissenting members of the HRDC, were in favor of the plan, and the English department seemed favorably disposed toward accepting me into the department.

Having contacted the Yale Dramat, the HRDC had concluded that I was hostile to undergraduate drama. I believed that if I could talk to members of this club, I could persuade them of my sincerity and of the advantages my proposal offered to undergraduates. A few days later I got my chance. Accompanied by Jonathan Miller—himself a Harvard graduate and former board member of the HRDC—I conversed frankly with the students, telling them I wanted to be as forthcoming as possible and asking of them only an open mind. I went over my background as a teacher of undergraduates at Cornell, Vassar, and Columbia, and explained my relationship—obviously a source of disquiet to them—to undergraduate theatre at Yale. My mandate as dean of a professional school, I told them, was to run a training program, not an undergraduate theatre; under a different mandate I would have an entirely different commitment. I tried to describe the attractions of our plan to all Harvard undergraduates: new courses, training in theatre, supervisory resources, help with construction of sets, discounted tickets to professional productions, opportunities for work with a professional company. Then I opened up the floor to questions.

These began with an adversary tone. Most of the questions still had to do with my reputation for indifference or contempt toward undergraduate theatre. Was it true I had tried to evict the Yale Dramat from the Drama School? Was it true I had never met its current president? The first allegation was untrue; the Dramat's stage time, in fact, had been increased well beyond the terms of the original agreement in 1927. As for the second, well . . . I had to admit that *was* true. I hadn't attended a single board meeting of the Dramat all year—I was busy looking for a job; I was more worried about neglecting my own School. Gradually the atmosphere of the room began to lighten. One young student actress spoke up passionately about what she called the absurdity of the opposition. They were like children protecting a sandbox. Couldn't they see the *advantages?*

When the meeting was over, Jonathan Miller and I were applauded and thanked for our frankness. On the ride back to New Haven, Jonathan told me he expected there would be two HRDC reports: a majority opinion in favor of our plan, and a minority opinion articulating the lingering objections of the still-disgruntled members.

I was feeling very high. Everything had led me to believe that this was an extremely important hurdle. Students at Harvard exercise considerably more influence on decisions than at Yale, and approval by the HRDC appeared to be crucial. President Bok had not yet given his final consent to my plan, and strong student opposition might cause him to draw back.

I believed, therefore, that I had cleared a significant barrier. But on the Sunday night following my Friday meeting with the HRDC, a reporter from the *Crimson* called to tell me that the board had voted five to two *against* the proposal. Did I have any comment? Holding the phone tightly, I said No. "That's the ball game," I said to Norma. We held each other very close, too dejected that night to think of alternative plans.

The next day, however, the *Yale Daily News* ran a story headed HARVARD CONSIDERS BRUSTEIN TO LEAD UNDERGRAD DRAMA. It reported the student opposition, but also quoted President Bok as saying he was "undisturbed" by my lack of popularity with undergraduates. "The situations are entirely different," he said. "We have lots of graduate Deans at Harvard and they are not particularly concerned with undergraduates. . . . Students here could benefit from the right kind of supervision and encouragement, and Boston could use a first-rate theatre." It was a remarkably encouraging statement, especially when you consider that Bok had hitherto refused any comment on the matter. I was also encouraged by a follow-up in the *Crimson* which cited swelling support for my appointment and growing opposition to the HRDC vote from theatre-oriented Harvard students.

On November 7 President Bok finally gave his approval. All that was required now was the endorsement first of the fellows of the university and then of the Board of Overseers. A few days later—despite rumors of serious opposition from one of its members from Yale—the fellows unanimously endorsed the proposal; and Rosovsky now told me my chances were eighty–twenty. As a bookmaker, he was a tough customer, and the contract we were beginning to negotiate was so complicated and hedged with caveats that it reminded me of a treaty between nations. But I could understand why Rosovsky had been offered the presidency of Yale. His candor and straightforwardness were enormously impressive, especially after my recent experiences. So was that of the entire Harvard administration. They had never misled me; they had never given me false hopes. They drove a fearfully hard bargain, but when they made an agreement, it was observed to the letter. I was beginning to regain some confidence in human institutions. To judge from my own experience, Harvard was a moral and principled university.

There was still a possibility that the Board of Overseers might reject—or, at least, postpone—the decision of the president and the fellows. Nevertheless, I finally allowed myself to believe we were going to make it to Harvard. For me, the process of decision had been agonizingly slow. Friends at Harvard told me that nothing in their memories had ever moved so fast. Whatever the case, I now felt so happy that all my past anxieties were forgotten. The *Yale Daily News* called me for a comment on the story, and I—unable to suppress an unworthy impulse to gloat—replied that "were this to happen, it would be an appointments matter, not a policy matter. I will say no more lest the *News* conclude that I am manipulating the press." The *News* failed to publish my statement, which was just as well; no need to rub it in. Norma, as ecstatically happy as I was, giggled throughout the entire day. I wrote in my diary: "The only thing that can mar our joy is ill health."

The Board of Overseers approved my appointment as director of the Loeb Drama Center on December 7, following approval by the English department of my appointment as professor of English. It didn't go without a hitch. A last-ditch campaign was launched against me by some former members of the Loeb Advisory Committee. One wrote a letter to the president questioning my interest in undergraduates. Another—an American playwright whose plays I had panned—alleged I had no interest in American playrights. Others were upset over not having been consulted. I worried that other people I might have previously antagonized (such as the president of the Rockefeller Foundation) might try to block my appointment from their seats on the Board of Overseers.

Furthermore, the *Crimson*—which had been publishing favorable comment on my appointment, along with an extremely eloquent editorial about the brightening future of Harvard theatre—was also featuring articles with titles like BRUSTEIN BOOSTERS BEWARE and BRUSTEIN WANTS HARVARD BUT DOES HARVARD WANT BRUSTEIN? which cited sour comments from the Yale Dramat about my contempt for undergraduate theatre. During a speech I made to the Harvard Signet Society, I tried to formulate a jocular response to these charges by confessing a secret appetite for eating undergraduates and offering my recipe for baking college actors in a stew (Cover; simmer; serves ten). "If the Board of Overseers votes positively tomorrow morning on my proposal," I concluded to a good-natured chorus of hisses and boos, "I may not be able to improve the quality of theatre in the area, but I can guarantee that the quality of the cuisine will be recognized and valued throughout the world."

I awaited the decision of the Board of Overseers in the Harvard press office; it was delayed. When word finally came of a unanimously positive vote, I was in the john, a fitting place to learn of the conclusion of such a long and arduous process. Glen Bowersock—the associate dean of Arts and Sciences who had guided the whole thing through so tirelessly and patiently—confessed that getting me appointed was "like bringing the *Queen Mary* into port—backwards." But I was now secure in my berth and whooping like a ship's horn. Reunited in New Haven that same night, Norma and I talked of the future into the early hours of the morning, our arms around each other. The Idea was vindicated, the Theatre was saved. And so, incidentally, were we.

The next day I spoke to the somewhat anxious students of the School, telling them the rumors were true—I was being dragged away to Harvard, "kicking and screaming," to start a theatre in 1980. "My resolution to do this," I added, "is motivated by a determination to preserve an Idea—an Idea which could not be continued at Yale, regardless of who is chosen dean. For anyone taking this position has a right to his own Idea, and the freedom to put it into operation. The institution called the Yale Drama School will certainly go on

—let us hope forever. But it will inevitably be different, and change will inevitably come. A number of exciting people have been rumored for the next dean of the School, and there is every reason to hope, partly thanks to your efforts, that a significant *professional* appointment will now be made. But whoever enters these halls as dean and/or artistic director ought to have his choice of faculty, as I was allowed when first I came. The company members and faculty and students I will be approaching soon to join the new company in Cambridge will be those who I believe belong to the Idea. Some, of course, belong to the institution and therefore are more appropriately situated here. But I can assure you there will be no tumultuous upheavals in the future, no mass exodus of faculty or students. Our theatre in Cambridge should be considered, rather, as another employment possibility for Yale graduates— especially those who, like yourselves, have had some contact with the Idea." I told them I would be visiting Yale frequently the next year to watch their progress, comforted by the knowledge that the Idea would still live with them in New Haven, and that they would continue to be part of it even while engaged in the new Idea coming to Yale.

All this talk about the Idea was fine enough, but what was happening to the Theatre during my voyages back and forth to Cambridge? It was continuing to function all right, not very effectively. The School was in good administrative shape, following the replacement of a frazzled Howard Stein by Jonathan Miller as associate dean. Miller calmly and confidently put all the programs on course while Stein, though offered a place in the playwriting program, decided to take an academic position at the University of Texas. But if the School was running smoothly, my preoccupation with Harvard had left the Rep a little rudderless. Andrei Serban had informed me the previous summer that, taxes being what they were, he couldn't afford to remain at Yale for another year on the salary we paid, and so he accepted a three-play contract with Joseph Papp at a whopping fee. Although Serban had promised to do one production for us in the fall, Papp wanted an exclusive on him and refused to release him to any other theatre. I called Papp to ask him to make an exception for us, reminding him of how I had agreed to release Serban to him in 1977, when he was already committed to Yale. Papp remembered, all right, but insisted on his exclusive. He thought a monopoly on Serban necessary for the identity of the Public Theatre. The whole conversation brought to mind the way contract players were once treated in Hollywood—I felt like David O. Selznick negotiating with Louis B. Mayer over Clark Gable in *Gone With the Wind*—but considering my own efforts to keep actors bound to the Repertory Theatre, I was hardly in a position to criticize Papp. That season at the Public Theatre, Serban did a workshop production of *The Master and Margarita* and two other shows including a musical version of *The Umbrellas of Cherbourg*. But for most of that year (and the next) he was being handsomely paid not to direct.

Unable to wait for Serban's manumission, we hired Keith Hack, a young English director whose work I had admired during my year abroad; he was appointed associate director of the Rep. That fall, Hack staged Odon von Horvath's *Tales from the Vienna Woods* in its American premier, and a chamber version of *Mahagonny*. Not much liked by the New York critics, the von Horvath production was a biting re-creation of pre-Nazi Vienna in all its seamy, fleshly rot, and it had some excellent performances by John Glover, Clarence Felder, Elisabeth Franz—and Norma, in the touching role of a corpulent, middle-aged tobacconist hungry for love. On the other hand, *Mahagonny*—which the New York critics liked much better—was, to my mind, something of a travesty, all glitz and no substance, in a truncated adaptation for which I felt compelled to apologize to Lotte Lenya. I didn't like this production much, and I didn't much like the production that preceded it— an evening of original one-acts, including one of Durang's short plays misdirected by our stage manager. The season was suffering from neglect. I was too engaged in planning my future to watch the store.

Consequently, once my Harvard appointment was secure, I resolved to pay more attention to the Theatre. I tried to plan a spring season that would serve as a strong conclusion to our thirteen years. Among the plays selected was Sam Shepard's powerful new work, *Buried Child,* directed by Adrian Hall of the Trinity Square Playhouse in Providence; Edward Bond's *The Bundle,* directed by John Madden; an experimental version of *As You Like It,* directed by another Rumanian artist, Andrei Belgrader; and Chekhov's *The Sea Gull,* directed by me. *The Sea Gull* was one of the plays being considered for Serban. When he fell out of the season, I chose it for Norma.

Norma had played her first featured role in *Tales from the Vienna Woods,* and played it brilliantly. It was our last year. She had served the Rep selflessly and faithfully in a number of thankless roles and understudy assignments. All her life she had wanted to play Arkadina, and I believed she had the quality, the talent, the intelligence, and the courage to do it. I wanted to compensate my wife for all the disappointments she had endured, all the sacrifices she had made, all the credit she had been denied. I also wanted desperately to make her life happy again. I felt deeply ashamed that out of fear of attacks on her or on me I had denied her roles that would have been the normal expectation of any actress in the company. This would be her last opportunity to act at Yale. She deserved to have a good one.

When I finally was able to convince my skeptical wife that she was really being cast in her favorite role, she was euphoric. Immediately she began researching and studying the play, and within a period of weeks, she entered Yale–New Haven Hospital for cosmetic surgery on what she called the "Fu Man Chu" lines between her cheeks and chin. For years she had talked about having a face-lift, but I—loving her face and loving the way she was aging— had always opposed it. Now I knew I could oppose it no longer, even if my opposition had any persuasive force with her. She thought she needed to look younger in order to play Arkadina; I thought she had to look younger for her sense of self. When the bandages were removed, I was relieved to see that her face was unchanged by the surgery, except for a new firmness in the chin and cheeks. Norma used to worry about her appearance, but she was not narcissistic; her beauty had come to her late, after a period of adolescent awkwardness, so she always regarded her face as if it belonged to someone else. Now, once again, I saw her examining herself in the mirror with detached admiration. It was not the surgery, however, but her pleasure in her new appearance that gave her such a fresh, luminous beauty.

We spent the Christmas vacation in the Caribbean, one week rusticating in a Grenada resort, the next week cruising through the Grenadines on a chartered sloop. We shared the boat with the Styron family. Bill had just completed *Sophie's Choice,* and had brought the manuscript on board for us to read. Norma—keeping her raw, sutured face protected from the sun—grabbed the book first and devoured its contents, handing pages to the rest of us as she finished them. All of us shared her admiration for the strength and precision of this novel, so obviously a major contribution to classical fiction. At night, rolling at anchor, we played charades and word games. And at bedtime, I played surgeon to my wife—Danny acted as my nurse—removing her sutures with tweezers while improvising Walter Mitty fantasies ("pocketa pocketa queep").

It was a lovely trip we took from St. Vincent through the islands to Grenada; it had been many years since we felt so carefree. Styron, having just completed ten painful years of labor, was in a warm, funny, expansive mood. He promised us a play for our second season at the Loeb—a stage adaptation of a screenplay he had written with John Marquand. Norma was also in a literary mood during that vacation. She had begun work on a novel about the career of a delicately poised big-band singer named Mona, who marries into the academic life with the chaplain of a large Eastern university. In the final chapters she planned to describe the conflict between her husband and the university president, a sinister character she had named V. Standish Gambino.

Returning to New Haven following our trip, we read in the *Times* that A. Bartlett Giamatti had just appointed a new dean for the School of Drama. It was Lloyd Richards, Broadway and television director, Hunter College professor of acting, and artistic director of the Playwrights' Unit of the O'Neill Theatre Center in Waterford. We were not entirely surprised by the choice. Richards had been rumored for the post for some weeks, no doubt because two members of the search committee were connected with the O'Neill: its president, George White, and its resident critic, Edith Oliver. It was a sensible choice, we thought, and offered some guarantees that the School would keep its professional status. I knew of Richards as an excellent teacher of acting (whom we had once tried to recruit for Yale), as the capable director of *Raisin in the Sun,* and as an experienced administrator. He was also a pleasant, likable man. The School seemed to be in competent hands; it was possible that my public conflict with Giamatti may have influenced the president's decision to choose a professional. It may also have persuaded him to postpone, if not cancel, his plan for bringing undergraduates into the School's acting program.

At any rate, when my Yale sabbatical was formally approved, I decided to turn it down. I did this as a matter of principle, but for practical reasons as well. I now wanted to start my work at the Loeb during the coming year, instead of in September 1980, as originally planned. Harvard was agreeable to the change, providing I could raise my own salary. Consequently, I wrote to thank the Yale provost, Abraham Goldstein, for the leave—and to reject it.

I sent a copy of this letter to Giamatti and to all members of the corporation, accompanied by another letter explaining my action "to you, as principal officer of the University and as principal catalyst of the decision."

I chewed over the recent events again, and concluded sharply: "During my twelve years at Yale, I have had the privilege of serving under two Presidents of unimpeachable character, honor, and integrity. At present, I do not believe I am associated any longer with an ethical institution. I do not question your right to shape the direction of any school or department in the University; what I find insupportable is your continued denial of what you told me about your plans for changing the direction of the Drama School.

"I am inclined to place a great deal of value on the importance of truth—a quality to which Yale also pays service in its mottoes, inscriptions, and prayers—and I do not need to say how much I value my own reputation for honesty. . . . After Watergate, it has become very difficult to tolerate deception in high places, especially in the administration of a University—even when accompanied by considerable charm and wit. For this reason, I find it necessary to sever my relationship with Yale on June 30th, when my commitments to students, faculty, and my theatre there have been completed. I will leave this institution with some regret, but with even more alarm over what your treatment of me bodes for the University as a whole."

To this Giamatti responded, about ten days later, with a letter that might have been written by a lawyer. It was addressed exclusively to the question of my contract. He enclosed copies of the Brewster-Brustein correspondence, now offered as evidence that I had *turned down* an offer of another five-year term. He concluded by saying, "Your insistence that you could determine how long you would serve as Dean is not substantiated by anything except your insistence."

I really had to take my hat off to this talented scholar of Machiavelli. He had reduced the whole issue to a legalistic question of whether I had a right to two more years as dean—an option I was making no effort to exercise—and thus managed to obscure the real issue of our policy disagreements and his denials of them. He had even sent me copies of my own evidentiary documents, accompanied by his own extraordinary interpretation of their contents. Was he anticipating a lawsuit? Was he preparing a defense? Whatever the case, he was a real high-stepper, this president; I had to admire his nerve. But for me the matter by now had grown boring, so I broke off any further communication with my pen pal, and never wrote to him again.

After opening Adrian Hall's extremely powerful production of *Buried Child,* we set about rehearsing *The Sea Gull.* The Shepard play was warmly received; our audiences, we thought, were finally beginning to share our respect for this unusual playwright, and so was the Pulitzer Prize Committee, which that year gave *Buried Child* its drama award. As for *The Sea Gull,* it was the first major Chekhov we had scheduled since *Three Sisters* in 1968 (*Ivanov* we did not consider a "major" play, since it was performed much less often than the others), and it was a formidable challenge. We had avoided plays of this kind out of fear that they were so familiar to audiences they were no longer being *seen,* just as the faces of our loved ones tend to blur a little from overfamiliarity. The task now was to demystify a great and well-beloved play —to present it, in short, as if it were a brand-new work. To accomplish this, it was necessary to examine and reexamine the text, looking for fresh perspectives, obliterating all previous versions from memory, ignoring the commentaries. I exhorted the cast to ask continual questions of themselves and of the play. I posed one as an example: What is a sea gull doing around an inland lake?

We managed to identify two central images in *The Sea Gull* that would influence not only the acting but Michael Yeargan's setting. These were the lake and the stage. First and foremost, *The Sea Gull* is a play about theatre. It features two actresses (Arkadina and Nina), two playwrights (Trigorin and Treplev), and two approaches to theatrical style (conventional melodrama and the avant-garde dream play). The theatrical household of *The Sea Gull,* moreover, has attracted a variety of characters who share varying degrees of interest in the profession of acting. It was no accident that the first thing Chekhov exposes to the audience is two workmen in the act of building a stage.

The stage was a metaphor for the theme of art, but an equally important strain in the play was the theme of love, nature, life. This was embodied by the lake—that "magic lake" that so enchanted Dr. Dorn. It was the lake that almost hypnotically exerted its influence on the characters during the summer months, stimulating their desires and passions. But the quality of the lake does not remain constant. Although the first three acts take place during a thick, hot, fly-buzzing summer, the final act is an epilogue occurring one year later when the waves on the lake are high and the wind is fierce.

The third important element we identified in the play was its dream quality. Treplev's strange first-act playlet, he tells us, was written to show not life as it is but "life as we see it in dreams"—it is, in other words, an experimental dream play in imitation of Maeterlinck. Nina doesn't understand it, nor do any of the other characters (though Dorn, at least, is sympathetic to the attempt), but she is nevertheless caught up in a dream of her own. It is a dream of great fame and of great love—"It's a dream," in fact, are the words with which she concludes the second act, following her amorous encounter with Trigorin.

We decided to approach *The Sea Gull* as if it had been written by Treplev —in short, as a dream play. For this purpose, Michael Yeargan created an environment not hobbled by realistic canvas flats and doorframes but permeated by the central images we had discovered in the text. He designed a stage floor made entirely of Mylar, a shiny substance that caught the light with rippling intensity; our production would take place not just around the lake but actually *on* it. As for Treplev's jerry-built stage, this would appear and reappear in every act of the play. It would also be the final image of the production, revealed to the audience with Treplev's body sprawled lifelessly across it, gun in hand. For we had decided to end *The Sea Gull* not with Dr. Dorn's melodramatic announcement, "The fact is, Konstantin Treplev has just shot himself," but rather with Nina's disembodied voice speaking the dooms-day lines from Treplev's play-within-a-play—no longer a self-indulgent mono-logue, but now invested with a special, ultimate significance. But the last lines of all would be those of Treplev and his mother. As we watched the wind blow through the tattered curtains of the decaying stage over Treplev's dead body, Arkadina's voice was to be heard saying, "I smell sulphur. Is that in the play?"

Treplev. Yes.

Arkadina. Oh, I see, a stage effect.

Treplev. Mother!

In this production I was again trying to show that characters in great dramas assume in the course of time an almost mythic significance—which means the capacity to develop a life beyond the play in which they are born, to become the very images of our dreams and waking thoughts. To help achieve this, I interpolated a "promenade" at the beginning of the play—accompanied by Steve Reich's shimmering, repetitive "Music For Eighteen Musicians"—in which Chekhov's characters were each "introduced" to the audience as they wandered around the lake enacting a particular emblematic gesture: Arkadina making sweeping bows, Trigorin taking notes, Nina leaping across the back of the stage to meet her appointment; Masha so bent with melancholy her body almost touched the ground, etc. The challenge of our rehearsal process was not just to explore objectives and intentions—the psychological side of these cha-racters—but also to extend character into more universal areas, which is to say, into *Gestus.*

To take one particular example, Sorin seemed to us to be engaged, through-out the four acts of the play, in a protracted death scene. He enters, in the first act, dazed and groggy, having slept badly, perhaps in the early stages of a stroke; in the second act, he is already walking with the aid of a cane; in the third, he is in a wheelchair; in the fourth, on his deathbed. Our work on this part, which Jeremy Geidt played with heartbreaking tenderness, was to ex-plore how Sorin moves toward his death: how the color of his face changes, how his movements are affected, how his eyes and voice thicken, and, finally, how he fingers his shroud. We were obliged to determine not only how these characters behaved in the world of this wonderful play, but also how they behaved in this strange and dominating stage environment.

Rehearsals were a pleasure. I enjoyed working with our amiable troupe of older players and, in the younger roles, with our talented, well-trained third-year class. Free of worries about the future, Norma and I had the luxury of being able to concentrate entirely on the process of *The Sea Gull.* She was in a very merry mood working on her favorite role. For the first time since we came to Yale, Norma agreed to be interviewed by a newspaper; at last, she believed that she was entitled to the publicity. The New Haven *Register* published a very appealing story, accompanied by a handsome photograph showing her being fitted for one of her costumes. She looked radiant and happy; clearly, some of her self-esteem was returning. She also adored the costumes designed for her by Dunya Ramicova. At last, she could look beautiful onstage again after years of playing ancients, crones, shrews, and maiden aunts with mustaches.

Much of the rehearsal process was devoted to improvisations. It is Chekhov's method to leave the direct action out of the play proper; most of the plot takes place between the acts. To extend their knowledge of the characters, the actors had to explore these hidden events by inventing them in rehearsal: Nina's love affair with Trigorin; Masha's sour marriage with Medvedenko; Dorn's relationship with Polina. In one such improvisation, Norma did a scene with Michael Wager in order to determine how Arkadina might have behaved when Trigorin, having abandoned Nina and their infant child, returned to ask his old mistress to take him back. When Wager approached sheepishly and tentatively, luggage in hand, Norma—savoring his embarrassment—fixed him with a sardonic look and said, "What have you got in the suitcase? Diapers?"

Improvisations were also taking place in the Cabaret around this time. The students were doing satires in an attempt to work off some of their anxieties about the unsettled future of the Drama School. One third-year student— Richard Grusin—playing the part of Giamatti, asked the audience for questions regarding his conduct as president. Never one to be reticent or tactful, Norma piped up: "Why did you fire my husband?" Grusin, who was wearing a Red Sox cap to suggest Giamatti's well-publicized passion for this Boston team, immediately answered, "Because he puts on plays during the baseball season."

Norma's passion for Chekhov was without limit. She had just guided her first-year class through a Chekhov collage in the Cabaret as an end-of-term project; now she was absorbed with Arkadina. Although she knew the part intimately, she was having trouble with a particular scene—the one in which Arkadina discovers that Trigorin is about to leave her for Nina, and implores him to stay. Chekhov has her flattering Trigorin shamelessly about his talent as a writer while telling him how meaningless her life would be without him; he ends the scene with Trigorin's surrender and Arkadina's triumphant aside to the audience: "Now he is mine." We found it difficult to determine the extent of Arkadina's sincerity in acting out the episode. I thought that this old-style actress was playing a part, perhaps from one of her previous successes, but Norma was convinced that Arkadina was genuinely panicked over the possibility of losing Trigorin, no matter how melodramatic or false her lines. The trouble was that her breathing, lately a source of difficulty for her, was too shallow to sustain the high pitch at which she wanted to play the scene. We tried it over and over, each time a different way. It was a crucial scene for the character; Norma despaired of ever getting it right. One night, after rehearsal, she emerged from the bathroom, tears in her eyes, to tell me she thought she was letting me down. I thought I was letting *her* down. I didn't know how to help her.

Norma's ego, always tender, was particularly vulnerable in the later stages of rehearsal. She had waited so long to play a substantial part that she feared she no longer knew how to do it. If I worked with her too much in front of the others, she complained that I was singling her out for criticism; yet she clearly wanted help with this difficult moment of the play. Finally she found the solution by herself. Calling on her considerable fund of wit and humor, she played the scene as if she were completely in charge of the relationship—throwing herself over Trigorin and holding his body helpless on the couch as she smothered him with kisses. During this long embrace, Trigorin let his arm fall limply by his side; he had no choice but to surrender to this devouring, overpowering woman.

Two days before we opened, Danny, sensing his mother's anxieties, sent her a Valentine: it said, "You will be wonderful." And she was. An Italian rehearsal the afternoon of the opening yielded the hoped-for results in size and pace; and that evening the production went extremely well, except for a few shaky moments in the final act. Although some of the reviewers were bothered by the concept, most of them agreed that it enhanced a neglected side of the play, and Norma shared excellent notices with the rest of the cast in all the local dailies, including the Hartford *Courant* and the Providence *Journal.* Nevertheless, five days after the opening, I dreamed that Norma and all the actors had fallen off a high platform while I watched in terror, powerless to save them.

That was the night that Richard Eder came to see *The Sea Gull.* His review appeared two days later. I was in New York at the time, having enjoyed a thrilling evening with Tadeusz Kantor's *Dead Class* at La Mama. My sleep had been troubled because I knew the *Times* review was about to appear. First I dreamed it was bad; then I dreamed it was good; and finally I dreamed it was awful.

It was worse than awful; it was ghastly. After his treatment of *The Wild Duck,* I was hardly expecting praise for my own work, but I was totally unprepared for his attack on Norma. After accusing me of having produced an ineffective parody of Serban, Eder then went on to devote two full paragraphs to Norma's acting, not only in *The Sea Gull* but in every other production he had seen her: "Norma Brustein," he wrote, "who is the director's wife, plays the central role of Mme. Arkadina but generates none of the oppressive charm that allows this character to rule the play. She is simply oppressive. Mrs. Brustein has played important roles in a number of the company's productions and, at least in the ones I have seen, she has tended to sink them.

"She has technical gifts but she lacks the central gift of impersonation. As Mme. Arkadina, she is glittery and charmless. She conveys anger, imperiousness, and frustration; but aggressive misery is certainly not the part that Chekhov wrote. It is not what holds Trigorin, the successful but weak-willed writer, and prevents him from taking more than a fatal glancing shot at Nina."

I read this notice at seven in the morning in my mother's apartment in New

York. By eight-fifteen, having risked fatal collisions and traffic tickets, I was back in New Haven. I found Norma on the bed, the review in her hand; she had been reading it over and over. In her eyes was the terror of a bird who has been shattered by buckshot. We talked it out; we tried to rationalize it. I couldn't console her with the letters and reviews that were praising her performance. All she could think of was being called "glittery and charmless," of being identified as a director's wife who had sunk all our productions with her "important roles."

Norma went to the theatre that night and played Arkadina with high spirits. Backstage, she scoffed at Eder's review, and tried to cheer up the others, telling them that, regardless of the *Times,* they were in a distinguished production. It was a brave effort, but it drained her energy. Norma always believed in maintaining a cheerful demeanor in public, no matter how she felt in private. This time, however, she was suspended between anger and despair; she could find no adequate expression for her conflicting, and disguised, emotions. Finally she did find one. She wrote a letter to Eder.

The letter made no effort to dispute his estimate of her acting. What she wanted explained was why he had felt compelled to identify her as "the director's wife" and what the other "important roles" were that he had seen her in. "You have a right to loathe my acting as much as you please," she wrote. "You have no right to make false and irresponsible remarks about the size of the roles I have played at the Rep, or to spread insinuations about the way I earned them."

I tried to dissuade Norma from sending this letter; I was not successful. A year before, she had composed a note to Eder protesting his persistent attacks on the acting of Max Wright and Austin Pendleton, and I had been able to talk her out of sending it. But this time her reasons for writing were more personal, and obviously more crucial to her sense of self. I had no right to interfere, but I no longer believed there was any profit in fighting the press. To be honest, I suspected I had brought on this attack by my own previous efforts to hold reviewers accountable; I couldn't shake off the feeling that Norma had intercepted a volley that was really meant for me. On the other hand, it was obviously necessary to Norma's psychic balance to find some retaliatory outlet, if only to channel her destructive despair into a positive expression of anger.

Eder's reply came a few weeks later. It recognized that what he had written might be "painful," but insisted on describing Norma's other roles as "important." It was obvious this correspondence was fruitless. Nevertheless, Norma composed another letter. She asked him to count up Mrs. Sörby's lines in *The Wild Duck* and to try to find any lines at all for the Fiancée in *The Ghost Sonata.* "I consider all my parts important," she wrote. "But my question to you is whether they are important enough to sink productions. . . . At the risk of being even more 'oppressive,' I still would appreciate an answer as to why you felt you had to identify me as 'Mrs. Brustein, the director's wife.' Did I hide my identity in the program? Is this stage relationship offensive to you?"

Soon after Eder's review of *The Sea Gull* had appeared, Norma and I went up to Boston with a few of our colleagues; Kevin White was giving a reception for the American Repertory Theatre, which is what we had decided to call our new company in Cambridge. It was a festive affair in the elegant Parkman House, marred only by Norma's irrational fear that everybody had read the *Times* review and was looking at her strangely. We stayed at the Ritz in a resplendent room overlooking Boston Common. The city had just been hit by an ice storm; the trees in the Public Garden had turned to glass. I tried to warm up Norma's frozen spirit by talking about the future. The Boston papers were vibrating with excitement about the American Repertory Theatre, the first major company to take up residence in the Boston area for years. I had resolved that one of the four productions of our pilot season would be *The Sea Gull,* with Norma playing Arkadina. That weekend her mood lifted somewhat when we rode through the icy streets of Cambridge looking at houses. One in particular had taken her fancy, and we decided to make an offer.

But by the time we left Boston for a short vacation in the Bahamas, Norma had begun to act strangely. We had a week on Salt Cay, a lovely secluded island off the coast of Nassau, and we were among loving friends. The weather was fine and so was the conversation, but Norma spent most of the time in her room or in the hammock reading. One afternoon, after we had skinny-dipped in the ocean off one of the island's private beaches, she emerged from the surf in terror, having hallucinated that she was carrying her older son, Phillip, in her arms, and he was only three years old. That night at dinner she broke down and had to leave the table. She feared she was losing her mind, losing track of time. She awoke from her sleep that night, under the impression that somebody was trying to kill her.

When we returned to New Haven, Norma went back into *The Sea Gull.* The audiences continued to enjoy the show, and Norma continued to grow in her role. Playing the part was giving her pleasure, and the praise she received after each performance was restoring some of her confidence. During this time I had the opportunity to introduce Lloyd Richards to the School. The students were beginning to feel somewhat abandoned, partly because of my absences, partly because the new administration had not yet informed them of its policies. I was eager to assure them that their work was still being supervised, and that Richards would provide a smooth transition. The students received the new dean-designate warmly; they also expressed their affection for me.

But I remained concerned about my family. During spring vacation, with *The Bundle* onstage, I took Norma, Danny, and Phillip to Vail for a skiing vacation. It was lovely and exhilarating on the peaks of the Rockies. Norma had much trouble breathing (was it the altitude? was it her smoking?), but she enjoyed the purity of the air, the outdoor swimming in the heated pools, the skiing instruction she was receiving from her older son. I, too, felt marvelous on the slopes, alive and clear-headed in this awe-inspiring environment. One night, however, I was depressed; I don't know why; I felt like a failure. This time it was Norma's turn to provide some cheer. She told me how proud she was of what we had achieved, and how important it was to persevere. "We are a minority theatre," she said. "We mustn't compromise." At night, however, she slept fitfully; I was the watchman of her troubled dreams.

And while she slept I stayed awake to study the part of the Ferryman in *The Bundle.* For the actor playing the part was about to leave for another job, and the replacement we hired couldn't come until a later date. Because of our repertory scheduling, this left only one performance without a Ferryman. We could cancel the show, which wasn't exactly popular anyway, or we could ask the understudy to go on for one performance. Unfortunately, the listed understudy was me. I was in no mood to work up a long part—one more burden when I was desperate for free time. Rob Orchard talked me out of canceling the performance by reminding me what a bad example it would be for student understudies; Norma offered to help me learn my lines. Reluctantly, and in a bad temper, I committed to memory that long role, and when I finally played it—my last appearance on the stage of the Rep—I really enjoyed the experience, especially the response of the students who had come to watch and applaud. I even heard one voice shout "Bravo" above the din. It was Norma, sitting proudly in the audience like a mother watching her Bobby in a school play.

On the weekend of April 6 we went to Cambridge to take another look at the house we wanted to buy and to negotiate a final agreement. Danny came along to look at Cambridge schools. Everything about the new venture was promising. Eight members of the third-year class had been invited into the company; seven had accepted. The foundations were willing to consider proposals from the American Repertory Theatre—if not as the new incarnation of the Yale Repertory Theatre, then at least as an already established company. The HRDC was growing reconciled to the situation; the rest of the Cambridge community was enthusiastic. The Harvard administration had worked out an agreement that guaranteed us five years at the Loeb and the probability of permanent residence following a review. The people we were meeting invariably impressed us with their graciousness and cordiality. Cambridge was like a European city, cultured, civilized, beautiful. The Promised Land was almost within our grasp.

Norma had to return to New Haven Friday night for a performance of *The Sea Gull.* I returned the following day, having stayed behind to talk to a Harvard group. I found Norma with another Eder letter in her hand. It described in measured tones why he had felt compelled to identify her as the director's wife. A political journalist, he wrote, would also be obliged to tell his readers what relationship "an imaginary Senator Brustein" might have to somebody else on her staff named Brustein.

Norma's blood was boiling again. She was particularly incensed about Eder's "imaginary Senator Brustein," since there were no women currently in the Senate. She found the analogy forced and evasive. So she wrote a reply:

"I must say I find your explanation strange as to why you had to identify me as the director's wife. . . . You seem to believe there is some kind of political conflict of interest involved in my acting with the Rep.

"Perhaps your lack of experience as a theatre reviewer is responsible for this false comparison. If a Senator Brustein, elected by the people and supported by taxpayers' money employed 'her' relative as an assistant, then it would be your duty as a reporter to name that relationship. But my husband was appointed to his office, raises all the money for the Theatre, and is accountable to the University, which clears all appointments and positions.

"If you think that a director or producer or playwright husband who employs his wife is guilty of some misdemeanor, then I feel it is my duty to inform on a number of my colleagues in the theatre, so that you can expose them in your future reviews: Laurence Olivier and Joan Plowright, Elia Kazan and Barbara Loden, Jules Irving and Priscilla Poynter, Herbert Blau and Beatrice Manley, Michael Langham and Helen Burns, Robert Whitehead and Zoe Caldwell, Harold Clurman and Stella Adler (and later Juleen Compton), Guthrie McClintic and Katherine Cornell, Ed Sherin and Jane Alexander, Jean-Louis Barrault and Madeleine Renaud, Anton Pavlovich Chekhov and Olga Knipper. Even in our corner of Connecticut you have the opportunity to point out these relationships: Arvin Brown and Joyce Ebert (Long Wharf); Del Tenney and Margot Hartman (Hartman), Lloyd Richards and Barbara Davenport (O'Neill Foundation).

"I was not aware that it is now *Times* policy to name the relationships between husbands and wives who worked in the same place. I looked in vain in the bio of Barbara Gelb, after reading her excellent article on Joe Heller, for some mention that she was married to your editor, Arthur Gelb."

I thought it was a good letter, but once again I asked her not to send it. We would soon be moving out of the orbit of the New York press, and I wanted to finish with it. My own quarrels had only proved damaging to our theatre; they had damaged Norma as well. It was a momentary relief to respond to bad or unfair notices, but theatre people would always be vulnerable to critics and we had to harden our skins. I had been pretty harsh myself in my time. I suggested to Norma that she consider changing her stage name; for a few moments she thought about it, then said, "No, dammit, my name is Norma Brustein." She agreed, however, to put the letter aside for a few days and think the matter over. It was the last letter she ever wrote.

That night she gave her final performance in *The Sea Gull.* Stella Adler appeared, unannounced, at dinnertime, and so did Alvin Epstein and Rocco Landesman. Stella was the last person Norma wanted to see her play Arkadina; she thought the role belonged to Stella, even though she had never had the chance to play it. But when we all went out to dinner before the show, she displayed a calm and serenity that were almost preternatural. Her performance that night—indeed, everybody's performance that night—was inspired. Stella was so wrapped up in the production that at the end, after Dorn says that Treplev has shot himself, she put her hand to her mouth and shouted out loud, "Oh my God!"—this despite the fact that she knew every line of the play backwards. The audience applauded the show for a full five minutes.

Norma, in her curtain call, was astonishingly beautiful.

Alvin stayed with us overnight to tell us of the agonies he was suffering at the Guthrie. By coincidence, Norma and I had recently had simultaneous dreams about Alvin—she dreaming that he had a big success, I that he was in big trouble. Norma's dream was more charitable, but mine was more accurate. Alvin felt overwhelmed by his job and crippled by lack of support from the staff. He had proceeded with the innovations he had promised, but now the Guthrie board was discovering it didn't want them. The local reviewers were hostile; attendance had fallen by a few percentage points; the current staff, resenting the people Alvin had imported, were calling the place the "Yale Repertory Theatre." Norma offered her counsel to Alvin, as she had always counseled me. She advised him to take firm charge of the theatre, and warn the people plotting against him that he had the power to fire them. Alvin departed that morning, having resolved to establish his authority at the Guthrie or leave it.

In the afternoon we went to Michael Wager's house in Roxbury for a festive end-of-the-play party. The house is a handsome converted barn with extensive grounds, a swimming pool, and a tennis court, and while Norma laid out the chopped chicken liver she was contributing to the lunch, I played a few sets of tennis with a student in the cast. Toward the end of the game I heard that shrill, raucous voice she always used when pretending to be a Jewish sea gull: "*Bobbee!*" The lunch was ready. We ate it greedily and, after, told of funny things that happened in the last production, outlandish stories of productions past.

When we awoke the next morning, Norma didn't feel like having breakfast with me; she preferred to stay in bed. I called from the School an hour later; she was up then and sounded lively, but when I returned home late in the afternoon, she was in bed again. "You feeling all right?" I asked her. "I *think* so," she replied uncertainly. I told her of the big news of the day. We had acquired the house in Cambridge; our offer and down payment were accepted. This immediately vitalized Norma, who got on the phone to tell all her Cambridge friends. I called after her to come down for our evening drink together, and we talked of the nice days to come.

After dinner I left home to watch the tech rehearsal of our last production at the Rep, Andrei Belgrader's experimental version of *As You Like It.* I had chosen this festive comedy in order to celebrate spring and in order to celebrate the Theatre. It featured the entire company and all the graduating class. The rehearsals had been so creative, the concept so original, and the acting so attractive, that I was left with very little to do as a producer. With the show in such good shape, it was not necessary for me to stay long at the tech, and I told Norma before I left that I would return early by 10 P.M. to watch the Academy Awards with her. Christopher Walken had been nominated for his role in *The Deer Hunter* and we wanted to see him win. At twenty minutes to ten Danny telephoned me at the theatre: "Call an ambulance. Mom thinks she's having a heart attack."

I arrived at the house exactly ten minutes later; the ambulance was right behind me. Some firemen lugging oxygen equipment followed me up the stairs. We found Norma sitting on the bed, holding herself under the arms. She told us she had unbearable pains in the back, in her armpits, across her chest. Danny looked on helplessly; I waved him out of the room. When the paramedics arrived a few minutes later, she couldn't take the oxygen. She fixed me with a terrified stare: "My chest is bursting," she said. Moments later she went into seizure, and died.

In modern medicine, nobody is dead until the doctors say so. For hours the paramedics worked over Norma with their machines while I kept my hopes alive by watching blips on the ECG tape—only ventricular fibrillation. Finally they took her to the hospital in an ambulance, Danny and I following behind in a Yale police car. How odd, I thought, we are going so slowly. When we arrived at Yale–New Haven, we waited silently in an anteroom, joined later by Jeremy Geidt, until medicine was ready to tell us that my dearest friend was dead.

The thing is, I didn't believe it. As Danny and I hugged each other in a mutual effort at consolation, I kept thinking, I must go to sleep so I can wake from this dream. When we returned to a house that seemed even bigger now than before, I looked for Norma in the bathroom, in the closets, in my study. Where could she be hiding?

The next day all of the rooms of the house were filled with people—just as I had once dreamed. Not only our immediate family but students and friends —people from New Haven, people from Yale. We had always thought ourselves to be friendless there, apart from a small tight circle, and Norma had suffered from my failure to give more time to social relationships. If only she could have read the letters that were now coming in, over seven hundred of them, from people she had touched. She was never aware of how devoted people had been to her, how important she had been to their lives. I was full of regret for so many things, but mostly because she never knew how much people had loved her.

I had not allowed an autopsy; I couldn't bear the thought of anybody cutting into her dead body. And because I couldn't bear the thought of Norma's flesh decaying, I had her body cremated. The doctors speculated that she had died of pulmonary edema, a massive blockage in the main arteries of the heart. It was unusual for a woman to succumb to this condition, especially at the age of fifty—they diagnosed an undetected heart condition, aggravated by "unbearable stress." Other doctors suspected that the antidepressant drugs had helped to kill her, taken in combination with dietary indiscretions. Whatever the medical explanation, I knew that she had named the real cause in the last sentence she uttered. Pushed to its limit, her heart had burst.

At her funeral two days later she was memorialized by her friends John Hersey, Jeremy Geidt, and Maggie Scarf, all of whom paid tribute to her charm, selflessness, wit, and warmth of spirit. Phillip read Sonia's last speech from *Uncle Vanya,* concluding with the line "We shall rest."

With Phillip, Danny, and Danny's girl (Danny had a girl!), I went down to Salt Cay for the weekend where, in that lovely, haunted spot, I looked for signs of my own girl along the beaches and the dunes. Phillip, a working actor in New York, was now expressing a desire to join our company in Cambridge, though he had always refused to go to School at Yale. And I thought, Yes, that's right, that's exactly right. He'll act with us, and he'll take up some of Norma's teaching duties, and anyone who mentions nepotism must be made to understand that the theatre is a laying on of hands.

Norma's main worry about our future in Cambridge had to do with our ability to attract financial support during difficult economic times. Now the money was beginning to come in, and I couldn't tell her about it. I told her anyway, finding myself talking to Norma while shaving, after a game of tennis, over the newspaper at breakfast, just as in the past. I searched my diaries for memories; fresh ones I recorded. I feared losing track of her face, her gestures, her intonations, but I needn't have worried; whoever dies young and vital, before her time, never fades from the mind. One day, leaving the house, I heard her voice, the Jewish sea-gull voice, crying *"Bobbee!"* When I looked, I saw a little black bulldog on the grounds, a stranger to the neighborhood. We stared at each other for a full three minutes in silence until the dog trotted away with a wiggle of its ear.

For his final English paper at Foote School, Danny wrote a story about a boy who plays Treplev so realistically that in the last act he actually commits suicide. He dedicated it to "My Mother for whom *The Sea Gull* was life." His was one of many memorials. The biggest one was held exactly where she would have wanted it—on the stage of the Yale Repertory Theatre. On April 30 the seats of the Theatre she had helped to build were filled with former students, present students, family members, friends, and actors. Alvin and Stella, both unable to attend, sent telegrams. Others read tributes. Bill Styron spoke of the encouragement she had given him as the first reader of *Sophie's Choice;* Phillip remembered how his mother had taught him to ride a bicycle; Rocco Landesman read Chekhov's letters to his "little actress," Olga Knipper; Peter Evans, who had been in Norma's undergraduate acting seminar, recalled how she had brought him chicken soup when he was down with the flu in London; Jeremy Geidt told of her selflessness as a company actress; Judy Feiffer read portions of Norma's unfinished novel; her beloved third-year acting class reminisced about her late entrances and sang songs by Purcell and Jacques Brel. I tried to speak, too, of what Norma had done for me, but was barely able to complete my remarks. And the service ended with a rowdy rendering of the Bilbao song from *Happy End* sung by Chuck Levin, Joe Grifasi, Paul Schierhorn, Walt Jones, and Jeremy Geidt. It summed up the spirit of the memorial, it summoned up the spirit of Norma: "It was fantastic, beyond belief."

Out of some biblical fear that I would not make it out of the desert, I had taken a stress test early in the fall. I wanted to know how well my heart would bear the strains of the coming year. My heart was pronounced entirely sound; instead, it was Norma's heart that gave out. I had worked all year to carry her out of that lonely place, and just short of success, I had lost her. She had seen the Promised Land from a peak in Pisgah, and then left us to complete the journey alone.

The rest of the year is a bit of a daze. Giamatti's provost, Abraham Goldstein, resigned his post over a scandal in the *Yale Daily News* regarding the cost of renovations on his university house, though these, along with renovations on the president's house, had been approved by the corporation. In his letter of resignation, Goldstein suggested that Giamatti had failed to support him, despite his earlier commitments, and as a result, "I do not wish to continue serving in his administration." Giamatti responded to this letter by hastily calling the deans to a meeting, where he told us that he was demanding Goldstein's resignation immediately, rather than in September, as offered by the provost; he cited "differences of perspective" that had arisen between them over the last few months. "In other words," I remarked, summoning enough energy to make a small scene, "Goldstein didn't resign—you fired him." When I later spoke to Goldstein, whose disgrace had by now spread to *The New York Times,* he told me he knew nothing of any "differences of perspective"; in fact, the president had just offered him a new appointment and praised his past performance. Not long after, an "unnamed university official" began revealing to the press that the renovations to Goldstein's house were well in excess of $100,000; the cost of Giamatti's house renovations has never been revealed.

Other events from this time: The students of the Drama School completed production after production, including a brilliant third-year project, directed by Lee Breuer, of Jean-Claude van Itallie's *Naropa.* A mammoth surprise party took place at the Rep after Jack Kroll, on the pretext of doing an interview with me on the new Cambridge company, led me into the Theatre to be greeted by over five hundred people while Willie Ruff's band played "Take the A Train." (In a state of shock bordering on paralysis, I embraced friends and students from all thirteen years—learning only later that before she died, Norma had helped Jan Geidt to plan the event.) At the Drama School graduation ceremony, I had the pleasure of awarding the acting prize to the entire third-year class—the first (and last) group to complete the whole new training, and soon to be the nucleus of the American Repertory Theatre in Cambridge. And at the Yale graduation ceremonies, I made my final scene in New Haven—I refused to tip my cap to Giamatti when presenting the Drama School graduates, and I refused to address him as "Mr. President." It was a petty gesture, but it fulfilled an earlier pledge I had made to Norma. (In a gesture that was at least equally petty, Giamatti later retaliated by forbidding his daughter to join Danny and some of her other friends from Foote School on a boat ride in Martha's Vineyard or to accompany them to the Fair.)

On the night of graduation I attended the final performance of the final production of my final year at Yale; it was an evening of last things. The show was that wild and nutty *As You Like It,* and that night the performance was totally abandoned. Near the end of the play, when Hymen—her head adorned with phalluses, her body with four female breasts—struck up her song in praise of wedlock, who should appear but our resident bat, buzzing the heads of the startled audience as if preparing to join the festivities, too. As the cast lined up to take their bows, one of the actors—costumed to look like Shakespeare and riding a simulated horse—pranced down to my seat to present me with a rose, and to invite me onstage to join the company call. It was the most moving farewell I could imagine. Overwhelmed by many emotions, I couldn't speak. But I knew as I stood there, surveying the friendly faces of the audience and holding the warm hands of the actors, that something had been accomplished in those thirteen years at Yale.

The weeks following graduation had the quality of a valedictory. Officially I was still dean until June 30. But although I still went to the office, it was mostly out of habit. There was nothing much to do there; Othello's occupation's gone. The *Yale Drama Alumni Newsletter* announced in its summer issue that the offensive red color in the greenroom would be changed, and that in future the Yale Repertory Theatre would feature plays by women and minority groups in an effort to reach out more to the community: a year later the Theatre would disband its permanent company, move out of rotating repertory and produce a play on Broadway. Lloyd Richards was also telling interviewers that contrary to what had been said in the press, the Rep was going to be more professional than ever; and although this somewhat muddied the issue (my concern was over the deprofessionalization of the *School*), it was a sign that he was going to be alert to any incursions from the central administration. Money was going to be a problem for the future dean, as it had been for me, but I had the satisfaction of completing my term with the most successful Rep season, financially, in our history—6,200 subscribers (60 percent of them students) and $310,000 in earned income. I also took satisfaction, at the end of that year, in watching our graduates and former company members dominate the Obie Awards. Danny graduated from Foote School in a new three-piece white suit. Remembering how I used to drive him to school from the time he went to kindergarten, remembering the day I had absent-mindedly driven past him crying on the porch, remembering when he first walked to school by himself pencil box in hand, I thought of all the history he embodied in his fifteen-year-old frame. How proud Norma would have been of this lanky ninth-grade graduate—and how angry that he didn't know all the words of "The Star-Spangled Banner."

Everybody, it seemed, was having happy dreams of Norma. One of her students dreamed that she needed a wig for a part, and Norma encouraged her to steal it. Lillian Hellman dreamed that she met Norma on the street and suggested that they swap clothes, but Norma couldn't because she was late for an appointment with the hairdresser both of them used in New York; later that same hairdresser told Lillian that she had dreamed about Norma and Lillian walking together on a street! Another student dreamed that Norma came to her, smiling, to tell her what it was like to be dead. And I—I dreamed of her constantly, kissing her soft hair, touching her soft flesh, together with her in an endless summer of moist, limpid nights.

Alvin Epstein, whom we had been urging to direct *A Midsummer Night's Dream* as the premiere production of the American Repertory Theatre, called in late June to accept the assignment. The Guthrie had decided not to renew his contract after the next year, and Alvin had decided to resign immediately. He was greatly relieved to be free of the job; it had been an awful mistake. Carmen de Lavallade agreed to play Titania for us, and other friends were beginning to join the company. We were regrouping our forces, forming ourselves anew.

At the end of June, having sold our New Haven house, Danny, Phillip, and I moved our belongings to Cambridge. I was a little hesitant about leaving our home of thirteen years, but only because the rooms were full of Norma. When the sewage backed up in the cellar the day before closing because some leaves were blocking the drains—and we almost lost the sale—I took it as an omen. The gods were telling us to get the hell out of there, fast, without looking back. Entering the new house in Cambridge, I felt it embrace me. It was a mansard building on a quiet tree-lined street with brick sidewalks, less than a mile from the Loeb; it was also just three houses away from the former residence of George Pierce Baker. It had affectionate, sunlit rooms, and a greenhouse where I could keep Norma's plants, a bucolic place in which to sit in the morning over a cup of coffee and look at the local birds. Norma was not there yet, but she would come, and meanwhile I was being welcomed by scores of loving friends.

Norma was everywhere on the Vineyard when we arrived a few days later —in the hammock, in the rooms, on the tennis court, everywhere. I had been warned that I would feel more loss in this sylvan place so intimately tied to her memory, but instead I felt strengthened, on my way to being restored. In accordance with what I knew to be her wish, I had mailed her last letter to Eder. Now I learned that Eder had been replaced on the *Times* by Walter Kerr, as Barnes had been replaced by Eder. Oh, well, I thought, it doesn't matter. Time to forget about critics and their fortunes; time to start a less embattled life.

I had found the place where I would bury Norma's ashes—under a sturdy beech tree, near our stone wall, with a view of the sea and the garden she loved. The Vineyard property had been our real home together all these years, and it would be the family resting-place. I arranged with a local stonecutter for a marker to be made; it bore an inscription from *Three Sisters* that was full of hope.

On Father's Day, just one day short of ten weeks since her death, I put Norma's ashes into the ground, along with a coral necklace made by a friend. I felt strangely peaceful, almost elated. Opening the receptacle in which they had been stored, I was relieved to see that her ashes really *were* ashes, mixed with just a few small pieces of bone. As I was sifting through them with my hand a wind blew up from the ocean, so I covered them quickly with soil.

One night in midsummer, I was amazed to discover—hovering in the leaves of the beech tree that sheltered her remains—over a hundred fireflies, the more remarkable because only one or two had ever been seen there before. Their small specks of light created an eerie effect in the tree, making it iridescent in the night. I thought it was hallowed ground.

Epilogue:
1979-

No epilog, I pray you . . . for when the players
are all dead, there needs none to be blamed.

—A Midsummer Night's Dream

The players were not all dead. Although I had survived to tell the story, I had not, like Ishmael, survived alone. Over four hundred people had gone through our training program, all of them part of an extended family we would be calling on for years. We had staged more than ninety productions in the thirteen-year life of the Yale Repertory Theatre; these would also be a reservoir for the future. The Rep had lost its mother, but its offspring were healthy and fit and ready to start anew.

About thirty-five actors, directors, designers, dramaturges, technical staff, playwrights, and administrators eventually joined us for the maiden season of the American Repertory Theatre in the spring of 1980. But from July 1979 on, the Loeb was being run by a skeleton staff, headed by Rob Orchard, engaged in planning productions, raising funds, and negotiating with Harvard. I was on a semester's leave during these first few months, working on this book, so I had no official duties. But the leave gave me time to outline the courses we had promised, and to try to get credit for them from the Faculty of Arts and Sciences. I had been told to expect a great deal of opposition from a community with a history of indifference to courses in performance, but discounting a few grumbles, we passed the various committees with remarkable ease. Once my appointment had been cleared, the rest was easy: the thing was carried forward by its own momentum. By March of 1980 the Committee on Dramatics had been empowered to make appointments in the theatre and to pass on a curriculum. Soon after, this Committee had given approval to five instructors from our staff, and twelve courses for credit in the art, craft, and literature of the stage.

The lingering opposition of the undergraduates had melted away as well. The hostile president of the HRDC had graduated, giving way to a more responsive student, and she in turn had been succeeded by a wonderfully mature and gracious woman officer. The supportive arguments of this new president, and the board with which she served, were very helpful in persuading the various committees of the viability of the new program. No longer our antagonists, the members of the HRDC were now our allies—and, increasingly, our colleagues in the administration and rehearsal of the productions. The new president worked in the box office; one HRDC board member acted as assistant designer to Michael Yeargan; about ten students on work study joined us in the administrative offices; over a dozen others took roles in our plays; and one young Harvard senior—twenty-two-year-old Peter Sellars—was assigned to direct one of our four major productions. There was considerable talent in the undergraduate community, which we were having fun identifying. And the new theatre courses in the Harvard catalogue were a guarantee that other talented people would soon begin to apply.

Just as encouraging as the support for our programs from the Harvard faculty and undergraduates was the enthusiasm of the Boston-Cambridge community. As soon as we announced our four-play pilot season, we were besieged with inquiries, and when we started our subscription campaign, the mails and the phones were very busy. In New Haven we had never had more than three thousand adult subscribers (not counting student passes); in Cambridge—in our very first season, and before we had mounted a single play—we had to stop accepting subscriptions at thirteen thousand. We would play to packed houses at every performance, and to warm receptions. The area was like a piece of parched earth that soaked up plays as if they were rain.

We had always considered ourselves a minority theatre; now we were in danger of entering the mainstream. Of the four productions I chose for a season that would be dedicated to Norma's memory, two had already been tested—*Happy End* and Alvin's *A Midsummer Night's Dream*—but two were designed as experiments: a new play by a Yale playwriting student, Mark Leib, called *Terry By Terry* and a strikingly original version of Gogol's *The Inspector General* by our young Harvard discovery Peter Sellars. The mix of experimental work and revivals from the repertory was something I hoped would be a pattern in future; it provided a solid base of appeal without compromising our need to move forward, and it would be supplemented by an adventurous cabaret. We were no longer one of two resident theatres in a town of 150,000. We were now the leading professional company in a major urban area. Boston had never been able to support a resident theatre for very long before; I think I knew why. The city had a great symphony orchestra (the BSO), an adventurous opera (Sarah Caldwell's Opera Company of Boston), and a rising dance group (the Boston Ballet). It demanded a theatre of commensurate cultural quality. But serious theatres take a long time to develop, and Boston audiences are impatient. Local corporations were cautious about doling out even very small grants to arts groups, and individual sponsors soon tired of supporting theatres that were taking time to reach maturity.

On the other hand, we had the great advantage of coming to Boston following a thirteen-year development period. Although financial support would always be a problem, especially in a crippled economy, we were familiar with national funding sources; although actors would always be reluctant to leave the opportunities offered by New York and Hollywood, we knew a large number of performers; and although we had no guarantee that our old work would please our new audiences, we had a large backlog of successful productions on which to draw. Furthermore, we were excellently managed and we were experienced. All things being equal, the odds were in our favor. For the first time in our history, it was possible to be sanguine about the future.

Looking back, I realized that however difficult the Yale years had been, they formed the basis for what we had become. New Haven was one of the few places in the country where it was possible to sustain a theatre in its formative stages. There were no distractions there from the work, and the School was a marvelous breeding ground for talent. True, we were still always subject to the depredations of the culture and regular visits from the press. But if we felt the pressures constantly, we were under no constraint to yield to them. Walt Whitman once said about New York, "You don't go there to grow fruit; you go there to sell it." In New Haven we were able not only to grow the fruit, but also to try new seeds, develop hybrids, weed and nourish the garden.

My amiable feelings toward New Haven reflected a general mood of euphoria. I enjoyed being at Harvard; I loved Cambridge and Boston. I was entranced by the Charles River, and my heart leaped whenever I rode along Memorial Drive and saw the lovely bridges, the strolling lovers, the shells cutting through the water. " 'Tis new to thee," said one of my Harvard colleagues when I spoke of my enchantment with the place, and I suppose I was exaggerating its virtues. But the mood continued throughout the year. Free from harassment and protected from envy's tooth, I was in serious danger of becoming a benevolent individual—though I returned to my old post as theatre reviewer for *The New Republic* lest I lose my reputation as a spitting critic.

Thirteen years had passed, the last of them marked by pain and loss and anguish, but I couldn't complain. I still had my sons with me. I had had a crack at doing something that excited me, and I had never once been bored. I had depended a lot on the young talent of this country; I still had the chance to find it and work with it. At Harvard we now had theatre courses; next, we would have a theatre major; perhaps, someday, a conservatory. And we had preserved our repertory theatre, which, when all was said and done, was still the best place for me to make my scenes.

On March 21, 1980, we opened *A Midsummer Night's Dream,* the initial production of the American Repertory Theatre at the Loeb Drama Center. It was the first day of spring, and it rained.

New Haven
Martha's Vineyard
Cambridge
1979–1980

Yale Repertory Theatre Productions 1966-1979

* **World Premiere**
\+ **American Premiere**

1966–67

DYNAMITE TONITE! An Actors' Opera, by Arnold Weinstein, music by William Bolcom, directed by Paul Sills
VOLPONE by Ben Jonson, directed by Clifford Williams
* PROMETHEUS BOUND by Aeschylus, adapted by Robert Lowell, directed by Jonathan Miller

Guest Companies:

Theatre of the Living Arts, Philadelphia: *Endgame* by Samuel Beckett, directed by Andre Gregory
The Open Theatre, New York: *Viet Rock* by Megan Terry, directed by Joseph Chaikin
Irene Worth and John Gielgud: *Men and Women of Shakespeare*

1967–68

'TIS PITY SHE'S A WHORE by John Ford, directed by Kenneth Haigh
* WE BOMBED IN NEW HAVEN by Joseph Heller, directed by Larry Arrick
HENRY IV by Luigi Pirandello, translated by Eric Bentley, directed by Carl Weber
THE THREE SISTERS by Anton Chekhov, translated by Tyrone Guthrie & Leonid Kipnis, directed by Larry Arrick
CORIOLANUS by William Shakespeare, directed by Larry Arrick and Jeff Bleckner

Guest Company:

The San Francisco Mime Troupe: *L'Amant Militare* by Carlo Goldoni

1968–69

* GOD BLESS by Jules Feiffer, directed by Harold Stone
* THE GREAT CHINESE REVOLUTION by Anthony Scully, directed by Ali Taygun
* THEY TOLD ME THAT YOU CAME THIS WAY by David Epstein, directed by Michael Posnick
\+ SAVED by Edward Bond, directed by Jeff Bleckner
* STORY THEATRE, conceived and directed by Paul Sills
BACCHAE by Euripides, adapted by Kenneth Cavander, directed by Andre Gregory
* GREATSHOT by Arnold Weinstein, music by William Bolcom, directed by Paul Sills

Guest Companies:

The Living Theatre: *Mysteries and Smaller Pieces, Antigone, Frankenstein,* and *Paradise Now*
Jean-Louis Barrault and Madeleine Renaud, *Happy Days* by Samuel Beckett and *Words and Music from the Court of the Sun King Louis XIV*

1969–70

THE RIVALS by Richard Brinsley Sheridan, directed by Alvin Epstein
* OVID'S METAMORPHOSES, conceived by Paul Sills, translated by

Arnold Weinstein, directed by Larry Arrick

*** TRANSFORMATIONS (3 one-act plays): **The Rhesus Umbrella** by Jeff Wanshel, **Clutch** by David Epstein, **Iz She Izzy or Iz He Ain'tszy or Iz They Both?** by Lonnie Carter, directed by Richard Gilman

CRIMES AND CRIMES by August Strindberg, translated by Evert Sprinchorn, directed by Robert Lewis

THE GOVERNMENT INSPECTOR by Nikolai Gogol, translated by Peter Raby, directed by Ali Taygun

DON JUAN by Molière, translated by Kenneth Cavander, directed by Robert Brustein

Guest Company:

The Negro Ensemble Company: *Song of the Lusitanian Bogey* by Peter Weiss

1970–71

*** STORY THEATRE REPERTORY, conceived by Paul Sills: TWO SAINTS, **Gimpel the Fool,** by Isaac Bashevis Singer, adapted by Larry Arrick, and **Saint Julian the Hospitaler,** by Gustave Flaubert, adapted by Kenneth Cavander; and OLYMPIAN GAMES, adapted by Kenneth Cavander from Ovid's *Metamorphoses;* directed by Larry Arrick

THE REVENGER'S TRAGEDY by Cyril Tourneur, directed by Robert Brustein

* WHERE HAS TOMMY FLOWERS GONE? by Terrence McNally, directed by Larry Arrick

MACBETH by William Shakespeare, directed by Robert Brustein

WOYZECK by Georg Buechner, translated by Theodore Hoffman, and PLAY by Samuel Beckett; directed by Tom Haas

+ TWO BY BERTOLT BRECHT AND KURT WEILL: + The Little Maha-**gonny,** translated by Michael Feingold, directed by Michael Posnick; and **The Seven Deadly Sins,** translated by W. H. Auden &

Chester Kallman, directed by Alvin Epstein

1971–72

WHEN WE DEAD AWAKEN by Henrik Ibsen, translated by Michael Feingold, directed by Tom Haas

* THE BIG HOUSE by Lonnie Carter, music by Maury Yeston, directed by Robert Brustein

CALIGULA by Albert Camus, adapted from the French by Justin O'Brien, directed by Alvin Epstein

*+ REPERTORY HOLIDAY: TWO BY BRECHT AND WEILL, **The Little Mahagonny** and **The Seven Deadly Sins** by Bertolt Brecht and Kurt Weill; + PASSION by Edward Bond and *STOPS by Robert Auletta, directed by Michael Posnick; JACQUES BREL: SONGS, directed by David Schweizer

LIFE IS A DREAM by Pedro Calderón de la Barca, English version by Roy Campbell, directed by Jacques Burdick

+ I MARRIED YOU FOR THE FUN OF IT by Natalia Ginzburg, translated by John Hersey, directed by Roger Hendricks Simon

+ HAPPY END by "Dorothy Lane," translated by Michael Feingold, lyrics by Bertolt Brecht, music by Kurt Weill, directed by Michael Posnick

1972–73

THE BOURGEOIS GENTLEMAN by Molière, translated by Michael Feingold, directed by Alvin Epstein

* A BREAK IN THE SKIN by Ronald Ribman, directed by Arthur Sherman

* ARE YOU NOW OR HAVE YOU EVER BEEN by Eric Bentley, directed by Michael Posnick

* IN THE CLAP SHACK by William Styron, directed by Alvin Epstein

* THE MIRROR by Isaac Bashevis Singer, directed by Michael Posnick

BAAL by Bertolt Brecht, translated by William E. Smith and Ralph Manheim, directed by Tom Haas

+ MACBETT by Eugène Ionesco, translated by Charles Marowitz, directed by Alvin Epstein, William Peters, and John McAndrew

+ LEAR by Edward Bond, directed by David Giles

1973–74

THE TEMPEST by William Shakespeare, directed by Alvin Epstein

* DARKROOM by David Epstein, directed by Michael Posnick

* WATERGATE CLASSICS by Robert Barnett, Robert Brustein, Lonnie Carter, Jules Feiffer, Jeremy Geidt, Jonathan Marks, Philip Roth, Isaiah Sheffer, and Maury Yeston, directed by Isaiah Sheffer

* THE TUBS by Terrence McNally, directed by Anthony Holland

THE RISE AND FALL OF THE CITY OF MAHAGONNY by Bertolt Brecht and Kurt Weill, translated by Michael Feingold, directed by Alvin Epstein

+ GEOGRAPHY OF A HORSE DREAMER by Sam Shepard, directed by David Schweizer

AN EVENING WITH DEAD ESSEX by Adrienne Kennedy, directed by Andre Mtumi

* SHLEMIEL THE FIRST by Isaac Bashevis Singer, directed by Isaiah Sheffer

* THE FROGS by Aristophanes, newly adapted and directed by Burt Shevelove, music and lyrics by Stephen Sondheim

1974–75

+ THE POSSESSED, Andrzej Wajda's adaptation of Albert Camus's dramatization of Fyodor Dostoyevsky's novel, translated by Justin O'Brien, directed by Andrzej Wajda

* THE IDIOTS KARAMAZOV by Christopher Durang and Albert Innaurato, directed by William Peters

* STORY THEATRE IV: VICTORY, a story theatre version of Joseph Conrad's novel by Alvin Epstein and Walt Jones, directed by Alvin Epstein

HAPPY END by "Dorothy Lane," lyrics by Bertolt Brecht, music by Kurt Weill, translated by Michael Feingold, directed by Michael Posnick

THE FATHER by August Strindberg, directed by Jeff Bleckner

* THE SHAFT OF LOVE by Charles Dizenzo, directed by David Schweizer

A MIDSUMMER NIGHT'S DREAM by William Shakespeare, music by Henry Purcell *(The Fairy Queen),* directed by Alvin Epstein

1975–76

A MIDSUMMER NIGHT'S DREAM by William Shakespeare, music by Henry Purcell *(The Fairy Queen),* directed by Alvin Epstein

DON JUAN by Molière, translated by Kenneth Cavander, directed by Robert Brustein

DYNAMITE TONITE! by Arnold Weinstein, music by William Bolcom, directed by Alvin Epstein and Walt Jones

* WALK THE DOG, WILLIE by Robert Auletta, directed by Walt Jones

BINGO by Edward Bond, directed by Ron Daniels

GENERAL GORGEOUS by Michael McClure, directed by Lawrence Kornfeld

TROILUS AND CRESSIDA by William Shakespeare, directed by Alvin Epstein

Guest Company:

Patrick Magee in *An Evening with Samuel Beckett*

1976–77

JULIUS CAESAR by William Shakespeare, directed by Alvin Epstein

* SUICIDE IN B-FLAT by Sam Shepard, directed by Walt Jones

IVANOV by Anton Chekhov, translated by Jeremy Brooks and Kitty Hunter Blair, directed by Ron Daniels

* THE VIETNAMIZATION OF NEW JERSEY (A American Tragedy) by Chris-

topher Durang, directed by Walt Jones

* THE DURANGO FLASH by William Hauptman, directed by Kenneth Frankel

* MR. PUNTILA AND HIS CHAUFFEUR MATTI by Bertolt Brecht, music by William Bolcom, lyrics adapted by Michael Feingold, translated by Gerhard Nellhaus, directed by Ron Daniels

+ WHITE MARRIAGE by Tadeusz Rozewicz, translated by Adam Czerniawski, directed by Andrzej Wajda

Special Holiday Production:

THE BANQUET YEARS, conceived by Carmen de Lavallade, Robert Gainer, Joe Grifasi, and Jonathan Marks (Texts by Alfred Jarry, Pierre Louys, Max Jacob and Erik Satie; original text by Jonathan Marks), directed by Robert Gainer

Guest Company:

Emlyn Williams as *Charles Dickens* and *Dylan Thomas Growing Up*

1977–78

THE GHOST SONATA by August Strindberg, translated by Evert Sprinchorn, directed by Andrei Serban

* REUNION (Reunion and *Dark Pony) by David Mamet, directed by Walt Jones

* TERRA NOVA by Ted Tally, directed by Travis Preston

SGANARELLE, an evening of Molière farces (The Flying Doctor, The Forced Marriage, Sganarelle, or The Imaginary Cuckold, translated by Albert Bermel; and A Dumb Show, loosely based on The Doctor in Spite of Himself), directed by Andrei Serban

MAN IS MAN by Bertolt Brecht, translated by Steve Gooch, music by William Bolcom, directed by Ron Daniels

* WINGS by Arthur Kopit, directed by John Madden

THE WILD DUCK by Henrik Ibsen, directed by Robert Brustein

Special Holiday Production:

THE 1940's RADIO HOUR, written and directed by Walt Jones

Guest Company:

Mabou Mimes: *The B. Beaver Animation,* directed by Lee Breuer

1978–79

TALES FROM THE VIENNA WOODS by Odon von Horvath, translated by Christopher Hampton, directed by Keith Hack

* MISTAKEN IDENTITIES: *'dentity Crisis, by Christopher Durang, directed by Frank S. Torok, and Guess Work by Robert Auletta, directed by Robert Gainer

MAHAGONNY a chamber version of *The Rise and Fall of the City of Mahagonny* by Bertolt Brecht and Kurt Weill, adapted by Keith Hack from the translation of W. H. Auden and Chester Kallman, directed by Keith Hack

* BURIED CHILD by Sam Shepard, directed by Adrian Hall

* THE SEA GULL by Henrik Ibsen, in a new version by Jean-Claude van Itallie, directed by Robert Brustein

+ THE BUNDLE by Edward Bond, directed by John Madden

AS YOU LIKE IT by William Shakespeare, directed by Andrei Belgrader

Special Holiday Production:

JACQUES BREL . . . A tribute to the author of *Jacques Brel Is Alive and Well and Living In Paris,* directed by Steve Lawson

Guest Company:

The Lucia Sturdza Bulandra Theatre company, Bucharest, Romania, performing *Elizabeth I* by Paul Foster, directed by Liviu Ciulei, and *The Lost Letter* by Ion Luca Caragiale, directed by Livui Ciulei

Index